50·00

TREATMENT WITHOUT CONSENT

SOCIAL ETHICS AND POLICY SERIES
Edited by Anthony Dyson and John Harris
Centre for Social Ethics and Policy, University of Manchester

EXPERIMENTS ON EMBRYOS
Edited by Anthony Dyson and John Harris

THE LIMITS OF MEDICAL PATERNALISM
Heta Häyry

PROTECTING THE VULNERABLE
Autonomy and Consent in Health Care
Edited by Margaret Brazier and Mary Lobjoit

**MEDICAL CONFIDENTIALITY AND
LEGAL PRIVILEGE**
Jean V. McHale

ETHICS AND BIOTECHNOLOGY
Edited by Anthony Dyson and John Harris

**LIBERAL UTILITARIANISM AND
APPLIED ETHICS**
Matti Häyry

CONTEMPLATING SUICIDE
The Language and Ethics of Self Harm
Gavin J. Fairbairn

TREATMENT WITHOUT CONSENT

Law, psychiatry and
the treatment of mentally disordered
people since 1845

Phil Fennell

London and New York

First published 1996
by Routledge
11 New Fetter Lane, London EC4P 4EE

Simultaneously published in the USA and Canada
by Routledge
29 West 35th Street, New York, NY 10001

© 1996 Phil Fennell

Typeset in Times by Florencetype Ltd, Stoodleigh, Devon

Printed and bound in Great Britain by
Clays Ltd, St Ives PLC

British Library Cataloguing in Publication Data
A catalogue record for this book is available
from the British Library

Library of Congress Cataloguing in Publication Data
A catalogue record for this book has been requested

ISBN 0–415–07787–7

To Jenny and James, and to the memory of my parents, Harold and Molly Fennell

CONTENTS

ACKNOWLEDGEMENTS

My largest debts are to two people: first, my colleague and good friend, Dr Clive Unsworth of Cardiff Law School, who has given unstintingly of his time and unrivalled knowledge of mental health legislation to offer constructive and inspirational criticism of draft chapters; and second, Catherine Young of the School of Social and Administrative Studies at Cardiff University for her invaluable and patient advice, in helping me to devise a coding frame to enable the data for the empirical study of statutory second opinions in Chapters 12 and 13 to be analysed, as well as for her assistance in entering and retrieving the data. Peter Alldridge, and Professors Shelia Maclean and Philip Bean have made many valuable suggestions. My thanks are due to the Nuffield Foundation, whose small grants scheme provided the necessary funding to carry out the empirical study; to William Bingley, the Chief Executive of the Mental Health Act Commission (MHAC) for arranging access to the data and for his helpful advice at various stages of the research; to Alison Cooney, the MHAC Administrative Manager for organising the photocopying of the relevant reports; and to Andrew Kay at the MHAC, who provided me with some of the more recent figures on the total numbers of second opinions during the biennium 1991–1993. Three Mental Health Act Commissioners, Dr Max Harper, Professor Elaine Murphy, and Ms Elaine Rassaby were kind enough to provide extremely useful comments on earlier drafts.

The research for the historical chapters of the book took me to a large number of libraries and research archives, whose staff were invariably helpful and friendly. These included the Public Record Office at Kew; the Royal Commission on Historical Manuscripts; the Radcliffe Camera; the Radcliffe Science Library;

the National Newspaper Library at Colindale; the Wellcome Institute; the Postgraduate Medical Centre Library at Whitchurch Hospital, Cardiff; the Library of the Royal College of Psychiatrists; Cardiff Law School Library; Cardiff Central Library; and the Bethlem Archive. Of these I should like to single out for special thanks Mrs Patricia Allderidge of Bethlem who helped me greatly with her infectious enthusiasm and encyclopaedic knowledge of her archive, and offered much useful scholarly advice about possible avenues of enquiry. I should also like to thank Mrs Ann Harris and Mrs Jean Walkden of Whitchurch Library for helping me to track down the annual reports of the Whitchurch group of hospitals. My thanks are also due to the many friends and relatives who offered me bed and board while I visited libraries in their vicinity, including Hazel and George Foster, Jill Russell and Charlie Sweeny, and Jacqui and Tony Wadling. Cheers to you all! Finally, I happily thank Jenny, not only because she told me to, but also for her wit, wisdom and support.

Phil Fennell
March 1995

INTRODUCTION

We are currently in an era, which effectively began in the 1960s, when consent to treatment is probably the central issue both in bioethics, and the growing speciality of medical law. Why is consent so important? Writing following the revelation of widespread medical experimentation on mentally disordered hospital inmates and others in the 1960s, the Princeton philosopher Paul Ramsey expressed the importance of consent to human experimentation as being what a system of checks and balances is to executive authority – the necessary limitation on the exercise of power.[1] From patients' point of view, seeking consent is a recognition of the autonomous right of all adult persons of sound mind to decide what shall be done with their own bodies, a right protected by the law of battery, summed up in Cardozo J's famous statement in *Schloendorff* v. *Society of New York Hospitals* that:

> Every adult person of sound mind has a right to determine what shall be done with his own body; and a surgeon who performs an operation without his patient's consent commits an assault, for which he is liable in damages.[2]

Bodily integrity and autonomy have been variously conceived as constitutional rights, fundamental human rights, democratic rights, and rights of citizenship. Once we move away from the principle of consent seeking and take treatment decisions away from the patient, we are effectively taking away a fundamental civil right and thereby creating new problems, among them the need to ensure that the people now making those decisions do so in the

1

patient's interests and do not underestimate the risks. The common-law right of self determination builds in an exception for people of unsound mind. This book is a history of treatment without consent, covering the changing treatments which have been given without consent, the changing basis on which people are treated without consent (because they are psychiatric in-patients, because they are detained patients, or because they are incapacitated), and the changing nature of consent itself.

In 1992–1993 I carried out an empirical study of just over 1,000 cases of treatment without consent under the Mental Health Act 1983, the results of which are summarised in Chapter 12. It revealed the sorts of treatments which are given today without consent: psychotropic medication and ECT. This history of psychiatric treatment without consent began life as an attempt to write a brief historical introduction to that study. This, I quickly discovered would not be a simple task.

Although W.L. Jones' book *Ministering to Minds Diseased*[3] gives a useful history of different treatment methods, and Elliot Valenstein's *Great and Desperate Cures*[4] brilliantly analyses the origins and history of the psychosurgery craze of the 1940s and 1950s, there was no history of psychiatric treatment which satisfactorily explained how treatment has developed over the 150 years since the dawn of the British psychiatric profession. Historians have tended to trace the beginning of modern psychiatry to 'Pinel's unshackling of the maniacal patients' in Paris in 1792. Weiner has shown that, despite its iconographic power for psychiatry, this legendary event, like many medical parables, was a myth. It was not Pinel but his assistant Pussin who removed the shackles in 1797, two years after Pinel had left the Bicetre. Pinel's true importance, according to Weiner, is that he was 'responsible for transforming French society's perception of the mad into that of sick and often curable men and women'.[5]

Having emerged from the dark ages, psychiatric histories then turn to late-eighteenth- and early-nineteenth-century treatments such as the douche bath (Chinese water torture), the 'bath of surprise' (plunging the patient unexpectedly into icy water), and the whirligig chair (for making patients sick with dizziness). Hunter and McAlpine's 1963 study contains an impressive collection of illustrations of these gadgets,[6] often shown at the beginning of lectures on modern treatments, implicit in the joke a demonstration of how far psychiatry has come. A steroptypical whig conception of psychiatric history would be that mechanical restraint was abolished in England in the middle of the nineteenth century, and that psychiatry has been making steady progress since. There was an exception: the period of experimentation with radical treatments, such as psychosurgery, coma and shock treatments, but these, with the exception of Electro Convulsive Therapy (ECT), were happily abandoned with the arrival of neuroleptics and effective antidepressants. Chapters 1–3 explain how psychiatry emerged from the 'dark age' of mechanical restraint, and Chapter 4 shows how in the 1880s there was a growing move to recognise mechanical restraint as an acceptable part of psychiatry's armamentarium, culminating in the development of a legal regime to allow it to be employed, subject to the safeguards in section 40 of the Lunacy Act 1890.

The history is not just of treatment, but of treatment without consent. Is this a late-twentieth-century question? Certainly, it is important to avoid the dangers of returning to the world of 150 years ago armed with the ethical concepts of the late twentieth century. Instead, care has been taken to seek documentary evidence of the views of doctors and official bodies about the importance of consent, and also the thoughts of those patients who were treated without consent. This book attempts to shed light on current law and psychiatric practice of treatment without consent through an examination of its history, an endeavour which has involved a number of different areas and styles of inquiry. Chapters 1 to 11 look at the history of treatment without consent and the importance attached to consent-seeking. Chapter 12 describes the operation of the statutory second-opinion procedures governing treatment for mental disorder without consent. Chapter 13 outlines current law and practice regarding emergency sedation, seclusion and restraint and the current law and practice regarding emergency sedation, seclusion and restraint and the current legal position, while Chapters 14–16 examine the development since 1989 of a sophisticated body of common-law rules and principles on treatment without consent.

The historical analysis was built up from learned medical journals, patient memoirs, files in the Public Record Office issued by the government, Lunacy Commission, and Board of Control, and treatment records in various asylums. Legal histories of psychiatry have tended to focus on powers and procedures of detention, not systematically on the actual treatment given to those detained and the relevance of consent. Until the 1980s and early 1990s, which have seen a plethora of statute and common law on treatment without consent, it is not possible to chart the development of treatment without consent through the traditional methods of legal history, which focus on Acts of Parliament and developing case law. This is because there was very little law. However, an examination of asylum medical case books, official papers, memoirs of patients and debates in medical journals shows that there was a great deal of treatment without consent, and that consent was an issue for doctors and patients as early as the beginning of the nineteenth century. In this sense the book is not so much a legal history but a legal and ethical archaeology, at times finding only traces of ideas of consent and consent-seeking, at others rich veins of material.

How has the law's role in relation to treatment without consent changed? In 1992 Lord Donaldson pointed out that seeking a patient's consent to treatment can have a number of purposes. From a therapeutic point of view a treatment may well prove more effective if the patient agrees to it. From a doctor's point of view it provides a 'legal flak jacket' in the sense that it gives legal authority to treat; a defence against criminal prosecution or civil action for battery.[7] For a doctor, the law may also have a predatory role as a source of legal liability. How has the balance between these roles changed over the period, and to what extent can and does law perform a third role of ensuring that patients are not harmed by treatment given without consent?

The year 1845 has been chosen as the starting point because it was then that the Metropolitan Commission in Lunacy – established to license and inspect asylums and private madhouses in London and its immediate environs – was transformed into a national Lunacy Commission, with jurisdiction over the detention and treatment of persons of unsound mind throughout England and Wales. The Lunatic Asylums Act 1845 also required the establishment of county asylums throughout England and Wales. Unsworth[8] describes the period from 1845 until the late 1860s as 'psychiatry's golden age'. During this time the Lunatics Act conferred control over the treatment of unsoundness of mind on the then-emergent psychiatric profession, and there was great optimism about the curative potential of asylums as Utopian communities based on philosophies of non-restraint. In June 1841 the Association of Medical Officers of Hospitals for the Insane was founded. In 1865 it became the Medico-Psychological

Association, and in 1926 received a Royal charter to become the Royal Medico-Psychological Association, the direct ancestor of the present-day Royal College of Psychiatrists, which received its charter in 1971.

From the 1840s onwards the medical officers had that most important attribute of a profession: a legal monopoly over a market. All asylums and private licensed houses had to have a medical attendant, and the superintendents of asylums were to be medical men. A further important sign of professional status and a weapon of occupational power came in 1853 when the Association launched their professional journal, the *Asylum Journal*. In 1856 it became the *Asylum Journal of Mental Science*, and from 1859 to 1962 was the *Journal of Mental Science*, after which it assumed its current title, the *British Journal of Psychiatry*. Andrew Scull sums up the period in the following terms:

> The advent of the Victorian era coincided . . . with the culmi-nation of a series of dramatic changes in society's response to madness. Some of the more obvious changes were: the state apparatus assumed a much greater role in the handling of insanity; the asylum became almost the sole officially approved response to the problems posed by the mentally disordered; and the nature and limits of lunacy were them-selves transformed. Madness was increasingly seen as something which could be authoritatively diagnosed, certi-fied and treated only by a group of legally recognised experts. And those experts were, of course, medical men, increas-ingly an organised and self-conscious specialism within the profession of medicine, known to their detractors as 'mad-doctors' and among themselves as 'alienists' or 'medical superintendents of asylums for the insane'. The clumsiness of the title at least captures the extent to which their pro-fessional identity was bound up with their institutional status.[9]

Victorian social policy on lunacy was based on the principle that the insane were best cared for in institutions, and that those institutions should be subject to inspection by a Crown-appointed central authority. To that end duties were placed on magistrates to build county asylums. Private institutions were required to be licensed and were subject to inspection. The whole system was placed under the supervision of the Commissioners in Lunacy and even those keeping a lunatic as a single patient had to notify the Commission.

Mid-nineteenth-century lunacy legislation created not only a system of institutions, but also a jurisdiction enabling the commissioners to influence the construction of asylums and to set down the moral boundaries for the treatment of their inmates. Ever since, with the exception of the period between the Mental Health Acts of 1959 and 1983, there has been a central authority to exercise this kind of supervision: the Lunacy Commission (1845–1913), the Board of Control (1913–1959), and the Mental Health Act Commission from 1983 until the present.

The Lunacy Commission and its successor, the Board of Control, issued streams of directives on the internal regulation of institutions, on matters ranging from drainage/sanitation of asylum sites and the diet of pauper patients to coercive practices like seclusion and the use of baths as a form of restraint.[10] This power to 'legislate' for the psychiatric system would come to play an important part in constructing a moral order for psychiatric treatment, and indeed in defining what treatment included. In order to understand fully the role of law *vis-à-vis* psychiatric treatment, it is important to adopt a broad concept of law which includes not only the legislative milestones provided by the Lunacy, Mental Treatment and Mental Health Acts, but also the subordinate rules and guidance, often developed in reaction to cases where individual patients died as a result of psychiatric treatment. The role of the circulars issued by the Lunacy Commission and the Board of Control is currently played by the Mental Health Act Code of Practice, the observance of which is monitored by the Mental Health Act Commission. The Commission has now started to issue guidance notes on particular treatments and on the implementation of various provisions of mental health legislation. These forms of 'soft law' seek to develop a system of psychiatric ethics, and part of the project of this book is to explore the principles on which that system is based.

Central authorities have always played an important role in defining what psychiatric treatment is. A major difference between psychiatric and other medical treatment is that it is frequently given to restrain patients who are, in the evocative Victorian phrase, 'furiously mad'. Restraint may be physical, by holding the patient down or using a restraint device; it may be achieved chemically by using sedative drugs; it may involve secluding patients

6

in solitary confinement; or it may involve combinations of these methods. However achieved, it is difficult to unravel the different strands of treatment, discipline and punishment interwoven in the Gordian knot of restraint. When chemical restraint is achieved using severe doses of drugs with unpleasant effects, patients see it as an exercise of disciplinary power by the doctor. Physical restraint is seen by patients as assault, mechanical restraint as bondage, and seclusion as solitary imprisonment or corrective isolation. However, the system of regulating seclusion is such that the perceptions of patients are of little importance unless it can be shown that the motive of the doctors and nurses imposing it was improper. Seclusion and restraint are to be used as last resorts, never as a punishment, and their continuation after the patient no longer poses a threat to the safety of others has always suggested to commissioners a punitive rather than a protective motive. With the exception of mechanical restraint in the early years of the Lunacy Commission, the strategy of central bodies has been to seek to exercise surveillance over the use of coercive interventions rather than to seek their total elimination.

Even if coercive restraint and heavy sedation were not viewed as recognised treatments *for insanity*, they were recognised treatments *of the insane* to control their disturbed behaviour, and the different commissions which have presided over the psychiatric system have played an important role in shaping the perception of what is acceptable. The Lunacy Commission in the 1850s saw seclusion as akin to restraint, but accepted that it might have a role in the management of severely disturbed patients and viewed it as less undesirable than mechanical restraint as long as it was kept within proper limits. Although recently there have been calls to ban seclusion, it is retained as an accepted psychiatric practice. The present-day Code of Practice on the Mental Health Act 1983, whilst not regarding seclusion as 'a treatment technique', describes it as falling within the broad legal definition of 'medical treatment' in section 145(1) of the 1983 Act, which includes 'nursing, care, habilitation and rehabilitation under medical supervision'.[11]

It is problematic to regulate treatment of mentally disordered people by stating that certain practices will be acceptable only if used with a therapeutic or preventative purpose rather than a punitive or disciplinary one. Regulation along these lines produces the paradox that the regulatory framework will provide authority for the continued use of those very practices it seeks to limit, as long as they are not applied with undue severity and the doctors and nurses are not acting out of improper motives. Emergency psychiatric medication and restraint both carry significant risks for the safety of the patient. Their very essence is that they are given without consent. This prompts two further questions. To what extent and for how long have consent to treatment and consent-seeking been ethical issues in psychiatry? How have ideas of consent been shaped and transformed over time?

There has been extensive debate about the point at which notions of consent (informed or otherwise) took root in medical practice.[12] The case of *Slater* v. *Baker and Stapleton*[13] suggests that it was well recognised in surgical practice by 1767. This was an action against a surgeon and an apothecary who had rebroken without consent a patient's leg which the surgeon had already set. Two surgeons gave evidence that they would not have rebroken the leg without the consent of the patient. In an early echo of contemporary legal debates it was argued that because the patient had been treated without any consent, the proper form of action was trespass or battery, not case, which was a form of action based on the defendant's ignorance and lack of skill. The judge dismissed this argument, noting that it appeared from the evidence of surgeons that it was 'improper to disunite the callous without consent'. Consent-seeking in such a case was 'the custom and usage of surgeons'. He went on to say this:

> [I]t was ignorance and unskilfulness in that very particular, to do contrary to the rule of the profession, what no surgeon ought to have done; and indeed it was reasonable that a patient should be told what is about to be done to him that he may take courage and put himself in such a situation as to enable him to undergo the operation.[14]

Whilst consent-seeking may have been viewed as important in surgery, we might not be surprised to find that this was untrue in psychiatry, because mental patients might be thought to lack the necessary judgment or capacity to give true consent. In fact there are strong traces of awareness of consent as an issue in psychiatric treatment in the 1820s from the memoirs of a patient, John Perceval;[15] in the mid-nineteenth century during the clitoridectomy scandal involving Isaac Baker Brown, described in Chapter 5; and in debates in the 1930s about sterilisation of the unfit, which are the subject of Chapter 6.

8

On what basis were people treated without consent? Until 1930 all people who were received into public asylums or into private care for profit had to be certified, and were subject to visitation by the Lunacy Commission. Certified status placed the patient in what Unsworth, following Castel,[16] has described as a 'tutelary relationship' with the asylum superintendent, a relationship where the doctors made decisions about their patients' treatment, subject only to any supervision exercised by the Lunacy Commission or the Board of Control.[17] Implicit in the status of psychiatric patient was the idea that patients were under doctors' orders regarding psychiatric treatment. However, as Chapter 5 shows, there is evidence from the 1860s and 1880s of the importance of securing someone's consent, even if it is not the patient's, where it was intended to carry out surgery. Concerns about consent also came to public prominence in the debates about sterilisation of 'the unfit' in the 1920s and 1930s. The Board of Control played an important part in these, and a committee presided over by its chairman, Sir Lawrence Brock, reported in 1933 recommending legislation to authorise sterilisation of mental defectives with their consent or that of their relatives.[18]

As far as psychiatric treatments were concerned, the advent of voluntary boarder status in the Lunacy Act 1890, and to a greater extent that of voluntary patient with the Mental Treatment Act 1930, raised questions about the lawfulness of treating without their consent in-patients who were not detained. Liability to compulsory treatment only existed if the patient was detained and was no longer an automatic consequence of being a psychiatric in-patient. Nevertheless, mental patients who were not detained but who were refusing treatment that was believed necessary by their doctors could always be detained in order for it to be given. The Mental Health Act 1959 introduced a new non-detained status for informal patients, including not only the truly voluntary, but also many who were 'non-volitional' (incapable of expressing acceptance or resistance), and who had been admitted without formality or compulsion by their friends or relatives. The assumption that detained patients could be treated for their mental disorder without consent met no serious challenge until the mid 1970s, when an extensive debate on the issue led to the provisions of Part IV of the Mental Health Act 1983 on consent to treatment, which makes it clear that detained patients can be treated for mental disorder without consent, subject to compliance with a statutory second opinion procedure.

Law has always played a fundamental role in providing authority for detention and in conferring the power to make decisions affecting psychiatric patients on other people. A central concern of historians of English mental health legislation has been the debate about legalism and medicalism.[19] Legalism focuses on the coercive aspects of psychiatry such as detention, forcible treatment and restraint, and seeks to regulate them by imposing due process safeguards. Medicalism seeks to take advantage of the ideological role of law to submerge these coercive dimensions of psychiatry, and encourage their perception as medical treatments whose administration should be a matter of clinical judgment rather than a subject for legal regulation. Kathleen Jones, whose work has been a great influence on thinking about English law and psychiatry, sees the history of mental health legislation in terms of the movement of a pendulum between the two extremes of legalism and medical discretion. For Jones legalism means procedural formalism and a 'mechanistic approach'.[20] She argues that 'open-textured law – enabling rather than regulatory, permitting the maximum of discretion within a loose framework of regulation – seems preferable', and she criticises those who have sought to limit psychiatric discretion by enhancing patients' rights as purveyors of 'resuscitated Diceyism'.[21] Underlying this critique is the assumption that a rights-based approach impedes effective pursuit of the welfare of the patient. Opponents of these views see Jones's 'open-textured' rules as leading to dangerous increases in the discretionary power of psychiatrists, putting them beyond effective control by traditional legal processes. Unless such controls are in place there can be no guarantee that psychiatry will use its compulsory powers for the best interests of patients. The fact that doctors mean well does not mean that they inevitably do good.

In his more recent work, Unsworth refers not to legalism but to 'juridicism', or 'adherence to an ideology embodying a preference for rule-bound relationships entailing rights, duties and other law-centred concepts'.[22] He counterposes the Lunacy Commissioners' 'bureaucratic juridicism ... directed to the utilitarian and humane operation of the system on the basis of a normative order which embodied sound practice' with 'traditional juridicism', represented by the activities of the patient-centred Alleged Lunatic's Friend Society. The latter, in Unsworth's characterisation:

[D]rew together a number of different currents, including 'juridical nationalism', a chauvinistic cultural pride in legally enshrined English liberties as being definitive of the national character, in contrast to the despotic tendencies of Continental European law and government, with invocation of resonant historical reference points such as Anglo-Saxon Law and Magna Carta. The common law and habeas corpus epitomized this mythical libertarian heritage.[23]

In the light of this description it is perhaps ironic that the most recent source of inspiration for juridicism should be the European Convention on Human Rights (ECHR). During the public debate prior to the passage of the Mental Health Act 1983, Larry Gostin the legal officer of MIND (the National Association for Mental Health) urged the introduction of greater procedural safeguards and tighter regulation of psychiatry, describing the reform proposals which he had drafted for MIND as based on a 'new legalism'.[24] Gostin argued that Jones's attacks were aimed at a cumbersome and technical legal formalism which few would support. His critique of the 1959 Act, which conferred wide discretionary power on doctors and state authorities, was put forward as serious institutional malpractice was revealed in a series of inquiries into abuses in psychiatric hospitals.

The 'new legalism' was based to a great extent on the ECHR. In the 1970s and 1980s Gostin and MIND had brought a series of test cases under the Convention before the Commission and Court of Human Rights, which highlighted the absence of possibilities for legal review of detention for many patients. The European Court upheld the legalist view of psychiatric detention as a form of arrest, holding that Article 5 of the Convention requires any decision to detain a person on grounds of unsoundness of mind to be free from arbitrariness.[25] In *Winterwerp* v. *the Netherlands* the Strasbourg Court held that three conditions must be satisfied in order for there to be a 'lawful detention of a person of unsound mind'. First, except in emergency cases, the individual must be reliably shown to be of unsound mind, entailing 'the establishment of a true mental disorder before a competent authority on the basis of objective expertise'.[26] Second, the mental disorder must be of a kind or degree warranting compulsory confinement. Third, the validity of continued confinement depends on the persistence of such a mental disorder.[27] If detention is to be prolonged, the authorities must satisfy themselves at reasonable intervals that the criteria for detention continue to be met. In *X* v. *the United Kingdom* the Court said this:

> [A] person of unsound mind compulsorily confined in a psychiatric institution for an indefinite or lengthy period is in principle entitled, at any rate where there is no automatic review of a judicial character, to take proceedings before a court at reasonable intervals to put in issue the lawfulness ... of his detention, whether that detention was ordered by a civil or criminal court, or by some other authority.[28]

In addition to traditional notions of due process, the two principles underpinning Larry Gostin's new legalism were 'the ideology of entitlement', that patients should have enforceable rights to the care which they need, and 'the least restrictive alternative', that they have a right to expect care in the least restrictive alternative setting.[29] The least restrictive alternative is based on the second *Winterwerp* criterion of lawful detention and, as Gostin points out, if taken seriously, 'would require the government to create a full range of community services including housing, crisis intervention, medical and nursing support, training and employment'.[30] It was envisaged that recognition of the ideology of entitlement and the least restrictive alternative would also entail the protection of mentally disordered people against discrimination and the creation of legal rights to appropriate care and treatment.[31] The Strasbourg Court has provided an important underpinning for the due process component of the 'new legalism' as far as psychiatric detention is concerned but, as we shall see, the scope for using the Convention to challenge coercive treatment or to uphold rights to adequate services has been extremely limited.

Whilst legalism concentrates on the coercive features of psychiatry, medicalism seeks to emphasise its therapeutic aspects and to approximate it to general medicine. The paradox of the medicalist perspective is that, in so far as psychiatry forces patients to accept treatment, it requires the law to give authority to clinical power, and yet is often reluctant to accept significant procedural or substantive limits on that authority. We shall see how, throughout its history the psychiatric profession has striven to establish, maintain, and expand the legal recognition of 'clinical authority' to treat, if necessary without consent. An important aspect of

clinical authority is the recurring theme of how far doctors are
protected against legal action in respect of acts done while caring
for and controlling patients, and the changing nature of the special
statutory defences for mental health professionals. The conclusion
examines current developments, including the Government's
Mental Health (Patients in the Community) Bill 1995, and the
proposals of the Law Commission for a new legal régime for the
treatment of adults who lack mental capacity.[32] It argues that
looking at the history of mental health law in terms of the promotion, development and legal recognition of clinical authority offers
a better perspective on the direction of reform than simply
portraying it in terms of a pendulum swing between legalism and
medicalism.

1
1845–1853:
THE BIRTH OF THE
LUNACY COMMISSION

The English tradition of supervising the treatment of the detained insane by commission is traceable to the Madhouses Act 1774, which provided for the inspection of private madhouses in London and its immediate environs by five commissioners appointed by the Royal College of Physicians. However, their powers and geographical jurisdiction were limited, and the medical commissioners' ineffectual approach meant that they offered scant protection for inmates.[1]

In 1814, scandal broke when Godfrey Higgins discovered in York Asylum (of which he was a governor) thirteen women in a cell twelve feet by seven feet ten inches, and that the deaths of 144 patients had been concealed.[2] The same spring, Edward Wakefield found a side room in Bethlem hospital where ten female patients were chained by one arm or leg to the wall, naked except for an unfastenable blanket gown. In the men's wing, in the side room, six patients were chained to the wall. In a lower gallery (traditionally the area of an asylum where the 'troublesome' and 'dirty' patients were kept), the pitiable figure of James Norris was found, confined in a dungeon, his body enclosed in a device of iron bars and chained to the trough where he lay. Norris died of consumption a few days after his release.[3]

The Parliamentary Select Committee appointed in 1815 in the wake of these cases was highly critical of the laxity of the Royal College commissioners' inspections. Eventually, in 1828, following a further Select Committee investigation in 1827, the Board of the Metropolitan Commissioners in Lunacy was established, consisting of fifteen commissioners of whom at least five were to be doctors.[4] Their functions included the licensing and frequent inspection of madhouses in the Metropolitan area of London.[5]

14

From November 1832 the chair was taken over by Lord Ashley, later to become Earl of Shaftesbury, and chairman of the Lunacy Commission from 1845 until his death in 1885.

The Lunatics Act 1842[6] extended the geographical jurisdiction of the commissioners to England and Wales as a whole, and the Lunatics Act 1845[7] renamed them the Commissioners in Lunacy. The Commission was to consist of three doctors, three barristers, and up to five unpaid lay commissioners. As Shaftesbury put it in his evidence to the Commons Select Committee on Lunatics in 1859:

> The lay element ... not only upon the Commission but among the visiting magistrates in the country is of the most indispensable importance, and without it, I am quite certain, the whole system of management of lunatics would fall into the greatest disorder and we should relapse into many of the errors from which we have been extricated.[8]

The Lunatic Asylums Act 1845[9] converted into a duty the power conferred on justices by the County Asylums Act 1808[10] to provide an asylum for each county. In conjunction with the Home Secretary, the Commission was to supervise the construction and management of the new county asylums.

A central function of the commissioners was licensing private institutions. The logic of the regulatory system was that no-one could be received into an institution as a person of unsound mind unless it was an asylum or licensed house which would be subject to frequent inspection. Under the Lunatics Act 1845, the commissioners had 'immediate jurisdiction' over licensing in the London area, and elsewhere the justices of the peace licensed houses within their county or borough.[11] The justices were to appoint three of their number plus one paid physician, surgeon or apothecary to act as visitors.[12] The clerk to the justices had to send a copy of any licences granted to the Commission.[13]

The Lunacy Commissioners visited private and public asylums and all single patients kept for profit. They also had to scrutinise all admission orders and supporting certificates which, together with a statement of the mental and bodily condition of the patient, were to be sent by the proprietor or superintendent of the asylum or licensed house to the commissioners within seven days of admission.[14] The same requirement applied to those who cared for single patients for profit in unlicensed houses.[15] The certificates of bodily condition often disclosed that patients being transferred from other institutions to asylums bore the marks of ill-treatment or lengthy confinement in fetters. In cases where it was believed that a patient was being kept under restraint as a single patient the Commission could apply to the Lord Chancellor for an order of visit.[16] The visiting justices and the commissioners could report any case of unlawful taking or confinement of a person as an insane patient, or of ill-treatment or wilful neglect, to the Home Secretary, who could direct the Attorney-General to prosecute.[17]

Jones describes Ashley's strong belief in the value of documentation as 'a safeguard against irregular practice'.[18] To supplement the central scrutiny of admission documents, visiting commissioners examined the medical visitation book and the medical case book which had to be completed weekly by the medical attendant of the asylum. The visitation book showed the number, sex, and state of health of all the patients in the house or hospital; the names of all patients under restraint, in seclusion, or under medical treatment since the last report; the condition of the house or hospital; and every death, injury or act of violence affecting any patient since the last report.[19] In 1846 the commissioners issued a circular specifying the information to be entered in the medical case book by the physician, surgeon or apothecary, including the mental state and bodily condition of each patient, and a correct description of the medicine and other remedies prescribed for the treatment of his or her disorder.[20]

All licensed houses were to be visited by at least two commissioners (a barrister and a physician or surgeon) at least four times a year if they were in the immediate jurisdiction, and twice if not. The justices had to nominate two visitors to visit every house licensed by them at least four times a year. The Commission was also under a duty to send a doctor and a barrister to visit every asylum in the country, and every gaol or workhouse where any lunatic was alleged to be.[21] The commissioners or visitors were required to visit every part of the establishment and grounds; to inquire if any patient was under restraint and why; to inspect the order and certificates for every patient received since the last visit. If the house was licensed by the justices, they had to consider the justices' observations in the visitors' book and to enter a minute in the visitors' book of the condition of the house and the patients therein; of the number of patients under restraint and the reasons thereof; and of any irregularities in the order or certificates. The 1845 Act required commissioners, on their visits to licensed houses and hospitals maintained by voluntary contributions, to ask 'whether there has been adopted any system of non-coercion, and, if so, the effect thereof?' It was a misdemeanour to give a false answer to any question.[22] Commissioners and visitors were also empowered to summon witnesses before them to testify on oath about any matter within their jurisdiction.[23] The commissioners could discharge individual patients if, after two separate visits seven days apart, they considered there was insufficient cause for detention.[24]

Hervey has raised the question of the influence of political theorists such as Bentham on the practical workings of the Commission, but he concluded that it is more important to emphasise the gradual evolution of the Commission, promoting internal change, initiating legislation and 'extending central control to the provinces, from a knowledge base founded on its field executives' experience'.[25] Although there is little evidence of the conscious adoption of Benthamite ideas, the *modus operandi* of the Commission shows strong parallels with Bentham's Panopticon; the model correctional institution where all the inmates could be viewed in their cells from a central point.[26] The Lunacy Acts conferred clinical power on psychiatrists, and created a limited zone within which it could be exercised – primarily public asylums or licensed houses, although anyone keeping a single lunatic for profit was also subject to supervision and visitation by the commissioners. Effective central surveillance required a measure of transparency, to be achieved by unannounced visiting and requiring records of key aspects of patient care. Visiting commissioners could then examine the records and pursue whatever lines of inquiry they suggested. Legal duties to keep documentary records in a standard form are essential for such a system, to show that those with the clinical power to interfere with a person's freedom have addressed themselves to the correct legal criteria and kept within the limits of their powers. This explains why commissioners from 1845 until today have invariably taken a serious view of failures to keep adequate records, from time to time attracting unfair charges of obsessional bureaucracy.

A principal occupation in the years following the 1845 Act was overseeing the establishment of public asylums for pauper lunatics. Only about 4,500 of the estimated 17,000 pauper lunatics were cared for in asylums and the establishment of asylums for every county was a priority. The commissioners' views on siting, architectural design and the command structure of asylums were strongly influenced by a series of articles in 1846 in the *Lancet* by John Conolly, the champion of non-restraint, which he expanded in a book in 1847.[27] Conolly recommended asylums capable of accommodating between 350 and 400 patients (although by the end of the century there would be many with populations of over 1,000). Contemporary asylum design had all too often reflected the style of the prison rather than the hospital. Conolly recommended that doctors should be involved in the design, the buildings should be on a healthy site in pleasant surroundings, well drained, admitting air, and there should be a school, a chapel and good hygiene. Patients were to be kept occupied, preferably on outdoor work in the gardens or on the asylum farm, and plenty of recreational activities and amusement should be laid on for them.

Each asylum should be under the direction of a medical superintendent, who in hospitals of less than 400 patients would need no more than one assistant to make up the drugs, and in larger establishments would require other medical assistants, either appointed by the physician or who would at any rate act under his instructions. Doctors were to be the officers, attendants the 'other ranks'. Even the matron would be under the superintendent's orders. In 1847 the Commission met a number of medical superintendents and together they developed a set of model rules along these lines, placing the medical superintendents in supreme command of the asylum, answerable only to the visiting committee and the Lunacy Commission.[28] The supreme power of the medical superintendents meant that there was one person whom the Commission could hold accountable for abuses in the institution. This internal command structure would endure until the Mental Health Act 1959. As Bynum, Porter and Shepherd put it, asylums would soon become thought of 'as a territory over which the alienist held suzerainty, an imperial colony or fiefdom to be managed with justice, economy, and administrative flair'.[29] Like its feudal analogue, this suzerainty not only conferred authority, it imposed duties too: to sanction, explain and record restraint or seclusion. The Lunacy Commission's jurisdiction over treatment reflected their origins in the Norris scandal. They were required by statute to inspect records of mechanical restraint.

The treatment philosophy of non-restraint dominated the psychiatric landscape from the 1840s until the 1880s. In 1792 William Tuke founded the Retreat at York, dedicated to the humane care of people of unsound mind.[30] Application of the principles of non-restraint in public asylums was pioneered at Lincoln asylum from 1835 onwards by Gardiner Hill, whose writings and experiences inspired John Conolly to introduce non-restraint at Hanwell in 1839 and develop it through his own teaching and writing into a comprehensive treatment philosophy. Non-restraint became the dominant psychiatric ideology of the 1840s and 1850s because its champions controlled the emergent professional body, the Association of Medical Officers of Asylums and Hospitals for the Insane, and its official organ, the *Asylum Journal*. At its inaugural meeting in 1841 the Association had resolved:

> That without pledging themselves to the opinion that mechanical restraint may not be found occasionally useful in the management of the insane, the members now present have the greatest satisfaction in according their approbation of, and in proposing their thanks to, those gentlemen who are now engaged in endeavouring to abolish its use in all cases.[31]

The abandonment of manacles, shackles and restraint devices was crucial to the professional project of the alienists because it was essential to differentiate themselves from mere prison warders. There are many surviving illustrations of prevalent treatments of the late eighteenth and early nineteenth centuries. During this period it was widely believed that physical and mental illness could not coexist in the same body and that severe shock and sudden terror to the body produced a tonic effect on the mind. Here was the therapeutic rationale for a bizarre range of treatments. It included restraint in such devices as the original tranquilliser, Benjamin Rush's chair, where the patient was strapped tightly to a sturdy chair which included a box to go over the patient's head. There was a bewildering array of machines, like the whirligig chair, where patients were revolved at high speed until they became violently ill and were reduced to a state of total collapse. Baths of surprise, where patients were suddenly and unexpectedly immersed in cold water, were still used during the first quarter of the nineteenth century, even though the dangers

19

of death from shock were well known. The predominance of this type of therapeutics militated against the alienists' desired image as doctors, rather than as a strange tribe of Heath Robinson engineers whose principal defining characteristic was a genius for developing weird and wonderful contraptions for the restraint or discomfiture of their patients.

Descriptions of contemporary treatment methods in the Minutes of Evidence to the Select Committee of 1815 show the defining characteristics of medical treatment as opposed to mere imprisonment.[32] Violent patients were purged and bled immediately on admission, and given 'vomits' regularly thereafter. Ultimately the order of the asylum rested on opium, described in standard texts throughout the nineteenth century as the 'sheet anchor', the heaviest anchor on the ship for use when all else fails. The metaphor is apt from more than one point of view, since the sensation of being hit on the head by a large heavy object characterises patients' descriptions of being on the receiving end of all the different drugs used by psychiatry down the years for emergency sedation. The drugs then in use to subdue disturbed behaviour were primarily hypnotics, most notably opium and cannabis. Emetics were also widely used not only for their properties of cleansing the digestive system but also because, if given in large enough doses, the frenzied state of patients' bowels rendered them helpless and compliant and acted as a corrective to unwanted behaviour. Other drugs such as digitalis and henbane were popularly used for their capacity to paralyse the minds and bodies of maniacal patients. By the end of the first quarter of the nineteenth century medicine had the pharmacological equipment to replace the mechanical genius of yore. To achieve the alienists' desired transition to a medical body, the old methods had to be stamped out. The Commissioners in Lunacy were required to record mechanical restraint and their reports provided the professional reformers with precious information about its continued prevalence.

As mechanical restraint came into disrepute, seclusion came increasingly to the fore. The Commission's report for 1843 noted that hospitals which professed wholly or partly to have dispensed with restraint, 'employ seclusion or solitary confinement', and that:

Seclusion or solitary confinement is now getting into general use in the treatment of the insane, and great numbers of the proprietors of public and private asylums throughout the country are fitting up and bringing into use solitary cells, and padded rooms for violent and unmanageable lunatics. ... Seclusion is found to have a very powerful effect on tranquillising and subduing those who are under temporary excitement or paroxysms of violent insanity. ... As a temporary remedy, for very short periods, in case of paroxysms and of high excitement, we believe seclusion to be a valuable remedy. We are convinced, however, that it should only be permitted for short periods, and that it should not be permitted as a means of managing and treating those persons who are permanently violent and dangerous ...[33]

The Commission's recommendation in 1843 that a register of seclusion should be kept as well as the register of mechanical restraint was partly taken up in the Lunatics Act 1845 requiring recording of the names of all patients under seclusion in the medical visitation book.[34]

The 1845 Act had not given the commissioners jurisdiction over Bethlem and the other charitable hospitals, much to Ashley's chagrin. In 1851 the certificate of bodily condition for a patient admitted to Northampton Asylum from Bethlem described her very poor condition, including extensive injuries from having been ill-treated, confined in a cell, and made to sleep naked on a bed of loose straw.[35] Four commissioners visited and inspected Bethlem under a special ministerial warrant.[36] The commissioners' report to Parliament deplored conditions in the 'back basement refractory wards' for wet and dirty patients. Apparently unknown to any of the responsible authorities or the institution's senior staff the practice of placing female patients naked to sleep in trough beds containing loose straw had prevailed for years, leading the commissioners to conclude that 'the most culpable laxity must have prevailed in the internal supervision of the hospital'.[37]

Although the Bethlem authorities complained about the vehemence with which the Commissioners had set about their investigation,[38] their findings could not seriously be disputed, and section 35 of the Lunatics Act 1853 brought the hospital under the Commission's jurisdiction. The 1853 Act also required the medical officer, on pain of a £20 fine, to make a special note in the medical journal of patients under restraint and seclusion, its means and duration, and the reasons for it.[39] Similar records were to be kept of patients receiving medical treatment for bodily disorders.

The 1853 Act completed the system of regulation which was to persist for the life of the Lunacy Commission and for most of the life of its successor body, the Board of Control. The rules of every asylum were to be submitted to the Home Secretary (in practice the Commission) for approval, and were to be 'printed, abided by and observed'.[40] In the 1870s the Lunacy Commission issued precedents of general rules for the government of asylums, in an effort to impose a national standard.[41] The Commission and the Board of Control would between them issue more than 1,000 circulars on various subjects, some seeking information about different treatments, others seeking to regulate conduct, and together with the model asylum rules they may be seen as forerunners of the contemporary Code of Practice in the Mental Health Act 1983.

During this period, from a doctor's point of view, treatment without consent was primarily a practical rather than an ethical issue. This is revealed by the instructions to use Haslam's Key, a popular device during the early nineteenth century. The key was invented by John Haslam, the apothecary of Bethlem, who described the rationale of his invention in these terms:

> Presuming that some good is to be procured by the operation of medicines on persons so affected, and aware of their propensity to reject them, it becomes a proper object of enquiry how such salutary agents may most securely, and with the least disadvantage, be conveyed into the stomachs of these refractory subjects.[42]

It was intended as a humane alternative to 'spouting', whereby medicine was administered forcibly by thrusting the spout of a metal medicine jug into the patient's mouth. Haslam's inventive talents had been inspired by the cases of a number of upper-class women patients who had been 'restored to their friends without a front tooth in either jaw'.[43] In the world of humane alternatives, everything is relative. The key was used by placing the head of the patient between the knees of the user. If a strait waistcoat was not used, a second assistant secured the hands and a third kept down the legs. The key would be inserted as soon as the patient's mouth was opened, which could be accomplished by 'blindfolding, a pinch of snuff causing him to sneeze, or tickling his nose with a feather'.[44] The key pressed down the tongue, and kept the jaws sufficiently asunder to admit the medicine, while the person using the key held the patient's nose in his left hand.

The days of devices such as Haslam's key were numbered when an Edinburgh doctor, Alex Wood, introduced in 1843 the subcutaneous injection of morphia as a treatment for nervous disorder.[45] This was followed by the invention of the hypodermic syringe in 1854, and injections of morphia would soon be seen to have many advantages over orally ingesting opium, including ease of administration to the unwilling, rapid action, less risk of constipation, and certainty of dose, since much might be spilled in trying to force a patient to take opium by mouth.

John Perceval's account of his treatment in the early 1830s testifies that patients felt acutely the dehumanising effect of being treated without consent. Whilst acknowledging that at the time of admission he required hospital treatment Perceval objected that, throughout his lengthy confinement:

> Men acted as though my body, soul and spirit were fairly given up to their control, to work their mischief and folly upon. My silence, I suppose, gave consent. I mean that I was never told such and such things we are going to do; we think it advisable to administer such and such medicine, in this or that manner. I was never asked, do you want anything? have you any objection to this or that? I was fastened down in a bed; a meagre diet was ordered for me; this and that medicine forced down my throat, or in the contrary direction; my will, my wishes, my repugnances, my habits, my delicacy, my inclinations, my necessities, were not once consulted, I may say thought of. I did not find the respect paid usually even to a child.[46]

In relation to treatment without consent the Lunacy Commission's concerns were primarily with restraint and seclusion. The Commission always declared that matters of pure medical treatment were for the individual judgment of the medical officers. Although treatments given to individual patients were to be recorded in the case books, there were insufficient commissioners to make possible any more than the most cursory perusal. The years after 1853 would see the Commission playing an important role in advocating non-restraint, and also in attempting to determine where medical treatment ended and assault began.

2

1853–1880:
THE TRIUMPH OF
NON-RESTRAINT?

As Nancy Tomes has observed: 'From the 1840s to the 1880s the non-restraint philosophy was a powerful force shaping English asylum practice.'[1] Battle lines were drawn. The *Asylum Journal* was edited by James Bucknill, medical superintendent of Exeter asylum, an ardent follower of Conolly, who was a frequent contributor. The opponents of non-restraint found expression of their views in the *Journal of Psychological Medicine*, founded by Forbes B. Winslow, a proprietor of a private licensed house, who edited the journal until his death in 1863 when it ceased publication. As Tomes puts it:

> Winslow's journal provided a continuous critique of the non-restraint party and commended those superintendents ... who defied its allegedly fanatical excesses. In disputing non-restraint, the *JPM* not only attacked the extremists in the specialty, but also questioned the Lunacy Commission's judgment in pressing their ideals too vigorously.[2]

On the other side, Bucknill and the *Asylum Journal* waited to pounce if the commissioners appeared to lack resolve in denouncing all forms of restraint.[3]

The Lunacy Commission issued a circular in February 1854 seeking the views of all asylum superintendents on restraint and seclusion and the extent of its employment, and the same year published the results in their eighth annual report.[4] In November 1854 Conolly began a series of four articles on the Commission's report,[5] which provided some raw material for his most famous book, published in 1856, *The Treatment of the Insane Without Mechanical Restraint*.[6] Although some medical officers continued to believe that non-restraint was ineffective and expensive, leading

24

to assaults on other patients and attendants and damage to bedding and windows, Conolly was pleased to report that the majority professed to have discontinued mechanical restraint at their asylums. He found the picture in the 128 private asylums more gloomy, however, with 'much reason to believe that mechanical restraints are used in no fewer than 91 of them'.[7]

The non-restrainers were not averse to using coercive methods short of mechanical restraint. One of the strongest opponents of non-restraint and the centralising tendency of the Commission was James Huxley, medical superintendent of the Kent asylum. When he suggested in a letter to the *Asylum Journal* that earlier intervention with mechanical restraint would have helped one of his very restless female meloncholic patients at Kent who died of her exertions, Conolly responded with the advice: 'A blister behind the nape of the neck, a tepid shower bath, not too violent, sedative medicines, variously prepared food, and very patient persuasion, have certainly often succeeded at Hanwell.'[8] A blister behind the neck was often an effective treatment for 'restlessness' because if the patient was clad in a garment with a coarse woollen collar, abrupt or violent movement would cause considerable pain. Judicious use of sedatives would of course reduce the need for other kinds of restraint, and in later years the question would arise whether chemical restraint had replaced the mechanical means.

The non-restraint party was also criticised for over use of seclusion, employed at Exeter asylum by Bucknill, who vigorously supported its use in his reply to the Commission circular. He now 'descended from the editorial stool' to elaborate his view in an article in the *Asylum Journal*, denying that seclusion was, as some alleged, an 'alternative' to mechanical restraint, but merely 'one of a range of more enlightened treatments' which had replaced it:

Instead of the periodic bleedings and vomitings that were formerly used, aperients, hypnotics and stimulants are now employed pro re nata [as the circumstances dictate]; and these are pointed at as substitutes for restraint. Instead of the torture of the cold douche, now happily obsolete in this country, moderate shower baths are used to cool hot heads or give tone to hysterical nerves, and they become, in their turn, the scape goats of restraint.[9]

All three of the interventions mentioned in Bucknill's article: purgative and sedative drugs, showers, and seclusion were widely used where restraint would have been used before. Although nowhere near as overtly barbaric as treatment by chains and floggings which left their outward marks on the body, in many ways restraint by chemicals was more sinister in that it restrained from within and affected the whole person, body and mind. Moreover, the drugs used by psychiatry down the ages have three basic characteristics. First, almost without exception, they have been highly dependence forming. Second, in many cases, intoxication with the drug or its abrupt withdrawal produces symptoms which mimic those of acute mental disorder. Finally, whatever their benefits, the powerful sedatives used as 'sheet anchors' have acutely unpleasant physical and psychological effects. This means they have been open to abuse for corrective purposes or as a form of chastisement.

The Commission's attitude to seclusion is revealed by the following extract from their eighth report:

> The disuse of prolonged solitary confinement ought perhaps to rank next as an important improvement in the treatment of the insane. Nothing impedes the recovery of a patient so much, or tends to confirm bad habits already contracted, as the abuse of solitary confinement.... Seclusion is chiefly used during the acute stage of mania, and in chronic cases for short periods of time as a mode of discipline when a patient has committed some act which he knows to be a breach of good order, or proper subordination.[10]

So, although the Commission discouraged its prolonged use, they accepted seclusion for short periods as a form of corrective isolation.

In 1856 the *Asylum Journal of Mental Science* published a summary of the annual reports of county lunatic asylums for 1855, noting that there was only one asylum (Kent) 'to which those who employ mechanical restraint in licensed houses and in private practice might look for countenance'.[11] Denying any desire 'to trample upon a fallen foe, and thrice to slay the slain', Bucknill concluded by noting that no single report published during the year contained 'the slightest or most indirect defence of the old methods'.[12]

As Tomes has pointed out, Huxley was prepared to offer a defence of mechanical restraint. His view was that the motivation of the doctor in imposing it was all important. Although unacceptable as a means of *punishment*, it was legitimate as a form of *treatment*, and an 'indispensable adjuvant to treatment'.[13] Once motivation becomes the central question the conundrum of where treatment ends and restraint or punishment begins becomes almost insoluble, as the Commission would soon find out.

Although the Commission always denied itself a role in decisions about medical treatment, there were many forms of treatment which could be used as restraint, including not only sedative and purgative drugs but also cold baths. The Commission was soon confronted by the question of whether cold baths were medical treatment and therefore wholly within the discretion of the medical officers. In 1856 they ordered the prosecution of Charles Snape, the medical superintendent of Surrey asylum, for manslaughter of a 65-year-old patient, Daniel Dolley. Snape had himself carried out a post mortem on Dolley, pronouncing the cause of death to be 'extensive disease of the heart', a conclusion upheld by the coroner's jury.[14] However, following an anonymous letter to the Commission, various witnesses were summoned to attend a special board of Commissioners which found that on the day of his death Dolley had hit Snape, who had ordered him to be placed for half an hour in a shower bath within a cabinet nineteen inches square and eight feet tall. The door was barred and between twenty and forty gallons of water per minute was deluged on the patient through perforations in the roof. Dolley had been placed in this bath for periods varying between five and fifteen minutes on several occasions during the weeks preceding his death. Snape regularly used shower baths to 'subdue excitement'.

Enraged by the assault, Snape ordered that Dolley should also be given four tablespoons of tartarised antimony, an extremely powerful emetic, and in a dose sufficient to produce uproar in the digestion of a horse. Both treatments were unprecedentedly severe in the experience of the attendant left to carry out these orders. They were clearly too much for Dolley, who died two minutes after being removed from the shower and given the purgative.

The Commission's investigation was commendably thorough. They had the bath examined by civil engineers who concluded that the volume of water would have made it extremely difficult for Dolley to breathe, and the holes in the ceiling were so large that the shock of the water would have been unnecessarily severe. The attendant who gave the bath said that he had opened the door at five minute intervals to allow some air in. The independent doctor engaged by the Commission found the cause of death to have been the shower bath and the tartar emetic.

The Commission assembled an impressive array of expert witnesses. Apart from Conolly himself, there were the medical superintendents of Bethlem and St Lukes, Drs Hood and Stevens, and Dr Forbes Winslow, editor of the *Journal of Psychological Medicine*. Winslow had been approached with a view to his appearing for the defence but, believing the shower and the emetic to have caused Dolley's death, he had refused. When the matter came before a grand jury to decide whether a bill of indictment for manslaughter should be preferred, the recorder at the Old Bailey astounded the Commission by favourably contrasting shower baths with out-dated modes of restraint, and by proceeding to consider the matter as one of treatment. 'The jury would have to inquire,' he said, 'if the treatment adopted by Mr Snape was accompanied by a reasonable degree of knowledge of his profession, attention and caution.' The illness of counsel forced the deferment of the proceedings, and when they were reconvened in September the recorder sought to rectify his earlier partiality by telling the grand jury that the matter was of public importance. He advised them to prefer a bill of indictment so that it could be investigated further by a petty jury. The grand jury nevertheless dismissed the indictment.

Incensed by the recorder's remarks and the collapse of a 'cast-iron' case, the Commission protested that they would not have prosecuted if they had thought for one minute that what happened to Dolley could on any possible view be considered as medical treatment given for his own benefit. Their injury was compounded when the visiting committee of Surrey asylum, having suspended Snape whilst he was under indictment, reinstated him. Accepting the view that the matter was one of strictly medical experience, the Committee had delegated the decision to a jury of six doctors – three of their own choosing and three of Snape's – which concluded that 'Mr Snape's conduct in the case in question was neither so rash nor so injudicious as to deprive him of the confidence of the magistrates'.[15] The Commission informed the Secretary of State and the Lord Chancellor that they viewed the decision to reinstate Snape by 'medical men not without note' as being of 'most dangerous import'. The Snape prosecution was a tremendous setback and clearly had a profound psychological impact on the Lunacy Commission. For neither the first nor the last time in the history of psychiatry, it highlighted the difficulties of unravelling the tangled skein of treatment and punishment. The Commission felt that Dolley had received pure punishment, and the only sense in which it could be described as medical treatment was that it was treatment ordered by a medic. It illustrates perfectly the problem of 'double effect' in this area. Both showers and emetics were recognised therapeutic agents in the treatment of mental disorder, but as both would be experienced as a form of torture by the hapless patient, they could also be used punitively. Clinical power was disciplinary power.

The Commission immediately issued a circular demanding answers to various questions about the use of baths. Huxley refused to answer, believing the question to be entirely one of medical judgement. From the responses, the Commission concluded that, however valuable shower baths might be as a remedial agent in the treatment of insanity, 'in which light alone we think they should be regarded':

> ... the distinction in many cases made between its use as
> such, and its use as a moral means of repressing excitement,
> and of correcting faulty habits, is vague and undefined; and
> that as a general rule, sufficient precautions are not taken
> to guard against its being resorted to as a punishment.[16]

The responses revealed that prolonged use of shower baths for periods of up to five, ten, fifteen or twenty minutes was occasionally given in some asylums and, more worryingly, 'systematically adopted' in a few.

In 1857 the Commission issued a set of regulations in the form of 'Suggestions to Medical Officers having care of the insane', suggestions which if not adopted might of course lead to the Secretary of State not approving the asylum's regulations. These provided that in no case should any kind of bath be used as a punishment. The authority of one of the medical officers would be required for any bath not given for the purposes of cleanliness alone. Baths could only be used as a medical agent or for subduing excitement in the presence of a medical officer or his assistant, the matron or deputy matron or a head attendant. Where a therapeutic shower or bath lasted more than three minutes, a medical officer had to observe the effects and report its exact duration in the case book. Drawing on the lesson of Dolley's death, they required that where a frame and door for the shower were used, they were to be constructed to allow the patient to be easily seen and air to be readily admitted. A record was to be made of all baths for medical purposes and their exact duration. When not in use, shower baths were to be locked and the key kept by a superior officer. The fact that Dolley had met his death as a result of the direct orders of the asylum's superintendent did not deter the Commission from continuing to rely on the senior ranks in the hospital hierarchy to police baths which lasted longer than three minutes.

When it came to restraint which was unvarnished with the tint of treatment, the Commission's approach was unyielding. In cases of recalcitrance by a medical superintendent of an asylum, they would pressure the visiting justices to dismiss him. In cases involving licensed houses, they would order the removal of patients under restraint to the asylum, and in extreme cases would recommend that the Lord Chancellor revoke the licence. These expedients were very rarely resorted to. In 1857 they secured the dismissal of Dr Millard, the medical officer of Haverfordwest asylum in Wales, for refusing to abandon restraint, and for failure to record it in the medical journal.[17] The visiting commissioners had on several occasions remonstrated with Millard for his excessive use of restraint devices. In the course of their September 1857 visit, they found one woman restrained in long iron sleeves and another in a restraint chair, one of many still in use in the asylum despite repeated recommendations from commissioners that they should be destroyed. Although the woman had been restrained on several other occasions in recent weeks, there was no record of any of these in the medical journal.

The visiting commissioners recommended that as many as possible of the more harmless cases should be moved to the workhouse (normally they recommended removal from workhouse to asylum of insane inmates), 'where they would certainly be more comfortable than at this place'. When their report was discussed centrally, the Lunacy Commission recommended to the Secretary of State that he urge the Committee of Visitors to suspend Millard forthwith. On receipt of the Home Secretary's letter, the Haverfordwest Committee immediately replaced him.

The following year the Commission again descended on Millard. He had fallen back on his other source of income, a private hospital called Portland House at Whitchurch in Herefordshire, where he had been proprietor for the past twenty-five years. In the immortal words of the Commission, 'it was built at a time when the requirements of the insane were imperfectly understood'. The Commission catalogued the deficiencies of this hospital, including unrecorded restraint with strait waistcoats, leather straps and dark, dungeon-like cells. As Millard had repeatedly failed to heed their strictures, the Commission now called in the Lord Chancellor to withdraw his licence. If the Snape prosecution had been a disaster for the Commission, Millard's fate must have been a powerful lesson to superintendents of asylums and licensed houses of the dangers of crossing them.

Recorded use of restraint certainly diminished during the 1850s and 1860s. Bethlem Royal Hospital recorded that no restraint was used between 1851 and 1870.[18] The 1862 Annual Report of the Commission summarised the use of restraint and seclusion in county asylums, indicating that mechanical restraint, although still used, was employed in very few places and on very few occasions.[19] Seclusion, on the other hand, was used in the majority of asylums with varying degrees of frequency. At Haverfordwest the new superintendent was praised for the fact that there was much less restraint and seclusion that had prevailed in Millard's time. At Bucknill's Devon county asylum, in the interval between Commission visits there were eighteen periods of seclusion for men, and fifty-three on the female side, for 'varying, but chiefly short' periods. At Kent, where Huxley was medical superintendent, five males and thirty-five females had been secluded, the commissioners finding a patient there who had been restrained and secluded for a period of four months and another who had been secluded naked for over twelve months. The Kent justices offered a robust defence of their medical superintendent, in effect telling the Commission that this was none of their business,[20] but the Commission returned to the fray in 1863, complaining about the excessive numbers of patients in strong canvas dresses. Huxley resigned, to be replaced by Dr John Kirkham, a strong devotee of non-restraint.[21]

In 1873, the Commission recorded that in thirty-eight of the fifty-four asylums visited by them, there was no record of any mechanical restraint. In the cases of twenty-two patients distributed over ten asylums, it had been reported for surgical reasons, such as to prevent patients removing dressings or during force feeding. In six asylums it had been used to counteract violent, suicidal or destructive propensities.[22] In Wandsworth asylum over a period of sixteen months, thirty-three men and twelve women had been restrained by hand gloves for destructive propensities. Dr Sheppard, the medical superintendent of the male department of Colney Hatch, singled out as having used an 'amount of restraint without precedent in any English asylum', put up a spirited defence of his use of 'robust canvas dresses', wrist straps and gloves. The Commission published their reply observing that 'such uninterrupted use of mechanical restraint, if not unjustifiable, is at least indicative of great poverty of remedial resources which is not creditable to the superintendent of a county asylum'. The visitors to the asylum replied, assuring the Commission that they had again impressed upon Dr Sheppard their desire that mechanical restraint be resorted to only in cases where he was convinced that it was for the benefit of the patient, and that 'during such restraint they require him to observe personally the progress and condition of the patient and to report the same fully in his diary'.[23] Unlike Millard and Huxley, Sheppard lived to fight another day.

There can be little doubt that this period saw a dramatic reduction in the traditional forms of restraint by chains and shackles. However, at the same time new methods of treatment were introduced which involved physical restraint but which initially were not defined as mechanical restraint. One of the most widely used was wet-packing, introduced into English psychiatric practice in 1858 by Dr C. Lockhart Robertson, medical superintendent of the Sussex lunatic asylum, as a treatment for acute mania.[24] A wrung-out wet sheet would be rapidly wound round the patient, enclosing his arms. He would then be swathed in blankets and left for an hour and a half or so following which he would be rubbed vigorously with a dripping wet sheet and the process repeated. Initially, commissioners accepted it as a form of medical treatment rather than mechanical restraint. In 1862 the medical superintendent of Somerset county asylum reported that packing in a wet sheet had often proved 'of great utility in producing sleep where opiates, given in as large doses as deemed prudent, had failed'.[25] In February 1864 James Snashall, one of Lockhart Robertson's patients, died following wet packing and the administration of digitalis as treatments for mania. He had been left in the wet-pack from 10 a.m. until 6 p.m. a week before his death, and the more likely cause of death was the digitalis rather than the wet-pack. Robertson defended himself vigorously, and successfully, in the pages of the *Asylum Journal*,[26] and both wet- and dry-packing entered more widespread use.

In 1868 wet-sheet packing was found to have 'accelerated' the death of another Sussex asylum patient, Emma Hoad. The Commission told the asylum committee that neither packing in a wet sheet nor Turkish bath should be ordered prior to examination of heart and lungs and a conclusion being reached as to its safety. Patients who were packed should be seen by a medical officer from time to time during the process, and especially before affusion in a bath.[27] In 1873 wet-sheet packing made the transition from medical treatment to mechanical restraint when the Lunacy Commission informed Robertson's successor at Sussex, Dr Williams, that packing was henceforth to be entered in the medical journal under the heading of mechanical restraint. Williams protested that the practice had been introduced more than ten years previously with the full knowledge and consent of the commissioners, and that water was a recognised therapeutical agent. Packing was initially discontinued following the commissioners' visit because the asylum staff did not wish to be using a practice stigmatised as mechanical restraint. This fastidiousness soon wore off, however, and it was resumed some weeks later. The wet-pack question showed how a psychiatric intervention could make the transition from treatment to restraint. It also serves as a reminder that the records of the prevalence of mechanical restraint are to a certain extent dependent on how restraint is defined. The other question which must be considered is the extent to which seclusion was a substitute for restraint.

The Commission included in its 1858 annual report a definition of seclusion and a statement about its use. All seclusion, defined as any amount of compulsory isolation in the day time, whereby a patient is confined in a room and separated from all associates, was required to be recorded in the medical journal. The Commission felt this had produced a beneficial effect in private houses where seclusion had been an ordinary and daily occurrence, because attendants were compelled to bring it to the attention of the medical officer, thereby producing its discontinuation. The visiting commissioners would note the total amount used in the visitors' book. Failure to record was a serious matter, and commissioners would also inspect the seclusion rooms. The Commission was forced to admit that in some asylums seclusion was still carried on to 'an injurious extent', and for reasons of convenience or economy rather than on medical grounds. They also emphasised that, in the opinion of many doctors, it was a most valuable agent in the treatment of insanity, and therefore they did not wish to offer any opinion as to its merits or demerits when employed within moderate limits. Their only desire was to secure a 'strict record of every instance where it is resorted to and to prevent its being adopted not from medical reasons, but from reasons of economy, and as a substitute for the watchfulness and care of properly qualified attendants'.[28]

Throughout the 1870s the Commission continued to insist on proper records for seclusion[29] and, where it was properly recorded, they would simply note the fact. The annual report of Bethlem Royal for 1870 contains the following quotation from the Commission Report:

According to the Medical Journal, since our last visit 6 male and 9 female patients have been secluded, on account of their violent excitement; the former altogether on 8, and the latter on 74 occasions.[30]

Their only adverse remark was that the ventilation in some of the padded rooms was imperfect.

If the commissioners considered seclusion in a particular hospital to be excessive, their standard approach was to express their great regret and their hope that the situation would be remedied in the future.[31] Use of seclusion increased gradually during the 1870s. The Commission's 1873 report showed that in only four asylums had it not been used at all. In twelve others, its recorded use was described as 'very rare'. In the remaining thirty-eight, it was more frequently used, prompting the Commission to state formally that although seclusion could be useful 'in certain cases of excitement', its value was much exaggerated and it was often resorted to unnecessarily and to an injurious extent, and for periods which were quite unjustifiable. Noting that patients usually regarded seclusion as a punishment, they declared that it was too readily used for cases of temporary excitement which might be dealt with by less repressive treatment. Its frequent use also led to attendants shirking their responsibilities. Their conclusion was that the repeated resort to seclusion could only be attributed to defective organisation or asylum management, especially regarding the adequacy of properly trained staff, and that in all cases 'persevering efforts should be made to diminish its employment and to keep it within reasonable limits'.[32]

When patients died in seclusion, the Commission took an understanding attitude towards the hospital, unless there was evidence of ill-treatment or neglect. In 1876 a Bethlem patient killed himself in seclusion. Although he did not appear to have been visited between 8 p.m. and 6 a.m. when he was found dead, the commissioners were uncritical, finding that 'even if he had been visited, the suicide might not have been earlier discovered, as he had covered himself up with the sheets'.[33] By their own definition, which applied only to day-time solitary confinement, he was not even in seclusion at the time of death. In 1880 another Bethlem patient, Martha Cristo, died in seclusion, and the Commission wrote to Dr Savage, the medical superintendent, recommending that the hospital's regulation as to frequent visitation of secluded patients be reduced to writing.[34] Although open to abuse, seclusion was clearly viewed as a more acceptable alternative than mechanical restraint, subject to a requirement that it be recorded and explained.

Between 1845 and 1880 the Lunacy Commission attempted to develop a system of ethics governing psychiatric treatment, a hierarchy of acceptability from which much modern thinking about what is permissible derives. Although it was not always clear what the concept included, mechanical restraint was frowned upon. Seclusion was allowed but had to be recorded assiduously. The method which the Commission adopted to regulate seclusion, bathing and restraint was to place them under medical control, producing the paradoxical result that whilst intended to limit their use it also legitimised them as medical interventions. The precedents issued by the Commission in 1879 to be used by local asylum committees in drawing up their local rules for approval by the Secretary of State stated that 'no patient shall be placed in restraint or seclusion except by the order of the superintendent, unless found necessary in cases of extreme violence, when the fact shall be immediately communicated to him. . . . No patient shall be subjected to a bath without a like order, except for the purposes of cleanliness'.[35]

Restraint by drugs was not mentioned. Anne Digby has shown how, during the 1870s and 1880s, sedatives such as chloral and bromides were used on an extensive scale at the York retreat, which ranked with Hanwell as a symbol of non-restraint and moral management.[36] By the late 1870s there was growing concern that chemical restraint had replaced chains and strait waistcoats.

3

CHEMICAL RESTRAINT

In the 1870s and 1880s the use of drugs to restrain patients was extensively debated. There was evidence that heavy doses of medicines with unpleasant effects were used to deter patients from misbehaviour and that many patients were kept in a permanent state of over-sedation. Motivation was all important. Administration of strong sedatives was acceptable if given with the intention to quieten a disturbed and potentially violent patient, but not as a form of punishment. Nor was routine sedation permissible simply to make life easier for the attendants. Although doctors were required to enter the drugs given to each patient in the case book, chemical restraint was clearly viewed by the Commission as medical treatment, and a matter of medical judgment, unless there was clear evidence of punitive intent. Nevertheless, the debates of the 1880s and 1890s clearly reveal the importance of drugs as a vehicle of disciplinary power in institutional psychiatry.

Although other hypnotics were widely used, opium was the traditional standby for the mad doctor, described by Bucknill and Tuke in the 1858 edition of their *Manual of Psychological Medicine* as the 'sheet anchor' of the alienist physician. 'It was the right hand of the physician in the treatment of insanity,' waxed Bucknill, 'a true balm to the wounded spirit, a sedative in mania, and a restorative in melancholia.' By the late 1850s the addictive properties of the drug were well known. The annual report of Lincoln asylum for 1858 remarked upon the high number of admissions of melancholic opium addicts due to the prevalence of opium eating amongst the people, and it pleaded for philanthropic endeavour to eradicate the addiction. Although opium was used initially as a remedy against ague (malaria), the disease had now

37

been eliminated by the draining of the fens. Many fen dwellers were now hopelessly addicted, and a goodly number were showing up in the asylum statistics as suicidal melancholics.[1] By the end of the 1860s opium was being supplanted by morphine. Because it was many times more powerful than opium, smaller doses were needed, and morphine was felt in the early stages to be a non-addictive substitute for opium. It was some time before what should have been expected sank in; that morphine was more addictive than opium. Like opium, although it was a medicine of last resort to sedate maniacally excited patients, morphia was also used routinely as a sedative and a sleeping draught.[2]

Overcoming the absence of an asylum inmate's consent to drugs during this period was still a practical rather than an ethical problem, and a giant stride towards resolving this was afforded by the invention of the hypodermic syringe in 1854. In 1876, John Diarmid, assistant physician at Perth asylum in Scotland, published an article extolling the many uses of morphine injections for acute mania, melancholia, and general paralysis of the insane. He described the importance of the hypodermic in maintaining asylum order in the following terms:

> The restraining influence which the knowledge that medicine can be administered to them, whether they are willing or not, exercises over many of the insane is very potent; while the defiant and triumphant attitude of mind which such patients frequently assume after an ineffectual attempt to give drugs by the mouth is most subversive of the quiet and order of an asylum.[3]

Drugs other than morphia enjoyed periods of intense popularity until they had been in use long enough for their limited value to become evident, and then they would be supplanted by a new fashion. Ether and chloroform were popular in the late 1850s and 1860s and Cannabis Indica was used throughout the nineteenth century.[4]

Medawar describes how potassium bromide was first recommended by 'the aptly named Sir Charles Lowcock', who had used it for epilepsy and remarked on its welcome incidental effect as a libidinal suppressant.[5] By the 1860s the bromides (bromide of ammonium and bromide of potassium) came into widespread use and remained extremely popular well into the twentieth century. Bromide is slowly excreted, so patients on regular high doses could accumulate large quantities in the body, sufficient to cause bromism (bromide intoxication), which was first observed in 1850 and a common phenomenon by the mid 1860s. Bromism merited scant mention in the spate of articles on bromides in the 1865 issues of the *Journal of Mental Science*, which dwelt on their advantageous sedative effect not only on cerebro-spinal functions, but also on the libido.[6] The symptoms of bromism mimicked closely those of mental disorder, including restlessness, disorientation, paranoia, and hallucinations. Medawar describes how this established a 'vicious cycle' whereby:

> Patients who behaved abnormally because of bromide intoxication were treated with more bromides, or perhaps with sedative hypnotic-drugs of other kinds. This phenomenon continued unnoticed for many years.[7]

Bromide was still being used as a staple in psychiatry and in general medicine throughout the first half of the twentieth century. In 1927 a simple test was developed for measuring the level of bromides in the blood. Yet Medawar reports that this brought no early reduction in hospital prescribing, nor in general practice where, in 1930, bromides were included in four prescriptions out of ten. By 1942 *Price's Textbook of the Practice of Medicine* was warning that:

> The symptoms of intoxication must be watched for with more than usual vigilance when bromide is being given, because if unrecognised as such they may lead to certification – for an avoidable, drug made psychosis.[8]

Given the extent of the bromides' hold on medicine over virtually a century, countless thousands of people may have ended up in a psychiatric hospital as a result of bromism.

Another wonder drug made its first British appearance in 1869, when Dr Lockhart Robertson reported to the Medico-Psychological Association that he had begun using chloral hydrate, a hypnotic drug which is still in use today although on a much smaller scale. Lockhart Robertson believed that it would enable the complete abandonment of restraint.[9] Within eighteen months of its introduction around fifty million doses were dispensed in England alone. Chloral would soon come to supplant opium and morphia as the sheet anchor of psychiatric treatment.

As bromides produced bromism, so chloral brought chloralism into the language, defined in the Oxford English Dictionary as 'a morbid condition induced by the long continued use of Chloral'. In the 1872 *Journal of Mental Science* Dr Richardson spoke of the need for care in the administration of the drug, suggesting safe limits for dosage and describing the dangers of 'chloral poisoning' whose symptoms included 'great mental irritability and muscular prostration, uncertainty of movement, tendency to fall forward, caprice of appetite and frequent nausea'. Richardson concluded that: 'It is certainly not because a patient is quieted by it that he is necessarily benefited by it.'[10] The same issue contained a summary of a paper lauding chloral's virtues by Dr J.B. Andrews, assistant physician at the New York state lunatic asylum. Andrews listed only the less serious effects, to which the author of the *Journal of Mental Science* abstract interposed that, 'from experience in this country might be added – death from the administration of doses not approaching the magnitude of some given by Dr Andrews'. Andrews' answer was dismissive. 'What medicine can be named which has been used so extensively, which allows of such variable limits in dose and which has passed into common use, even in the hands of nostrum vendors, and against which such a small number of casualties can be adduced.'[11] Knowledge of the dangers did not diminish chloral's popularity. The *Dispensary of the United States* for 1878 said there was 'probably no remedial agent more universally employed throughout the civilised world'.[12]

The dangers of chloral were well known by the early 1870s. In 1873 the *Journal* printed an abstract of a German article prompted by 'the numerous cases where bad symptoms or death have occurred after the administration of Chloral, the difficulty of determining the minimum dose which may induce symptoms of poisoning'. Guidance was given on pumping the stomachs of those who had been poisoned by chloral, on giving fluids, artificial respiration, injections of strychnine and caustic ammonia, and even on blood transfusions.[13] There was much doubt about what was a safe dose and there were numerous cases in the medical literature to prove that even what was reckoned a small dose might be dangerous.[14] Two doctors had reported deaths to the *Lancet* and the *British Medical Journal* following doses of five grammes, and others had observed dangerous effects after two grammes. Doses of chloral then were about twice the dose prescribed by doctors today. In 1876, a leading North American alienist, Thomas Story Kirkbride, announced that he had seen several unexpected deaths of patients taking chloral and argued for extreme caution in its use, adding that he would rather his medical friends not administer it to him.[15] Chloral would remain widely used in psychiatric hospitals well into the 1930s and is still in use today. Chloral addiction could lead to certification. Chloral certainly led to the downfall of Andrew M. Sheffield, the authoress of the letters collected and edited by John Hughes in *Letters of a Victorian Madwoman*.[16] Andrew was kept supplied with chloral by a doctor who had effectively enslaved her. Her father shot the doctor and persuaded her to burn down the house. The matter was resolved by committing Andrew to hospital where she spent the next thirty years.

By the late 1870s the proud boast of English alienists that they had vanquished mechanical restraint was being met with the accusation from their foreign counterparts that the victory had been won only by drugging patients into submission. In 1879 Conolly's son in law, Henry Maudsley, launched an attack on chemical restraint,[17] and in the same year Dr George Savage, since 1878 the chief medical officer of Bethlem, published an article in the *Journal of Mental Science* on the use and abuse of chloral. Savage had worked at the hospital for five years as assistant to Dr Rhys Williams, who had gone to the Lunacy Commission. He already had a high reputation and soon became a co-editor of the *Journal of Mental Science*. He would later leave Bethlem for a successful career in private practice, during which time he treated Virginia Woolf, and he became one of the models for the society psychiatrist Sir William Bradshaw in Woolf's novel, *Mrs Dalloway*.[18] Savage acknowledged the dangers of chemical restraint, considering chloral to cause as much insanity as it alleviated and to be a prominent cause of physical ill health, often being used as restraint rather than treatment in violent cases.[19]

In 1881 Pritchard Davies, medical superintendent of the Kent county asylum warned readers of the *Journal of Mental Science* that 'Chemical is following mechanical restraint.'[20] The term 'chemical restraint' drew attention to the Lunacy Commission's fixation on mechanical restraint and seclusion to the exclusion of restraint which could be termed medical treatment. As Pritchard Davies put it:

The Commissioners ... seldom omit to notice the presence or absence of excitement among the patients in the asylums they visit, and, as it is generally regarded as evidence of skilful treatment to have the wards quiet, any and every means could be adopted to make them so. If this desired result were obtained by means of a strait waistcoat and a gag, or by hitting the patient on the head, public opinion, if not the law, would soon put an end to the practice. But is it more humane to compel the restless and noisy patient to be quiet, by simply crushing them under the stupefying action of drugs?[21]

Pritchard Davies referred to the 'exquisitely simple' remedy for wet, dirty, and destructive lunatics which he had recently seen advocated – the administration of a ponderous dose of hyoscyamine – and sarcastically recommended that its advocates consider 'garotting' as at least a justifiable alternative.[22] He felt that chloral had now become 'the sheet anchor of a large number of medical men called on to treat nervous excitement'. As far as he was concerned it had set back the rational treatment of insanity many years, because its undoubted action in subduing even the most aggravated excitement, if given in large enough doses, had led many to regard it almost as a specifically efficacious remedy for all forms of mental disorder, and to be blind to its many dangers. 'Every period of quiet produced by chemical agency,' said Pritchard Davies, '[was] but another blow to the already enfeebled organism ... inevitably leading to its ultimate destruction.'[23] The Lunacy Commission made no enquiry into the number of patients taking chloral, morphia, or any other 'soothing medicine'. Pritchard Davies felt that this information ought to be juxtaposed in their reports against any description of the state of excitement of the patients.

In 1881 Daniel Hack Tuke delivered the presidential address for the fortieth anniversary of the Medico-Psychological Association, a wide-ranging retrospective of the development of psychiatry over the period.[24] He listed the treatments used, including: hypodermic injections of morphia, the administration of the bromides, chloral hydrate, hyoscyamine, physostigma (the poison from the calabar bean), cannabis indica, amyl nitrate, conium (hemlock), digitalis, ergot, pilocarpine, the application of electricity, the use of the wet pack and the Turkish bath and other

remedies too numerous to mention, all of which had their stren-
uous advocates. Polypharmacy was widespread, and Rhys Williams
and Savage at Bethlem had experimented with administrations of
one drug at a time, including conium (hemlock) and digitalis.
Whilst acknowledging that in the majority of cases the drugs used
'simply quiet for a time, merely knocking the patients down, but
in no way relieving the disease', they felt that experimenting with
one drug at a time might ultimately bring some degree of certainty
as to what to give in certain conditions. They had also experimented with poor results in the use of galvanism, applying an
electrical current via a negative terminal applied to the nape of
the neck and a positive to the forehead. Pre-eminent among the
drug treatments was chloral. In his presidential address Tuke
called it 'the spoilt child of psychological medicine', noting the
view of its critics that whilst the bromides had slain their thousands, chloral had slain its tens of thousands.[25]

By the 1870s another drug, hyoscyamine had taken its place on
the roll of honour of psychiatry's sheet anchors. Neither Tuke nor
his close friend Savage were averse to using this drug to restrain
patients. In 1879 Savage had written an article on the use of
hyoscyamine (otherwise extract of henbane), a poisonous alka-
loid used by many as a sedative. He found the drug useful as a
means of 'quiet restraint in violent and dangerous cases', especially those that were homicidal. The effect of large doses, given
'as occasion requires' was in his view better in every way than
regular administrations. Regular administrations were secreted in
food and patients who suspected they were receiving the drug
would refuse to eat anything at all. When given in a large single
dose as a method of 'quiet restraint', to use Savage's phrase, it
was given forcibly by hypodermic injection. Its intended impact
was as a shock to the system, and that impact would be lost by
routine administration. Savage emphasised that he did not
consider chloral or hyoscyamine to be curative in any sense. He
believed that nutrient remedies, general hygiene and tonics would
be the most powerful aids in nervous disease. He concluded with
these words:

I do not believe that whipping a tired nervous system with
strychnine is good, nor deranging an already deranged brain
by belladonna, opium, chloral or hyoscyamine will lead to
happy results. We may make a desert and call it peace.[26]

43

The Bethlem Case Books of the 1870s and 1880s show Savage practising what he preached, and in each year small numbers of patients received a large dose of hyoscyamine in response to violent or manic outbursts.

In 1883 the *Journal of Mental Science* carried a series of articles on all kinds of restraint, including chemical, by the medical superintendent of the Lothian asylum, Robert Cameron. In response to the charge that only 'the free use of stupefying drugs' had brought victory over mechanical restraint, Cameron admitted that:

> It cannot be gainsaid that, by the use of toxic remedies, noisy and violent patients may be as effectually controlled for the time being as by any species of mechanical appliance; nor can it be denied that in many of our asylums narcotics and sedatives are employed in such doses, so continuously, and for such purposes as to justify the appellation of 'chemical restraint'.[27]

Whilst denying that he employed chemical restraint, in the next breath Cameron revealed his particular regard for hyoscyamine, which, although devoid of curative power, 'judged as a means of restraint', had 'no equal in the pharmacopoeia'. His description of the effects of an injection leaves no doubt why this was:

> A general relaxation of the voluntary and involuntary muscular systems with loss of control over the bladder and rectum; paralysis of the legs with staggering gait and ultimate inability to stand; paralysis of the muscles of articulation manifested by increasing difficulty and finally complete loss of the power of speech, the phenomena being not unlike what are seen in some stages of general paralysis. The pupils are widely dilated, the respirations become slower and deeper. There is usually great flushing of the face. The effect on the heart is very much like that produced by digitalis – the pulse beats are reduced in frequency and increased in strength and volume. The subjective symptoms are impairment of vision, a feeling of dryness and suffocation about the throat, confusion of ideas, delirium with hallucinations deepening into stupor and coma.[28]

Although he admitted that hyoscyamine's long term effects could not fail to be disastrous, Cameron believed it to be safe in comparison with chloral, morphia and conium.

Cameron's article concluded with an open plea to recognise the need to punish patients at times. He viewed hard work as the best cure, and if a patient obdurately refused to work there was only one thing for it:

> ... the infliction of punishment is imperatively demanded in the patient's own interest. A dose of hyoscyamine administered especially hypodermically is in most cases a speedy and effectual remedy ... Epsom salts with tincture of asafoetida may be advantageously given, the efficacy being all the greater if, as is generally the case, recourse must be had to the stomach pump.[29]

Cameron's psychiatry of the recalcitrant was indeed red in tooth and claw. Other punishments from his repertoire included strong emetics, shaving the patient's head, and compelling him to carry a heavy bag of sand on his back. Hyoscyamine injections could also be used to punish mischievous behaviour which was 'the outcome of wilful malignity rather than purely the result of mental disease'. Cameron's opinion was that his position was perfectly ethical since: 'These are instances where the infliction of punishment ... is indicated, and it is justified as being truly treatment calculated to improve the mental condition of the patient in the manner most conducive to his own welfare and that of the community'.[30]

These views provoked a hostile response in the next issue of the *Journal*, and Cameron was rebuked by the editors (Tuke and Savage) for believing that punishment had any place in the treatment of the insane. In a letter in the same issue Cameron tried to defend himself by denying that he had ever practised any of the punishments he had advocated (which was obviously not true), but was 'merely throwing out suggestions as indicating what he considered to be a rational mode of treatment in certain cases'. He still maintained, however, that there were occasions when the insane needed to be 'frightened into good behaviour'.[31] The editorial strongly repudiated this stance:

> To punish by drugs is the saddest punishment of all. It is a degradation of medicine, and a double wrong to the patient. A whip scores the skin, and a treadmill tires the limbs; but to poison the brain with hyoscyamine, as a mere punishment, till the lunatic is paralysed and comatose, and can

afterward recall the condition only with abject terror, is a cruel injury. Such means might perhaps be justifiable in dealing with an infuriated animal, but to expect a punishment like this to restore reason, self respect, and self control to a human soul is a monstrous and melancholy mistake.[32]

This was all very well, but how could we tell the difference between punishment (unacceptable) and hyoscyamine treatment to quiet a disturbed and violent patient which to opinion formers like Savage and Tuke was entirely acceptable? Patients would see it as a punishment, and Savage's own practice shows that he intended it, if not as a punishment, at least as a corrective and deterrent. Two female cases from his Bethlem Case Book for 1885 illustrate how the desired effect was achieved. In the first, the note records that the patient was highly vindictive towards the medical superintendent who ordered hyoscyamine, after which the patient became 'very frightened'. Her pupils became dilated and she complained that the dose was too strong. The note concludes: 'Today is much more cheerful and self-controlled. Does not want to have any more medicine.'[33] In the second case the woman became violent and excited when given the hyoscyamine, and Savage reported that 'she is terrified when she sees the syringe and says the last dose nearly killed her'.[34]

Throughout the nineteenth century the consensus was that nothing tended to improve the temper and cut short a mental crisis better than 'the proper regulation' of a patient's digestion. Emetics and purgatives were widely used not just in small doses to regulate digestion, but also in large doses as a method of behaviour control, alienists not having been slow to note a direct empirical correlation between amenability and laxity of the bowel. The drug preferred by psychiatrists to achieve this was croton oil, a violent purgative derived from the East Indian castor oil plant, and widely acknowledged to produce a remarkable effect on disturbed patients.

The Commission generally became involved in questions involving drugs only if there was an accidental overdose leading to death. In 1905, five patients died from an accidental overdose of chloral, due to an error in making up their sleeping draught.[35] Following the inquest an investigation by two commissioners recommended the appointment of a duly qualified dispenser, or the placing of one of the assistant medical officers in charge of the safe custody of drugs, surgical instruments and appliances.

Paraldehyde was developed in 1882, and although it had a powerful sedative effect, it was dangerous in overdose. Accidentally administered overdoses of paraldehyde soon began to make regular appearances in the Lunacy Commission reports as a cause of patient deaths. The commissioners' accounts reveal how the nasal tube had become an important method of giving treatment without consent. In December 1913 the Lunacy Commission censured the 'regrettable and unfortunate want of care' whereby an elderly woman suffering from senile dementia was killed by an overdose of paraldehyde. The patient had refused a dose and the nurse placed the tumbler on a bedside table. Shortly afterwards one of the assistant medical officers, on his way to his room with a glass containing a much larger quantity of paraldehyde, was informed that the patient had not taken her medicine, and forcibly gave her the contents of his own glass by mistake through a nasal tube. Despite repeated administrations of aromatic spirits of ammonia and injections of strychnine she died soon afterwards.[36]

The concerns expressed about chemical restraint from the late 1870s onwards did not significantly diminish the use of powerful drugs to subdue patients in psychiatric hospitals. The criticism of the continental psychiatrists was well directed. Under the guise of medical treatment, troublesome patients could be paralysed with powerful narcotics, and yet an asylum could appear from the register of restraint and seclusion to be a very model of non-restraint. With such powerful chemical restraints there was no need for mechanical ones. But Savage and others were using various devices to restrain patients, including wet-packs, which they considered should not be prohibited. We might expect a return to mechanical restraint in the 1880s in an effort to reduce psychiatry's dependence on sedatives. Other factors were a growing therapeutic pessimism and the determination of the new generation of alienists, spearheaded by Savage, not to be 'shackled by any rigid doctrines' such as non-restraint.

4

1880–1913:
THE RETURN OF
RESTRAINT

From the 1870s onwards there was an increasing belief that insanity was an intractable problem, accompanied by fears that its incidence was steadily increasing, and the human and institutional resources available to tackle it were unequal to the task, as evidenced by the large numbers of insane in workhouses. A large chronic population in ill-staffed institutions contributed to the perceived need for coercive treatment, as well as to the perception of asylums and licensed houses as places of dread. The last three decades of the nineteenth century saw a struggle between the new generation of psychiatric empiricists who believed the deployment of both physical and chemical restraint to be matters for clinical judgment, and the remaining followers of Conolly who adhered to the view that psychiatric practice should be constrained by moral precepts such as the philosophy of non-restraint.

By the late 1870s it was clear that mechanical restraint was on the increase. In 1879, soon after Savage's appointment as chief medical officer, the commissioners reported that in addition to the usual quota of seclusion at Bethlem, four patients had been wet-packed, four dry-packed, and one patient was wearing 'strong clothing' at night.[1] In 1880 they found that: 'Mechanical restraint by the gloves has been used in two cases to prevent destruction of clothing or self injury, and one patient was wet packed on three days for three or four hours at a time. Fourteen patients have been in seclusion: 4 males and 10 females; and on 25 occasions.'[2] In 1881 they noted that: 'The Medical Records tell us of a woman who was dry packed three nights – on each night for six hours, and of seclusion employed in the case of a male patient once for three hours and with seven females for an aggregate of 110 hours and on 29 occasions.'[3]

Despite this evidence to the contrary, in their *Thirty-Sixth Annual Report* (1882) the Lunacy Commission maintained that: 'The general abolition of instrumental or mechanical restraint in all English Asylums, Hospitals and Licensed Houses, renders unnecessary any remarks on a "system of non-coercion".'[4] Yet their visits to other hospitals during the 1880s were also revealing that in addition to other instruments of restraint, wet and dry packs were in widespread use. Indeed, on occasion, the Commission actually encouraged mechanical restraint. In 1884, following the death of a patient in Glamorgan asylum as a result of broken ribs sustained while he was being physically restrained, the medical superintendent was informed that in such an extreme case mechanical restraint might have been used without impropriety and with advantage.[5]

In August 1888 the Commission's bubble finally burst when a controversy about mechanical restraint surfaced in the correspondence columns of *The Times*. Bethlem was the focus of the debate. Conolly was now dead, but his old friend and chief propagandist Bucknill was now a member of Bethlem Board of Governors. Bucknill had noted the increase in recorded mechanical restraint at Bethlem, and having received no satisfaction either from Sir James Lawrence, president of the Royal Hospitals, or from the Lunacy Commission, he wrote to *The Times* complaining that Savage had revived the use of mechanical restraint at Bethlem.[6] Bucknill noted that the reasons given for restraint were insufficient; they included destructiveness, dirty habits, self abuse and striking a nurse. In reply, Savage was unrepentant. He professed himself not to be governed by any dogma of non-restraint, his overriding concern being to do what was best for the individual.[7] He regretted that Bucknill had chosen to air the matter in the press. Although Bucknill replied that he had only invoked the support of *The Times* because he had exhausted all official means, including the Lunacy Commission, his *Times* letters suggest a certain personal animosity towards Savage. Inevitably the Lord Chancellor asked the Commission for their view of the matter.

They were in an embarrassing position. Whilst the visiting commissioners' entry in the visitors' book had noted that the 'use of mechanical restraint has been very considerable', it went on to say that they could not judge 'how far it was expedient in individual cases, but we cannot either condemn it as being bad treatment. We would only remark that it should be used with judgment, and in no case without occasional interruptions to see if the patient can be managed without it.' Savage's former boss, Rhys Williams, was the medical commissioner, and he and his colleague had accepted Savage's explanation that more mechanical restraint was to be expected given the high number of acute patients in the hospital,[8] a point hotly disputed by Bucknill. Savage later claimed that the reason for increased restraint was his own deliberate decision to free himself from the ties of the doctrine of non-restraint. When the president of the Bridewell and Bethlem Hospitals pointed out that the commissioners' entry appeared to condone restraint, the Commission's tone became simultaneously embarrassed and menacing. Asserting that the entry in the visitors' book had been referring to 'the principle of mechanical restraint of the insane', they warned that if on future visits 'it is found that restraint is excessive in quantity or is resorted to for insufficient reason, such steps will be taken as circumstances may dictate'.[9]

Apart from one letter to *The Times*, Savage refused to take part in the extensive discussion in the daily press. Instead, he described and justified his means of restraint in *The Lancet*. He stated that strong dresses, in which the limbs were free to move but the hands were enclosed in padded gloves, enabled disturbed patients to be restrained 'without the annoying constant presence of attendants'. Side arm dresses, where the arms of the patient were enclosed in pockets at the side, were used for patients who were persistently masturbating or self mutilating. Wet and dry packs were also used for the maniacally excited. Savage maintained that 'every physician with experience has the right to private judgment in the treatment of his cases, and that is practically what I claim and for which I suffer abuse'. In Bethlem there were no strait waistcoats, handcuffs or 'true instruments of restraint'. No patients were ever kept quiet by drugs and it was 'rare for patients to be held by attendants after the first day or two'.[10] Savage believed that as the profession of alienist could not yet lay claim to any fixed principles, they must be guided chiefly by experience. He explained his position as follows:

> I felt restrained from doing what seemed likely to be useful to my patients because of this so-called principle of non-restraint; But during the past two years I have gained

confidence from experience, and I have tried the experiment with results that have justified my actions, and with Dr Yellowlees of Glasgow, I would say that I acknowledge no principle of 'non-restraint', but only the higher one of humanity and humane treatment which, if it means anything, means the use of every method likely to restore health. . . . [T]hough the slavery of restraint is over, its service as a handmaiden to the physician will continue to have its place and be better understood.[11]

Savage had already resigned as medical superintendent on Bethlem before the restraint controversy arose, and he left to enter private practice. His departure from Bethlem was marked by a dinner attended by Daniel Hack Tuke, Savage's co-editor on the *Journal of Mental Science* and a former president of the Medico-Psychological Association. In his final annual report to the governors, Savage called for restraint to be used:

like any other surgical or medical measure, after careful consideration of the whole consequences, and to the very best judgment of the man who ordered it. On no account should it be allowed to be used but by direct medical order in every case, and on every occasion of use, just as a dangerous medicine is used.[12]

Redefining certain forms of restraint as permissible, if given subject to a medical order, entailed accepting the view that restraint could be a form of medical treatment.

Among the psychiatric luminaries who added their voices to *The Times* debate was the former medical superintendent of Colney Hatch, Edgar Sheppard, now professor of psychological medicine at King's College London, who extolled the magical tranquillising properties of the wet-pack, which was in danger of being eliminated by the unwillingness of many practitioners to blot their 'medical diary' with an entry of mechanical restraint.[13]

Conolly's friend and disciple W.H.O. Sankey rallied to Bucknill's side at the standard of non-restraint. Sankey emphasised that non-restraint was just as much, if not more, about general kind treatment as it was about not using mechanical restraint, and it was the failure to recognise this which had led to a 'gliding back into the old and severe treatment'.[14] He considered ordinary attendants 'too prone to resort to mechanical instruments for preventing the free use of the limbs to save themselves trouble', but for 'an officer to allow of such indicated a distinct misunderstanding of the primary principles of non-restraint'.[15] The success of non-restraint had been achieved largely because many of the first wave of medical superintendents had been Conolly's protégés, and the medical members of the Lunacy Commission were of the same school. Conolly's original disciples were now dying off and being replaced by a new generation of medical superintendents.

The Commission's response to the Lord Chancellor noted that, although restraint was not forbidden, it was discouraged by lunacy statutes, and that both the statutory provisions requiring records to be kept and the actions of the Commission had largely reduced its employment. The Commission now claimed that the general consensus of opinion favoured a sparing use of restraint, under proper restrictions and conditions, and that to condemn its use in every case would be adverse to the interests of the insane. Mild forms of mechanical restraint were less objectionable than manual restraint, which often proved fatal for the patient. One of the most frequent causes of patient death given at inquests was fractured ribs sustained whilst being restrained by attendants. Finally, the suggestion that restraint should be prohibited except in surgical cases was firmly rejected by the Commission, although they expressed strong disapproval of its use as a means of achieving 'economy of attendants'. The question of mechanical restraint became bound up in the extensive public debate about lunacy law reform of the 1880s, and the distrust of alienists and all their works made it inevitable that the question would be addressed in any new legislation.

Throughout the late 1870s and the 1880s there was increasing dissatisfaction with lunacy laws, with much criticism directed against the private sector. In 1877 a parliamentary select committee was appointed under the chairmanship of Thomas Dillwyn to consider the operation of lunacy law, following highly publicised cases of wrongful confinement. Shaftesbury, the chairman of the Lunacy Commission, was passionately anti-legalist in his views, arguing that whilst it was plausible to say that a lengthy and detailed inquiry should take place before a citizen was forcibly deprived of liberty, the symptoms would have to be so pronounced by the time this step was finally taken that a clear and unequivocal finding of insanity could be made. By that time, he maintained, the patient would 'have got pretty nearly into the category of the incurable'.[16] Although the committee found that allegations of *mala fides*, or of serious abuse, were not made out, Dillwyn introduced a bill in 1880 to require judicial certification in all cases, private or pauper. The bill was not passed in that session, but it was the first in a succession of similar measures. The *cause célèbre* of Georgiana Weldon, who was successful in an action for damages against the doctor who had certified her at the behest of her husband, an official in the royal household, proved influential in steering public opinion towards judicial certification procedures.[17]

On St Patrick's Day 1885, Shaftesbury resigned from the chair of the Lunacy Commission in protest at Dillwyn's bill. Although the Lord Chancellor, Halsbury, persuaded him to return with promises that there was no chance of legislation that session, Shaftesbury was in very poor health and died in October 1885. He had presided over the Commission since 1832 when, as the young Lord Ashley, he had taken over the chair of the Metropolitan Commission in Lunacy. Venerated by the informed public, his reputation as a philanthropic champion of the vulnerable extended far beyond the lunacy system, and his death removed a significant obstacle to reform along the legalist lines proposed by Dillwyn.

During the late 1880s the Lunacy Commission had suffered a number of blows to its credibility. Not least was losing a leader of Shaftesbury's stature. Their Annual Reports continued to give details of cases where lunatics were treated improperly, and where suicides occurred which might have been prevented by closer supervision. As a *Times* leader put it in 1889: 'These cases appear not infrequently to give rise to a collision of authority and a conflict of opinion between the Commissioners and the local managers of asylums, and we must say that, in some instances, the latter seem to show a rather imperfect application of their duties and responsibilities.'[18] The saga over restraint at Bethlem had earned the Commission a reputation with the press as ineffectual and enjoying too cosy a relationship with those whom it was supposed to regulate. The popular press was especially antagonistic. At a meeting in 1889, several commissioners complained about a 'defamatory' article which had appeared in *Titbits* in January 1888, and which was typical of the criticisms made. A 'humanitarian', who said he had recently worked as an attendant in a London private asylum, wrote as follows:

I could plainly see how much in the interests of proprietors it was to 'hold on' to their patients as long as possible. I was also present at one of the visits of the Commissioners. A cursory glance at each room of 7 or 8 patients seemed to satisfy them, and they would have passed on to the next room, had not one patient, whom I often thought from his patience and general intelligence ought not to have been there, stopped them and said, 'How much longer am I to be incarcerated in this dungeon?' A Commissioner said 'Oh yes! You will be better presently, good day,' and passed on. Sir, it was heart-breaking to see such a scene of blighted hopes. I am inclined to think that the public would not be satisfied to allow these Commissioners to quietly assist in draining the public purse if they knew how their duties were performed. I should like to ask your numerous readers whether it has ever come to their notice that the Lunacy Commissioners are in the habit of 'dining out' with a certain asylum proprietor previous to making their official visit.[19]

Another scandal blew up at Bethlem in 1889, this time over the restraint of Sophia Thornhill without the keeping of necessary statutory records. The Commission sent a letter to the medical superintendent (copy to the Lord Chancellor) expressing its regret at 'the omission of so important a statutory duty as that of recording mechanical restraint, and trusting that greater care will be exercised in the future'.[20] A conference was held to mark the coming into force of the 1890 Act under the auspices of the Lunacy Law Reform Association, an organisation including former patients, wherein it was agreed to press for the abolition of licensed houses and their replacement with paying wards in public asylums. The Lunacy Commission was denounced as 'hopelessly effete', and its abolition was also recommended, with its functions to be devolved to local bodies; an outcome which would not be achieved until 1959.[21]

Pressure for reform finally bore fruit with the Lunacy Acts (Amendment) Act 1889, consolidated with other lunacy legislation into the Lunacy Act 1890. The new Act bore a strong legalist stamp. It provided that patients could not be received or detained in any institution for lunatics except under the provisions of the 1890 Act.[22] If a patient was to be detained there had to be a 'reception order' made by a judicial authority, a magistrate or a county court judge. The reception order would be made on the petition of the husband or wife if possible, supported by two medical certificates, one from the patient's usual medical attendant if this was practicable. People who were of unsound mind and not under proper care and control could be admitted by a justice of the peace. Although patients were not entitled to be seen by the judicial authority before admission, any who were not had the right to be taken before or visited by a different judicial authority, unless the medical officer of the institution notified the Commission within twenty-four hours of admission that to exercise the right of hearing would be prejudicial to the patient. If no such notification was made, patients were to be told of their right to a hearing within twenty-four hours, and if they applied for one, their application was to be forwarded to the clerk of petty sessions. Pauper patients did not enjoy such extensive rights, but could only be admitted on order of a justice. An order from an officiating clergyman or poor law officer would no longer do. The policy of the Act was to favour public over private provision. No new licences would be issued for private houses, and asylums were empowered to establish departments for private paying patients.

The Commission's documentary scrutiny functions increased significantly. Certificates of bodily condition still had to be forwarded with the certification documents. In addition, a further report on the medical condition of every private patient was to be sent at the end of the month following reception. For the first time, the 1890 Act provided that reception orders would expire at the end of a year unless the institution manager furnished a special report and certificate to the Commission. Acceptance of the report by the Commission would renew the order for a further year, and it would be renewable for first two, then three, and thereafter for successive periods of five years. If the commissioners were not satisfied with the report, they could discharge the patient.[23] The Commission retained its power to direct discharge of patients from asylums, and two commissioners – one medical and one legal – could discharge a patient from any hospital or licensed house after only one visit.[24]

It is not hard to see why Jones describes the 1890 Act with its emphasis on judicial certification as representing 'the triumph of legalism'.[25] However, whilst much about the Act would support such a characterisation, many aspects did not. Section 330, included in response to a 'certification strike' by doctors following the Weldon case, provided that:

> ... anyone doing anything in pursuance of this Act shall not be liable to any civil or criminal proceedings whether on grounds of want of jurisdiction or any other ground if such person has acted in good faith and with reasonable care.[26]

The Act further provided that proceedings were to be stayed if there was no reasonable ground for alleging lack of good faith or reasonable care. This combination of defence and procedural hurdle came to be construed generously by the courts in favour of those operating the admission procedures.[27]

Despite the criticisms levelled at commissioners, their role was significantly increased under the 1890 Act. They continued to exercise visitatorial functions, their scrutiny of documentation grew, and under section 40 of the 1890 Act they were placed in charge of mechanical restraint. How should section 40 be characterised in terms of legalism and medicalism? On the legalist side, it prohibited mechanical restraint. However, it was medicalist in that it permitted restraint in a form approved by the Lunacy Commission and necessary for purposes of surgical or medical treatment or to prevent the lunatic from injuring himself and from hurting others.[28] Section 40(2) required in every case a certificate signed by the medical attendant to be obtained as soon as possible, stating the means of restraint used and the reasons for its imposition. Full records were to be kept, and were to be forwarded to the Commission every quarter.[29] Whilst appearing to limit them, section 40 in fact increased the scope of medical treatment and thereby of medical judgment.

Commissioners were alert to the danger that regulation of restraint would be seen as authorisation, legitimising it through subjection to legal procedures. Consequently, the first regulation on the subject, issued in April 1890, was prefaced by a cryptic preamble that their discharge of the duty to define mechanical restraint did not imply 'any greater countenance to this mode of treatment than they had hitherto given it'. They considered that the obvious intention of section 40 was to discourage the employment of mechanical restraint in treatment of the insane, except in cases of urgent and manifest necessity, so that its application should be restricted within the narrowest limits possible, and 'by the most humane means that could be contrived'. It should not be long continued without intermission, and should be discontinued as soon as it had effected the purpose for which it was employed. 'Mechanical means of bodily restraint' were defined generally to include 'all instruments and appliances whereby the movements of the body or of any of the limbs of a lunatic are restrained or impeded'. All such appliances were to be produced for inspection by the commissioners on their next visit.[30]

The death in 1894 of Thomas Weir, a patient in Holloway sanatorium, following confinement for four days in a dry pack, led to the regulations being amended. Weir's body was completely enveloped by a blanket and webbing secured by five straps, the blanket then being sewn back around his nose and mouth to permit breathing. Two commissioners made a full inquiry at the hospital, taking evidence upon oath, and recommended that the use of this type of dry pack should not be permitted as the leather straps had 'added a serious danger to a form of restraint which was already not unattended by it'.[31] They also stipulated that mechanical restraint should not be applied in any institution except on the direct authority and direction of the medical superintendent or deputy superintendent; that where patients were completely restrained, they should be under constant observation; that 'the appliances for mechanical restraint should be under the charge of medical staff, and that their first application at least should be made under his personal superintendence, and as a means of *medical treatment* [emphasis added]'.[32] Any subsequent application of restraint should be effected in the presence of the head attendant, who should immediately report to the medical superintendent both its use and any struggle with the patient.[33] Yet again the mode of regulation fostered a perception of restraint as a form of medical treatment.

In 1895 the Commission issued new regulations in response to the Weir Case. Although they did not go so far as to require prior medical authority for restraint, the need for a medical certificate was stressed. The general definition of 'Mechanical means of bodily restraint' remained unchanged, but permissible forms of mechanical restraint were now specifically listed, including straitjackets which had to be of a type approved under seal of the commissioners. The list also included fingerless gloves fastened together at the wrists, baths where the patient was closed in save for an aperture for the head, the wet or dry pack, and sheets or towels when tied to the sides of the bed or other object. With wet or dry packs the outer sheet was to be sewn or pinned, not strapped or tied. Patients in wet or dry packs were to be released for 'necessary purposes' at intervals not exceeding two hours. A later amendment in 1913 allowed jackets or dresses of some other pattern approved under the seal of the commissioners, as long as a sample bearing the seal was kept in the institution or work-house for inspection.[34]

The regulation ordered frequent visits by a medical officer and continuous special supervision by an attendant, except where gloves were the means of restraint. Under no circumstances were patients to be left unattended.[35] At the same time the Commission requested that all notices of patient deaths specify whether mechanical restraint was used in the seven days preceding death.[36] They obtained returns for 1894 of mechanical restraint from all the 155 asylums, hospitals and licensed houses. In a total of fifty institutions no mechanical restraint was used. The older form of dry pack was used in three institutions, and the wet pack in twenty-four. In the rest, the amount of restraint was 'very small and the means used were the sleeved jacket and dress, gloves, and occasionally belt and armlets'.[37]

By specifying the types of restraint apparatus which would be allowed, the amended regulation showed the Commission declaring types of restraint which fell outside its terms to be illegal, and they did so with reference to 'muffs' at Suffolk asylum, a device involving a strap and chain at the Grange, Rotherham, a mackintosh in which a Cardiff patient was trussed to remove him to the asylum, and padded belts with wrist straps in several other asylums.[38]

The Commission had a number of sanctions at its disposal. It could prosecute for failure to comply with section 40, or for ill-treatment or wilful neglect. It could also continue with its previous policy of pressing for the removal of patients under restraint from hospitals or licensed houses to asylums. From 1890 onwards, the Lunacy Commission pursued a vigorous policy of prosecuting attendants under section 315 of the Lunacy Act for ill-treatment. At the same time, however, the worst a doctor would get for trans-gressing section 40 and the Commission's rules would be a warning. In 1897 a patient died in Wadsley asylum having been placed in 'severe restraint' immediately before admission. The Commission directed a letter 'to be sent to the medical man who applied the restraint pointing out the impropriety'.[39] This contrasts with the fate of Mrs Buchanan, who was not a doctor, and who had allegedly ill-treated her daughters by placing them in prolonged restraint without medical authority. She had written to the Commission on a previous occasion in 1886, asking about the use of restraint on her daughters, and her medical attendant had been asked by the Commission to give particulars of the treatment and of the nature of the restraint that was applied. On that occasion she and her husband were convicted of ill-treatment. The Commission again prosecuted her in 1901, and she was convicted at Warwickshire Easter Quarter Sessions in 1902 of a misdemeanour under section 40. She was fined £20, and other charges of ill-treatment were not pursued.[40] No doctor was prosecuted by the Commission under section 40.

The Commission had also issued detailed rules regarding seclusion. In 1899 a nurse was dismissed for secluding a patient without an order from the medical officer, without removing the patient's clothes, and without observing her at intervals of less than fifteen minutes. The patient committed suicide in the seclusion room.[41] In January 1901, the Commission issued a circular drawing attention to their definition of seclusion as 'the enforced isolation of a patient by day, between the hours of 7 a.m. and 7 p.m. by the closing, by any means whatsoever, of the door of the room in which the patient is'.[42]

Any seclusion was to be authorised by the medical officer and recorded. The patient was to be observed at irregular intervals. Seclusion could be authorised to prevent injury to others or to ensure the patient's safety. It was also permitted for those who were in bed for medical treatment for physical disorder, and on a voluntary basis for those who wished to have privacy. However, patients in solitary confinement between 7 p.m. and 7 a.m. were not secluded according to this definition, and the rules regarding observation and recording did not apply during this period.

At the turn of the century there was a controversy about seclusion in Broadmoor. In 1895 Dr Richard Brayn, previously medical governor of Woking and Aylesbury prisons, was appointed superintendent of Broadmoor. He was to remain until 1910, and was the first of Partridge's 'men of iron' who ruled Broadmoor for a generation.[43] In 1896, 200,000 hours of seclusion were logged, involving 159 men and 39 women; and three years later 164 men and 39 women had been secluded for a total of 177,000 hours. This systematic solitary confinement began to alarm the asylum visitors who, in their report to the Home Secretary for 1899, asked for the policy to be reconsidered. However, the average hours of recorded seclusion remained around the 200,000 mark until 1901, by which time the visitors had accepted Brayn's main contention that Broadmoor was not a hospital but a prison, a description which would earn a sharp rebuke from modern medical directors of the institution. Partridge remarks that after 1901 'the annual sum of secluded hours sinks with astonishing rapidity until in 1907 only 15 patients were secluded against their will for 1,500 hours and the total for all classes was only 18,000 hours, and most of those were allotted on medical grounds'.[44] By Brayn's retirement in 1910, the number of hours spent in seclusion had risen again to 40,000 per annum.

Brayn's successor was Dr John Baker (1910–1920), another former prison medical officer. By 1914, the amount of solitary confinement was reduced to less than 10,000 hours per annum. Seclusion is still used extensively in the special hospitals, which may be as much due to the legacy of this repressive culture as to the difficulties of dealing with the more disturbed type of patient to be found there. What is interesting about this saga was that neither the visitors nor the Commission were able to achieve a significant reduction in seclusion through their efforts, since the decision to seclude was seen as a matter for medical judgment.

Throughout the early 1900s the Commission's minutes show a steady stream of admonitory letters to doctors for using unlawful forms of restraint. They also show that a small number of patients died as a result of restraint, in some cases physical restraint by attendants rather than restraint of the mechanical kind, and most of these deaths occurred in the workhouses.

As Parker has noted, in 1890 14 per cent of workhouse inmates were deemed to be insane.[45] Whilst lunatics in workhouses had been visited by the Lunacy Commission, the management of workhouses came under the jurisdiction of the Local Government Board (LGB). There was a certain amount of liaison between the two bodies. In 1906 the Commission received a letter from a former assistant medical officer of Newcastle Upon Tyne workhouse, stating that lunatics in the workhouse were placed in seclusion on the authority of the attendants alone. The Commission communicated their displeasure to the LGB who informed the local Poor Law guardians, who in turn issued an instruction that a telephone link between the doctor's office and the wards should be installed and the medical officer was to be summoned immediately any patient was put in a padded room.[46]

In the same year, a patient attempted suicide in a padded room in Southampton workhouse, having sustained a fractured jaw at the hands of the attendant in charge, who was dismissed forthwith by the local guardians. The LGB criticised the chief attendant of the workhouse for allowing the strait-jacket to be used without the explicit instructions of the medical officer but, because of his exemplary record, he escaped with a warning that any repetition would inevitably lead to dismissal.[47]

The rising number of pauper lunatics in workhouses was now causing serious concern within the Lunacy Commission. In October 1907 a patient died in a workhouse after being admitted in a drunken state, placed in a restraint jacket and then struggling with the attendants all night. The LGB reminded the local guardians that the Lunacy Commission, had on many occasions, recommended the building of a padded room at the workhouse, and urged that this now be carried immediately into effect.[48] In 1910 the Lunacy Commission's seclusion regulations were extended to workhouses when the LGB issued a circular requiring a careful record to be made of cases where inmates were detained in padded rooms in workhouses.[49] The Board added that in no case should such detention happen unless it had been previously ordered or subsequently approved by the medical officer. Meanwhile, the Commission actively promoted the construction of fully padded rooms in workhouses and asylums. In 1910, at Wakefield asylum, a patient died having dashed himself repeatedly against the unpadded floor of the padded cell, and the Commission urged that floor pads now be added.[50]

Much recorded use of mechanical restraint was for the purpose of force feeding patients – mainly women suffering from depression who were refusing food and drink. The Lunacy Commission acknowledged that the decision to force feed was a matter of clinical judgment. In the celebrated suffragette case of *Leigh* v. *Gladstone*[51] in 1909, Lord Alverstone CJ ruled that the prison authorities had a duty to preserve the health and lives of prisoners and it was therefore lawful to force feed them. Evidence of the prevalence of force feeding in contemporary psychiatry was given by Dr Craig, a former senior physician at Bethlem, who testified that he had administered forcible feeding 'thousands of times', sometimes eight or nine times a day.[52] In his view force feeding did not demand great medical skill, and he had never known a case of detriment or injury arising from it, even though in some cases it had to be continued for two years or more.

From the patient's perspective, tube feeding offered a different prospect. In the account of her seventeen weeks in private madhouses, Marcia Hamilcar, a fifty-seven-year-old teacher who was admitted for depression, describes it thus:

> The other attendant sat on my trembling legs, whilst she pinioned my shaking arms. Then Stiles roughly opened my mouth and thrust a tube down my throat, causing me intense pain. The choking sensation was indescribably horrible. To swallow was impossible, and a sickening sensation of suffocation almost robbed me of consciousness.[53]

Following the death in July 1913 at Denbigh asylum of a female patient who had been tube fed and who was suffering from acute melancholia and exhaustion, the commissioners issued the following statement on force feeding:

> The Commissioners fully recognise that the decision as to the proper moment when resort should be had to tube feeding must, of course, always remain with the medical man in whose care the patient is, that each case must be considered on its merits. . . . With a view to affording you support when any such case arises, the Commissioners direct me to add that . . . when the patient's life is apparently in danger on the one hand from the possibility of starvation, and on the other from some unusual risk involved in tube feeding, they are of opinion that, speaking generally, it is preferable – as the only means of saving life and promoting recovery – to incur the latter danger, and that, under the circumstances, the risk run is justified.[54]

In 1913 the Commission amended their mechanical restraint regulation to allow other mechanisms than those listed if deemed necessary by the patient's doctor in exceptional circumstances and provided the Commission had given prior authority.[55] The regulations also became more detailed, clearly a result of commissioners being asked knotty questions on their visits as to whether this or that form of restraint was covered. The 1913 amendment provided that it would not be deemed mechanical restraint if splints, bandages, and other appliances were used in accordance with surgical practice for the treatment of fractures or other local injuries, if the aperture in a bath cover for the patient's head was large enough for his or her body to pass through it, if gloves were fastened so as to be removable by the wearer; if unfastened sheets were used to restrain patients during forcible feeding; if trays or rails were fastened to the front of chairs to prevent adult or child patients from falling or injuring themselves, as long as the adults were able to remove them under their own power.[56] In the last ten years of the Lunacy Commission's life, definitions of restraint and seclusion became increasingly detailed. In a pattern of regulation which is strongly echoed in the modern Mental Health Act Code of Practice, the Commission issued exhortations to use restraint and seclusion as last resorts, requiring that the reasons be recorded and patients be observed at frequent intervals. The Lunacy Commission then examined these records, and a typical report on a hospital would state that mechanical restraint (without specifying what type) was used on so many occasions with so many patients, and a similarly brief account was given of seclusion. Placing the instruments of restraint and the prescription of seclusion under the control of doctors had an important effect. Restraint and seclusion, albeit regulated, came to be perceived as part of the medical repertoire of psychiatry, permissible if authorised by a doctor; a perception which remains firmly entrenched to the present day. The Lunacy Commission had established a pattern of regulation whereby it exercised central authority through a combination of visits and documentary scrutiny over an asylum system governed at a local level by visiting committees and medical superintendents.

One provision of the 1890 Act which certainly could not be described as legalist was section 229. In retrospect it was the foundation for achieving the medicalists' most earnest desire, accomplished in the 1930s, of introducing the new status of voluntary patient. Section 229 allowed managers of licensed houses, with the permission of the Commission or the licensing justices, to receive as boarders 'any person who is desirous of voluntarily submitting to treatment'. Boarders had to be produced to the Commission and the justices on their visits. They could leave on giving twenty-four hours' notice, and detention beyond twenty-four hours rendered the proprietor liable to a fine of £10 per day. The Lunacy Acts (Amendment) Acts 1854 and 1862 had made limited provision for voluntary boarders but this had not been widely employed. Under the 1890 Act the admission of voluntary boarders remained confined to licensed houses and only extended by implication to registered hospitals. The consent of the commissioners or licensing justices was still required. The slow expansion of the voluntary boarder provisions marked the effective beginnings of legislative provision for voluntary admission.[57] It was also important for another reason because it broke the necessary connection between asylum inmate status and subjection to compulsory powers, raising the question of whether they could be secluded or restrained physically or chemically without their consent.

Initially, the Commission's view was that section 40 provided authority for mechanical restraint to be applied, but only to patients who had been certified or received as single patients under a reception order. It did not apply to voluntary boarders, and in 1892 the Commission ruled that if continuous restraint was to continue to be applied to 'idiot children' in Chorlton workhouse, they would all have to be certified under the Lunacy Act. In other words it was necessary to certify patients in order to restrain them lawfully.

In 1910, a change of policy took place. The Commission were asked about the lawfulness of mechanical restraint of an uncertified patient, and adopted a rather evasive and legalistic tone, replying initially that they felt it inadvisable to express a view. However, they then concluded that section 40(1) prohibited mechanical restraint of any lunatic, certified or not, unless it was necessary for purposes of surgical or medical treatment, or to prevent the lunatic from injuring himself or from hurting others. They concluded that the machinery in the other subsections, which required medical certificates stating grounds for restraint and records to be forwarded to the Commission, was only applicable to lunatics in an asylum, in a workhouse or those who were single patients. Despite one commissioner's efforts to re-open the question by pointing out that Mrs Buchanan had been convicted in 1901 for restraining uncertified patients, the interpretation was confirmed at the next meeting. This meant patients in licensed houses could be restrained, as long as the restraint was for a permitted purpose and of a permitted type, but there was no need to record it on the statutory form or to notify the Lunacy Commission. This marked the effective beginning of a legalist paradox, that patients who were detained were entitled to greater safeguards that those who were, in theory at least, voluntary. It presaged more contemporary concerns about the medical treatment of informal patients. By the end of the Lunacy Commission's life in 1913 it was officially accepted that the psychiatric armamentarium included restraint for a wide range of purposes in forms permitted by the Commission, seclusion according to procedures set out by the Commission, and practically unlimited authority to prescribe sedatives. Whilst it was unquestioningly assumed that certified patients could be restrained, secluded, and forcibly medicated, consent in psychiatry was not a complete nonissue. There was evidence that, by the end of the nineteenth century, surgical treatment of mentally disordered patients was viewed in a different light.

5

SURGICAL TREATMENT
AND CONSENT

The first test for the importance of consent to surgery on psychiatric patients came in the extraordinary saga of Dr Isaac Baker Brown, who in the mid 1860s took it into his head that he had discovered the surgical answer to epilepsy, mania and other forms of insanity.

Baker Brown founded the London Surgical Home in Stanley Terrace, Notting Hill in the mid 1860s. In December 1866 *The Times* carried a short article describing how 'in addition to the ordinary maladies which come under the head of physical diseases, women are received who are of unsound mind. . . . In it the great experiment is being carried out of endeavouring to cure mental disease by surgical operations.'[1] The article claimed high rates of success and described how the treatment not only benefited the patients but also the medical profession by strongly stimulating a neglected branch of surgery. It did not mention that 'the neglected branch of surgery' was clitoridectomy.

The Times piece could scarcely have been more favourable to Baker Brown had he written it himself, listing the distinguished visitors to the home and stating that, although in its infancy the home had attracted great opposition, those who had opposed it were now among its most ardent supporters. This was not entirely accurate. Although Baker Brown did have supporters, there was strong and bitter opposition to clitoridectomy within the profession, and if he had hoped to sway opinion by engineering the publication of *The Times* article, it was a strategy which was to backfire. The background was that earlier in 1866, Baker Brown had published a book[2] claiming a 70 per cent success rate for clitoridectomies in the treatment of epilepsy, catalepsy and hysteria in women; claims which were treated with scepticism by

66

the *Lancet* reviewer, who felt that similar success could be achieved by 'blistering or some other less objectionable procedure than excision'. The reviewer felt that:

> The irritation being due to external friction, it seems reasonable to conclude that if such friction were rendered impossible for some length of time, the exaggerated sensitiveness of the parts would gradually diminish and finally disappear. If in the meantime, moral influences could be brought to bear, they might help in restoring the mental tone and thus assist in bringing about a cure.[3]

This was the heyday of theories portraying masturbation as both a cause and a symptom of insanity, and the controversy about clitoridectomy which followed the publication of Baker Brown's book revealed much about how epilepsy and 'masturbatory insanity' were treated. In June the *Lancet* carried a letter from a Dr Moore describing a twenty-six-year-old patient currently under his care who had been epileptic since the age of four. She had been referred to the London Surgical Home, underwent the 'operation as before' and, thirteen weeks after admission, she was discharged. However, within a month her fits had returned with an unprecedented severity. Moore believed that if other doctors wrote in with their experiences, it would soon be revealed that permanent cures were few and far between.[4]

Baker Brown's registrar and assistant surgeon, Granville Bantock, took issue with Moore's description of the operation as 'questionable', and invited him to explain the difference between 'applications of lunar caustic or actual cautery and extirpation of the organ'.[5] Moore's reply was that the application of caustics was 'much more desirable' because the effect of the caustic could be kept up for as long as the medical attendant desired, and if necessary could be reapplied, whereas extirpation ran the risk that 'directly the part was healed peripheral irritation may be had recourse to again over the remaining branches of the pudic nerve'.[6] Caustics and blistering may have been less permanent than clitoridectomies but they were only marginally less horrific.

Moore's view was that 'we have no more right to remove a woman's clitoris than to remove a man's penis'. He also raised the issue of the validity of the consent obtained from the patients:

I am sorry that females have not so much knowledge of the clitoris as we have, for if that were the case I am sure there are very few who would consent to part with it, and when questioned about it afterwards say, 'Oh I have only had a little knot removed.' Verily, they know not the nature of that 'little knot'.[7]

The question of consent was further elaborated in a letter from Dr Charles West. West felt that clitoridectomies were therapeutically useless and that few doctors would dissent from the opinion that the removal of the clitoris with neither the cognisance of the patient and her friends, nor a full explanation of the nature of the proceeding, nor the concurrence of some other practitioner selected by the patient or her friends, was improper in the highest degree.[8] In December 1866, one week before the fatal *Times* article, the *Lancet* carried a report of a discussion at the Obstetrical Society at which clitoridectomy had been debated in 'a remarkably bold manner', given the delicate subject matter. No detail had been spared. As the *Lancet* correspondent put it:

Even the winter of life failed for once to command the respect which is ordinarily considered its due, and the habits of sundry ladies more than seventy years old were expatiated upon in a way to prove that, although age may induce continence, it is not necessarily accompanied by chastity.[9]

The opinion at the meeting was strongly against Baker Brown, although there was a general disposition to allow that, whilst mistaken in his premises, he was nonetheless genuine in his opinion and open in his mode of proceeding. There were at the same time strong protests that the operation was nothing short of a mutilation, which it seemed had often been performed without the knowledge or consent of the patient or her friends. The meeting concluded with an observation that more convincing proof would be needed if the profession were to follow Baker Brown 'in a proceeding which if it be useless is a lamentable mistake, and if it be unnecessary is a cruel outrage'.[10]

At the end of 1866 the storm clouds looming over Baker Brown finally erupted. More and more evidence was coming to light that he had not secured the consent of the women or their relatives. On the very day in December 1866 when *The Times* published its favourable article on the London Surgical Home, West had a further letter published in the *Lancet* describing a case where Baker Brown amputated a woman's clitoris whilst operating on her for an anal fissure. She was left in physical and mental anguish, only finding out some time afterwards what had been done. Adding insult to injury, she 'had the humiliation of discovering that the justification was that she was assumed by the surgeon to be addicted to a vice with the very name and nature of which she was unacquainted'.[11]

The Lunacy Commission had been given a copy of *The Times*' article and, following calls in the *British Medical Journal* for them to investigate, they were anxious to know whether Baker Brown had indeed received women of unsound mind at the surgical home, since the premises were not licensed under the Lunacy Acts. Under the advice of his solicitor, Baker Brown sought to distance himself from *The Times*' article, which had appeared with no by-line. In direct contradiction of the case studies in his book, he now denied that he had received any patient for treatment for unsoundness of mind. This was a fatal error. Whilst he might have been able to survive attacks on his clinical practice, telling a bare-faced lie to the Lunacy Commission was guaranteed to bring him in conflict with the code of the medical gentleman. This, and the question of consent, would be the main factors contributing to his downfall. The following week a *Lancet* editorial attacked not only clitoridectomy, but also Baker Brown's view of medical ethics, and it called on the Obstetrical Society to investigate the question urgently. In the same issue, there was a letter from Baker Brown emphatically denying that he had treated without her consent the woman mentioned by West. He claimed, instead, that he had been sworn by the woman not to communicate to her husband and friends the true 'cause' of her illness (masturbation). Baker Brown concluded his letter with an undertaking '[i]n deference to the opinion of many members of the profession', not to perform the operation in any case 'without the sanction of the patient and her friends, nor without consulting another medical practitioner'.

At issue now was not only the probity of clitoridectomy, but the manner and circumstances in which it was being performed. Consulting physicians and staff began to leave the Surgical Home in increasing numbers. Further evidence against Baker Brown surfaced in the nullity action, *Hancock* v. *Peaty*, in January and February 1867 where the wife, 'an unfortunate lunatic', had been placed under the care of Baker Brown, who 'unknown to her husband, performed a most cruel and barbarous operation upon her'.[12] Her husband said in evidence that: 'I never gave the smallest sanction to her being taken to Mr Baker Brown's establishment, and I am even now in the dark as to what the operation was that was performed on her.'[13] On 19 January the *British Medical Journal* ran an editorial calling on the Obstetrical Society to discharge its duty to professional honour and public morality and to consider the moral and professional aspects of the charges which had been made. On 7 February the secretary of the London Surgical Home inserted a note in the *Lancet* announcing that: 'Solely in deference to the opinion of the medical press on the subject of clitoridectomy', the surgeons had determined not to perform the operation 'pending professional inquiry into its validity as a scientific and justifiable operation'.[14]

On 3 April 1867 the Obstetrical Society met to consider a motion to strip the errant surgeon of his fellowship. The charges against him were threefold: that he had operated without the knowledge and consent of the patients or their friends; that he had lied to the Lunacy Commission; and that he had carried out clitoridectomies without the knowledge of the patients' own doctors, some of whom were present during surgery. This last charge was viewed very seriously. Baker Brown's answer to it was that he took the responsibility on himself, but the patient's own doctor was seen as having an important role in safeguarding the interests of patients during surgery, as can be seen from this description by the president of the Society, J. Hall Davis:

> If a medical man is in a room with another who is the ordinary medical attendant of the patient, and who perhaps enjoys the patient's entire confidence ... if an operation of this serious nature – mutilation, for it can be called nothing else, is to be performed without the consent of that medical man; when it is all over, and by and by disappointment arises, then the patient and friends begin to find fault and consider who was in fault. She says, 'There was my friend, my ordinary medical attendant: Why did he not protect me from this mutilation?' The medical attendant says, 'It was done by Mr Brown on his own responsibility. I had nothing to do with it.' Is that an answer? I ask if any woman or person in the world would accept that as an answer or a vindication of a medical man who had been deceived and compromised

against his will. [Applause] The proper course is, it appears
to me, Mr Brown, and it must appear so to every honour-
able man, that if a surgeon feels that he is morally bound
by his own convictions to carry out his own practice and
his own operation, he should say so plainly to the medical
attendant and give him an opportunity of retiring, or
protesting, or placing the case fairly before the friends
of the patient and leaving them to decide whose advice they
will follow.[15]

Nor were the sexual politics of the debate lost on its participants,
much ink being spilt in the correspondence columns of the medical
press on whether the analogy between amputation of the penis
and the clitoris was misleading. The broad consensus was that it
was not. Baker Brown considered the parallel unjust, maintaining
that it was 'neither more nor less than female circumcision'.[16]
(Female circumcision in fact involves the removal of the inner
labia.) A telling intervention in the debate had come from one
Dr Oldham. After a blow-by-blow description of a clitoridectomy
he had seen done by Baker Brown, frequently interrupted by
cries of 'Enough!', Oldham went on to say that when he subsequently spoke to the patient she clearly did not know what
had been done to her. The nature of the operation had not been
explained to her, nor had she been asked for her consent. 'It
appears to me,' he concluded, 'that we must eliminate clitoridectomy performed under the conditions under which Baker Brown
performs it, or we really must fall down and become worshippers
of Priapus.'[17]

The vote to remove Baker Brown from his fellowship was
carried by a majority of 194 to 38. He died within two years of
the Obstetrical Society hearing.[18] The *British Medical Journal*
carried a full account of the meeting and an editorial in which
the issue of consent featured prominently. The editorial pointed
out that women were unlikely to gainsay a doctor who said they
needed an operation to preserve their reason, their health or their
life, but at least where they had agreed to it, there consent existed
by whatever arguments it had been obtained. In such a case the
editors continued:

It would be difficult to draw the line between unscrupu-
lousness and indiscretion, between fanaticism and fraud.
But there were charges that operations had been performed

upon women – mutilations they may be called – without the knowledge and consent of the unfortunate women or their husbands. Hysterical and weak-minded women are easily enough persuaded to submit to almost anything which they are assured will benefit them; but the mutilation of persons incapable of judgment without the consent of their natural protectors, and of conscious and intelligent women without their knowledge and consent, is a proceeding which the profession justly holds in horror.[19]

Although there was little compunction amongst alienists about giving drugs without consent, the clitoridectomy scandal shows how important consent was in the context of surgery. It also gives an insight into ideas of what consent to treatment entailed. Where women were capable of consenting, their own consent was required, but when they were incapable of judgment, their 'natural protectors' would make the decision for them.

The Baker Brown saga did not completely eliminate the use of clitoridectomy, nor did it completely displace the idea that insanity might be tackled by other operations to the sexual organs of women and men. In an interesting postscript to the affair, the *Journal of Mental Science* published a brief review of the 1866 correspondence between West and Baker Brown, which concluded that the operation is justifiable 'only in very exceptional cases, where there is strong reason to anticipate a good result and when every other remedy has been tried'. The note also mentioned that Professor Gustav Braun of Vienna had performed the operation 'in two cases with the best results'.[20]

Shortt describes how, in the late Victorian period, leading alienists such as Maudsley, Tuke, Bucknill, and Clouston 'assured their readers of the prevalence and validity of masturbatory insanity as a clinical entity. . . . Not until the close of the century was the causal nexus between masturbation and insanity disputed.' We have seen how Baker Brown and his colleagues sought to inhibit female masturbation. In the mid 1870s Dr Yellowlees, medical superintendent of Gartnavel asylum in Scotland and a close friend of George Savage, developed a surgical procedure for the insertion of a silver wire through the foreskins of male prac-titioners of 'the solitary vice'. Shortt says that this was widely taken up for a while, but what he describes as the 'technical difficulties' were immense. Not surprisingly, patient opposition was a big problem, and the risk of post-operative infection high, so the practice was soon abandoned.[21]

The Lunacy Commission's involvement in the Baker Brown affair had been somewhat peripheral, but in the 1880s they became more directly involved in sanctioning operations without consent. In 1880 a case was reported in the *Journal of Mental Science* of menstrual epileptic mania treated by oophorectomy. The patient's ovaries were removed by Dr Lawson Tait FRCS, the consent of the Lunacy Commissioners having been obtained. The operation had resulted in an improvement in the patient's condition. At the Medico-Psychological Association meeting, Dr Bacon reported that, apparently without the prior approval of the Commission, he had castrated two male epileptics, with the result of an improvement in one case. Hack Tuke asked under what conditions such an operation would be indicated and Bacon replied 'in cases of confirmed masturbation in incurable cases of epileptic insanity'. The president of the society considered the paper suggestive and

illustrative of the importance of what he had long urged, an increased attention to the state of the sexual organs and functions in insane females. In various forms of insanity the thorough investigation of these by a person with special skill ought to be a matter of routine practice. Surgical procedures such as those adopted by Mr Lawson Tait and Dr Bacon, ought only, of course, to be resorted to in extreme cases and with great caution.[22]

In 1886 George Savage, who was president of the Medico-Psychological Association that year, reported that a new departure had been made at Bethlem during the previous year in performing operations upon some insane patients, but that:

A difficulty in these cases arises from the insanity of the person which prevents him giving consent himself and when the operation is of a very serious nature it is difficult to satisfy oneself as to who should give the authority.[23]

Savage said that his practice had been to obtain the consent of the nearest relative including the relative who signed the order for reception, to communicate with and get the sanction of the Lunacy Commissioners, and to act on the surgical opinion that life was at stake and that without the operation the patient must die. The two cases where operations were carried out, by surgeons at St Thomas's, both involved women. In one, an ovarian tumour was removed from a thirty-three-year-old woman, and although her physical condition improved after removal of her ovary, she was discharged uncured. In the other, a growth of hair on the woman's chin was removed. It had caused her to contemplate suicide. Savage said that he contemplated further operations with the object of removing 'causes of unrest'.[24] The Commission was not only now being seen as the arbiter in cases where surgical treatment had to be given without the patient's consent, but also as a form of insurance against possible liability. The accepted view was that consent to surgery on psychiatric patients could be given by the relative who had signed the application for certification, or by the Commission.

Further emphasis of the importance of consent in general surgery was provided by the 1896 case of *Beatty* v. *Cullingworth*.[25] The patient had undergone surgery to remove one diseased ovary, but when she was under the anaesthetic the surgeon found both ovaries to be diseased and so he removed them both. The plaintiff brought an action against the surgeon on the basis that she had not consented to removal of both ovaries. The action failed on the grounds that she would have been presumed to have consented had she been confronted with the knowledge that she had two severely diseased ovaries. The *British Medical Journal* emphasised the 'obvious moral of the case' which was that the sole weakness of Dr Cullingworth's position arose from the fact that the consent given to him was 'tacit, implied, not even verbal much less in writing'. Mr Bidwell, the doctor who had written to Cullingworth stating that Miss Beatty consented to the operation, could not remember whether it was 'Miss Beatty or her sister or someone else' who had authorised him to do so. The moral was this:

> Before doing an operation, surgeons should be careful to explain what they propose to do and get unequivocal consent from the patient, or if the patient is not in a condition to give consent, from the patient's nearest friends. Such consent should either be in writing or distinctly expressed before witnesses.[26]

Although there was no pronouncement from the English courts to the effect that the consent of a relative was sufficient, the decision of the Supreme Court of Illinois in *Pratt* v. *Davis* provided support for this view.[27] This was another case where it was sought to relieve a woman's mental disorder by surgery on her reproductive organs. Mrs Davis was a forty-year-old-woman with four children who had suffered from epilepsy for fifteen years with increasingly frequent seizures in the years leading up to 1896. Her husband placed her in a sanitarium where Dr Pratt gave her a pelvic examination and discovered that her uterus was contracted and her lower rectum was diseased. He operated on her for these complaints with the consent of her husband, admitting that he did not tell Mrs Davis the whole truth about what he proposed to do, and that he told her husband the operation would be a trifling one. After the first operation her condition did not improve. Mr Davis contacted Dr Pratt who instructed him to return his wife to the sanitarium 'for the finishing work'. The day after her return the surgeon again operated on her, this time removing her ovaries and uterus. Neither operation was a success in improving her mental health, which deteriorated to the extent that she was adjudged insane and admitted to a state asylum in 1898. She was awarded $3,000 for trespass to the person, and the decision was upheld by the Supreme Court of Illinois which found that her husband had not consented to the second operation.

Pratt v. *Davis* was also important because the lower courts delivered a number of statements on the principle of consent which would be referred to in a clutch of US cases in the early 1900s. They included the famous and influential New York Court of Appeals' 1914 decision in *Schloendorff* v. *Society of New York Hospital*, often cited by the English courts in the consent cases of the 1980s and 1990s. The most resounding of these statements links consent to the concept of a free society thus:

> Under a free government, at least, the free citizen's first and greatest right, which underlies all others – the right to inviolability of his person; in other words, the right to himself – is the subject of universal acquiescence, and this right necessarily forbids a physician or surgeon, however skilful or eminent, who has been asked to examine, diagnose, advise and prescribe ... to violate, without permission, the bodily integrity of his patient by a major or capital operation, placing him under anaesthetic for that purpose and operating on him without his consent or knowledge.[28]

The contemporary edition of the American commentary *Kinkead on Torts* based the consent principle on natural law theory:

> The patient must be the final arbiter as to whether he will take his chances with the operation, or take his chances of living without it. Such is the natural right of the individual, which the law recognises as a legal one. Consent, therefore of an individual must be expressly or impliedly given before a surgeon has the right to operate.[29]

It was from such statements that Cardozo J. distilled his famous principle in *Schloendorff* that:

> Every patient of adult years and sound mind has a right to determine what shall be done with his own body; and a surgeon who performs an operation without his patient's consent, commits an assault for which he is liable in damages.[30]

This statement has been widely quoted as the basis of the common law of consent on both sides of the Atlantic.

Medical treatment for mental disorder was ethically and legally constructed and reconstructed between 1845 and 1890 in a process of interaction between psychiatric practitioners and the Lunacy Commission. There consent was not an issue. Given that the safeguard of the requirement for consent was taken away, the question remained as to what treatments could be given without consent. Coercive interventions such as restraint and seclusion could be legitimised by the fact that they were ordered by a doctor.

The concept of consent is subject to a similar process of construction and reconstruction through case law and through the interaction between medical professionals and official bodies. By the end of the nineteenth century it was clear that there was a legal and ethical requirement of consent to surgical operations, but there was also a widely held view that where a patient was incapable of giving consent others could give it on her or his behalf. The views expressed in the course of the Baker Brown affair showed that even if the patient's own consent was not possible, the consent of her 'natural protector' was necessary, whether that was her husband, or if she was under anaesthetic, her own attending physician. When he sent his patients for surgery in the 1880s Savage secured the consent of the relatives who had placed the patient in the asylum and the Commissioners in Lunacy, and in the 1890s the *British Medical Journal* was promulgating the view that the consent of patients or their next friends was necessary. In 1913 the Lunacy Commission was replaced by the Board of Control. The new Board took supervision not only of the care of the insane, but also of mental defectives, and questions of treatment without consent would soon arise for both groups.

6

THE BOARD OF CONTROL
AND STERILISATION
OF 'THE UNFIT'

By the time the Mental Deficiency Act 1913 replaced the Lunacy Commission with the Board of Control the numbers of legal and medical commissioners had already been increased from three to four of each. The new Board retained this arrangement, the main change being that instead of five unpaid lay commissioners, the Board now had up to four paid and three unpaid lay members.[1] Existing Lunacy Commissioners were transferred across. The first chairman was Sir William Patrick Byrne, formerly an assistant under secretary at the Home Office, and a member of the Royal Commission on the Care of the Feeble-Minded whose recommendations had formed the basis of the 1913 Act.[2]

The Ministry of Health Act 1919 transferred responsibility for the Board from the Home Office to the newly formed Ministry of Health, and its subsequent chairmen were all former senior civil servants from that department. The Board exercised an administrative and policy-making role as well as inspectorial and quasi-judicial functions in protecting the 'liberty of the subject' including those inherited from the Lunacy Commission under the 1890 Act.

The new Board was more than the Lunacy Commission in a new guise. From 1913 to 1948 it was the central department responsible for the development and administration of mental health services, assuming supervision and control over the administration by local authorities of their powers and duties under the Mental Deficiency Act 1913. It was directly responsible for establishing and maintaining state institutions for defectives of violent or dangerous propensities, and also administered grants to local authorities and voluntary bodies to develop provision for 'mental defectives' under the 1913 Act. The local

78

authorities' duties under the Lunacy Acts were placed under the Board's supervision, and it was the medium of communication between the authorities and the Home Secretary.[3] By the Home Secretary's directions, the Board issued circulars to local authorities concerning their duties to 'ascertain' and provide for mental defectives.[4]

The Board was reorganised in 1930 into a two-tier authority consisting of a chairman and four senior commissioners based in London, and fifteen assistant Commissioners with visitatorial functions.[5] The new Board had a significantly medical bias. Two of the senior commissioners were to be medical, one legal, and the fourth could be a legal or lay member. The chairman and the senior commissioners appointed the other commissioners, so that in a sense the Board became self-perpetuating. When the National Health Service Act 1946 came into operation in 1948, the Board's administrative functions were vested in the Ministry of Health, and section 49(5) of the 1946 Act enabled the fourth senior commissioner, who previously had to be lay or legal, to be another doctor.[6] From 1948 onwards, most of the Board's members also acted as officers of the Ministry of Health, performing mental health functions for the minister and for the Board. By the 1950s the Board's main statutory functions related to the liberty of the subject: scrutiny of documents, discharge of patients (rarely exercised) and the visiting of hospitals. During this final period, the Board consisted of a civil servant as chairman, one senior legal commissioner and three senior medical commissioners. In addition to their powers of review and inspection, they managed the three special state hospitals: Broadmoor, Rampton and Moss Side.[7]

A significant anxiety behind the Mental Deficiency Act 1913 was 'the high rate of propagation of mental defectives', and the possible ways of countering the threat they posed of national degeneration. This is how the arguments were summarised by one of the medical investigators employed by the Royal Commission on the Feeble Minded,[8] Dr A.F. Tredgold, in a speech which Winston Churchill, then Home Secretary, placed before the Cabinet in 1911: 'The chief evil that we have to prevent is undoubtedly that of propagation, for so long as it is allowed to go unchecked it is plain that no measures can really be considered satisfactory.' Tredgold was later to become a medical member of the Board of Control. His view was that building colonies to provide productive work and segregate mental defectives from society was the answer:

> Society would thus be saved a portion, at least, of the cost of their maintenance, and, more important, it would be secure from their depredations and from the danger of their propagation. Colony life would at the same time protect the feeble minded against a certain section of society and protect society from the feeble minded.[9]

The 1913 Act required local authorities to provide colonies and arrangements for supervision in the community to enable society to be protected from degeneration. The new legislation was much wider in scope than previous acts relating to 'idiots' and 'imbeciles'. The 'feeble minded' were brought under the aegis of the Act, thereby casting the net of control extremely wide to include people who would nowadays be viewed as having only mild learning disabilities.

Soon after its establishment, the Board began to receive inquiries about the lawfulness of sterilising psychiatric patients. In January 1917 the former medical director of Bethlem, now Sir George Savage, asked for the views of the Board of Control as regards sterilising by X-ray (a) a patient suffering from sexual mental disorders and approaching the menopause, and (b) a young person. Savage had a particular patient in mind, a forty-one-year-old woman suffering from melancholia who had been detained under the Lunacy Acts for a number of years. Savage described her as 'persistently guilty of masturbation'. The Board of Control's reply indicates the importance of consent:

> Sterilisation for ... mental illness can at present only be regarded as in the nature of an experiment and that this being so they do not think it should be performed upon any person who is incapable of giving a valid consent.[10]

Three commissioners, including the chairman, were deputed to interview Savage and express the Board's disapproval of the sterilisation of patients certified to be insane. Twelve years later, in 1929, the Board's inspectors reported that the patient was still under care and was frequently depressed and morose. There was '[n]o mention of immoral tendencies' and no record of whether she had in fact been sterilised.[11]

Soon after the end of the First World War, it became clear that institutional provision was not keeping pace with the growing number of defectives being 'ascertained'. In July 1919 the Board considered a letter forwarded by the Ministry of Health suggesting legislation that would permit sterilisation of the 'unfit'. They replied expressing their disapproval of the proposal.[12] In June 1923, Derby County Council passed a resolution that the Board of Control should be asked to consider the introduction of legis-lation (a) to empower a court to order the sterilisation of mental defectives convicted of sexual offences and (b) for the voluntary sterilisation under proper safeguards of any unimprovable male defectives who were unfit to become parents. Unlike later council resolutions, this one applied only to males. Later that year, the attention of the Board of Control was called to F.W.B., who had been admitted to an English mental hospital at the age of twenty-seven having been deported from Canada. He was seen by a medical commissioner, who found that he had been castrated. The hospital at Hamilton in Canada said that, owing to persistent masturbation, which weakened him both physically and mentally, it had been decided to perform the operation. The Canadian medical superintendent could not say under what statute the oper-ation had been performed, but it had been done on a number of people. There was no question of it being carried out with the intention of improving the patient's medical condition. As the secretary of the Board of Control sardonically observed: 'this in fact did not happen, but it is suggested that it alleviated the masturbation'.[13]

Interest in the legal position regarding sterilisation increased in the 1920s. The Eugenics Education Society took the lead in pressing for sterilisation of 'the unfit'. One of their pamphlets, by Cecil Binney, a barrister, entitled *The Law as to Sterilization*, became widely accepted as the definitive statement of the legal position. Binney concluded that to sterilise a sane person, even with his consent, might be a crime under the Offences Against the Person (OAP) Act 1861 (malicious wounding, or common assault), but 'what crime was committed would depend upon a minute and, from a medical point of view, ridiculous inquiry into the means used'.[14] His view was that, quite apart from the 1861 Act, it might well be an offence at common law to perform the operation, regardless of the method used, and, even if sterilisation was not itself criminal, a conspiracy to sterilise might be.[15] To sterilise a mentally abnormal person was at least as criminal, to Binney's eyes, as to sterilise an intelligent person. Regarding the ability to give consent, he said that 'in the case of an idiot or lunatic, the operation is always illegal, but it would be an overstatement to say this of any defective person'.[16] Binney took the view that in the case of children, sterilisation was clearly illegal, but that, given consent, the operation was certainly lawful in any adult case where it was necessary for the patient's health. If the operation was not necessary for the patient's health, he considered that this amounted to maiming under section 18 of the OAP Act 1861, and consent was no defence.

The British Medical Association (BMA) devoted a part of their conference in Portsmouth in July 1923 to sterilisation. Tredgold had succeeded in persuading the BMA Council to seek counsel's opinion from Sir Travers Humphreys QC.[17] The BMA Council resolved in 1925 to publish the opinion, with a disclaimer that it must not be taken necessarily to reflect their own views.[18] The main point on which they wanted advice was this:

> Whether what is suggested can be done with legal justifica-
> tion and protection in the case of a child or an adult who
> is suffering from mental deficiency or epilepsy. If it can, then
> the position is clear and free from legal difficulty. If it cannot,
> the question arises of whether an indemnity could be taken
> out.[19]

Humphreys' opinion was unequivocal. There could be 'no justifi-
cation for operating to sterilise a defective. A doctor who does so acts illegally and without any lawful justification.'[20] Moreover, there could be no indemnity for liability for carrying out an illegal purpose.

By the end of 1925 it was clear to the Eugenics Education Society that legislation would be necessary to carry their project through. One of their members, the Conservative MP, Wing Commander Sir Archibald James, reported the rapturous recep-
tion given by the 1925 Tory Party Conference to a eugenic speech calling for certificates of fitness before marriage, and the penalty of sterilisation for unlicensed persons who produced children.[21] Certificates of fitness for marriage were also a pet project of the Board of Control during the 1920s. Trombley describes how the euphoric support of the Conservative rank and file led Major Leonard Darwin, the fourth son of Charles Darwin – and from 1911 to 1928 the president of the Eugenics Education Society –

to write an article entitled 'Race Degeneration and Practical Politics'. This marked the beginning of the Society's all out effort to bring American-style legislation to Britain.[22] Darwin advocated what he called 'voluntary sterilisation', but his definition of 'voluntary' did not actually require the patient's consent. He said: 'Sterilisation should be regarded as a legitimate and humane alternative; provided that it is only performed on those who finally consent, *or who are incapable of understanding the nature of the operation.*'[23]

From the end of the First World War, the Board of Control had been grappling with the gross inadequacy of colony provision to accommodate the large numbers of defectives being 'ascertained'. From 1919 onwards they received a steady stream of letters from doctors and local authorities demanding legislation to allow sterilisation of the unfit. Because of the inadequacy of institutional provision, many people ascertained as mental defectives had to be looked after under guardianship or on licence from institutions. It was here that the dangers of race degeneration were perceived most acutely. A Board circular of April 1925 strongly urged managers of institutions that where mental defectives were allowed out on licence:

> Frequent visits should be paid by an experienced visitor and any tendency to form friendships likely to lead to marriage or immorality should be reported at once in order that recall to the institution or a change of guardianship can be effected in time.[24]

The Board issued a form that would be submitted to it by the Committee for the Mentally Defective of any borough where it was proposed to discharge a mental defective from hospital. It included the question: 'Is it considered that the control available would suffice to prevent the defective from procreating children?'[25]

In January 1926 there was a flurry of correspondence in *The Times*, with ten doctors supporting sterilisation of mental defectives,[26] and counter arguments being put by Sir Leslie Scott on behalf of the Central Association for Mental Welfare.[27] This was followed in February 1926 by a meeting between representatives of the Ministry of Health and the Board of Control to discuss amendment of the 1913 Act. Among the questions discussed was sterilisation, and the fact that many states in the USA had laws permitting sterilisation. Neville Chamberlain, the Minister of Health, considered that before any steps could be taken 'public opinion must be allowed time to form itself'.[28] Later in 1926, the Board of Control received identically worded petitions from numerous local authorities. They read:

> In view of the increase of mental defectives in the country and the heavy and necessarily increasing cost of maintaining and extending institutional treatment, the effect of which is usually most unsatisfactory, this Council urge the Government to take such compulsory measures as it may deem best for preventing the spread of this condition, by sterilisation, by compulsory segregation, or by other measures.[29]

Despite these motions and Darwin's efforts, the Bill introduced in the Commons in July 1926 made no reference to sterilisation or to certificates of fitness to marry, both considered far too controversial. The Bill had attracted enough opposition already from Colonel Wedgewood, the veteran campaigner against extensions of the scope of mental deficiency legislation, and the government had already been forced to make extra time available to cope with his wrecking amendments.[30]

By 1927 the Eugenics Education Society had prepared their own draft Bill. Acknowledging its amateurish drafting, Darwin passed a copy to Sir Frederick Willis, the chairman of the Board of Control from 1921 to 1928.[31] Willis offered to prepare a draft Bill for the Society, but insisted on secrecy because of his position. The original draft was entitled: 'An Act to prevent the practice of sterilisation when morally or socially objectionable, thus safeguarding its use for the preservation of the races.' It was a eugenicist's paradise of rules and regulations.

It would have allowed sterilisation of mental defectives and the insane with the consent of parents, guardians, the Board of Control or the detaining authority, making it an offence to be concerned with the sterilisation of a mentally defective person without the permission of the Board of Control or the guardian. The increased freedom for the patient would 'be likely to be beneficial to the patient and the nation'. This open-ended formula would have left no room to challenge a sterilisation in a climate where there was ready acceptance in medical circles that racial deterioration was a real problem, and that eugenic sterilisation was the solution. The Bill would have made it a misdemeanour to 'intermarry with a person known to be certified as mentally defective or insane', though the sane spouse would have had a defence if he or she did not know the person was certified. Such provision was a pet project of the Board of Control in the 1920s and early 1930s, and was frequently advocated in its annual reports.[32]

In May 1927 Willis replied that it would be quite simple to say in an Act of Parliament that:

> With the consent of the parent or guardian and the consent of the Board of Control it shall be lawful to sterilise any insane person or any mental defective when under an order of detention. Perhaps this would give effect to what you want.[33]

After two meetings during 1927, Willis forwarded a draft to Darwin, emphasising that, because of his position, he wanted his involvement to remain secret, and that it did not necessarily reflect his own views. He may have wanted to use the Bill as a stalking horse to give public opinion a further opportunity to 'form itself'.

His draft also contained provision for 'voluntary' sterilisation as the price of discharge from detention. Clause 2(1) stated that 'at the request of any patient who is about to be discharged from an asylum ... the Visiting Committee may undertake his sterilisation subject to the condition that the form of operation has been approved by the Minister of Health'. The operation was to be performed at the expense of the visiting committee and it was envisaged that the patient would be detained in the asylum until the medical superintendent certified that he was in a fit condition to leave.

Meanwhile, throughout 1927 Darwin busied himself seeking to persuade doctors to carry out sterilisation by X-ray, an operation subsequently revealed to be extremely hazardous. He sought, unsuccessfully, to persuade the X-ray department at Guy's Hospital to give this treatment to patients selected as suitable by the Society. Trombley describes how Darwin was:

> Undeterred by his failure to persuade hospital authorities to carry out eugenic sterilisations of poor women, [and] drew up a plan to create a hospital for voluntary sterilisation which failed when doctors proved unwilling to take on the legal question. He then tried, in 1929, to mount a less ambitious project of sponsoring sterilisation beds in London teaching hospitals, but the medical profession would not co-operate.[34]

Although the pro-sterilisation lobby vehemently denied that saving money was their prime objective, they never hesitated to provide estimates of the great savings to be made. In 1929 Lord Riddell published a pamphlet advocating sterilisation of the unfit and pointing out that the country could save the cost of maintaining 225,000 unfit persons. He estimated that their maintenance included capital costs of £29 million and an annual expenditure of £16 million.[35] The anonymous reviewer for the *Journal of Mental Science* tartly remarked that Lord Riddell had underestimated the national inefficiency which would result from the spread of venereal disease by sterilised defectives, which might turn out to cost more than the savings made.

Opinion within the ranks of psychiatrists was divided. A strong opponent was Professor Joseph Shaw Bolton of Birmingham who had been president of the Medico-Psychological Association in 1928. His speech on the subject, at the Society's Midlands division, attacked the aristocrats like Riddell who were presuming 'to improve the breed of human beings'. He said that it was 'only the law of entail which had preserved a small number of families in positions of power and responsibility and, with a few notable exceptions, their stock is, if anything, worse than that of the run of men'. Referring to the argument that sterilisation was cheaper than colonies, so too, he said, was 'the lethal chamber'. His words proved chillingly prophetic, since the Nazis would later take racial purity polity to this very extreme. Disquiet was also expressed about the ethics of making sterilisation the price of release from institutions. In the course of the discussion a Dr Russell revealed that he knew of several women who had had illegitimate children who had been informed that they could obtain their discharge from the workhouse only if they agreed to sterilisation.[36]

As the Eugenics Education Society gathered itself to bring its Private Member's Bill before Parliament, cases came to the Board's attention indicating the increased enthusiasm for sterilisation among members of the medical profession. In October 1930, a commissioner of the Board of Control visited the Gateshead Public Assistance Institution and found that the medical officer there had castrated three inmates: a certified imbecile aged twenty-two; a boy, aged fourteen, who had been charged with indecent assault; and an eight-year-old epileptic imbecile who was unable to talk. In the first and third cases it was stated that the operation had been performed on the initiative of the parents, and in the second with the agreement of the mother and step-father. Only the first was detained under the Mental Deficiency Act.

The Gateshead Poor Law Authority were advised by the Minister of Health that castration was illegal unless the operation could clearly be proved to have been performed for the medical welfare of the patient. The surgeon was told that, in the absence of such proof, neither the consent of the patient nor that of the parent or guardian would be of any help to a surgeon in a prosecution for unlawful wounding. If death ensued, the surgeon would presumably be guilty of manslaughter. A surgeon who contemplated castration for therapeutic reasons would, in the circumstances, be well advised not to proceed without obtaining a second opinion. The medical officer gave an undertaking that he would not in future perform such an operation and no further action was taken. The 'Gateshead reply', as it came to be known, outlined the legal principles which the Ministry and the Board of Control considered to apply. It became the standard reply to requests for advice concerning sterilisation for both men and women.

On 21 July 1931 Major Archibald Church, a Labour MP with strong eugenicist sympathies introduced the Eugenics Education Society's Bill, based on Willis's draft, under the ten minute rule. Although purportedly on 'voluntary sterilisation', the Bill's real purpose was to sterilise those who were refusing consent or who were incapable of consenting. Although the Bill failed, the majority against, 167 to 87, gave great encouragement to the Society.

One of several cases referred to the Board in the early 1930s was that of Ida Hudson. It led to a confrontation between the Board of Control and the Ministry of Health on the one side, and the asylum and mental deficiency authorities in Staffordshire on the other. In 1931 the medical superintendent of Cheddleton Mental Hospital in Leek, wrote asking if the Board would consent to Ida's father and stepmother being appointed guardians so that she could live at home. He asked if a sterilisation might lawfully be performed.

Ida had been in the Stoke on Trent Mental Deficiency Home at Stallington Hall and was alleged to have become suicidal, although she said that she only broke a window in a rage. She had been moved to a public assistance institution, which had its licence terminated under the 1913 Act. When the Board of

Control asked the Stoke on Trent Mental Deficiency Committee to have her back, they refused to readmit her to Stallington Hall, feeling that her influence would have a bad effect on the other patients. Ida's stepmother had attended a Committee meeting of the Stafford Mental Hospitals Board and expressed a desire that Ida be sterilised. The medical superintendent went on to say that:

> The Committee had ascertained from both the step mother and the patient that she fully understood the meaning and object of the term, and I have now received a request in writing asking me to employ a competent surgeon. The Committee expressed the view that if sterilisation could be performed, this would be a suitable case and were satisfied that the applicants were reliable people who would do their best for the girl.[37]

Before the medical superintendent consulted a surgeon he wanted to find out whether the Board had any objection to the step-mother being guardian so that Ida could live at home. He concluded by posing this stark choice:

> If you are opposed to any such proceeding on the presumption that it is an illegal operation even when voluntarily performed or that a mental defective has no power to give permission, then there is no use proceeding any further with the negotiations as the girl would have to continue to live here although she is perfectly quiet, harmless, well behaved and a good clean worker.[38]

The Board replied that their consent was not required for guardianship, that their intention was to persist in seeking her admission to Stallington Hall under the 1913 Act, and that a sterilisation would be illegal unless the operation could clearly be proved to be for the medical welfare of the patient, whether or not he or she consented. A surgeon who contemplated the performance of the operation for pathological reasons would, in the circumstances, be well advised not to proceed without first obtaining a second opinion. The advice was a copy of the letter that was sent in the wake of the Gateshead castrations.

In early December the Stoke on Trent town clerk reiterated the Committee's refusal to admit Hudson to Stallington Hall and continued in provocative vein:

The Committee also considered the sterilisation of Hudson, and I was instructed to inform the Medical Superintendent that they raise no objection to the course proposed by him as they consider that the operation could clearly be proved to have been performed for the medical welfare of the patient. I am also to state that arrangements will be made for the operation to be carried out in the course of the next few weeks.[39]

The matter had clearly gone beyond the stage where a standard form letter would resolve it. The Board secretary, Frederick Chanter, referred the case to Sir Laurence Brock CB, who had taken over the Board's chairmanship from Willis in 1928. He informed Brock that this was the first case of a local authority definitively stating that it proposes to cause a mentally defective woman to be sterilised, that 'the approved draft' letter from the Board's sterilisation file had had no effect, that 'the insistence of the local authority in this case appears to be open to grave objection, and the Board may desire to consider whether representations in stronger language should not be addressed to them'.[40]

Brock obliged with a strong letter to the town clerk saying that sterilisation unless necessary on medical grounds was illegal, and further admonishing the Stoke on Treat authority that:

The Mental Deficiency Committee has no jurisdiction to decide whether the operation is necessary for the patient's medical welfare, and no resolution which they may pass would be admissible as evidence on this point. It seemed to me so serious a matter for a local authority to authorise an operation of this character that I am sending the correspondence to the Ministry of Health, and would strongly advise you not to allow any further action until you hear from them.[41]

The town clerk replied that the Mental Deficiency Committee had been advised that the operation in question was in the patient's best interests, and that the medical officer, Dr Menzies, seemed disposed to take the responsibility for the operation.

The Board received a letter from Menzies himself in January 1932, reporting that, as a result of the opinion of the Board, 'the London and Counties and the Medical Defence Union had both refused to assoil the surgeon and himself in the event of a criminal prosecution'. Describing himself as a 'moderate', Menzies said this:

> I would use sterilisation as a means of saving money in certain carefully selected cases of high grade mental deficiency who were sufficiently civilised to live outside provided it were certain that they could not propagate their race. I would also permit voluntary sterilisation in the case of psychosis or a tendency thereto ... I would sterilise the proven dominants against their will if it would save them being kept expensively in an institution, this choice they would have.[42]

The crux was that Menzies was offering himself as a sacrificial victim to prosecution by the Board, declaring that he would 'go to considerable lengths to have this question decided in a court of law before I have to give up work', the inference being that a significant proportion of that work already consisted of sterilising mental defectives. He proposed that the Board should 'enter into explanations with the Medical Assurance Committees' with a view to the latter 'indemnifying the defendants in the case of a heavy fine'. Menzies envisaged a procedure whereby

> the Board would prosecute us and the case would if necessary be carried to the House of Lords. I do not see any other way of settling the matter decisively because the opinion of the Law Officers of the Crown is after all, only provisional.

Not surprisingly, the Board would have nothing to do with this scheme, and Menzies' fantasy was never realised. By 1931 two strategies for legalising sterilisation of mental defectives had been tried and failed. The first was the BMA's attempt to get the backing of counsel's opinion for the practice. The second was Menzies' quixotic offer to be the victim of a test prosecution, which, probably luckily for him, never came to anything.

In February 1932, the Ministry of Health received a deputation from various associations of local government bodies stating that, whilst they had reached no final conclusion upon the desirability of sterilising 'mental deficients', they considered the time had come at which a full enquiry should be made into the whole question in view of its national importance.[43] At their last public health congress a special session had been devoted to the sterilisation question. In Birmingham:

> [L]arge sums were being spent on mental patients and mental deficients, but the city council was still being pressed by the Board of Control to provide more accommodation. There was a waiting list of 1,000. In such circumstances it was natural that the possibility of sterilisation should be considered.[44]

On 9 June 1932 the minister, Sir Hilton Young, announced the establishment of a departmental committee, chaired by Sir Laurence Brock, to consider the value of sterilisation as a preventive measure.[45] Some of the membership, which included Dr Tredgold, were known to hold strong views on sterilisation, and Brock was sensitive to the charge that it was packed with eugenicists. In an internal civil service memo Brock confessed 'a slight prejudice in favour of sterilisation in theory, and a doubt of its efficacy in practice, combined with a strong dislike of the controversial methods of certain eugenicists of the baser sort'.[46] The other members were Wilfred Trotter of the Medical Research Council and Sergeant Surgeon to the King, Professor R.A. Fisher, head of the Galton Laboratory in London University, Miss Ruth Darwin, senior commissioner of the Board of Control, Dr E.W. Adams from the Ministry of Health, Dr R.H. Crowley from the Board of Education, and Dr E.O. Lewis from the Board of Control. The Board of Control secretary, Mr F. Chanter, was also the Committee secretary. Brock later explained that the Ministry's choice of members was aimed at getting different types of expert opinions. Since the top experts all had expressed their views, this meant trying to secure that 'opinions one way or the other were evenly balanced'.[47]

Within a week of the Committee's appointment, *Cull* v. *Chance*, a case involving sterilisation without consent, was reported in *The Times*.[48] Mrs Cull was thirty-two years old and since the age of fourteen had suffered from epileptic fits at intervals of twelve to eighteen months. She had had one healthy child, a second who died of pneumonia at ten months, and a third who was stillborn. In 1929 she again became pregnant, and went to hospital. She was examined and returned home. Various discussions ensued during which Butler, the consultant surgeon, proposed removal of her uterus. Eventually Mr and Mrs Cull agreed with their family doctor that she should not be sterilised, but should go into hospital for a curetting operation. The family doctor wrote to the hospital to this effect stating that she refused to have her uterus removed. This letter went to the assistant hospital surgeon, but somehow became detached from the notes. The consultant who carried out the operation did not see the letter, and removed Mrs Cull's uterus. The operation made her much worse, and ever since she had experienced fits once a month. Butler, the consultant surgeon, said in evidence that since September 1928 he had performed 128 operations of the same character as that performed on Mrs Cull. The jury found the hospital authorities negligent and in breach of contract and awarded £120 against them. They also found that Butler had committed a trespass and awarded damages of one farthing against him. There could not have been a more timely reminder of the importance of consent to sterilisation.

The Committee's first meeting in June 1932 was devoted to the question of whether voluntary sterilisation was legal in Britain.[49] Brock referred to Binney's pamphlet and Humphreys' opinion. Tredgold insisted that Humphreys's opinion of sterilisation as *ipso facto* unlawful was solely concerned with a mental defective who was incapable of giving consent. Brock referred to *Cull* v. *Chance* and said that the case showed there was a 'clear legal reluctance to recognise sterilisation unless on the grounds of greatest urgency'.[50] In October 1933 Brock sought confirmation of the Committee's view on the legality of sterilisation from the Ministry of Health Solicitor, E.J. Maude.[51] The point which he wished to clarify was whether a eugenic (i.e. non-therapeutic) sterilisation was legal if done with the patient's consent. Responses to enquiries made by Brock at some of the larger hospitals indicated that doctors generally viewed sterilisation to be illegal except for 'therapeutic reasons'. 'At any rate,' he said, 'it is never done except for a few cases at one hospital, which I believe to be Leicester, and even then it was only done *sub rosa*.' Brock felt that the hospitals' reasons for not doing sterilisation operations might partly be fear of upsetting their subscribers. Observing that: 'In the absence of any decided cases, the position seems exceedingly obscure', Brock added that he had been told:

that there are surgeons of doubtful reputation who make big fees for sterilising persons who seek sterilisation solely as a permanent method of contraception. If in fact sterilisation with consent is not illegal, it seems strange that the number who are willing to do it should be so limited.[52]

Maude, who had advised the Ministry in the Hudson case, replied that in his view sterilisation for non-therapeutic reasons was indeed contrary to section 18 of the 1861 Act, since it was done 'with intent to disable'. In the absence of legislation this would represent an authoritative declaration of the legal position.

The Brock Committee's remit required them to look at experience in other jurisdictions, and they drew on extensive experience in the United States, where twenty-seven States had sterilisation laws. The first had been California, which introduced a law in 1909, and where 8,504 of the 16,066 sterilisations done in the United States up to 1 January 1933 had been carried out; 6,999 on males and 9,067 on females. The Brock Committee considered that less use of these statutes had been made than was anticipated, blaming in part constitutional doubts which had only recently been resolved in the landmark decision of the Supreme Court in *Buck* v. *Bell*.[53] Carrie Buck had been chosen by Dr A.S. Priddy, the superintendent of the Lynchburg Colony, Virginia, to be the test case by which the constitutionality of the new Virginia sterilisation law would be determined.[54] Carrie's mother had been suspected of prostitution and had herself been admitted to Lynchburg. Carrie had been admitted there following the birth of a baby daughter, conceived as a result of rape by the nephew of her foster parents. Although Carrie, her mother and her daughter were all described as 'feeble minded' there was no reliable evidence of this, and indeed her daughter would later appear on the roll of honour at her elementary school before her untimely death at the age of eight.

In no sense could *Buck* v. *Bell* be described as a genuine challenge by Carrie Buck. The case had been manufactured by Priddy, and Carrie was represented by a lawyer member of the governors of the colony who was an ardent advocate of eugenic sterilisation. It was no surprise when, by an eight to one majority, the Supreme Court upheld the constitutionality of the Virginia sterilisation statute. The case is remembered chiefly for the extreme remark of the eighty-six-year-old Supreme Court justice and leading legal theorist, Oliver Wendell Holmes, that 'three generations of imbeciles are enough',[55] particularly insulting since, in the light of subsequent evidence, it proved entirely false. Holmes would later remark that he felt that, with this decision, 'I was at last getting to the principle of real reform'.[56] A challenge had been concocted which successfully clothed the policy of eugenic sterilisation in constitutional legitimacy for the next half century in the US, and it is estimated that 60,000–70,000 men and women were sterilised under state sterilisation legislation.[57]

The Brock Committee met thirty times over two years, taking evidence from sixty witnesses including biologists, geneticists and psychiatrists.[58] They received evidence from the Eugenics Education Society, the Central Association for Mental Welfare, and other bodies. The Eugenics Society sought legalisation of 'voluntary sterilisation' for mental defectives. The Royal Medico-Psychological Association declined to give evidence as a body, there being no unanimity on the subject.[59] The Parliamentary Committee for the Legalisation of Sterilisation[60] agreed with the BMA that neither medical nor public opinion was sufficiently advanced to warrant sweeping proposals for compulsory eugenic sterilisation, but that 'sterilisation should, with adequate safeguards, be legalised so that this form of preventative medicine should be available in a defined sphere'.[61] The Parliamentary Committee's bill would have authorised sterilisation of mental defectives. It required consent of the defective, and envisaged that the Board of Control and the judicial authority under the Mental Deficiency Act would, between them, determine whether the defective was capable of validly consenting. The Brock Committee ultimately proposed a similar system, but instead of the safeguard being the requirement of sanction from the judicial authority, they opted for administrative approval by the minister and the Board of Control.

The Brock Committee Report distinguished between operations performed in the interests of the patient's health, what today might be called therapeutic sterilisations, and operations not necessary for the patient's health, but which were necessary to prevent 'the propagation of unsound offspring', which they defined as 'eugenic sterilisations'. The legality of a sterilisation which was necessary for the patient's benefit was not disputed in principle. The Committee emphasised that the sterilisation of mental defectives on eugenic grounds was currently illegal, and the arguments applied equally to persons suffering from mental disorder.[62]

On the question of consent, they recorded that 'most authorities hold that the consent of the patient would not be a good defence, even if he or she were capable of giving consent, a point which, in the case of some defectives and many mental patients might well be open to question'. If a mental defective were to be sterilised, the Committee's view was that, apart from the possibility of proceedings being taken under the OAP Act 1861, under section 55 of the Mental Deficiency Act 1913, or, in the case of a child, under section 1 of the Children and Young Persons Act 1933, 'in the event of the patient's death it would seem that a charge of manslaughter might lie against the operating surgeon'.[63]

As to the eugenic sterilisation of 'persons of normal mentality' the Committee reported the view commonly adopted by the medical profession and acted on by the hospitals that it was illegal:

[W]e understand that the medical defence organisations agree in refusing to indemnify any practitioner undertaking eugenic sterilisation. In theory the point is not entirely free from doubt, but in practice it appears to be almost universally accepted that eugenic sterilisation is illegal and involves the surgeon concerned in the risk of legal proceedings, even though the full consent of the patient has been obtained.[64]

Although the Brock Committee estimated that the number of defectives living in the community was 'in round figures a quarter of a million',[65] they felt that 'grave as the problem is, there is no ground, in our view, for the alarmist views expressed in some quarters that there is wholesale racial deterioration'.[66]

Whilst favouring eugenic sterilisation, they rejected compulsion, refuting the argument made by many that sterilisation would serve as a substitute for institutional provision, as it was estimated that only three or four per cent of in-patients could be discharged if they were sterilised. Institutional patients were, in the Committee's view, 'virtually sterilised' anyway, and they could not accept the view of some American experts that the sterilisation of institutional patients was justified by the greater measure of freedom within the bounds of the institution which could then be allowed. The case for sterilisation was stronger in relation to the large number of defectives living in the community than for the limited number who from time to time were sent out from institutions. However, even if the justification of saving on institutional provision was illusory, the Committee did not accept that sterilisation had no social value: 'Defectives make inefficient parents; if only for social reasons they should not have children.'[67] Only three of the sixty witnesses who had appeared before them had opposed sterilisation. The Committee recorded as follows their unanimity on the desirability of sterilisation:

> We know . . . that mentally defective and mentally disordered parents are, as a class, unable to discharge their social and economic liabilities or create an environment favourable to the upbringing of children, and there is reason to believe that sterilisation would in some cases be welcomed by the patients themselves. This knowledge is in our view . . . more than sufficient to justify allowing and even encouraging mentally defective and mentally disordered patients from adopting the only certain method of preventing procreation.[68]

A small number of witnesses favoured compulsory sterilisation. They included Professor Berry of the Incorporation of National Institutions for Persons Requiring Care and Control who was medical director of Stoke Park Colony at Bristol. Menzies, the doctor who had offered himself as a test case in the Ida Hudson case, advocated compulsory sterilisation in 'a few selected cases' as a condition of discharge from institutional care. The Brock Committee assumed that the legislature would not feel justified in compelling anyone to submit to sterilisation 'unless it could be shown beyond reasonable doubt that some at least of their offspring would either be mentally defective or develop mental disorder'.[69] In the present state of knowledge, no such proof could be produced. Also it was likely to be unworkable and would 'drive defect underground, as parents of defectives might become more reluctant to let their offspring enter institutions, and it would add to the difficulties experienced by local authorities in carrying out their duty to ascertain the number of defectives in their area and provide for them.[70]

The report dismissed criticism that mental defectives would be so suggestible that their consent would be meaningless, advocating the introduction of a procedure for 'voluntary sterilisation'. Though they agreed that patients might be incapable of understanding 'the sociological implications' of sterilisation, nevertheless in the Committee's view:

It by no means followed that ... they were incapable of understanding what it means and of making a rational choice. To a large extent this must depend upon the attitude and explanation given by those around them, and this we believe to be true of other people in the community besides defectives.[71]

The Committee recommended a procedure whereby eugenic sterilisation could be performed on two medical recommendations, one from an expert approved by the Minister of Health, and one from the family doctor.[72] When the medical recommendations had been obtained, the committee envisaged that the papers would be submitted to the Minister of Health who, in cases involving mental patients, would exercise his functions after consulting the Board of Control, and the written authorisation of the minister should be required before sterilisation was performed. Although they proposed that the Ministry and the Board would act primarily by scrutinising the papers to see that everything was in order, it was also proposed that they should have the power, not merely to require any necessary amendment of the forms, but also to cause the patient to be medically examined if it was considered advisable. They did not anticipate that the necessity for special examination would be a frequent occurrence, but the fact that the minister or the Board could order such an examination would afford an additional safeguard against the possibility of error or abuse.[73]

Because of worries that the scheme would break down if doctors were anxious about legal action against them for signing a certificate recommending sterilisation, the Brock Committee had entered into discussions with Sir Henry Brackenbury and Dr C.G. Anderson, the chairman and secretary of the BMA, to discuss providing legal protection against suit by aggrieved parties. Not surprisingly, the doctors were emphatically of the view that protection against 'vexatious' proceedings should be provided. Under section 330 of the Lunacy Act 1890 the courts had the power to stay an action against a doctor who had signed a medical certificate for detention unless there was evidence that the doctor had acted without good faith or reasonable care. Following vigorous lobbying by the medical bodies, section 16 of the Mental Treatment Act 1930 had introduced a requirement of leave for such proceedings to be brought, and provided that leave must be refused unless the judge was satisfied that the doctor had acted in bad faith or without reasonable care. The Committee recommended that doctors should have the same claim to protection in the case of sterilisation recommendations, declaring that they 'could hardly ask for more protection than [was] afforded by section 16, but they will certainly not accept less'.[74]

The Brock Committee knew that the fundamental weakness of their proposals was the difficulty of ensuring that consent was truly voluntary. They therefore recommended that in all cases where patients were capable of giving consent, they would have to sign a declaration of willingness to be sterilised, and one of the two medical recommendations, preferably that of the family doctor, would have to include a statement that the effect of the operation had been explained to the patient and that, in the doctor's opinion, he or she was capable of understanding it. It was clear, however, that the Committee envisaged the giving of 'voluntary sterilisations' to patients who were unable to consent, if the full consent of the parent or guardian was obtained. If there was no such person, the consent of the person responsible for the maintenance of the patient would suffice. What was proposed was a procedure for sterilising those who were capable of giving their own consent, and also for those who were not, with the consent of their parent or guardian. The sterilisation of children would always require the consent of the parent or guardian. As to the method of sterilisation, the Committee could not recommend as safe the X-ray method proposed by the Eugenics Education Society in the 1920s, as the levels of radiation needed to sterilise young women presented a serious danger to health. It was suggested that operations should be not be carried out in mental deficiency hospitals, to avoid the suggestion that sterilisation would be the inevitable result of admission to such an institution.

The Brock Committee Report was published in an inauspicious climate. Before it could be debated in Parliament, the Nazi Law to Prevent Hereditarily Sick Offspring had come into force in Germany on 1 January 1934, permitting voluntary sterilisation on eugenic grounds and providing for compulsory sterilisation of persons suffering from 'congenital mental deficiency, schizophrenia, manic depression, hereditary epilepsy, blindness and other inheritable conditions'. All practising doctors were obliged to notify cases of patients thus afflicted to medical officers of health, who could demand sterilisation if it was not already demanded by the person concerned or a legal representative. A special tribunal was set up to order sterilisations with a legal president and two medical members, one of whom had 'special competence in cases of hereditary diseases and racial hygiene'. The other was a medical officer of health, who not only presented cases for sterilisation but sat in judgment on them as well. The medical members of the panel could initiate proceedings, and together could outvote the legal member. There was an appeal on medical grounds only to a High Court of Eugenics. As Weindling puts it, the Nazi state:

> ... established primacy over reproduction, but left the operation of the controls to the medical profession ... [T]he medical profession and especially psychiatrists benefited greatly from the drive for sterilisation. They had responsibilities in training, administering and adjudicating the law in 250 tribunals. These enhanced status and also income, since the work paid well.[75]

Weindling describes the assiduity with which the Nazis hunted down their prey, not only developing 'an extensive institutional machinery of hereditary censuses and surveys', but also commandeering health records to scour them for information about the 'hereditarily ill'.[76]

British newspapers and public opinion were clearly influenced by events in Germany. On 19 January 1934, the foreign press were invited to the Propaganda Ministry in Berlin to hear an explanation of the new German law from Dr Gütt, the medical architect of the new arrangements. A long-time Nazi who had been admitted to the SS in 1933 as a reward for his enthusiastic pursuit of the cause of eugenic sterilisation, Gütt is credited with coining the term for hereditary and racial welfare, 'Erb- und Rassenpflege'. On 20 January 1934 all English national newspapers carried reports of the German law. Gütt emphasised that the sterilisation law was applied on the decisions of doctors only, and there was a right of appeal from the first medical tribunal to a higher one where the necessity for sterilisation was contested on medical grounds. The government attitude was that the law was ethical and the state had to decide who should have children and who should not. Germans with religious scruples would have to submit to it in the same way as others. Gütt thought the guarantees against the violation of conscience in the law were adequate. Those who had objections could enter institutions at their own expense where they could be isolated, and the operation thus avoided.[77]

The *Daily Express* noted that Catholic priests were being taken to concentration camps for speaking out. The *Daily Mail* quoted the chairman of the BMA Council, Sir Henry Brackenbury, who said that sterilisation would never advance the improvement of the human race. He did not believe it could ever become eugenically effective, and argued that even if you sterilised every mental defective in the country, the number of mentally deficient would be the same in a generation or so. He did agree, however, that voluntary sterilisation, under the safeguards suggested by the Departmental Committee, would be useful in certain special cases. The *Daily Mail* reported 'informed comment' that there was little likelihood of legislation: 'Parliament rightly fights shy of legislation in this area.' The next day, the *Empire News* reported that the Vatican had taken a definite stand against Hitler's 'programme for the sterilisation of 400,000 Germans', ordering all Catholics to fight against Hitler's measure.[78]

Events in Germany heightened the already widespread concern that the Brock Committee's recommendations had strained the concept of voluntariness beyond breaking point. The *Sunday Express* denounced Sir Hilton Young and Brock for 'delivering the poor into the hands of the Eugenists'.[79] They had captured the Ministry of Health, and the Board of Control was packed with Ministry bureaucrats. How could mental defectives consent if they were incapable of understanding the meaning of sterilisation? 'Their consent and the consent of their parents and guardians was only another form of compulsion. . . . The real public danger,' the report concluded, 'was mental deficiency in high places. How many peers and politicians might be certified as sub-normal and morons. Even Sir Hilton Young appears to be slightly deficient in common sense.' More soberly, the *Public Assistance Journal and Health and Hospital Review* expressed similar concerns that the Brock proposals clearly imply 'that there might be cases where sterilisation might be adopted without the real consent of the person affected'.[80]

The Ministry of Health cuttings file bulged with reports of this nature. Scarcely surprising, then, that when the Brock Committee Report was considered by the Commons in February 1934, the government retreated to its previous line that there would be no legislation until public opinion had been given the opportunity to declare itself. This involved weathering a storm of demands for legislation from some Conservative MPs, but this was less risky than the high seas of public opinion.[81]

Judging by the number of articles in the *Lancet* calling for action and offering the congratulations of 'all interested in racial welfare' to the Brock Committee,[82] medical opinion was strongly in favour of sterilisation. In February the Cambridge Union debated a motion that: 'This house would welcome the compulsory sterilisation of the unfit in this country.' However, opposition from outside the medical profession was also rallying. On 9 March the *Catholic Times* reported that the Catholic Union of the Archdiocese of Glasgow had sent a petition to the Prime Minister representing 200,000 Catholic voters, and reminded its readers that eugenic sterilisation was a mortal sin.

By now reports of the first cases in the German courts were beginning to come through. When asked during an interview in March 1934 about sterilisation in Germany, George Bernard Shaw replied: 'Why Germany? America began it. Chatter about "the unfit" and "the benefit of the human race" is for fools; we know nothing about it.'[83] In April the *Catholic News* carried a report on a scandal in Michigan where sterilisation had been legalised in 1929 and where an inquiry instituted into abuses in state asylums had heard allegations against institution directors. According to evidence, many of them had carried out operations against the will of the persons concerned and in some instances they had persuaded parents to sign the necessary forms by pretending they were documents demanding the release of the children. Altogether 900 children were reported to have been 'thus mutilated'.[84]

In May 1934 the Mental Hospitals Committee of the London County Council met to discuss the Brock report and decided by majority to recommend to the Council that mental defectives in its institutions should be allowed to offer themselves voluntarily for sterilisation.[85] However, the full Council rejected the Committee's proposal. The opposition was led by Herbert Morrison, the Labour politician, who felt it was fundamentally wrong that sterilisation should rest on the will of a person admittedly unable to make the decision. 'You may, in due course make out a case for compulsory sterilisation, but we have no right to take liberties to experiment upon people not in a condition to make a decision for themselves.'[86] Morrison was praised in both the *Catholic Times* and the *Catholic News*, for having shown that, 'like Sir Hilton Young, he was aware of the religious objections of Catholics'.[87]

By June 1934 sterilisation legislation was a dead duck. Sir Hilton Young said that although the Brock Committee had been unanimous, it would be wrong to propose any national policy until there had been time for the national mind and conscience to become clear on the subject. Although the lunacy figures had increased, they were deceptive. This was a disease of advanced years. The population was growing older, and the increase was probably due to the increased age of people rather than any advance of the disease. In the same month the *Lancet* carried a series of essays on 'Eugenics in Practice' which acknowledged the uncertain prospects for legislation, but 'at least the protagonists of eugenic sterilisation could feel for the first time that they stood upon indisputably firm ground'. Legalisation of eugenic sterilisation had 'been definitely put on the map'.[88]

In 1934 and 1935, Professor J.B.S Haldane gave many widely covered speeches against the Brock proposals. A key point of his attack was that the demand for mental defectives to be sterilised came from those who consider such a measure to be cheaper than segregation and to whom this consideration is paramount.[89] Mainly for these very reasons, the local authorities were still firmly in favour of implementing the Brock Committee proposals. They were being pressed by the Board and the Ministry to carry out their statutory duties of ascertainment, but the increased numbers ascertained were filling the colonies to overflowing. In July, the Executive Council of the County Councils' Association approved the Brock recommendations, and the Mental Hospitals' Association added their support. Although there was strong support amongst some local politicians for compulsory sterilisation, opposition was mounting. The Mental Hospital Workers Union put forward a resolution to the TUC in 1934 protesting at any measure for the legalisation of sterilisation until there had been a royal commission on the subject.

By 1935 reports of the vigorous enforcement of German law effectively killed off any remaining hope for legislation. On 5 February 1935 the *Daily Telegraph* quoted a report from the German legal periodical, the *Jurist's Weekly*, that between 180,000 and 200,000 sterilisations had been ordered by German courts during the past year. Inherited feeble mindedness was the reason given in most cases. The report went on to warn travellers to Germany of the Supreme Court's decision that foreigners resident in Germany might be sentenced to sterilisation if they were a 'danger to public safety', and the fact that foreigners were liable to deportation need not, it was said, prevent the performance of the operation. This fate had already befallen an Italian subject resident in Wiesbaden.[90]

The quarterly meeting of the Medico-Psychological Association in November 1935 was devoted to a discussion of the Brock Committee Report. Discussion was opened by Carlos Paton Blacker, the secretary of the Eugenics Education Society, who had only that day been admitted to membership of the Medico-Psychological Association. Brock also attended. He wanted the Association to support legislation. He informed the meeting that, although a government Bill was unlikely, 'there was every reason to believe that sooner or later such a Bill would be introduced, perhaps a good deal sooner than some of those present expected'.[91] At the end of the meeting Brock's hopes of an immediate expression of support were dashed when it was agreed to circulate not one, but two questions to members: (1) would you support a Bill along the lines proposed by the Brock Committee; and (2) do you regard as a more important measure effective research on the heredity of mental disease and disorder?

In April 1937 came the Private Member's Bill anticipated by Brock. Wing Commander James, a member of the Parliamentary Committee for the Legalisation of Sterilisation, 'the gallant airman' as the *Catholic Herald* called him, proposed the introduction of legislation on the Committee's report.[92] The Bill was sponsored by the County Councils Association, the Association of Municipal Corporations, the Mental Hospitals Association and the Eugenics Education Society. Whilst denying that he was doing so, James sought to make capital of the public expense which might be saved. He pointed out that the total expenditure on mental defectives by London County Council was £1,698,633. 'If sterilisation were legalised,' he said, 'the immediate effect would be small. But if any part of the present enormous expenditure could be diverted to other channels and social services, the community as a whole would benefit.' He claimed the active support of the Central Association for Mental Welfare, the Royal College of Surgeons, the Royal College of Physicians, and the Society of Medical Officers of Health. Despite this, and a large number of resolutions from different county councils calling for the implementation of Brock, the Bill was not passed.

After the defeat of James' Bill, the question of legislation lost further ground on the political agenda, despite continued interventions from Bishop Barnes and the secular efforts of the Eugenics Education Society and the County Councils. The Brock Committee had established a view of the existing law which suggested that sterilisation was lawful if done for the medical benefit of the patient. This left the way open for a compromise solution where sterilisations could be carried out on mentally handicapped women for sound health reasons, and the permanent contraceptive effect would also be achieved, although it was not the primary aim. There is no accurate information on the number of sterilisations of mentally handicapped women carried out on these terms, especially after medicine claimed dominion over women's monthly cycle, and menstrual management became an accepted goal of medical intervention.

In 1939 the Royal College of Surgeons and the Royal College of Physicians obtained a legal opinion from Norman Birkett and Sir Walter Monckton that sterilisation without consent rendered the doctor liable to a charge of malicious wounding, and this applied also where patients were incapable of giving 'rational consent'. However, as Trombley puts it, they considered that the legality of the operation depended on 'sound medical opinion as to the likelihood that the patient will beget diseased or unhealthy children unless he is so sterilised'.[93] Although a copy of this opinion found its way into the Eugenics Education Society archive, it was marked 'strictly confidential' and *secreta collegia*.

During the Second World War attitudes to mental deficiency softened further, many of the 'higher grades' having carried out essential war work. Also the full realisation of the horror of the Nazis' crimes against humanity put legislation out of the question. Blacker and the Eugenics Education Society sought to revive Monckton's opinion to persuade doctors that eugenic sterilisation was lawful. In January 1950, Doris Kindred, a Birmingham mother of six, was charged with neglect of her four-month-old son and placed on probation after agreeing to sterilisation. The surgeon at the local hospital refused to perform the operation and it was never carried out. A spokesman for the BMA said that: 'Medical ethics would prevent a doctor from performing the operation unless it was absolutely necessary for the patient's health. As the law exists today, there is no legal protection for the doctor.'[94] Blacker and others sought in vain to use this as a case for legalising sterilisation to prevent neglect, ill-treatment and suffering of children.[95]

In February 1952 a further petition to the Ministry of Health came from the Association of Municipal Corporations, the County Council's Association, and Staffordshire County Council, in the van of activity since the Ida Hudson affair in 1931. The Councils had moderated their tone since the 1930s. They called for the establishment of a Royal Commission to look at the whole question of mental deficiency, and urged the Ministry to recognise that the value of sterilisation in the case of the mental defective 'rests largely on the freedom it will afford the defective of high grade who wishes to marry, and the apparently normal person who may produce a mentally defective child', going on to say that:

> It would appear that in both cases, the *right* to sterilisation as recommended by the [Brock] Committee is reasonable. In addition, a wide general application of the practice might, in the course of time, secure some reduction in the incidence of mental defectiveness in the community.[96]

Sterilisation had now become a right to enable the patient to live a freer life, a concept which would find some acceptance in the English case law of the 1980s and 1990s. The Ministry was not impressed with this attempt to broaden the concept of best interests beyond medical ones. They were compiling their own departmental shopping list of reforms. The Prime Minister was publicly committed to avoiding unduly controversial legislation. As Sir Percy Barter, the chairman of the Board of Control, put it: 'The Government will not in any event contemplate legislation on sterilisation. At any time, the subject is fraught with controversial issues of the most far reaching type, medical, social, ethical and religious.'[97]

The case of *Bravery* v. *Bravery* in 1954 had revealed that the legality of sterilisation as a method of contraception remained doubtful.[98] Denning LJ voiced his strong objections to accepting the lawfulness of a sterilisation performed on contraceptive rather than therapeutic grounds. He accepted Binney's argument from the 1920s that it amounted to maim. Gillian Douglas has noted how:

This view remained influential in discussion of the legality of sterilisation in the criminal law, and undoubtedly made doctors reluctant to perform the operation in the absence of strong medical reasons. Indeed before 1960, advice given to doctors by the BMA was that sterilisation could only be done lawfully for therapeutic reasons (i.e. to improve health).[99]

In 1960 the secretary of the Medical Defence Union took counsel's opinion after hearing of a case where the same serious hereditary defect was transmitted to two consecutive children of the same family, and acting on that opinion advised doctors that sterilisation was legal as a method of birth control.[100] The Abortion Act 1967 permitted abortion if there was a serious risk that the child, if born would suffer serious mental or physical handicap.

There has been a profound change in our way of thinking, marked by the legal acceptance in the 1960s of sterilisation with consent on contraceptive grounds, and of consensual abortion on what in the 1930s would have been seen as eugenic grounds. These developments have undoubtedly contributed to the elision of medical, eugenic and moral considerations, so that present day case law acknowledges that best interests do not extend merely to medical interests, but include the mentally handicapped person's right to live a freer life, and to be freed from the burden of childbearing. The sterilisation debate undoubtedly heightened awareness about consent to treatment and incapacitated people. But Herbert Morrison's widely publicised dictum that 'we have no right to take liberties to experiment upon people not in a condition to make a decision for themselves' was not extended to psychiatric in-patients. The 1930s may have seen the defeat of proposals to legalise sterilisation without consent but they also ushered in an ethos of free experimentation with hazardous physical treatments for mental disorder.

7

THE BOARD OF CONTROL AND THE MENTAL TREATMENT ACT 1930

During the early 1900s there was a strong movement amongst psychiatrists, supported by the Lunacy Commission and Board of Control, to extend the limited provision for voluntary boarders to a fully fledged voluntary patient status. In 1915 the London County Council obtained Parliamentary authority to receive voluntary patients 'suffering from incipient insanity or mental infirmity' in the newly completed Maudsley Hospital, built with a gift from Henry Maudsley.[1] The extension of voluntary treatment gave hope that a certain percentage of patients could avoid long-term institutionalisation if they could present themselves for treatment before they deteriorated so far as to be certifiable under the Lunacy Acts. In 1920 a Bill to extend voluntary admission to hospitals, approved by local authorities, passed the Commons but was narrowly defeated in the Lords on second reading.[2] However, if voluntary admission was to be widely taken up and psychiatry was to lose its 'Cinderella' status by moving closer to other branches of medicine, some hope of cure had to be offered, and asylums had to lose their image as places of incarceration, dread, punishment and stigma. Asylums had to become hospitals where people spent a comparatively short period, rather than human warehouses for large numbers of long-term chronic patients.

Clive Unsworth has described the 'bitter war' in the 1920s over the direction for lunacy law reform. On the one hand the psychiatric and medical establishments, including the Board and the Medico-Psychological Association were assiduously portraying psychiatry as 'a modern enlightened dynamic therapeutic enterprise', insanity as an illness 'analogous to and often inseparable from somatic illness', and legal safeguards as 'largely unnecessary in their stigmatising, quasi-penal connotations'.[3] Opposed to this formidable alliance were those who considered that equating psychiatry with other branches of medicine was mere window dressing for essentially custodial and punitive practices, and who believed in increasing rather than reducing legal safeguards.[4] The latter group included a small number of dissident doctors, some old-style radical MPs, mainly from the Independent Labour Party, including the redoubtable Colonel Josiah Wedgewood and the National Society for Lunacy Law Reform, an organisation of ex-patients and their sympathisers founded in 1920 by Robert Montgomery Birch Parker, a non-practising barrister. As Unsworth observed, societies and campaigns based around patients who have had negative experiences of psychiatry 'have consistently failed to make any real impact on the legislative process'.[5] He offers the following explanations:

> [T]he hostile views of ex-patients towards their former curators were liable to be discounted as the residual effects of mental illness. Secondly, ex-patients who felt sufficiently strongly to combat the existing system on the basis of their personal experiences were often so incensed at the treatment they had received at the hands of what they perceived as a medical and bureaucratic autocracy whose unresponsiveness to the resistance of 'deluded' patients was impenetrable, that they were prone to intemperate attacks which tended to confirm their misguidedness in the eyes of officialdom. Thirdly, the demands of these societies were often unclear. Were they opposed to the conceptualization and treatment of insanity as a *medical* condition? Did they accept this, but object to coercive psychiatry?[6]

Whilst the psychiatric system, including the Board of Control, was used to dealing with critics who were patients – they usually listened at length and then patronisingly informed the patients that their whole experience was a product of their mental illness[7] – criticism by doctors was harder to deflect.

In 1921 Dr Montague Lomax published *Experiences of an Asylum Doctor*, a scathing attack on inhumane conditions in mental hospitals, based on three tours of duty carried out in two different asylums in 1914, 1917 and 1918, when Lomax was a junior doctor. It painted a picture of asylum life wholly at odds with the gleaming medical projections of the Board of Control and the Medico-Psychological Association. Without going so far as to say that asylums were receiving prior notice of Board visits, Lomax referred to the 'mysterious telepathy between asylums' which meant that an hour or two's warning was generally forthcoming during which the asylum was made ready for the commissioners. Patients confined in single rooms (in seclusion) were dressed and sent to the wards and the rooms scrubbed and disinfected. Lomax summarised the scene at a typical visit in these terms:

> The usual number of hopelessly insane patients pressed for their immediate discharge; the usual number of patients with real grievances, which they knew too much to mention, sat gloomily silent. . . . The hurried and blasé Commissioners; the bored and indifferent Superintendent; the constrained and anxious attendants; the composed and critical lunatics, who realised well enough that the whole drama was staged for their especial benefit, and were not disposed to applaud the performance.[8]

Lomax also described over-medication of patients and punitive use of drugs, particularly purgatives. He described chloral, bromide and croton oil as still being 'the sheet anchors of all asylum medicinal treatment, and the worst in its effects of the three is possibly croton oil'.[9] With croton, 'the bowels are not merely opened, they are scoured out, and not only scoured out but flayed'.[10] It could only be prescribed on a medical order, but Lomax described how the attendants in the hospital where he worked would recommend a certain number of patients each day for 'crotons', some of whom were genuinely constipated, but many of whom were simply troublesome or refractory. In his view the drug was used far too frequently and indiscriminately, and often as a punishment. There was a long tradition of its use in the asylums where he worked. Having himself taken the standard (and very strong) dose in his hospital of two minims in order to experience its effects, Lomax vowed never to prescribe it except for severe and intractable constipation in young healthy subjects. He said it was often dissolved without the patients' knowledge in their food. Many patients refused their food when they suspected its presence. Lomax believed that croton was probably responsible for the other intestinal complaint endemic in asylums, 'asylum dysentery',[11] and that untold numbers of patients had had their lives cut short and health wrecked by being sent out in wet airing courts during croton treatment.

Lomax's book caused a storm. An editorial in the *Journal of Mental Science* dismissed him as a trouble-maker, declaring that his book would be chiefly remembered for the acute controversy it aroused, not to mention 'the growth of a miasma of slander and mendacity regarding the character and conduct of mental nurses and the treatment of patients in mental hospitals'.[12] The horrified public reaction made inevitable a proper investigation of Lomax's allegations. Unless his criticisms could be repudiated, the perception of a modern medically oriented psychiatry which was being so assiduously cultivated by the Board and other official bodies would be irrevocably damaged. The Board of Control, scarcely an independent investigator, ordered two of its medical members, Dr C. Hubert Bond, the president of the Medico-Psychological Association, and Dr A. Rotherham, to visit Prestwich, the main asylum referred to in Lomax's book. The wording of their report bespeaks a predisposition to disbelieve Lomax, and a determination to find all his allegations unfounded.[13]

They emphasised that their visit to Prestwich, from 27 to 29 September 1921, was made 'direct by train from London and entirely unannounced'. On the allegation of punitive use of croton oil, they found that there was a 'strict rule that no aperient medicine of even the simplest kind was to be given without a medical order'. 'Close inquiry' had revealed to them no evidence of its breach.[14] Bond and Rotherham must have been encloseted for most of their visit with the medical records, since they claimed to have examined all the prescriptions for the period of Dr Lomax's service and for the current year, and found that neither the doses given, nor their frequency were 'in any way excessive'. Although even this paper exercise turned up 'some slackness in the past in signing medical orders for "Crotons"', they were quick to accept the hospital's assurances that, 'even if the medical officer had omitted to sign them, they had been brought to his notice'.[15]

They found plenty of evidence that croton oil was extensively prescribed: 540 doses between January and June 1914, 396 between April and September 1917, and 333 between October 1917 and March 1918 (of which, they pointedly noted, 253 were prescribed by Lomax). This did not in any way contradict Lomax, since it was prior to the time when he decided to stop prescribing crotons. Despite the frequent use of the drug, Bond and Rotherham went on to say that croton oil had been given by the medical staff for years, and still was, and they were 'satisfied that it was only given for strictly proper medical reasons and certainly not as a punishment'. They had concluded this following 'close questioning of the medical officers', 'conversations' with patients who had been given the draught on several occasions (who could of course be believed when they were supporting the status quo rather than complaining about it), and after 'a scrutiny of record books which showed that there was no *systematic* relation between the ordering of the drug and the patients' unruly conduct'.[16]

The evidence unearthed by this process verified Lomax's claim that he ceased to prescribe croton during his final ten-month stint in the hospital in 1918, but even this was turned into a criticism, in that on only eighteen days during that period did he prescribe any medicine of any kind. As for the allegations of 'window dressing' at visits by commissioners, Bond and Rotherham – commissioners themselves – found 'no evidence at all' to support it. Even then they were forced to admit that, in 1919, the figures 'perhaps' suggested that patients usually kept in bed in single rooms might have been got up on account of the presence of commissioners. However they were easily reassured: 'A satisfactory explanation was given us and the notion was otherwise contraindicated by the figures of other years.'[17] It is an indication of how far a bureaucratic mentality had overcome the commission, that an 'investigation' could be based almost entirely on records kept by the hospital.

But public opinion would not so easily be subdued. In December 1921 the Minister of Health appointed a Departmental Committee consisting of: Sir Cyril Cobb, MP for West Fulham and former chair of the London County Council; Dr Percy Smith, a consultant specialising in mental disorders from St Thomas's Hospital; and Dr Bedford Pierce, former medical superintendent of the Retreat. They were to investigate and report on Lomax's charges, and to make any recommendations which might be necessary and practicable without amendment of the Lunacy Laws. Lomax himself refused to give evidence as he considered the committee to be biased in its constitution. He judged that the terms of reference did not enable it to look at the root of the evil, which were the Lunacy Laws, and the committee had the power to resolve itself into camera. Among those who gave evidence were a number of patients, of whom the most convincing was a former Metropolitan Police inspector, Charles Cox, whose evidence was completely written off as the product of his illness, although lucidly put to two commissioners who had investigated his earlier complaints, and to the Cobb Committee.

Corroboration of Lomax's picture of asylum life comes from the reminiscence of a nurse from the 1920s, in Peter Nolan's *History of Mental Health Nursing*, who remembers as a lowly trainee scrubbing out the side rooms (seclusion rooms) that were filthy from the faeces of patients who had been prescribed large amounts of the 'white mixture'. *Experiences of an Asylum Patient* by Rachel Grant-Smith was published in 1922, with a foreword by Lomax. At one hospital Grant-Smith was required to drink one-third of a breakfast cup of the laxative, cascara, for 'bad behaviour'. If she did not take it, she 'knew it meant being forcibly laid down and three or four nurses pulling my mouth open and pouring it down'.[18] Often a fresh dose was prescribed before there was time to recover from the last one. One criticism voiced by Grant-Smith which would be taken up by the Cobb Committee, was that the nurses were left with power to administer aperients and sedatives as they thought fit, and that 'the doctors of asylums have no right to place such dangerous weapons in the hands of unskilled and possibly vicious people'.[19] This was done by PRN prescribing. Every patient would be 'written up' for sedatives and aperients *pro re nata* – as the circumstances dictated – and nurses would be left to decide when, what and how much the circumstances did dictate. By this 'casual delegation' of their duties to the nurses by the doctors, said Grant-Smith:

> I prove my point that these asylums can only be regarded as places for detention not for cure. Would any doctor in a general hospital contemplate such interference in his treatment by a nurse? Would he think it right to keep his patient in a continuous state of muddle and melancholia and induce great constitutional weakness by the frequent use of opening medicine in large doses? Would he not also be afraid of setting up the narcotic drug mania, thereby filling instead of emptying the asylums? And would he threaten a patient with a morphia injection for any disobedience of his or his nurse's directions? But this 'treatment' is the common experience of many asylums and . . . in their estimation of their charges the officials never regard them in any other light than as

112

automatons or 'waxworks' whom to poison by excess drugging could never be regarded as a serious crime.[20]

The low calibre of nursing staff was a central theme of the
Cobb Committee Report issued in August 1922.[21] As to Lomax's
allegations of punitive treatment and abuse they accepted the
Bond/Rotherham version of events, thereby, as the Board of
Control put it, 'disposing in the main of the allegations which
have been made against the administration of public mental hospitals',[22] and echoing the Board and Medico-Psychological
Association party line about early voluntary treatment. There
were some criticisms of the Board, such as the need for a more
precise definition of seclusion, and more monitoring of the level
of sedative and aperient medication. But the medicalist view
of psychiatry was confirmed as the official one, although the
complaints in Lomax's book, especially those concerning punitive
treatment of so-called refractory patients, resurfaced throughout
the 1920s, especially at the instigation of the National Society for
Lunacy Law Reform.

The committee was nevertheless critical of aspects of the system,
such as large prison-like hospitals like Prestwich. There were,
at the time, 97 hospitals in the country, with 108,646 beds.
Whittingham Hospital had 2,838 beds and the Committee recommended a limit of 1,000 beds, with smaller villa-type units spread
through the grounds (the hallmark of psychiatric hospitals built
in the 1930s). They also criticised the calibre of mental nursing
staff, a situation which had been aggravated by the war. Training,
run by the Medico-Psychological Association, was inadequate.
Attendants were paid a pittance and subject to many petty tyran-
nies. Little wonder that they might visit similar treatment on
their charges. There were several strikes in the early 1920s, one
at Nottinghamshire County Mental Hospital, where the patients
and nurses joined to repel the police sent to restore order. An
inquiry into a patient's death at Salop Mental Hospital revealed
'grossly substandard' nursing practices.[23] In 1924 an official inquiry
into nursing in county and borough mental hospitals was
published, advocating not merely improved nurse training, but
also measures to make the career more attractive to a better
calibre of applicant.

In 1922 the Board again called for the introduction of a new
status of 'voluntary patient', a plea persistently echoed in their

annual reports throughout the 1920s.[24] In May 1923 a Mental Treatment Bill was introduced in the Lords, based on proposals of the Board and Medico-Psychological Association for voluntary treatment. Although it did not pass, it was clear, as Unsworth says, 'that by 1924 . . . reform of the lunacy laws was already firmly on the legislative agenda'.[25] In 1924 a Royal Commission was appointed to look into the question. The precipitating event was the famous case of *Harnett* v. *Bond*[26] in which a patient alleged eight years' wrongful detention and where one of the defendants was none other than Dr Hubert Bond, sued in his capacity as a commissioner of the Board of Control. The other defendant was the manager of an institution. Together they had revoked the patient's leave on the basis that he was unfit to be at large. The jury found the manager to have acted without reasonable care and Bond to have acted with neither good faith nor reasonable care, hence depriving them of the defence of section 330 of the Lunacy Act 1890. Harnett was awarded £25,000 damages. On appeal the manager was found not to have been liable and a new trial was ordered in the case of Bond to reassess the damages, because his decision had only caused illegal detention for a period of hours.

Public confidence in the lunacy system was severely shaken by the fact that one of its leading lights had acted without good faith, and the court's decision triggered a 'certification strike'. In July 1924, Arthur Henderson, the Labour Home Secretary announced the appointment of a Royal Commission under the chairmanship of the Rt Hon. Hugh Pattinson Macmillan KC LLD, later Baron Macmillan. As Unsworth notes: 'This response possessed the capacity not only to placate or reassure public opinion, but also to shift the question from that of legal safeguards to that of early treatment, which was the established preoccupation at government level.'[27]

The Board proposed that non-volitional patients, those who were incapable of making or expressing a decision to accept or refuse treatment, should be received for six months without certification, a period which could be renewed once. Unwilling patients, they proposed, should be detainable for up to twenty-eight days for observation and treatment without certification, a proposal which would not find legislative favour until the Mental Health Act 1959. Voluntary patients would be received without any formality beyond signing a form to the effect that they were willing to accept treatment. Moved by their colleague Bond's unpleasant experience, the Board strenuously advocated 'more effective protection to medical men in the bona fide discharge of their duties under the Lunacy Acts'.[28]

Robert Montgomery Booth Parker, as the chairman of National Society for Lunacy Reform, was allocated substantial time to give his evidence, and much of it concentrated on the punitive aspects of hospital treatment, including the use of croton oil and the widespread practice of maintaining more austere regimes in 'back wards' for 'refractory' patients. The Macmillan Commission expressed itself in favour of the careful monitoring of the administration of croton, and in 1930, in a bizarre piece of pharmaceutical cataloguing, the Board of Control added it to their circular requesting information on the use of sedatives.[29]

The decision to remove a patient who behaved badly from more congenial surroundings to the back wards was considered a matter of medical judgment for the medical superintendent, and therefore a question of treatment. As so often before, motivation was the crucial element in distinguishing between punishment and treatment, but the distinction was so blurred as to be meaningless for practical purposes. The Commission favoured 'disciplinary relegation' as a reformative measure and as a deterrent against future misconduct, but deplored its use as a punishment. Unsworth refers to the 'thoroughgoing moralism' of psychiatrists' evaluations of patients and the accounts of treatment in their evidence to the Macmillan Commission; an approach supported by the Commission which lent its support to 'the infantilization of patients and disciplinary methods of normalization'.[30] The Commission recommended that disciplinary relegation should remain a matter of medical judgment and rejected suggestions that the question should be entrusted to the visiting committee and governed by rules.[31]

Although the National Society for Lunacy Reform brought forward a number of former patients who wished to give evidence, the Commission resolved itself into camera after the first day of hearing them, feeling that the atmosphere had degenerated into one of 'recrimination and controversy'.[32] Having heard the evidence, they did not feel that it made 'any constructive contribution'. They spared little or no time for the investigation of individual cases, and most of the evidence they heard came 'from official or semi-official sources'. Jones views this as an indication of 'the growing remoteness of twentieth century administration',[33] and Unsworth says it shows how the Commission was 'clearly intent upon purging its own proceedings of legalism', and ensuring that the 'modern, informed, enlightened and rationalist concept of mental disorder and its treatment' was not obscured by the publicity which would be attracted by sensationalist allegations.[34]

Much to the relief and satisfaction of the Board of Control, the Macmillan Commission rejected suggestions that there were widespread infringements of liberty and found that, although there might be isolated incidents of patient abuse which might be lessened by administrative reforms and better training for nurses, 'ill usage was not deliberately or systematically practised in mental institutions'.[35] Although they did not recommend its abolition, 'certification was to be the last resort in treatment, not [its] prerequisite'.[36] They recommended voluntary admission on the written application of the patient without medical recommendation but, once admitted, discharge would be subject to a requirement of seventy-two hours' notice. They proposed a new compulsory Provisional Treatment Order to be granted by a Justice on the basis of one medical recommendation, which would last for one month initially and would be renewable by the Justice for up to five months. It would differ from certification in that the patient would not be described as 'of unsound mind and a fit person to be detained', but instead the patient's mental condition would make it expedient for his or her own welfare or that of the public that he or she be detained under observation, care and treatment.

The Commission also proposed increased protection for doctors by shifting the burden of proof to the complainant and increasing it to require substantial grounds (rather than a prima facie case) for the contention that the practitioner had acted in bad faith or without reasonable care. Whilst the Commission could not ignore the criticism which had been directed at the Board of Control, they considered most of it ill-informed, and that any legitimate dissatisfaction was the result of 'defects in the existing system rather than any want of zeal on the part of Commissioners'.[37] Perceiving one of the principal problems as stemming from the fact that Board members were constantly on visits, the Commission recommended restructuring the Board into two groups: a core of four senior commissioners who would remain at headquarters and who would deal with any queries or complaints, and fifteen assistant commissioners who would take over the visiting function. The proposed new categories of uncertified patient would be within the Board's jurisdiction. The Commission rejected suggestions that decisions about discharge of detained patients should be judicialised and placed in the hands of Justices of the Peace.

The Mental Treatment Act 1930 introduced voluntary admission by written application to the person in charge of the hospital. No medical recommendation was required except for a minor under sixteen years, who could be received on the application of the parent or guardian, with a medical recommendation from a doctor approved by the Board or the local authority.

Instead of the Provisional Treatment Order advocated by Macmillan or the Board's recommendation of a twenty-eight-day procedure without certificate for observation and treatment, the 1930 Act provided for 'temporary' compulsory admission without judicial certificate of patients who were 'incapable of expressing themselves as willing or unwilling to receive such treatment'. This revived proposals made by the medical professional bodies and by the Board for special provision for the 'non-volitional'. Applications for temporary admission could be made by the husband, wife or other relative, or by a duly authorised officer of the local authority supported by two medical certificates.[38] One of the doctors giving a certificate had to be recognised by the Board of Control as having sufficient psychiatric expertise for the purposes of the Act: an 'approved doctor'. The Board issued a circular offering observations on the type of patient who would be suitable for temporary admission noting that a refusing patient, no matter how irrational, could not be temporarily admitted, though persons could be if they were confused and incoherent to the extent that they were willing one minute and refused the next.[39] Applications were made not to a judicial authority but to the person in charge of the hospital. Even though there was no 'full certificate of insanity', patients who were temporarily admitted as non-volitional were still formally admitted. If they did not recover their volition within six months of admission, they had to be certified under the Lunacy Acts, unless the Board authorised an extension for a maximum of a further six months.[40] If they did recover volition, they could not be detained for more than twenty-eight days, unless they were certified under the Lunacy Acts. Whilst extensive use was made of voluntary admission, despite encouragement from the Board, there were only ever about 500 patients under temporary admission at any one time in England and Wales, and the procedure never accounted for more than 4 per cent of all admissions.[41]

The provisions for voluntary and temporary admission without certification represented success beyond the expectations of the medical and psychiatric professional bodies, and their lobbying during the passage of the 1930 Act was mostly directed towards strengthening the legal defence against proceedings brought in respect of acts done pursuant to the legislation. The medical bodies secured an increased onus on plaintiffs by requiring them to show substantial grounds before commencing their action. As Unsworth puts it:

> Whilst the Ministry was advised that placing the procedural barrier at the very outset would not appreciably increase the degree of protection above the Macmillan level, the view prevailed that the new form of words might have the right psychological effect from the medical point of view in deterring actions.[42]

The medical profession would come to interpret section 16 of the 1930 Act as not merely extending to the actions of doctors in signing statutory forms, but also to the administration of treatment, and to their actions in respect of voluntary patients.[43]

Voluntary patients effectively remained under doctors' orders because they had to give three days' notice before leaving the hospital, to allow for certification where necessary. In 1937 Dr Douglas Macrae, medical superintendent of Glengall hospital, Ayr and president of the Medico-Psychological Association described his practice in the following terms:

> After showing the patient to his accommodation and getting him clearly to understand that in agreeing to come under my medical care he was faithfully to abide by medical orders and so help me in securing his recovery, it was then explained to him that should he wish to leave at any time I required three days' notice to send for his relatives and, if necessary, two doctors, for the express purpose of his being detained should we all agree that he was not well enough to go home. The patient, thus realising the position from the outset, never runs the risk of bearing resentment.[44]

Unsworth sums up the political importance of the 1930 Act in these terms:

> [It] marked a transition from formal to therapeutic liberalism, from the primacy of abstract political liberty to the primacy of a concrete, substantive, socially defined liberty, which had to be positively created by expert intervention lubricated by informal, flexible, discretionary procedures.[45]

The 1930 Act also created a favourable legal and ideological climate for a period of experimentation with a wave of new psychiatric treatments in which a central aim was to make a reality of the representation of mental hospitals as places where people were admitted for a short period of treatment and then discharged.

8

THE BOARD OF CONTROL AND TREATMENT FOR MENTAL DISORDER, 1913–1930

English psychiatric treatment before the 1930s continued to rely heavily on sedatives. Dr William Sargant recalls in his memoirs how, up until the Second World War, many hundredweights of bromide a year were dispensed at the National Hospital in London 'to relieve the tensions of unresolved nervous states and the milder depressions of outpatients who came asking for help'.[1] Together with Dr Eliot Slater, Sargant would later co-author the influential textbook, *Introduction to Physical Methods of Treatment in Psychiatry,* which ran to five editions between 1944 and 1972, and the pair were to become the foremost proponents of physical treatments in the United Kingdom.[2] Sargant was, by his own account, one of the pioneers in England of Electro Convulsive Therapy (ECT) and was instrumental in introducing leucotomy. His zeal in pursuing radical physical treatments must be seen in the context of his horror, as a young locum in 1934, at the way in which hospitals were little more than warehouses for large numbers of drugged and zombified people. Referring to rows of patients with drooping heads and salivating mouths, he said:

> You could generally tell the heavily drugged patients during a ward round because you could pat them on the backs of their heads when they were sitting in rows. This was because their relaxed heads fell so far forward on their chests. All these tranquillised patients were then using bromides in truly enormous doses.[3]

Bromism was now a recognised condition. In 1927 tests had been developed to measure bromide levels in blood, so that it could be determined whether bromide was the cause of symptoms of mental disorder. Use of bromides did not diminish appreciably with the discovery of their adverse affects, which had been well known since the 1890s. They were very effective behavioural and libidinal sedatives and, until the arrival of barbiturates, they would occupy a central place in twentieth-century psychiatry.

In 1930 Dr Saxty Good, president of the Medico-Psychological Association and a doctor with a reputation for enlightened practice,[4] detailed the consumption during 1929 of sedative drugs for his own institution, Littlemore Hospital (which had 688 admissions during the year). Morphine had been used roughly one hundred times during 1929, in doses of a quarter of a grain. Hyoscyamine had been used twice and strong purgatives around four times, but the most widely used sedative drugs were the bromides (84 lbs during the year) and paraldehyde (240 lbs).[5] Paraldehyde would be a popular sedative until well into the 1960s and is still used today, both as a sedative (rarely) and more frequently in the treatment of epilepsy. In 1948 the deputy superintendent of Devon asylum, Dr J.W. Fisher published a best selling guide to mental treatment for nurses, which described paraldehyde as 'the asylum sheet-anchor' which, despire its disagreeable taste, was 'the safest, cheapest and most convenient of all forms of chemical restraint for excited and troublesome cases'.[6] Although it stimulates before it depresses, patients would be unconscious within about fifteen minutes of administration. As paraldehyde dissolves rubber and plastics, glass syringes have to be used where it is given by injection.

Although, like its predecessor, the Board of Control disavowed any intention of interfering in clinical matters, it gradually became more involved in questions of medical treatment. The Board played two roles. First they undertook rudimentary central monitoring of treatments given. During the public concern about over-sedation and the use of purgatives following Montague Lomax's book, they required hospitals to submit returns of sedative drug use, giving the annual quantities and the number of sleeping draughts administered nightly. Their annual report for 1930 gave the results, showing a wide variation in practice, and that the order and tranquillity of mental hospitals bore no relation to the amount of sedatives used:

There is clearly no consensus of opinion in respect to the value of sedatives in the treatment of mental illness. Some institutions use hardly any, but it can be said that in no case

121

are the quantities used excessive. There is also little agreement regarding the value of individual drugs. Some given freely in one hospital are rarely, if ever, used in another. It is in no critical spirit that we draw attention to this divergence in practice, but we suggest that the subject is one which needs further study and investigation. Research is much wanted so that it may be possible to define more clearly the conditions in which sedatives should be prescribed.[7]

The following year the Board again reported wide variations in local practice and noted that, in relation to the average annual employment of sedatives per hundred patients, there was a considerable difference between the 'county hospitals' (the old asylums), registered hospitals and licensed houses. They did not, however, reveal which class of institution used sedation the most. The Board recognised that the use of sedatives presented 'problems of some complexity', that there were many factors in the choice of treatment, and that there might be differences in the kinds of cases receiving treatment in the different classes of institution. Although they said that they were 'following up' the statistics with personal enquiries in representative hospitals for each group, subsequent annual reports make no mention of the question.[8]

The second aspect of the Board's role was promoting advances in treatment. Early evidence of this came with the adoption of a two-part format for their annual reports, the first summarising their own activities, and the second collecting abstracts of research reports from the various asylums and hospitals under their jurisdiction. By the mid 1920s the research section came to rival and later outstrip the Board's own reports in terms of bulk. The Board also played a significant part in promoting the new physical treatments for mental disorder, a role which increased after 1930. In this, the Board followed the dominant trend within institutional psychiatry by allying itself firmly to somatic approaches to treatment. The Board's prime concern with the various treatments for mental disorder was to promote the use and safe administration of up-to-date treatments and research into their efficacy, rather than worrying about the patient's consent or its absence.

The theory of focal infection was a somatic approach which attracted many British psychiatric adherents in the 1920s. The idea that physical sepsis was the starting point for a condition of toxaemia which could end in insanity formed the theoretical basis for large-scale dental extraction and tonsillectomy in psychiatric hospitals. The connection between focal infection and certain forms of mental disorder had first been suggested by the British surgeon William Hunter in 1900.[9] Hunter's ideas were taken up and applied with vigour by the North American psychiatrist H.A. Cotton, the superintendent of Trenton hospital, New Jersey, in what Hunter himself described as a frontal attack on focal sepsis with 'artillery, horse and foot'.[10] Andrew Scull has detailed how in 1919–1920:

> Acting vigorously on these opinions, Cotton's staff extracted more than 4000 teeth ... and over 6000 the following year, taking time to enucleate the tonsils of at least 90 per cent of the patients coming under their care.[11]

Absence of consent from patients or their relatives was no obstacle to Cotton's zeal:

> If we wish to eradicate focal infections, we must bear in mind that it is only by being persistent, often against the wishes of the patient, [that we can] expect our efforts to be successful. Failure in these cases often casts discredit upon the theory, when the reason lies in the fact that we have not been radical enough.[12]

By 1923 Cotton's activities had extended to include radical surgery to the colon as one of the principal foci of infection, resulting in a 30 per cent mortality rate.[13] His cavalier attitude to consent brought him under investigation in 1925 by a state commission, which heard allegations of Trenton patients having been 'dragged kicking and screaming into operating rooms where they were subjected to mutilating experimental surgery'.[14] Although, in the USA, it was beginning to emerge that Cotton's claims of recovery rates were grossly overestimated, his theories were acclaimed in Britain when he attended the 1923 meeting of the Medico-Psychological Association, and a series of adulatory articles appeared in the *Journal of Mental Science*, including one by his ardent British disciple, T.C. Graves of Rubery Hill Hospital, Birmingham.[15] Cotton's second visit was in 1927 to a joint meeting of the Medico-Psychological Association (which had been given a royal charter in that year) and the BMA in Edinburgh, to celebrate the work of Lord Lister in pioneering antiseptic surgery.

Although there were many eminent doctors and psychiatrists who endorsed focal sepsis theory, it was not greeted with the universal rapture of the 1923 meeting, and the resulting debates in the *Journal of Mental Science* ended in humiliation for William Hunter. Hunter's extravagant claim that functional psychosis should be replaced by the term septic psychosis was described by D.K. Henderson as calculated to make British psychiatry 'the laughing stock of the world'.[16]

By the early 1930s the heyday of focal sepsis theory in Britain was past and its inflated claims were no longer accepted. In his 1934 presidential address to the Royal Medico-Psychological Association, D.F. Rambaut, medical superintendent of St Andrew's Hospital, Northampton praised 'intestinal lavage on the Plombiere system in psychoses of toxic origin', but pointed out that although every effort was made at Northampton to discover septic foci, few were revealed; no more than 3 per cent in three hundred cases.[17] Whatever excesses focal sepsis theory had spawned, its enduring importance was twofold. First, it encouraged greater attention to be paid to the physical health of psychiatric patients and was an important factor in securing the appointment of dentists and radiographers to many English mental hospitals. Second, it contributed towards establishing the ideological hegemony of somatic treatment in institutional psychiatry, helping to pave the way for the flurry of experimentation with physical treatments which was to take place in the 1930s. In contrast to the role it would later play in promoting other forms of physical treatment, in relation to the treatment of focal sepsis the Board of Control confined itself to commending hospitals for hiring their own dentists and radiologists, or for making good use of visiting specialists.

The Board's first, rather inauspicious, foray into actively promoting a particular therapy involved malarial treatment for general paralysis of the insane or advanced syphilis. In 1923 they issued a circular encouraging a programme of clinical trials for treating general paralysis of the insane by inducing attacks of inoculated malaria, a treatment which had originated in Austria in 1919. Their zeal must be seen in the context that there was no known cure for tertiary syphilis at the time. The disease was widespread amongst the psychiatric hospital population and there was evidence that high fever eradicated the syphilitic spirochetes in the patients' blood. The Board's circular informed doctors of the chief results and procedures to be followed in applying the treatment in mental hospitals. It had to be used with great caution as there was a high death rate, although early death was also likely if the patients were left untreated. The death rate was high in the early English experiments with the treatment because, as the Board acknowledged, 'in some cases the induced malaria in the inoculated cases in England has been of an unusually severe type accompanied by pronounced complications and a tendency to fatality'.[18] They had initially thought that the inoculated malaria would be mild, but were alarmed to discover that the infections proved just as severe as the naturally contracted disease. They hoped that a less virulent strain could soon be introduced, but in the meantime counselled regular blood monitoring since the onset of complications was preceded by a phenomenal increase of parasites.

The Ministry of Health had also found that the common English mosquito readily became infected from inoculated patients. The circular recommended that hospitals using the treatment should have malaria specialists, adequate laboratory facilities with qualified staff, and from the 1 April until 30 October patients undergoing the treatment should be kept in a mosquito-proof ward or under mosquito curtains while parasites remained in their blood. On discharge, their names and home addresses should be given to the medical officer of health for the district in which they would reside.

The Board enclosed with the circular a translation of an article which warned of the risk of spreading the disease. It also outlined the threat of death to patients and advocated measures to 'avoid bringing into discredit a therapeutic measure which is now reckoned as the best method of treatment for general paralysis'.[19] Professor Dr P. Muhlens advised that the treatment should be carried out only in hospitals which were perfectly free of bugs, lice and anopheles mosquitoes, and on individuals whose resisting powers were good and whose paralysis was not of long duration. In his view most of the reported deaths could be ascribed to the fact that the patients were 'ill-nourished elderly paralytics, where the infection was not monitored or not early enough treated with quinine'.

Over the next twenty years the Board returned to the question on several occasions. Following some further deaths in 1926, the Board asked all hospitals for particulars of malarial treatment carried out, and stated that it preferred treatment by infected

125

mosquitoes to that by direct inoculation of blood from another case, and stated that arrangements had been made with the Ministry of Health to comply with requests for inoculation by the mosquito method.[20] In 1935 one of the senior medical commissioners, Surgeon Rear-Admiral E.T. Meacher, published, through HMSO, a study of general paralysis and its treatment by induced malaria.[21] In the late 1930s the Ministry of Health carried out an extensive study in conjunction with Exminster Hospital in Devon. Whatever its efficacy, the use of this treatment also provided a ready pool of human subjects for research purposes, giving the opportunity to gather information on the disease process of malaria in controlled circumstances. The results of the Exminster study were regularly reported to the Malaria Committee of the League of Nations.[22] The treatment was still in use in 1944, when the Board issued a further circular noting reports that induced malaria was being used where wards and beds were not mosquito proofed, reminding hospitals of the need to protect the general public and informing them where they could acquire effective nets.[23] By 1945, penicillin was being used successfully to treat all stages of syphilis, and malarial therapy gradually died out thereafter. It was the earliest of the modern wave of physical treatments. Unlike many which would come after, it appeared to work and was one of the best available remedies until the arrival of antibiotics. It involved a significant risk that the patient would die, but since many would die anyway if the disease followed its natural course, this was viewed as acceptable. It also showed how the Board of Control could promote, co-ordinate, and give advice about a pioneering and controversial procedure, and in the process turn it into an accepted medical treatment.

Although the climate of security in legal immunity created by the 1930 Act was an important factor in stimulating experimentation with new and hazardous treatments, the Board was active in its encouragement before the new legislation came into force. The hierarchy within psychiatric hospitals remained largely the same as it had been since the 1840s, with the medical superintendents or chief medical officers remaining ultimately responsible for the condition of patients and the direction of their medical, surgical and mental treatment. They were also responsible for the careful dispensing and administration of all medicines, and had control over all officers, nurses, artisans and servants.[24] This wide clinical authority was subject to the overall supervision of the visiting committees which varied considerably in their willingness to allow experimentation with new therapeutic methods.

In 1929 the Board of Control made the following direct plea for visiting committees to be more adventurous:

> While the more enterprising visiting committees are fortunately ready to test new methods and adopt any therapeutic device which seems likely to be beneficial, others not unnaturally follow a conservative policy and will not adopt new methods or install new appliances until their utility has been demonstrated beyond any reasonable doubt.[25]

The Board described conservative policies as 'ultra cautious' and 'a mistake', advocating the adoption of treatments even though they were at an early or experimental stage on the grounds that, even if not of proven efficacy, such interventions inspired hope in patients and their relatives. They also encouraged the perception, which the Board were so keen to foster, of psychiatry as a branch of medicine. The actual efficacy of treatments was secondary. Scull has posed the question: 'What was it that made the mentally ill so vulnerable to therapeutic experimentation – often, as it subsequently transpires, of a singularly harmful sort?'[26] Undoubtedly the removal of the spectre of liability for unintentional battery by section 16 of the 1930 Act played its part. So too did the policy of the Board of Control. Their concern was to create in the minds of patients and their relatives the sensation that something positive was being done, as the following passage demonstrates:

> It is common enough in the enthusiasm for any new discovery to claim for it in all honesty more than later experience will justify; but even if too sanguine expectations may sometimes be disappointed, it is still worth while to try every new method which gives any hope of improvement. The results, expressed statistically, may be disappointing; but psychologically, it is worth while to inspire the patient and his relatives with the feeling that everything possible is being done to ensure his recovery. The public generally, and in particular the patient's relatives, will never regard mental hospitals as hospitals in the true sense until they are satisfied that vigorous effort directed to the individual patient is being made to effect a cure.[27]

We might have expected a central authority born out of concerns for protecting patients from maltreatment to have reined in the wilder excesses and enthusiasms of psychiatrists, but the opposite was in fact the case. The Board of Control presided over a period of unprecedented experimentation with physical treatments in the 1930s and 1940s whilst its medical members actively promoted many of these novel interventions, offering support to psychiatrists who tried them in the face of opposition from conservative visiting committees or medical superintendents. The most important sources of mental patients' vulnerability were the acceptance that they could be treated without consent, and the psychiatrists' desire to take active steps beyond sedation and analysis to relieve the acute misery of mental disorder.

The question of forcible treatment for detained patients was raised in March 1934 when the Board considered a report of a visit to Caterham mental hospital, referring to the fact that force had been used in obtaining a sample of blood from a high-grade mental defective who actively objected. The Board discussed the situation wherein a patient under detention objects to the taking of blood or cerebro-spinal fluid. They came to the conclusion that a blood test or lumbar puncture given against the consent of a patient could be defended only if the diagnostic method was necessary for the individual's treatment or for the protection of other patients, there being *prima facie* grounds for thinking that the case required further diagnosis. As far as the Board was concerned, medical treatment could be given without consent and by force if necessary, and this included diagnostic procedures. They told commissioners that they should bring all such cases to the Board's notice without further comment in the visitors' book, in case the hospital might think they had done something wrong. By the early 1930s it was clear that detained patients could be treated without consent, voluntary patients could be detained by assembling the necessary medical evidence to have them certified, and doctors felt themselves to be adequately protected from legal action. This was fertile legal soil for therapeutic experimentation.

9

THE AGE OF EXPERIMENTATION: THE BOARD OF CONTROL AND TREATMENT FOR MENTAL DISORDER, 1930–1959

The significance of malarial treatment for general paralysis was that it gave renewed credence to treatments of mental disorder which relied on administering a severe blow to the patient's physical being. This struck deep resonances. It had been the rationale of baths of surprise (shock) or whirligig chairs (inducing physical sickness). It became the rationale for shock and coma treatments in the 1930s and 1940s. In the 1920s and early 1930s psychiatry relied upon sedation to calm patients so that they could be worked with by psychological methods of treatment. Patients might be sedated by drugs, or by prolonged warm baths. Every modern early twentieth-century asylum had a large bath department where patients could be confined in a bath for most of the day. Although the modernists were anxious to differentiate their medical scientific endeavour from the mechanical inventions of their forebears, with the exception of psychosurgery, and stripped of medical jargon, the underlying rationale of physical treatments involved jolting patients out of, or giving them a rest from, their own disordered thoughts and behaviour.

The drugs most widely used to give patients a rest from their disorder were the barbiturates, which by the early 1930s were beginning to supplant bromides as the sedative drug of choice. Medawar sees this period as crucial in the formation of the modern pharmaceutical industry:

> By the late 1930s, the industry had mastered the commercial basics of drug innovation, and had established some

129

credibility with the medical profession. By then, the big companies were actively promoting their drugs to doctors – and systematically competing with each other, for the first time, through innovation of me-too products. The barbiturates were among the earliest me-toos – drugs which are chemically and otherwise very similar to existing products and therefore superfluous to medical need . . . me-toos have recently been renamed 'innovative chemical extensions'.[1]

By the 1950s, 2,500 different kinds of barbiturate had been synthesised and 'there was not a lot to choose between them – though most doctors could clearly be persuaded there was'.[2] In 1927 Sir William Wilcox of St Mary's Medical School, London, and consultant toxicologist to the Home Office, advised that barbiturates should only be given on prescription, the number of doses should not exceed six and patients should be warned against daily use. By 1934 he considered them 'to occupy the foremost place among the drugs of addiction'.[3] The addictive and toxic effects of barbiturates would not be widely accepted in psychiatry until the early 1950s, although there were plenty of warning signs in the literature. In the 1933 *Journal of Mental Science*, A.M. Meerloo of the City of Rotterdam Psychiatric Hospital wrote at length on the action of barbituric acid compounds, proclaiming the principal advantage of barbital therapy, that 'it brings rest in restlessness'. He observed that barbiturate intoxication mimics the symptoms of insanity, and considered that 'the therapeutic action was achieved by inducing barbiturate intoxication which affected ontogenetically old parts of the brain in such a way that withdrawal may influence psychotic processes favourably'.[4]

Barbiturates were used in institutional psychiatry both as a routine sedative, and in massive doses to produce modified narcosis. The 'bromide sleep' had been tried at the turn of the century as a treatment for acute mania, but the heavy doses required carried serious risks for patients.[5] Prolonged narcosis was pioneered in Austria in the 1920s by Jakob Kläsi using injections of somnifaine (di-allyl-barbituric acid). In the initial trials, with twenty-three female and three male cases, there was no reaction from the male patients as safe doses could not produce sleep and eight dementing women did not respond. However 'from 25–33%' improved sufficiently to be sent home or to resume work.[6] However, early exponents of the treatment reported a high mortality rate of 5 per cent.[7] As Jones puts it: 'Even with the highest standards of nursing care, the risks of pneumonia or suffocation or irreversible coma were not negligible.'[8] This did not deter psychiatrists from continuing the experiment.

Somnifaine narcosis was particularly popular in Wales, at Whitchurch, Cardiff and Cefn Coed, Swansea. Trials were carried out at Whitchurch from 1933 onwards. By 1938, 460 Whitchurch patients had been treated by this method.[9] In 1934, Drs Ström Olsen and McCowan presented a summary of their results at Whitchurch to the annual conference of the Royal Medico-Psychological Association claiming significant success. In the discussion, Dr Norman Moulson of Cefn Coed summarised the rationale of the treatment:

> The purpose was to make some attempt to break the faulty habit of thought into which the patient had fallen, first by putting his mind completely at rest, and secondly, by endeavouring, during the period of increased suggestibility which followed such prolonged narcosis, to approach the causes underlying the symptoms by psychological means. The post narcotic period should be made a starting point for new habits of thought. At this stage occupational therapy . . . had a proper place in the scheme of treatment. A close understanding must be achieved between the patient and the physician by prolonged private conversation.[10]

Moulson himself had used narcosis on involutional melancholics who struggled violently and consistently against the effects of the drugs.

In his annual report for 1934, Ström Olsen remarked that the majority of psychiatrists who tried the treatment had abandoned it because of toxic complications. However, 250 patients had been treated at Whitchurch, where they were maintained in narcosis for fourteen days, with 'a high proportion of cure and without serious toxic effects'.[11] This was ascribed to the administration of insulin and glucose as part of the treatment. Others could not replicate this success. Palmer, writing in 1937, contradicted Ström Olsen saying that he had met serious cases of collapse despite using glucose and insulin, and as far as he was concerned the treatment was sufficiently dangerous that the permission of relatives was always obtained in addition to that of the patient, unless the patient was too ill to have the treatment discussed with him.[12]

The following year R.S. Wilson and J.W. Gillman published their experiences with the Cardiff method and concluded that somnifaine narcosis 'remains a dangerous procedure'.[13] Despite this, prolonged narcosis continued to be used at Whitchurch throughout the 1940s and 1950s.

Other barbiturates like seconal and nembutal were used to achieve narcosis. In 1939 Dr W.P. Berrington described his experiences using narcosis induced by Sodium Amytal. If patients exhibited no response to the standard dose for achieving coma, repeated doses were given until they did. With shades of nineteenth century treatment rationales, Berrington explained how, with catatonic patients, the period of narcosis 'dislodges the catatonic mechanism'.[14] Although what is now described as 'modified' narcosis is still sometimes used in hospitals in England and Wales, none uses the deep sleep therapy (DST) carried out in Chelmsford Hospital, a private hospital in Sydney, Australia, between 1963 and 1979. DST was a form of continuous narcosis, and the Royal Commission chaired by Mr Justice Slattery into the events at Chelmsford noted that it had been in vogue at some centres in the USA and the United Kingdom. The treatment involved large doses of barbiturates (seconal, Sodium Amytal and tuinal), inducing coma. The Royal Commission found that DST had no benefits to counteract the substantial risks including the possibility of permanent brain damage and death. It found that at least 24 of the 1,127 patients at Chelmsford who underwent the treatment died as a direct result of it. Electro Convulsive Therapy (ECT) was given to 997 patients along with the DST.[15]

Insulin coma therapy, invented by the Austrian psychiatrist Manfred Joshua Sakel in 1935, also enjoyed a period of popularity in Britain from the late 1930s well into the 1950s. Insulin was used to sink the patient into a deep state of unconsciousness through loss of sugar in the blood stream. The theory was that the temporary lack of sugar circulating in the system had a tonic effect on the brain, and the induced coma broke the train of disordered ideas, giving the patient a short rest from madness.

Insulin coma had many risks and the medical superintendents, who held ultimate clinical authority, were reluctant to allow their medical staff to experiment with them. Sargant recalls how, at the Maudsley, his respected mentor Dr Mapother, would not allow insulin coma to be introduced until 1938 because he 'feared to risk the lives of voluntary [patients], especially with our fierce local coroner waiting to pounce on us at the slightest provoca-tion'.[16] In the face of such hesitancy, the Board of Control played an important role in promoting physical treatments. Dr Isobel Wilson, one of the new intake of medical commissioners appointed as part of the reorganisation under the 1930 Act, made a study of insulin coma therapy, and Sargant records how her encour-agement facilitated its introduction at the Maudsley.[17] During the Second World War, when supplies of insulin and glucose were short, comas had to be induced by other means, such as barbiturates.

After 1945 insulin coma therapy became widely used again, but it was strongly criticised in a famous article in the *Lancet* entitled 'The insulin myth' in which, as Jones describes it, 'the good results were ascribed to the strong suggestive effect of the technique, together with the enthusiasm of a dedicated staff, and the incul-cation of group morale in a special unit'.[18] Partridge's account of insulin coma therapy in Broadmoor supports this view, empha-sising the privileges attached to the fourteen-week courses of treatment. Patients went into a daily coma five days every week, but were rewarded with a special dinner and were allowed to play cards with patients of the opposite sex for an hour and a half before returning to the ward with a bottle of glucose and sweets. In the restricted world of Broadmoor these must have been strong inducements. There is some evidence of the importance of consent seeking. Partridge observed that at Broadmoor during the 1950s consent was always sought from patients and their next of kin, if available, stating that they were willing to incur the risk of the treatment, since 'a state of coma is in the nature of an ante room to death, and the treatment necessarily is not without danger'.[19] In 1957, another *Lancet* article demonstrated equal results from insulin coma and barbiturate narcosis, and the use of insulin declined sharply thereafter, a demise also hastened by the arrival of the neuroleptic drugs.[20] Sargant was convinced that, used in conjunction with Electro Convulsive Therapy, insulin was the most effective treatment of schizophrenia until the arrival of the neuroleptic drug, Largactil (Thorazine).[21]

The other theory behind physical treatments was that they 'jolted' patients out of their illness. Convulsive therapy by drugs was introduced in 1934 in Hungary by Ladislas von Meduna, acting on the belief (later discovered to be erroneous) that there was a negative correlation between epilepsy and schizophrenia.

The convulsions were induced by drug injections. Insulin could be used to induce hypoglycaemic shock. The Board of Control was actively involved in promoting shock treatments for schizophrenia. In 1935 a special study of insulin shock by Dr Isobel Wilson was published by HMSO, pointing to the benefits of the treatment.[22]

In 1937 the Board's attention was drawn to an alternative method of achieving the convulsions by injections of the drug pentamethylenetrazol, known as cardiazol in the UK and metrazol in the USA. Large doses of cardiazol had been found to produce similar effects to camphor, an epileptiform fit. The Board decided that cardiazol shock should be studied where it had originated and dispatched Dr Wilson and a senior medical commissioner, Dr Rees Thomas, on a study tour to Vienna, Frankfurt and Budapest. On their return the Board issued a circular on the subject, accompanied by the usual disclaimer that they did not

> desire to interfere with the discretion of medical superintendents or medical officers in charge as regards the treatment to be given in individual cases, but the inception of a new form of therapy such as this is a matter in which the Board are concerned and would be glad to be consulted.[23]

They felt themselves to be well qualified to offer help and guidance because of Dr Wilson's study and requested that they be informed by hospitals whether this form of treatment was in use. If there was a plan for its future use, the Board wished to be informed before it was started. They warned that shock treatment was attended by certain definite risks, that it was of the utmost importance that the proper safeguards be meticulously observed, and that those who proposed it should either study its operation elsewhere or should invite help from abroad.

The Board's annual report for 1937 extended a more unequivocal invitation to experiment with cardiazol. Whilst acknowledging that insulin and cardiazol treatment had been in use for too short a time to give 'any reliable indication of the permanence of the results obtained, in view of the claims of such striking results', the Board felt that they merited 'a careful trial', either separately or in conjunction with each other.[24] There had been considerable criticism of chemically induced shock on the grounds that the proven benefits did not justify the considerable physical risks to patients. The Board brushed these aside:

Without making any extravagant claims for either form of treatment, we feel that it is most encouraging that at last a determined effort has been made to devise some active treatment for a form of mental disorder which has hitherto, in spite of a certain percentage of spontaneous remissions, proved in general so intractable, and which has done so much to add to the permanent population of mental hospitals. Even if it be true, as some contend, that some of the recoveries claimed for the new methods might have been effected by older forms of treatment, the speeding up of recovery which these new treatments secure is in itself a substantial advantage.[25]

The *Journal of Mental Science* emphasised the Board's satisfaction at the great interest in shock therapy by insulin and cardiazol and at the large numbers of hospitals reporting that they were carrying out trials of these treatments. The *Journal* editorial concluded that a consensus seemed to have emerged that it was 'a useful addition to our armamentarium'.[26]

In 1938 the Board issued a circular and a questionnaire seeking information from hospitals about their use of insulin, cardiazol and triazol, and published the results in their report for that year.[27] A total of ninety-two institutions employed the treatment, of which sixty-one used cardiazol only, three insulin only, sixteen insulin and cardiazol combined, and twelve used both drugs but not in combination. Courses of treatment had been completed by 3,531 patients; 1,808 men and 1,723 women. Cardiazol was the most widely used, accounting for 2,875 or 81.4 per cent of the patients, 474 (13.5 per cent) having insulin and 180 (5.1 per cent) having combined treatment. There had been nineteen deaths. As to success rates, these were judged by the rather crude measure of patients leaving hospital with 'complete, incomplete or partial remission of symptoms', and 30.9 per cent of patients achieved this. A most important aspect of the treatment was that it fostered the very view of hospitals and hospital treatment which the Board was anxious to promote, and in relation to a group of patients – schizophrenics – who were generally regarded as prime contributors to the chronic population. However, the Board's figures could only be regarded as providing a rough and ready indication of success rate, and the story from individual hospitals reveals more about the impact of this treatment on patients and the difficulties of assessing its effectiveness.

It must have been terrifying for patients. The immediate effects of a dose required to induce a fit were violent heartbeat and pulsating of the larger blood vessels. Within ten seconds the first signs of the fit would appear:

> Sudden pallor, twitchings of the finger and movements of the facial muscle, which gave the patient the appearance of being suddenly terrified. Very often the terrified expression is followed by a few staring glances from side to side, dilation of the pupils and a cry or scream.[28]

The patient would then lose consciousness. This would be followed by the 'tonic stage', ten to thirty seconds of intense fitting, and finally the 'clonic stage' where fitting became more intermittent. After patients had slept off the immediate effects of the shock, they would be in 'a more compliant mood' to respond to psychological treatments.

Insulin and cardiazol shock treatment had been started at Bethlem in 1937. The medical superintendent, Dr Porter Phillips, reported that forty-two women and six men had received cardiazol or triazol shock in 1938. All the men were unchanged, whereas twelve of the women were 'recovered and home', eight were 'much improved', six were 'unimproved', and sixteen were 'unfinished'.[29] However, Porter Phillips himself acknowledged that although these figures showed a significant recovery rate for the women, they needed to be treated with caution for the following reasons:

> [O]ne should say that an appreciable number of cases that were not treated eventually recovered, but the percentage rate is difficult to assess. It is assumed, rightly or wrongly, by other observers that by treatment a higher recovery rate is obtained and the duration of illness is shortened. However, so much depends on the personal equation of the observer and whether the diagnosis is correct.[30]

One of the results of shock therapy was that it so terrified many patients that it rendered them more compliant to other more traditional approaches. Porter Phillips reported his experience that the treatment brought about an alteration in 'the mental state or attitude of such patients . . . more often with advantage so that nursing control and management is carried out with greater ease'.[31]

In his 1939 report, Porter Phillips again expressed reservations. Observing that each method of 'shock production' after trial appears to be 'withdrawn in favour of some other therapeutic agent more suitable and promising', he went on to say that there had been 'such varying results that in the absence of a reliable scientific explanation of their rationale, one cannot enthuse about their effectiveness in producing a stable recovery'.[32] At the time, Bethlem was using mainly triazol. Fourteen male patients received treatment during 1939, of whom three were discharged 'recovered' and two 'relieved'. Two others were 'brought out of stupor', but made no further recovery, and one relapsed after an initial recovery. One other was improving, but six had refused further treatment after a few injections and had shown no change. As previously, forty-two females had been given the treatment, with an average of twelve injections per patient. Of these, twenty-three had left the hospital recovered, three others were awaiting discharge, and ten had not improved at all or insufficiently to leave hospital. The importance of turnover of beds was emphasised by Porter Phillips' assistants, who actually carried out the treatment:

> With this a recovery rate of 61 per cent is recorded. Moreover, another important point presents itself in that the average stay in hospital is greatly reduced by this treatment, thus making it possible to treat a greater number of patients within a prescribed time with the same number of beds. The average stay of those cases designated 'recovered' was under four months from the beginning of treatment, which compares favourably with the average stay of patients generally.[33]

Whatever the true success rate of drug-induced shock treatment, its adverse effects and risks were indeed significant. It often caused hairline fractures of the spinal vertebrae, resulting in severe back pain, and the shocks induced acute terror in many patients. Partridge records how Broadmoor patients 'learned to dread it; and they would cower in corners and beg for mercy when their turn came again for the hypodermic needle'.[34] A survey by Kennedy published in the *Journal of Mental Science* in 1937 underlines the importance which he attached to keeping from the patients the true nature of the treatment:

It was found advisable for patients having the treatment not to see one another, especially in the latter stages, as in this way it was often possible to conceal from the patients that they had had convulsions.[35]

Kennedy also offered advice on overcoming patient resistance. In order to produce convulsions it was necessary to withhold all sedatives except paraldehyde and hyoscine. He had found hyoscine in particular to have no inhibiting effect on the convulsions: 'there seems to be no objection to giving the treatment to patients premedicated with this drug, and this may prove to be a valuable method in the treatment of resistive patients'.[36]

The safer method of inducing convulsions which was to sound the death knell of treatment by drug-induced shock was Electro Convulsive Therapy (ECT). Tourney describes the replacement of chemically induced convulsions by the use of electric current as 'a logical one'.[37] In 1938, after a lengthy series of experiments, the Italians Ugo Cerletti and Lucio Bini produced the first electrically induced convulsion in man, without consent, as Valenstein's account shows:

> The police commissioner had sent over a man, presumed to have been schizophrenic, who had been wandering round the train station in a confused state. When the current was applied to his head, his whole body jolted and stiffened, but he did not lose consciousness. Clearly the voltage was too low, and they decided to try again the next day. Overhearing the two doctors, the patient said, 'Not another one! It's deadly!' As those were the only comprehensible words they had heard from the patient, they ignored his protest and decided to try again immediately with higher current.[38]

The result was an classic epileptic convulsion, and it produced a happy ending, in the words of Cerletti and Bini:

> We observed with the most gratifying sensation the characteristic gradual awakening of the patient 'by steps.' He rose to a sitting position and looked at us, calm and smiling, as though to inquire what we want of him. We asked: 'What happened to you?' He answered: 'I don't know. Maybe I was asleep.' Thus occurred the first electrically produced convulsion in man, which I at once named electroshock.[39]

This has all the hallmarks of heroic medical discovery. Medawar has pointed out that when doctors talk about heroic treatments: 'They were not referring to the forbearance of the patients on whom the treatments were inflicted; the term rather implied that doctors were the heroes, because of their confidence in the drastic treatments they used.'[40] The common feature of these medical breakthroughs was that they were often performed for the greater good (and greater glory) of medicine, on patients who were incapable of consenting or who adamantly refused them, and who were certainly never told of the likely effects. In the world of 1930s psychiatric ethics, the patient's views were of little account. Again, Medawar sums this cast of mind up brilliantly: 'Evidence from around the world suggests that professional attitudes towards the mentally ill to some extent still reflect deep-seated notions of illness as an expression of personal fate, and of medical treatment as the next best thing to divine intervention.'[41] The discovery of ECT was announced with vigour, and its description had all the elements which make histories of medical discovery resemble accounts of religious experiences: the kindly parental doctor overriding the unreasoning objections of the patient to harness (at last) the power of electricity for the good of psychiatry, followed by the ceremonial christening of the new treatment. Electroshock!

ECT was cheaper and easier to administer. There was better control, reduced patient anxiety, and lower risk than with cardiazol shock. In the USA, it was used in 10 per cent of institutions in 1940, in 43 per cent by 1941, and its use rapidly increased thereafter. Many hospitals which had previously used a combination of insulin coma and metrazol shock switched to insulin plus ECT or ECT alone.[42]

In Britain, ECT was first used by Grey Walter and Golla at the Burden Neurological Unit in Bristol. Strauss and Macphail developed a practical ECT machine and used it on in-patients and out-patients at St Bartholemew's in London, and the treatment was taken up by Dr T.P. Rees at Warlingham Park in Croydon. In 1940 Bethlem took delivery of its first ECT machine, and in his annual report for that year, the physician superintendent said that since its arrival the apparatus had been 'in active use'. He went on to say that so far the results were very satisfactory, and several dramatic improvements had resulted. Many patients had shown improvement of their worst symptoms.[43] With ECT most of the unpleasant features of shock treatment for the patient could be avoided. By the end of the 1940s, curare was being used to eliminate the muscle spasms induced by the shock, offering the possibility to eliminate fractures.

In William Sargant's book, medical heroism was seen to lie in overcoming bureaucracy and bringing patients the latest available treatment. He tells how he was working under the clinical directorship of his co-author Slater at Belmont Hospital, and wanted to introduce ECT there. Although Slater was prepared to give permission, the London County Council (LCC) refused to put up the money for a machine. When Sargant acquired one as the result of a charitable grant, the LCC would not pay for its maintenance and upkeep. Nevertheless, he immediately started work with it, and though sending an electric current through a patient's head was always an 'anxious event', the machine was soon in extensive use. He recalls how he was asked by the medical director of St Ebba's Hospital Epsom, where the LCC had also refused to provide a machine, to bring his apparatus to treat an acutely ill schizophrenic patient. Although the patient was too malnourished to be given ECT without serious risk, Sargant asked to see any agitated depressives, and gave 'nearly the whole ward . . . the new electric shock treatment'.[44] He records that more than thirty of the forty patients treated made a quick recovery and were able to leave hospital.

The shock treatments were initially developed to combat schizophrenia, on the basis that epilepsy and schizophrenia could not coexist in the same person, and later continued with the more empirical rationale that they appeared to work – though it remains to this day unclear precisely why this should be. ECT is sometimes used in schizophrenia when antipsychotic drugs do not work, but the principal modern use is for depression, as the second line of attack when anti-depressant medication proves ineffective. It is also used as an emergency treatment when patients have deteriorated to a stage where their lives are at risk. Its precise success rate is hard to determine, but to this day, ECT is widely regarded as one of the most effective treatments for depression, and is extensively used in the UK and the USA. Like many psychiatric treatments, it is empirical in the sense that it is often tried to see if it works for a variety of different disorders without any clear idea of precisely how or why it works.[45]

When ECT was given unmodified (without muscle relaxant or anaesthetic), a practice no longer regarded as acceptable, it could produce serious physical injury. This happened in *Bolam* v. *Friern Barnet Hospital Management Committee*,[46] the well-known case which lays down the principle that, to avoid liability in negligence whilst exercising clinical judgment, doctors must act in accordance with *a* responsible body of opinion (not necessarily the majority) skilled in the speciality. The patient in this case was suffering from depression, and alleged that the doctor had broken his duty of care by failing to disclose the risks of giving ECT without a muscle relaxant, as a result of which the subject sustained a fractured pelvis. In the course of his instruction to the jury McNair J said this:

> You may well think that when a doctor is dealing with a mentally sick man and has a strong belief that his only hope of cure is submission to ECT, the doctor cannot be criticised if he does not stress the dangers, which he believes to be minimal, which are involved in that treatment.[47]

He then went on to say they might also take the view that 'unless the plaintiff had satisfied them that he would not have taken the treatment if he had been warned', there was nothing in the point about failure to warn. The doctor was found not to have been negligent. Although the case suggested that consent might be an important issue, where a patient suffered from mental disorder it afforded generous scope to 'therapeutic privilege', the discretion of a doctor not to warn if he or she considers the risk minimal when weighed against the potential benefit to the patient, and where because of mental disorder the patient might attach disproportionate importance to that risk. There was no suggestion of this in *Bolam*, but the giving of ECT unmodified and without anaesthetic was open to being used as a punishment or a deterrent because of its unpleasant effects, and allegations that it was being used in this way surfaced from time to time between the 1950s and the 1980s.

The most dramatic of the physical treatments was psychosurgery. As Elliot Valenstein reminds us:

> Psychosurgery was not a medical aberration, spawned in ignorance ... [T]he history of psychosurgery is a cautionary tale: these operations were very much part of the mainstream

141

of medicine of their time, and the factors that fostered their development and made them flourish are still active today.[48]

The desperation of institutional medical superintendents led them to adopt desperate remedies.

As these patients remained hospitalised for long periods, sometimes for life, and funding did not keep stride with the increasing patient population, economic considerations often became the factor determining treatment. Any suggested treatment that had the slightest chance of decreasing the patient population, and was relatively inexpensive to administer, had great appeal.[49]

Psychosurgery as a treatment for mental illness was started by Egas Moniz in Portugal in 1935, although a Swiss psychiatrist Gottlieb Burckhardt had experimented with surgical removal of part of the temporoparietal region in 1890, causing great outcry.[50] Having heard of experiments by the leading US physiologist John F. Fulton at Yale University in which the frustration and anger of chimpanzees disappeared completely if their frontal lobes were destroyed, Moniz, himself disabled by gout, trained his junior colleague, Lima, to undertake the procedure and they proceeded to leucotomise eighteen patients in a mental hospital near Lisbon.[51] Moniz gave an enthusiastic account of these experiments in a monograph published in 1936.[52] News of this surfaced in the British medical press via a brief note in a 1938 literature survey in the *Journal of Mental Science*.

Ultimately there would be twenty patients in the series. Moniz 'obtained' fourteen of the patients from the Manicome Bombarda asylum, and the other six from his own clinic or other asylums. Most of them were deteriorated, many were incapable of consenting to treatment, and some actively resisted. One woman was so disturbed that she pulled out the intravenous needle used to convey the anaesthetic, and after the operation tore at her bandages, screaming, 'They have tried to kill me twice but I'm still here.'[53]

Moniz himself claimed that of twenty cases, seven were recovered, seven were improved, and six unchanged. But Valenstein's careful analysis of the case histories indicates that claims of cure were inflated. Moniz, who was advancing in years and anxious to publish his results quickly, rushed into print before a proper evaluation could be made. There was an average of four days between the operations in the series, far too soon to evaluate post operative complication. Some of the observations on 'cure' were made a mere seven days after the operation, which was to say the least, premature:

> Moniz presented no evidence indicating that any of the patients was capable of living normally outside the hospital. In the majority of cases the major change was the reduction of agitation and increased 'calmness.' Yet neurologists and psychiatrists commonly described the evidence in Moniz's monograph as 'detailed' and 'impressive'.[54]

Guilty of this were the American review of Moniz's monograph and the summary in the *Journal of Mental Science*, which said that 'with deteriorated patients he had obtained slight or no benefit'; however, in ' "recent cases" the results were good, and some patients had left hospital and resumed their occupations.'[55]

The circulation of Moniz's results led to the adoption of leucotomies at psychiatric centres throughout the world. In the United States they were pioneered by Drs Walter Freeman (author of the laudatory review of Moniz) and James Watts in Georgetown University, Washington DC. Having obtained leucotomes from Moniz's instrument maker, Freeman and Watts carried out the first leucotomy in the US on 14 September 1936, on a sixty-three-year-old agitated and depressed woman from Kansas. She and her husband agreed to the operation, in preference to the alternative of institutionalisation. The woman changed her mind when she realised that her hair would have to be shaved, and only proceeded after Freeman had assured her that every effort would be made to 'save her curls'. Valenstein describes how 'The curls were not saved – but as Freeman observed, "she no longer cared." '[56] This was to be the most marked effect of psychosurgery, variously described as 'detachment', 'indifference', or 'insouciance'. The problem might still be there but the patient no longer worried about it. Freeman and Watts were more cautious than Moniz, emphasising that indiscriminate use of psychosurgery could cause vast harm, and and calling for limited trial.

> Prefrontal leucotomy should be reserved for a small group of specially selected cases in which conservative methods of treatment have not yielded satisfactory results. It is

extremely doubtful whether chronic deteriorated patients would be benefited. Moreover, every patient probably loses something from this operation, some spontaneity, some sparkle, some flavour of the personality.[57]

When Freeman and Watts presented their results in Baltimore, one questioner raised ethical and legal concerns about consent of patients, but Adolf Meyer, the doyen of American psychiatry, rescued them from adverse comment. Another powerful ally in the medical establishment was John F. Fulton, who, as Jack D. Pressman has shown, 'played a crucial behind the scenes role in helping to insure that the subject of psychosurgery would obtain a fair hearing and survive its controversial first few years'.[58] They were indeed turbulent years, and Freeman and Watts met strong criticism from within the profession, where some denounced them as criminals. Their ability to cultivate the media, and actually create a public demand from patients and their families for psychosurgery was a crucial factor in securing public support. In 1937 they invented a new procedure different from Moniz's, and the 'Freeman Watts cut' became the standard leucotomy for many years. By the early 1940s lobotomy, as Freeman and Watts called it, was widely covered in such publications as *Time Magazine*, the *Reader's Digest*, *Newsweek*, *Harper's*, and *Life*. The tone of the media coverage was almost uniformly adulatory, reporting miracle cures on a grand scale. One stated that: 'The fear, the worry must be very grave indeed before Doctors Freeman and Watts decide that the operation is the only hope.' Freeman was quoted as saying: 'We want a little indifference, a little laziness, a little joy of living that patients have sought in vain for so long.'[59]

On a visit to the United States in 1938, William Sargant examined three of Freeman's patients and, as he tells it with characteristic lack of false modesty:

> When I suggested to Freeman that he had not found a cure for chronic alcoholism, schizophrenia or depression, but for persistent chronic anxiety and obsessive tension, he was somewhat doubtful – not having thought of his operation in that light. But this proved to be the correct view ... [A]s soon as possible after my return to England in 1940, I began planning to try to develop modified techniques of leucotomy.[60]

Along with his co-author, Dr Eliot Slater, William Sargant later became one of the leading British propagandists of psychosurgery and, interestingly in the light of his claim to have informed Freeman that the procedure was not a cure for schizophrenia, Clare remarks how Sargant and Slater remained unabashed advocates of psychosurgery for schizophrenia until the 1970s, by which time all enlightened psychiatric opinion took the opposite view.[61]

When Sargant returned to England in 1938, he went to work at the Belmont Hospital where Slater, who was the medical superintendent, was willing to allow him to introduce leucotomies. However, the London County Council would not provide the necessary neurosurgical facilities. Sargant describes how he wrote to Professor Golla at the Burden Neurological Unit in Bristol saying that, if he would only introduce leucotomy at Bristol, he could use this as a precedent:

> Golla thereupon went ahead, and soon could point to the most successful results; so before long we won permission to use leucotomy on very occasional patients – always provided that every case had been vetted by my seniors – who sometimes proved very difficult to convince.[62]

The 'encouraging' results of a small series of eight cases carried out in Bristol in December 1940 were published in the *Lancet* in July 1941.[63] In 1943 Dr T.P. Rees, medical superintendent of Warlingham Park Hospital and a practitioner of psychosurgery, expressed his surprise that:

> [whilst t]he tonsils, the sinuses, the appendix, the clitoris, the ovaries and the testes have on numerous occasions provided the field of action for surgeons collaborating with psychiatrists ... [it was] surprising that the brain, the organ of the mind, has been left alone for so long.[64]

Within a short time leucotomies were being performed at psychiatric hospitals across the country, and the pages of the *Journal of Mental Science* were full of accounts of the procedure, complete with pictures of cross sections of brains, drawings showing where the holes ought to be made in the skull, and diagrams of the authors' own design of leucotomes.[65] The average mortality rate from the treatment was around 4 per cent, usually from haemorrhage, and there was a significant risk of permanent damage to the patient's personality. It should be remembered that in their heyday in the 1940s, these operations were being carried out in psychiatric hospitals across the country by people who were not qualified neurosurgeons. The US guru of psychosurgery, Walter Freeman himself, was not a surgeon. Given these risks, to what extent was consent an issue, whether consent by relatives or by the patient him- or herself?

The British patients selected for treatment in the early 1940s appear to have been the most deteriorated and behaviourally disturbed, regardless of diagnostic classification. Describing fifty cases operated on in Netherne Hospital in the second half of 1942, Cunningham Dax and Radley Smith said that they carried out the operation:

> With the primary object of relieving the most disturbed patients in the hospital, quite independently of their poor prognosis. They formed a large part of the most violent, hostile, noisy, excited, destructive or obscene cases in the hospital; the type who distress their relatives, upset the other patients and consume the time and energy which could be put to so much better use by the staff.[66]

In his study of leucotomy at Denbigh, North Wales, Crossley notes that selection of patients was influenced by behavioural disturbance, but also points out that media portrayal of psychosurgery as a miracle cure was leading patients' relatives to ask for the treatment. In 1942, McGregor and Crumbie offered the following advice for dealing with resistive patients:

> One of the intravenous anaesthetics is probably the anaesthetic of choice in non-co-operative patients. . . . Three times in our series of cases an electric convulsion was induced before the administration of the intravenous anaesthetic. This was done because the patients were so resistive that administration would otherwise have proved very difficult. In each case it proved a most satisfactory sedative . . .[67]

In March 1943 the Royal Medico-Psychological Association held a symposium on leucotomy which was attended by representatives from most of the major psychiatric hospitals. Only one voice was seriously raised against the treatment, that of Professor James MacDonald who said this:

[T]he frontal lobes represented the highest form of evolution, and if there was one thing which distinguished the human being from the anthropoid ape it was in the existence of the frontal lobes. He wished to know more about this suggestion of interfering with them; at one time he went further and called it vivisection; it was human vivisection because there was no definite basis for it; it seemed to be purely experimental. He was not against experiments that were rational, but he could not see the rationality of this at all ... [68]

Macdonald also referred to the apparently indiscriminate use of leucotomy:

A point which occurred to him was the generality of types treated; the operation appeared to be applicable to a great number of types of mental disorder. Was it so applicable?[69]

The Board of Control's interest in gathering information about new treatments was again in evidence in 1945 when, in view of the increasing extent to which prefrontal leucotomies were being performed in mental hospitals, they asked that they be notified of such operations and their results.[70] In 1947 the Board reported their pleasure that some form of such 'physical treatment' was used in every hospital to supplement psychotherapy and other approaches. They went on to say that:

Among the many forms of treatment the progress of which we have watched with interest, we have observed in particular the development of pre-frontal leucotomy; and in February 1947, the Board issued a report on 1,000 cases, this report being mainly the work of Dr Isobel Wilson. Some time must necessarily elapse before opinion can crystallise as to the precise place which this form of treatment can fill, but there seems reason to hope that for certain types of case the operation of pre-frontal leucotomy offers a probability of relief and the possibility of recovery.[71]

Meanwhile, in the United States in 1945, Freeman had pioneered the transorbital lobotomy, where an ice pick was inserted through the eye socket. This led to a split between Freeman and Watts in 1947, because of the latter's refusal to accept Freeman carrying out operations in the office. He used an electric convulsion to produce anaesthesia, and ECT just before psychosurgery became a widely adopted procedure because of his assertion that it enhanced the effectiveness of the operation. Freeman's rationale for the transorbital lobotomy, which he would maintain into the 1970s, was this. Prefrontal lobotomy required a neurosurgeon, and a large staff to care for patients during the long recovery period. Standard leucotomy was therefore reserved as a treatment of last resort, when shocks and comas failed, and this meant that, in schizophrenia in particular, an illness could become entrenched which could be curable by a speedy surgery. Transorbital lobotomy was viewed by Freeman as being a half-way stage between electroshock and prefrontal lobotomy.

From 1946 Freeman offered his services to hard-pressed hospital superintendents, and busied himself promoting transorbital lobotomy, touring the United States carrying out psychosurgeries in different hospitals as he went. By 1947 psychosurgery was in its heyday and Freeman was its foremost figure below Moniz. He organised the First World Congress of Psychosurgery in Lisbon in 1948, and Moniz received the supreme accolade of the Nobel Prize for Medicine in 1949, an indication of the acceptance and popularity of psychosurgery in mainstream world medicine.

Controversy about psychosurgery continued to rage, for two reasons: one was that there was a high death rate, and the other that 'the indifference' aimed for in many cases produced serious loss of social functioning. However, Kramer found that between 1936 and 1951 at least 18,608 lobotomies were performed in the US.[72] Between 1945 and 1954, 12,000 leucotomies were performed in England and Wales and reported to the Board of Control.[73] A survey carried out by the Ministry of Health showed that of 10,365 patients who underwent leucotomies between 1942 and 1954, 6,338 were women.[74] Of all patients having the operation, 64 per cent were schizophrenics, 25 per cent were suffering from affective disorder, and 11 per cent had other diagnoses. There were more women than men in all three diagnostic categories, but the difference was far the greatest for patients with affective states.[75]

What led to the decline of psychosurgery? As Valenstein says, it would be more pertinent to ask 'why did it survive so long?', given that it was a high risk procedure and results were often not good. When results were poor, surgeons did not give up:

Rather than abandoning psychosurgery, neurosurgeons much more commonly introduced some change in the operation in the hope of increasing the success rate. During the five years following the end of the War there was great prolif-eration of different psychosurgical operations – motivated partly by the desire to improve the results, and partly by the natural inclination of each surgeon to improve his procedure. Had the lobotomy procedure not been modified, the number of operations performed would probably have decreased rapidly. The hope held out for these new procedures was, however, the main reason interest in lobotomy remained high for another five years – until chlorpromazine was intro-duced in 1954.[76]

With the arrival on the scene of the neuroleptic drugs, of which chlorpromazine (largactil) was the first, psychosurgery was rele-gated largely to the sidelines, despite the evangelical attempts of Walter Freeman in the US and Sargant and Slater in the UK, which continued well into the 1970s. By the late 1950s the only physical treatment to survive in widespread use was ECT. The practitioners who gave these heroic treatments had a number of characteristics in common. They were usually struggling against bureaucracy, ignorance, professional jealousy, or over cautious colleagues. Over-punctiliousness about consent was a positive vice when set against the immense benefits to be reaped. In 1947, one of Freeman's patients who had come from out of town for an operation, became very unruly in a motel. The police would not enter the room without permission, but Freeman went to the motel, and decided that the patient could be calmed with a few bursts of ECT. The patient's relatives held him down while these were given, and while the patient was unconscious Freeman performed a transorbital lobotomy.[77]

Where consent was obtained it was usually that of relatives who, in the climate of enthusiasm for psychosurgery as a miracle cure, were keen not to stand in the way of their loved ones having access to it. Dr J.W. Fisher's best-selling *Modern Methods of Mental Treatment: A Guide for Nurses*, published in 1948, makes no mention of consent in relation to coma or shock treatments but, in relation to psychosurgery, insisted that 'the consent of relatives is necessary for the operation, which is not devoid of risk (mortality 1–5%)'.[78] Proxy consent by relatives was widely accepted in psychiatric practice, whatever may have been the legal view as to its validity.

As Medawar reminds us: 'The history of medicine reveals again and again the bias that exists towards proving the triumph of benefit over risk – and at times this has involved extraordinary denial of some unpalatable truths.'[79] This could certainly be said of the age of experimentation. In 1951 the president of the Royal Medico-Psychological Association called for facilities to carry out 'empirical shock treatments'. Empirical medicine, according to the Oxford English dictionary, is based on or guided by the results of observation or experiment. In psychiatry this meant one treatment would be tried to see if it worked. If it did not, something else would be tried. So many treatments were available that, unless a patient recovered, he or she would be lucky to get away having sampled only one. The detailed case histories in the psychiatric journals from the 1930s to the 1950s show how a patient might begin with prolonged narcosis or insulin coma, and if these did not prove effective, might then be given cardiazol shock or ECT. If these did not work, patients often ended up being leucotomised.

In 1958 Sargant publicly recognised that numerous patients had undergone psychosurgery because their illness was due to barbiturate intoxication and withdrawal. Although, during the 1940s, he had stated that barbiturates in moderate doses did not create true addiction, he now modified his view:

I am now seeing patients who have had one, two, or even three leucotomies performed for a chronic persisting tension and who have turned out, probably, to be cases of barbiturate addiction.[80]

Given the extent of barbiturate use in the 1930s and 1940s in psychiatric hospitals, both routinely and in large doses to achieve narcosis, there must have been many who suffered this fate. The physical treatments of the 1930s and 1940s shared another characteristic with the contraptions of the late eighteenth and early nineteenth centuries; they were invented and pioneered by individual doctors, working in the field. From the early 1950s, this would no longer be possible, as the drug industry established a firm foothold in institutional psychiatry. The age of psychopharmacology was about to begin.

10

THE AGE OF
PSYCHOPHARMACOLOGY

We have seen how, prior to the physical treatments, the theory was that drugs should be used as a way of calming patients so that the underlying causes of their symptoms could be worked with. These drugs were mostly sedatives, but from the 1930s experiments were carried out with what we, from our 1990s viewpoint, would call psychedelics: mescalin and LSD. In 1933 the Italian, L. Ceroni wrote 'Mescalin intoxication: a personal experience'. He took mescalin five times and noted among the effects, dissociation of the personality and 'not a few points of contact with the symptomatology of schizophrenia'.[1] In 1936, Erich Guttman of the Maudsley wrote an article in the *Journal of Mental Science* entitled 'Artificial psychosis produced by mescalin', and pronounced that it might have some therapeutic use. Even more important, he felt that it gave psychiatrists an opportunity of experiencing 'indescribable mental changes as a help in understanding the mental life of schizophrenics'.[2] Guttmann and Walter Maclay continued their experiments with Maudsley patients, by definition voluntary, and studied patients' drawings for their psychological significance.

In the early 1950s psychiatric hospitals in the US and the UK experimented with LSD. This was an event of great importance. Whilst Guttmann had only to thank his colleague in South America who provided him with his mescaline, the LSD experiments mark the beginning, in the UK at least, of researchers appending thanks to drug companies and their employees for advice, support and supplies of the drugs with which the trial was carried out. The drug companies were now highly visible in psychiatric hospitals, which of course had great potential as testing grounds for new drugs, as well as providing a potentially large (and captive) market.

The first American studies in 1952 compared the response of 'normal people' and schizophrenics to LSD and mescaline. They found that in both groups these drugs had the same effect of disorganising psychic integration and producing schizophrenia-like symptoms. This suggested that if naturally occurring equivalents could be found in the blood of schizophrenics they might be the causes of schizophrenia, but it did not suggest a therapeutic use for LSD. It was not long in coming. 1n 1952, Sandoz supplied Powick Hospital, Worcestershire with LSD for a therapeutic trial.[3] The subjects for their experiments were severe obsessional neurotics with a bad prognosis or who had been ill for a considerable time; twenty of the sample of thirty-six had been ill for more than six years. 'The outstanding symptom [was] that of extreme mental tension, and the majority of the cases would have been considered for rostral pre-frontal leucotomies.'[4]

One point had been clearly established in the earlier experiments. The 'LSD experience', as it was called, was personal to each individual. Memories of childhood would be recalled and relived. The hallucinations often included experiencing picture images which suggested that the drug put patients in touch with the collective unconscious. The LSD experience would trigger an upsurge of subconscious material into the consciousness, which could then be subjected to Jungian analysis. Although many had to be cajoled to continue, only one patient in the original study withdrew. There was a whole protocol for doctors and nurses to administer the treatment, provide care and support the patients without obtrusion. Patients were encouraged to write and draw while under the influence, and their art became the raw material of analysis. After the trip was over, patients were to be given nembutal to help them recover from the emotional experience, and were they to be observed if they showed any suicidal tendencies – a known effect of the drug, as were 'delayed reactions', perhaps an early description of flashbacks. There were therapy groups to foster *esprit de corps* and to enable patients to discuss their LSD experiences with each other (a strong contender for many people's idea of hell). The team claimed good results and, from 1952 until 1972, LSD treatment was carried out at Powick, in a purpose-built unit from 1958. At least 4,500 people in hospitals around Britain received LSD treatment during that period. Recently, patients treated with LSD have alleged that their consent was not obtained, that they were not properly monitored for side effects, and that they continue to suffer flashbacks and panic attacks.[5] The tests with LSD were soon eclipsed by a group of drugs which swept the world of psychiatry more comprehensively and rapidly than even psychosurgery; the phenothiazines.

Chlorpromazine was the first of the phenothiazine derivative drugs to be synthesised. Better known in England under its proprietary name of Largactil, it was originally intended for use in the management of general anaesthesia. Various articles on Chlorpromazine's psychiatric potential appeared in continental psychiatric journals during 1952 and 1953, and trials began in British psychiatric hospitals at about this time. In 1954 the *Journal of Mental Science* published the results of trials carried out by Dr Anton Stephens at Warley Hospital, Essex, and by Dr F.B.E. Charatan at Cane Hill in Surrey. Perhaps it is the fate of every new psychiatric treatment to be evaluated in terms of the treatment it replaces. Early descriptions of Chlorpromazine spoke of the 'chemical lobotomy' effect, because of its resemblance to the characteristic state following a pre-frontal leucotomy. Charatan described the key features of this state. Patients were:

> [M]otionless and relaxed; staring, disinterested, and remote, but not drowsy, and with consciousness unimpaired. They were disinclined to talk, and their responses were of the briefest. This state may perhaps be likened to the mental state described in patients suffering from encephalitis lethargica.[6]

Four of Charatan's group of eighteen patients showed this effect. Anton Stephens reported that two of his fifty patients showed an extreme form of this, presenting responses which were 'considered to represent a state of intoxication':

> Both patients entered a state probably best described as one of dissociation. They became dazed and bewildered, and unable to make effective contact with their environment, although apparently aware of it. Both became incontinent ... a state neither had exhibited previously. One showed marked perseveration in his speech, repeating words and phrases as though endeavouring to recall their meaning, the other became retarded almost to the point of mutism, with only occasional replies to questioning. Both had been

agitated and overactive and both had exhibited considerable press of talk. Both required full nursing attention in respect of hygiene and feeding and the comparison between the picture they presented and that sometimes encountered following a prefrontal leucotomy was independently made by several observers.[7]

Anton Stephens pointed out that 'personal sensitivity may have had a part', since larger doses had been given to others without the same effect. For both patients the effects had been triggered by their abrupt rise to daily doses of 200 mgm, and a change from oral administration to intramuscular injection. In his arguments for continuing use of lobotomy, Walter Freeman would often hurl the 'chemical lobotomy' jibe at his critics. But the physical effects described by Anton Stephens had been encountered long before the age of psychosurgery. They had also been produced by the wonder drug of chemical restraint in the late nineteenth century, hyoscyamine.

Anton Stephens' report mentioned many adverse affects of the drug. By the end of the first week of treatment patients developed an extremely pallid and pinched appearance. Hypotensive attacks were frequent during the first days, and for some patients these did not pass with time. Patients given the drug by injection showed a tendecy to develop hard, tender, circumscribed masses at the injection site. The drug slowed patients down, and this affected the rate of absorption from the injection site. This he described as 'the major drawback to using Chlorpromazine'.[8] For the first three or four days after administration, and occasionally throughout treatment, patients felt giddy and unsure of themselves on standing up. For this reason, patients on the early trials were confined to bed for anything from three days to two weeks from first administration. Dryness of mouth was a constant finding, but inconvenience could be minimised by ready supplies of orange squash.

In Anton Stephens' view, the most reliable clinical indication of the drug's activity was tachycardia and palpitation. The rise in pulse rate followed closely after the administration of the drug, and was tending to return to normal just before the next one. One of Anton Stephens' patients experienced cardiac distress, and he could 'imagine difficulty arising in this respect if it were wished to use doses of more than 200 mgm daily or to give

Chlorpromazine to subjects with cardiac insufficiency'.[9] A fifty-three-year-old manic depressive woman in Charatan's study did die of a heart attack, and little wonder. She had been given a long course of ECT in 1952. After some improvement, she had become manic, noisy, aggressive and destructive. She was on 300 mgm Chlorpromazine daily by intramuscular injection, which 'had no effect on her psychomotor activity'. She was then given a pre-frontal leucotomy in November 1953, 'without any effect on her excitement'. After ten days she was recommenced on not only 150 mgm of Chlorpromazine per day, but also 150 mgm of Phenobarbital three times daily. Charatan stated blandly

> The possibility at once arises that the hypotensive effect of Chlorpromazine and the leucotomy, together with the increased demands made on the myocardium from the tachycardia so often associated with the drug, led to the fatal coronary thrombosis.[10]

Not merely possibility, but virtual certainty, when the 'cocktail' effect of Chlorpromazine and barbiturates is taken into account. This was not known to Charatan, though he was also experimenting with narcosis treatment using Chlorpromazine to 'potentiate' the effects of relatively small quantities of barbiturates. Like other continental researchers, he found this unlikely to prove fruitful, as only one patient had shown any benefit.

Apart from his discussion of this death, Charatan scarcely refers to side effects, except to tell readers that patients in his study experienced the same effects as recounted in Anton Stephens' lengthy discussion. Given that there were so many side effects, what did Chlorpromazine have to commend it? In Anton Stephens' trial, its 'outstanding action' was its ability to produce rapid sedation and sleep in an acutely disturbed and excited patient, and schizophrenic, manic and confusional excitements responded equally well.[11] He chose the word 'somnolence' to describe chlorpromazine's sedative action, 'in order to invite comparison between it and physiological sleep, and to make a distinction with the sleep that follows barbiturates'. The principal psychiatric effect was what Anton Stephens described as 'psychic indifference'. Patients 'responding well' to the drug developed indifference both to their surroundings and their symptoms, 'best summarized by the current phrase "couldn't care less"'. This meant a reduction in tension, anxiety and distress. Patients' abnormal responses to hallucinations diminished because they 'lost interest in them'. There was also a lessening of preoccupational and hypochondriacal ruminations. In the presence of the 'fully developed response', even in the absence of somnolence, the patient 'lies quietly in bed, staring ahead, unoccupied and showing little or no interest in what is going on around him'.[12] The degree to which the desired 'indifference' was achieved varied considerably, but except for the overdose cases, the patients never needed special nursing attention. In fact, '[t]he lessening of disordered behaviour that inevitably accompanied the development of indifference reduced rather than increased the need for nursing supervision'.[13]

Charatan said that on the basis of his results, Chlorpromazine was 'the drug of choice in the management of acute excitement', and 'probably as effective as electroshock':

> The rapid reduction of aggressiveness, diminution in psychomotor overactivity, without the production of drowsiness or confusion, renders the drug particularly valuable in facilitating psychotherapeutic contact. Unfortunately tolerance quickly develops in some patients, so that the beneficial effect may disappear after 10–14 days. Despite this . . . Chlorpromazine represents a definite therapeutic advance in the treatment of excitement.[14]

Although Chlorpromazine (and the other neuroleptics) would later come to be viewed as an effective treatment *for* mental disorder, apart from its miraculous sedative effects, one of its primary virtues in the eyes of these researchers was that, like shock treatments, narcosis, and all the other drug treatments which had gone before, it rendered psychotherapeutic contact possible.

By the end of 1954 Chlorpromazine was being hailed as the new wonder drug for psychotic illness. Here is an author's abstract of a two-year follow-up study of Chlorpromazine which appeared in the *American Journal of Psychiatry*, declaring it to be established as a useful therapeutic tool:

> It is a relatively safe drug, and although side effects are many, serious or permanent sequelae are almost unknown. . . . It is palliative rather than curative. It can intensify anxiety and precipitate psychotic symptoms as well as alleviate them. Its major advantage lies in its tranquillizing

action without accompanying marked drowsiness or confusion. Its value as an adjunct to psychotherapy has yet to
be evaluated.[15]

The author concluded, like many of his contemporaries, that chlorpromazine had been 'a major force in firmly launching us into
the era of psychopharmacology', but cautioned that 'we are still
suffering, however, from all the uncertainties and hesitation of a
pioneer venture', and this should not inhibit further research and
progress. Further research and progress were not long in coming,
with a steady stream of articles demonstrating the wide range
of Chlorpromazine's applications in reducing the restlessness of
elderly mentally ill patients and, in mental deficiency institutions,
to control behaviour.[16]

The neuroleptic drugs (drugs which affect the neurones)
differed from previously known sedatives and tranquillisers in that
they were able to relieve the distress caused by psychotic symptoms of delusions, hallucinations and disordered mood or
behaviour. The early trials did not pick up one of the neuroleptics'
most serious side effects, which only became apparent as experience of long-term use accumulated. The neuroleptics produced
undesirable neurological symptoms. These include spasmodic and
continuous disorders of muscle tone (dystonia), abnormal movements (dyskinesia) and uncontrolled restlessness (akathesia) and
the tremors, rigidity and salivation of Parkinson's disease. These
last symptoms afflicted some patients in the permanent form of
tardive dyskinesia. Jones points out that these symptoms had last
been seen in the patients whose brains had been damaged in the
epidemic of encephalitis lethargica.[17]

Psychiatry had a new sheet anchor. Chlorpromazine soon
became widely used as an emergency tranquilliser for patients
exhibiting disturbed behaviour. Other neuroleptics followed.
Haloperidol came on the scene in 1959, followed in 1963 by
Droperidol, which gives rapid temporary control of extreme agita-
tion. For patients who were reluctant to accept medication, an
important development was 'depot neuroleptics', which could be
administered by injection in long-acting form, so called because
a depot is formed in the tissues from which the drug is slowly
absorbed. This offered the possibility for patients to be maintained
in the community, provided they continued to receive their regular
depot injection.

It is interesting to compare the rapid development of Chlorpromazine with that of Lithium salts as a treatment for manic depressive psychosis, following the observation that it made animals extremely lethargic and unresponsive to stimuli. Because it is a natural salt, and therefore unpatentable, the promotion of Lithium was slow. Lithium was nevertheless soon seen as a magic wand for mania, described by Jones as the 'first true psychoprophylactic'. Another problem in the development of Lithium was its poisonous effect on the central nervous system. For that reason, serum levels of Lithium in patients' blood have to be regularly monitored to ensure that toxic levels are not reached.

As Tourney wrote in 1968, the influence of the pharmaceutical industry on developments in psychiatry has grown rapidly:

> We are in the great age of psychopharmacology, in which industry has great stakes. Compounds that may have considerable therapeutic value but no presumed potential for commercial exploration, such as the use of Lithium salts in mania, were at first not presented seriously to the psychiatric profession. The physician has become increasingly dependent on brochures from drug companies rather than formal scientific reports.[18]

The mutual interdependence of psychiatry and pharmaceutical companies continues to increase. Restaurant lunches as the guest of drug company representatives are regular events in the diaries of many consultant psychiatrists. Psychiatric hospitals not only provide a market for pharmaceutical products, but also a testing ground. Educational events and conferences rarely take place without drug company sponsorship. Even conferences of the Royal College of Psychiatrists now have a prominent presence of drug company representatives plying their wares, assisted by promotional material.

The entry of psychiatry into 'the age of psychopharmacology', the buzz phrase of the mid 1950s, was important for a number of reasons. First, it suggested hope for rapid progress in the future, as the massive resources of multinational drug companies and the white heat of modern pharmacological technology would now be brought to bear on mental disorder. Second, never again would 'advances in psychiatry' come from therapeutic entrepreneurs like Cotton, Von Meduna, Sakel, Moniz and Freeman. Innovation would henceforth be pioneered in the laboratories of the drug companies. Psychiatric hospitals became extensions of those laboratories where the effects of the drugs on humans could be monitored. Psychiatrists became the customers and researchers of the pharmaceutical companies and this fortified psychiatry's already pronounced dependence on drugs, since it meant that henceforth innovation was likely to be pharmaceutical.

Criticism of psychosurgery, so little evident before, spread rapidly in the mid 1950s. In 1952, just as psychiatry was leaving leucotomy behind, the first British survey of patients' attitudes was published, having been carried out on 224 patients at Graylingwell Hospital. It found that no fewer than thirty-one patients were not aware that they had had an operation, and this was not attributable to memory. None of these was classified as improved. A total of twenty-two patients had a negative attitude, believing the operation to have been unnecessary or unsuccessful, including (a brilliant example of invalidation by diagnosis) 'two paranoid schizophrenics who regarded the operation as one of the many interferences they had been subjected to'.[19] Psychosurgery? Interference? Surely not! By 1960 psychiatrists were already speculating that psychosurgery, the miracle cure of the 1940s, would be chiefly of interest to medical historians. Psychiatry's self-consciously proud entry into 'the age of psychopharmacology' enabled a line to be drawn under the wilder excesses of the age of experimentation, and a process was begun whereby it could be portrayed as another dark age from which psychiatry had emerged. As with previous times, no survey of treatment during this period would be complete without some consideration of seclusion and restraint.

During the 1920s, restraint and seclusion were rarely mentioned by the Board of Control. In 1925 the Board 'rationalised' its requirements concerning clinical and other records kept in psychiatric institutions. It issued new regulations regarding seclusion and restraint, earning the approval of the *Journal of Mental Science* by expressing the view that in some cases seclusion could be 'a valuable form of treatment'.[20] Seclusion was redefined as 'isolation between 8.00 a.m. and 7.00 p.m. in a room the door of which is fastened or held so that the patient is unable to leave the room at will, but not if the lower half of the door is fastened but the upper half is left open'.[21] The total number of hours spent by a patient in seclusion or mechanical restraint was to be entered in the register, together with a statement of the reasons for it.

The 1925 amendment removed from the category 'mechanical restraint' any interventions which the Board described as purely medical treatments. These did not have to be recorded in the register as mechanical restraint, but did have to be entered in the notes. As medical treatments, they could only be given under medical order. This dispensation applied to continuous baths, widely used at the time in combating mania, as long as there was an aperture for the patient's head large enough to let the patient's body pass through. It also applied to the dry and the wet pack, as long as no straps or ligatures were used and the patient was released at two-hourly intervals for 'necessary purposes'. Splints or bandages used for surgical purposes were not restraint, and patients could be held down for force feeding by nurses using sheets or towels as long as they were merely held, not tied or fastened. Permitted forms of mechanical restraint included strong jackets, dresses, or strait-jackets of a design approved under seal of the Board, non-removable gloves fastened at the wrist, and sheets or towels tied or fastened at the side of a bed. The Board had discretion to approve in advance other methods of restraint if, in the opinion of the doctor giving the certificate under section 40, that method was necessary in exceptional circumstances. In such cases the prior permission of the Board was necessary and only for such a period as they might authorise. The Board's 'legislation' was drawing the boundary lines where treatment ended and restraint began.

In 1927 the Board commemorated the centenary of Pinel's death with a special section of their annual report on mechanical restraint.[22] They asserted that although restraint had never been abolished, 'by a gradual yielding to a growing consensus of opinion, and by statutory rules, it has been regulated within very narrow margins'.[23] Self-satisfaction was the order of the day, the Board declaring that:

So negligible is the amount of mechanical restraint, or of any form of physical coercion used in the mental hospitals of this country, that, although quarterly and other returns of such use continue to be requisitioned by us, its absence, save in isolated and exceptional cases, is so taken for granted that we frequently omit all reference to it in our entries. ... [D]uring 1927, out of 139,876 patients under treatment

... only 76 were subject to mechanical restraint and for a total of only 26,469 hours.[24]

This averages out at just over fourteen days per patient under restraint. Of course it would have been impolite to mention the hundredweights of bromide and chloral which had gone into achieving this happy state of affairs.

In 1928, in response to an enquiry from a psychiatrist, the Board issued a ruling on the applicability of section 40 of the 1890 Act to uncertified persons. After the usual disclaimer about not being entitled to give authoritative decisions on the law, they said that if restraint was used, only such means as were sanctioned in the cases of certified patients should be employed, and certification should be considered.[25] Although the Board always declared itself unable to give authoritiative rulings, their answers obviously were authoritative. Doctors would come to use the Board in the same way as they did their medical defence organisation, seeking in advance an opinion of the lawfulness of some proposed intervention. Who would criticise a doctor who acted in accordance with the advice of the central authority of the mental health system?

The introduction of voluntary status under the 1930 Act gave rise to initial concerns about the position regarding seclusion, restraint and forcible treatment of voluntary patients. In 1931, the Board was asked by the medical superintendent of Bracebridge Hospital whether he was entitled to restrain, seclude, forcibly feed, or administer drugs to a voluntary patient.[26] The Board accompanied the usual disclaimer with the rather legalistic advice that section 40 of the 1890 Act made no mention of voluntary patients, and Schedule 3 of the 1930 Act did not give the Board any power to apply the provision to voluntary patients. However, they suggested that, as the patient in question needed restraint and seclusion, he was scarcely suitable to be retained on a voluntary footing.[27] This became the Board's stock response to such an inquiry in the future.

This is an early manifestation of one of the central paradoxes of the psychiatric system in England and Wales, that whilst the rights of non-detained patients are in theory more extensive than those of the detained, the treatment of the latter has traditionally been subject to closer scrutiny and regulation. The assumption that the non-detained have their remedy by walking out of the hospital has never been borne out in reality. Even if they were capable of exercising this right under the 1930 Act, they had to give seventy-two hours' notice of discharge. Under subsequent legislation informal patients have been subject to a 'doctor's holding power' keeping them in the hospital for seventy-two hours if they are felt to need detention. Patients who are being pressured to remain in hospital and to accept treatment under the threat of detention are often referred to as *de facto* detained, and the paradox is that they would have greater procedural opportunities to challenge their treatment and to have their position reviewed if they were detained *de jure*.

Restraint and seclusion remained issues throughout the life of the Board. Sometimes forms of restraint were used in connection with the physical treatments. On a visit to Moorcroft Hospital the commissioners found that patients were strapped to a specially designed 'Gitter Bed' during insulin shock treatment. The Commossion informed the medical superintendent that they would approve this as a form of mechanical restraint for the purposes of the regulation, as long as it was used only in the course of insulin shock treantment.[28]

The lawfulness of restraining voluntary patients was again questioned in 1953 when an elderly voluntary patient at Goodmayes Hospital died following the application of a form of restraint not permitted by the rules, leading the Board to review its position.[29] A memorandum was written expressing the view that despite the absence of authority to restrain a voluntary patient, and although an unapproved method was used, the restraint could be excused because it was obviously necessary to prevent the patient doing herself an injury. In the Board's view, the method used was neither severe nor brutal, the restraint was recorded, and no attempt had been made to conceal it. The doctor in charge of the ward had obtained consent from the medical superintendent after discussion, and the Board concluded that they were obviously acting in the best interest of the patient. Finally, in a departure from its earlier position, the Board concluded that it 'could hardly take the line that if the patient were in need of restraint she should have been certified'.[30] The need for legal authority to restrain did not justify subjecting the patient to the 'stigma' of certification. Henceforth, the Board resolved to 'consider each case on its merits in the light of the circumstances prevailing at the time of action',[31] which on occasion led to disputes within its own ranks.

In 1954 a voluntary patient complained to the Board that he had been secluded eleven times in seven days for a total of twenty hours. One Board member suggested that, whilst it might occasionally be essential to seclude a voluntary patient in his own interests, when it was done so frequently and the patient complained of his confinement, 'the proper course for the medical superintendent to have taken would have been to arrange for the patient to be handed over to his relatives, or, if this were too risky or the relatives were unwilling, to certify him'. However, a medical commissioner, Dr Rees Thomas, thought the seclusion justified, on the assumption that a doctor had a power of detention over a voluntary patient. He suggested that the patient be thanked for his letter and told that seclusion was used entirely in his own interest and that the use of any violence other than necessary force had been denied. A reply to this effect was sent, although some dissent from Rees Thomas's general views on doctors' powers was also voiced. In its response to the hospital the Board maintained its view that regular or systematic seclusion of a voluntary patient would imply that he was unsuitable to remain on that footing.

With the arrival of the National Health Service, new Mental Deficiency Regulations were issued including provisions relating to seclusion and mechanical restraint, the last regulations to deal with these subjects.[32] Under the Mental Health Act 1959 seclusion and mechanical restraint ceased to be governed by any statutory regulations and were dealt with by local policies.

The age of experimentation did not end with the dawning of the age of psychopharmacology. As with psychosurgery, ECT and the physical treatments, the new drugs were pioneered on human subjects, many of them manifestly incapable of valid consent, and others clearly refusing. By the mid 1950s psychiatry seemed to have emerged from all its dark ages. Hazardous and irreversible treatments had been all but eliminated. Psychosurgery was very much a treatment of absolutely last resort. The staple treatments of the 'psychiatric armamentarium' were ECT and drugs, including neuroleptics, Lithium, antidepressants, anxiolytics, and hypnotics. The new 'sheet anchors', employed when a patient threatened the safety of the ship, were injections of phenothiazines and seclusion.

On 25 October 1953 Sir Winston Churchill announced the appointment of a Royal Commission on the Law relating to Mental

Illness and Mental Deficiency under the chairmanship of Sir Eustace Percy.[33] As with the Macmillan Commission of 1924, the Percy Commission was ostensibly established in response to libertarian concerns, this time about cases of wrongful detention under the Mental Deficiency Act 1913.[34] Yet again, however, the Ministries and the Board of Control had their own agenda of reform which had been under preparation since at least 1950.

Consensus in official circles was that fresh legislation was necessary because of the large number of different statutes relating to mentally disordered people, a position which had been further complicated by amendments introduced by the National Health Service Act 1946. From 1950 onwards a series of meetings was held between the principal secretaries of the Ministry of Health and the Home Office and the Board of Control, during which they mapped out a number of desired changes.[35] One of their main concerns was with the role of the central authority. From 1948, when the National Health Service Act 1946 came into force and the Minister of Health had taken over the psychiatric hospitals, the officials who made up the Ministry's Mental Health Division (in charge of providing the service), and the Board of Control (supposed to be its independent critic), were the same people.

As a result of the 1950 discussions a proposal circulated between government departments to set up a new body, consisting of a small group of officials, under the aegis of the Lord Chancellor's Department. It would deal with 'liberty of the subject questions', and would have a duty to examine reception documents, to exercise residual powers of discharge, and to deal with complaints of ill-treatment or improper detention. It would have power to visit any place or patient. It would be entirely independent of the service providers in the Ministry of Health. In 1953, Sir Percy Barter retired as chairman of the Board. A.K. Ross, a commissioner at the time, considered Barter to have been the last 'independent' chairman. His replacement, Frederick Armer, another deputy secretary of the Ministry of Health, was viewed by Ross as a 'Trojan horse' for the forces who believed that the Board no longer served a useful purpose and could be abolished.[36]

The Board's credibility as a body which protected the liberty of those detained was not helped by the 1956 case of Kathleen Rutty, who was granted habeas corpus because the Board had authorised her continued detention in excess of its powers.[37] She had been detained under section 15 of the 1913 Act as having been 'found neglected, abandoned, without visible means of support or cruelly treated', even though she was working as a resident domestic worker for Essex County Council. The ruling had wide ramifications because the Board had promulgated its wrongful interpretation as policy guidance, and as a result of the court ruling, more than seven hundred wrongfully detained patients had to be discharged.[38]

Clive Unsworth and Kathleen Jones have shown the great influence of the Board's evidence on the recommendations of the Percy Commission. It was compiled by Armer and Walter Maclay, a senior medical commissioner and principal medical officer at the Ministry of Health.[39] The Percy Commission proposed a radical reorientation of the legislation away from the legalism of the 1890 Act, and the abolition of the Board of Control. William Sargant describes Walter Maclay as 'largely responsible for carrying through Britain's new Mental Health Act, which has enabled us to lead the world in implementing sane and practical treatment policies'.[40]

The Commission's terms of reference expressly required them to consider the extension of voluntary admission, without certification. The great failure of the 1930 Act had been the provisions for temporary admission of non-volitional patients without certification. Many argued for its extension to unwilling patients, and for the abolition of judicial certification. This was in fact what Percy recommended and what the 1959 Act put into place.

Clive Unsworth describes the presentation of the 1959 Act thus:

[It was] a reaction against and negation of the Lunacy Act 1890, the late Victorian assumptions of which had only partially been ousted by the amending Mental Treatment Act 1930. The [Act] injected into mental health law a contrary set of assumptions drawing upon the logic of the view of insanity as analogous to physical disease and upon reorientation from the Victorian institutionally centred system to 'Community Care'. The libertarian and legalistic tendencies of the Lunacy Act were reversed, and expert discretion, the autocratic possibilities of which had alarmed the authors of its procedures, was allowed much freer rein at the expense of formal mechanisms incorporating legal and lay control of decision-making procedures.[41]

The 1959 Act brought mental illness and mental handicap together under one statute. It introduced a new 'informal' status embracing both those who were voluntary and those who would previously have been regarded as non-volitional. Instead of the provision under the 1930 Act whereby voluntary patients had to give three days' notice of their intention to leave hospital, a new holding power was introduced enabling the doctor in charge of treatment to detain an informal patient for up to seventy-two hours for the purpose of making an application for detention.

Judicial certification was abolished and two compulsory admission procedures for non-offender patients were introduced to replace it: admission for observation and admission for treatment. Neither involved a judicial authority. An application for admission could be made if there were two supporting medical recommendations, one of which had to come from a doctor with recognised psychiatric experience. The process was not wholly medical, however. The application had to be made by a mental welfare officer (social worker) or the patient's nearest relative. An unwilling patient could be admitted for observation for up to twenty-eight days, a belated enactment of the recommendation of the Board of Control to the Macmillan Commission in 1924. The required grounds of admission were that the patient was suffering from mental disorder of a nature or degree which warranted detention for observation in the interests of his or her health or safety or for the protection of others. Admission for observation was not renewable beyond twenty-eight days and if the patient was to remain in detention, he or she would have to be detained under the power to admit for treatment.[42] Patients could be admitted for treatment if they were suffering from one of four prescribed forms of mental disorder: mental illness, psychopathic disorder, subnormality, or severe subnormality. Detention for treatment had to be necessary in the interests of the patient's health or safety, or for the protection of others. It was for twelve months in the first instance, renewable for twelve months and thereafter for periods of two years.[43] There was also an emergency procedure allowing admission for observation for up to seventy-two hours on one medical certificate, convertible to a twenty-eight-day detention by the furnishing of the second medical opinion after admission.[44]

The Board virtually recommended its own abolition, suggesting that the inspection of hospitals be transferred to the Ministry of Health, and that an institutionally separate central authority should have a residual role as 'a last court of appeal' for discharge.[45] Instead of this, the Percy Commission adapted the idea of the Socialist Medical Association for a Mental Health Review Tribunal (MHRT). The Association's view of the role of such a body was as follows:

> Complaints of infringement of liberty ... are at present usually referred by the Board of Control to the person, such as the Physician Superintendent, alleged to be responsible for such infringement, and further first hand investigations are rarely made. We strongly recommend that in order to reassure the patient, his relatives and the public, that such complaints are carefully considered, that an independent tribunal should be set up with the duty to investigate all such complaints, the power to obtain independent psychiatric opinion, and to hold an inquiry whenever the patient or his relatives request it, subject to safeguards against abuse.[46]

Although not in favour of such a broad remit, the Percy Commission saw possibilities for the tribunal to perform the narrower role of reviewing the continued need for patients' detention. Hence a quasi-judicial safeguard could be made available, but instead of one which preceded admission and might operate as an obstacle to speedy therapy, the MHRT would come into play after admission and at the suit of the patient. With the last 'residual' function of the Board taken care of, the Commission recommended abolition for the central authority, and the 1959 Act redistributed the Board's functions among other agencies. The scrutiny of documents having been devolved on the hospital managers (health authorities), the jurisdiction to discharge was now vested in the newly established MHRTs. The MHRTs, whose task was to review, on application by the patient, the continued need for detention, consisted of a lawyer president, a consultant psychiatrist, and a lay member. Patients could challenge the lawfulness of their initial admission by judicial review or habeas corpus, and those detained for treatment or under hospital orders as offender patients would be entitled to seek review of the need for continued detention by applying for a MHRT hearing, once in the first period of detention and once in each period for which detention was renewed. Although tribunals had a discretion to discharge in any case, the burden was, and remains, on the patient to satisfy them that he or she is entitled to discharge.[47] Apart from the tribunals, no new 'liberty of the subject' body was established under the 1959 Act, and for the next twenty-five years the only central authority over the mental health system was the Ministry, later the Department of Health, supplemented by infrequent inspections from the Health Advisory Service and the National Development Team for Mental Handicap.

Questions of consent to treatment did not loom large in the Percy Commission's deliberations. When the National Association of Local Government Health and Welfare Officers tried to argue that judicial safeguards should remain because modern treatments carried the risk that periods of detention might be used to change patients' personalities, Percy accused the witness of stating 'the consequences of certification in an extreme and alarming form'.[48] We have already seen how consent was not routinely sought from detained patients, even if the consent of relatives might be obtained for the more serious treatments. The representative for the National Association of Local Government Health and Welfare Officers stated before the Commission that they had not found a single case where a certified patient had been asked whether he was willing to accept treatment.[49] The Percy Commission's view appears to have been that treatment was a matter of clinical judgment and no special safeguards were necessary in that regard.

One of the most significant, and underestimated, changes introduced in 1959 was the reinforcement of clinical authority. The Royal Medico-Psychological Association, the BMA and the Royal College of Physicians were all against devolution of clinical authority from the physician superintendent to someone holding consultant status, because that status was the creation of a hierarchical structure set up by the Ministry for the purposes of pay and conditions, which they thought might not endure.[50] Also they were worried that such a move would weaken the concept of 'medical authority' so resoundingly endorsed by the Macmillan Commission. As all three medical bodies put it, 'the preservation of "medical authority" is as necessary now as it was a hundred years ago, and for the same reasons. This opinion was endorsed by the [Macmillan] Commission, and [we] are in full agreement with the conclusions expressed in ... that report.'[51] They unanimously recommended that legislation should preserve the physician superintendent's existing power to discharge and to extend a patient's detention, on the understanding that his duty was to see that the law was carried out, rather than to act personally in every case.[52]

The 1959 Act solved the problem by devolving every aspect of the medical superintendent's powers, in respect of individual detained patients, to the senior medical staff of the hospital. Each detained patient would have a responsible medical officer (RMO), assumed to be, but not necessarily of, consultant status, and legally in charge of the patient's care and medical treatment.[53] Beneath the RMO would be a medical hierarchy of senior registrars, registrars and house officers. Unless the patient was a dangerous offender patient under Home Office restrictions, the RMO could prolong detention by sending a report to the hospital managers, or discharge from detention, or send on leave. The RMO also had authority over medical treatment. For the first time 'medical treatment' was defined in the legislation, section 147(1) stating that it 'includes nursing and ... care and training under medical supervision'. The *defining* characteristic was that it was under medical supervision. The protection of doctors from legal action in section 16 of the 1930 Act was re-enacted in section 141 of the 1959 Act. Seclusion and mechanical restraint were dropped completely from the legislation and they became matters for hospitals to have their own procedures on. Although this was presumably on the grounds that both were out of keeping with the modern ethos of psychiatry, seclusion would in fact remain the disciplinary bedrock of virtually every psychiatric hospital. It was little wonder that psychiatrists like Sargant thought the 1959 Act enabled them to lead the world. Far from holding psychiatry back, the law was now giving it free rein. This would not last. By the 1970s consent in relation to psychiatric treatment had surfaced as a critical issue.

11

THE MENTAL HEALTH ACT COMMISSION AND THE MENTAL HEALTH ACT 1983

Concerns about whether it was lawful to treat psychiatric patients, whether detained or not, without consent began in the early 1970s. Until then the main voices raised in protest had been those of former patients and their organisations. What prompted this upsurge of interest in consent? David Rothman has traced the rise of the bioethics movement and widespread concerns about consent in the United States to 'a critical period of change' between 1966 and 1976, beginning with the publication of Henry Beecher's 'Ethics and clinical research' in the *New England Journal of Medicine*. Beecher's article exposed abuses in human experimentation. As Rothman says:

> At its heart were capsule descriptions of twenty-two examples of investigators who had risked 'the health or the life of their subjects', without informing them or seeking their permission.... Example 16 involved the feeding of live hepatitis viruses to residents of a state institution for the retarded in order to study the etiology of the disease and attempt to create a protective vaccine against it. In example 17, physicians injected live cancer cells into twenty-two elderly and senile hospitalised patients without telling them the cells were cancerous, in order to study the body's immunological responses.[1]

Other broader developments between the mid 1960s and mid 1970s played their part too. The civil rights movement in the US, and the culture of protest and individual self-expression created a climate favourable to complaints by psychiatric patients about their situation of powerlessness and absence of civil rights. Fostered by the writings of R.D. Laing, there was also a certain romanticising of madness as a voyage of self-discovery, as a rebellion against, or reaction to, the contradictory demands of family life, rather than a true 'illness'.

Militant campaigning by patients and former patients was spearheaded by the Mental Patients' Union. Their concerns were similar to those of their predecessor organisations. By the early 1970s, Mental Patients' Unions had been established in major British cities. Two of their central concerns were over sedation and the punitive use of medication. As it was put by the Manchester Mental Patients' Union Pamphlet, *Your Rights in Mental Hospital*:

> TREATMENT CAN BE USED AS A PUNISHMENT TOO
> Most patients get a lot of tablets and injections. This makes the wards easier to manage. If there were more nurses, they could use fewer tablets. If you break the ward routine and they want to get you back in line, the doctors may order an extra injection. They use this to keep you quiet on the ward, and to train you to stay in line when you leave hospital.[2]

Doubts in official circles about whether detention under the 1959 Act suspended a patient's common-law right to refuse treatment surfaced in January 1973, when Sir Keith Joseph, Secretary of State at the Department of Health and Social Security, was asked a question about consent in Parliament. He said he was advised that, where detained patients were concerned, consent was not necessary but that it was normal practice to try to obtain the patient's agreement if he or she was capable of understanding the proposed treatment.[3]

In 1973 the Davies Committee on Hospital Complaints Procedure referred to 'the special difficulties' in connection with complaints about mentally disordered patients who had been given treatment, even though they objected. The Committee observed that if patients are in a psychiatric hospital of their own free will, 'their remedy against receiving treatment to which they do not consent is the same as that of any patient in any kind of hospital, they can sue for assault'. However, they had also been told about patients to whom this theoretical remedy was of no use, namely those who were informal and who objected to particular treatments, but who had nevertheless given their consent because, they were told, they would otherwise be 'put on an order' so that the treatment could be given. As far as the Committee could see:

> Detained patients who object to particular treatments do not appear to have the right to sue for assault. The law allows for such patients to be given treatment in their own interests, even when they object. It recognises that doctors should have such powers: but they must not be abused.[4]

The Committee heard of detained patients being given drug treatment to which they had been sensitive on previous admissions, 'objecting most rationally to treatment with the same drug and having their objections overruled with the results which they themselves had predicted'.[5] They proposed that there should be an independent second medical opinion in any decision to impose treatment upon a patient.[6]

One of the main reasons for the establishment of the Davies Committee was a series of inquiries into abuses in psychiatric hospitals, including Ely Hospital, Cardiff in 1969,[7] Farleigh in 1971,[8] and Whittingham in 1972.[9] These were to become frequent events in the 1970s and early 1980s. At the same time there was a marked shift in emphasis of the work at MIND (the National Association for Mental Health) towards advocacy of psychiatric patients' civil rights, due largely to the arrival in the early 1970s of Tony Smythe (formerly of the National Council for Civil Liberties) as director and Larry Gostin (an American civil liberties lawyer) as legal officer.

MIND's evidence to the Butler Committee, which reported on mentally disordered offenders in 1975, expressed concern about treatments such as ECT, the long-acting phenothiazines and forms of leucotomy. It urged that a second psychiatric opinion from outside the hospital concerned should be obtained whenever a patient objected to treatment.[10] The National Council for Civil Liberties felt that treatment without consent should be limited to emergency procedures, for example to curtail sudden outbursts of violence or to relieve an acute depressive state. They considered that to confer on doctors unqualified powers of treatment without consent was unsafe insofar as doctors might – even with the best intentions – abuse this privileged position in their enthusiasm to treat disorder. As regards irreversible procedures, even when the patient wished to accept the treatment, MIND felt that the freedom of choice and understanding of the consequences was often suspect, and that the consent of a mental health review tribunal (MHRT) should be obtained. In considering an application, the tribunal should, in their view, satisfy itself on three main points: first that the treatment was appropriate and that alternative treatments had been exhaustively tried; second, that the patient was giving his or her free and informed consent without promises of early discharge, and that he or she fully understood both the positive and the negative aspects of treatment; and third, that the suggested treatment was not 'inhuman or degrading' in the terms of Article 3 of the European Convention on Human Rights.[11]

The Butler Committee put forward a formula by which treatment without consent could be authorised:

Treatment (other than nursing care) should not be imposed on any patient if he is able to appreciate what is involved. Three exceptions should be allowed: treatment may be given without consent

(a) where not being of a hazardous or irreversible character it represents the minimum interference with the patient to prevent him from behaving violently or otherwise being a danger to himself or others; or
(b) where it is necessary to save the patient's life; or
(c) where (not being irreversible) it is necessary to prevent him from deteriorating.

Where, because of his disability, the patient was unable to appreciate what was involved, despite the help of an explanation in simple terms, the treatment may be given: but special considerations apply to treatments involving irreversible procedures.[12]

The Committee rejected any idea of proposing detailed rules of guidance to protect patients. However, because of the pressures on the patient, they saw force in some of the arguments for safeguards over and above the requirement of the patient's consent, especially in relation to irreversible procedures. They rejected the idea of the MHRT, but instead recommended that a second psychiatric opinion, independent of the treating hospital or prison, should be obtained, in addition to the patient's consent, if he is capable of giving it, before irreversible treatments are carried out on detained patients, unless delay would cause or increase danger to life.[13]

As to the existing legal position, the Committee considered that certain eventualities, such as the need to restrain a patient during a violent episode by the injection of a tranquilliser, or to use medical procedures to save the life of a patient who lacks understanding, would be covered by common law, treatment being justified on the grounds of presumed consent or necessity. However, to what extent compulsory treatment was authorised by the 1959 Act was not entirely clear. In the opinion of the legal advisers of the Department of Health and Social Security (DHSS), treatment considered necessary could be administered irrespective of the patients' wishes or those of their relatives. They also referred to section 141 of the 1959 Act, which provided that no-one should be liable in criminal or civil proceedings in respect of anything done in pursuance of the Act unless the act was done in bad faith or without reasonable care. This was felt to cover staff who gave treatment for, or in connection with, the mental disorder for which the patient was admitted, even if the patient did not consent, as long as the staff acted in good faith and with reasonable care. In practice, said the Department, forms of treatment 'involving special risk' were not given if the patient or nearest relative objected. We have already seen how quite serious risks could be viewed as routine, so the concept of special risk was not likely to rule out very much treatment without consent.

By the early 1970s faith in drug companies had taken a severe dent as a result of the Thalidomide affair. The Medicines Act 1968 introduced a requirement that manufacturers distribute to all doctors a data sheet including formally approved information about properties of the drug. As with the barbiturates before, experiments were undertaken with high doses of major tranquillisers, the so-called megadoses. Combinations of different drugs were used, with all the attendant risks of potentiation. Large numbers of different neuroleptics had been and continue to be developed, producing almost infinite scope for experimentation with different combinations of this or that drug to achieve the desired effect without unacceptable side effects. The reliance of psychiatry on pharmacology has led to a predisposition to prescribe a higher dose if the desired effect is not achieved at normal dose levels, and to prescribe a different drug or combination of drugs where one is not doing the trick. In a way these permutations were all experimental, a point not lost on the Mental Patients' Union, who protested that 'most of the treatments are experiments':

The hospital won't tell you that you're the guinea pig in their experiment, because they don't see it as an experiment. If they did, they'd be more careful to watch out for side effects. We have nothing against experiments, but you should have a right to know what's going on, and to choose whether to take part.[14]

Experimentation without consent became a hot topic in the United States in 1972 after the revelations of a study which had been carried out in Tuskegee, Florida into the effects of untreated syphilis. The study had begun in 1932 and as James Jones puts it:

The Tuskegee Study had nothing to do with treatment. No new drugs were tested; neither was any effort made to establish the efficacy of old forms of treatment. It was a non-therapeutic experiment, aimed at compiling data on the effects of the spontaneous evolution of syphilis on black males.[15]

Over the course of the study, 399 black males with syphilis were left untreated, This was scarcely justifiable before the availability of penicillin in the 1940s, and certainly not thereafter. There was a growing sensation that, in matters of ethics, the medical profession could not be left to its own devices.

In 1970 there were 300 psychosurgeries in the United States, a tiny fraction of the number in the heyday of the operation. However, it still had its exponents. As Valenstein records, the American public became aware of psychosurgery as a result of the book, *Violence and the Brain*, in which the authors, Mark and Ervin, argued that a great deal of violence in society was created by brain disorder and that modern surgery could eliminate it.[16] Controversy grew over the perceived use of psychosurgery as a method of social control. Then, in 1973, Senator Edward Kennedy conducted hearings on the 'Quality of health care – human experimentation', in which he heard from a Mississippi psychosurgeon who advocated psychosurgery for 'aggressive, uncontrollable or violent behaviour' that does not respond to various other forms of treatment. Kennedy established that the psychosurgeon in these cases made the decision, and was not subject to any regulation.[17] In 1973, Oregon passed legislation restricting psychosurgery to situations where it had been established on independent review that the patient had given truly informed consent and that all other possible treatments had been tried. Similar legislation followed in California in 1976.[18]

In 1975, MIND published the first part of *A Human Condition*, Larry Gostin's two volume critique of the Mental Health Act 1959. Gostin argued simply that whilst the 1959 Act authorised compulsory admission, it said nothing about compulsory treatment and accordingly did not 'alter the rights of the person to a common law remedy for medical assault'.[19] He argued for the right of patients to information about the advantages and disadvantages of treatment, and the right to make an uncoerced treatment decision without influence from threats (of punishment, detention or a longer stay in hospital), or inducements such as a promise of early release. Where there was no valid consent a multidisciplinary committee on the rights and responsibilities of patients would review the treatment programme to decide whether it would be given. These committees would also adjudicate complaints that patients had not received adequate treatment and would give advice to psychiatrists as to whether a treatment was hazardous, irreversible, or not yet fully established. Each institution would have an advocate whose task would be to ensure that recipients of psychiatric services were not being deprived of their rights under the law.[20]

Consensus was growing that the position on treatment of detained patients without consent should be clarified by legislative intervention,[21] and this was accepted by the DHSS in its review of the 1959 Act published in 1976.[22] The proposal that MHRTs should be involved was no longer viewed as realistic. The choice was now between Gostin's proposals and the system of medical second opinions favoured by the Royal College of Psychiatrists. The College advocated that the second opinion should be advisory rather than binding, since in their view only the consultant in charge of the patient's treatment – the responsible medical officer – could take the final decision about treatment, particularly if he did not accept the opinion of the second consultant. The Interdepartmental Review Committee did not think that the public would regard the obtaining of a second opinion as a safeguard if the responsible medical officer could disregard it.[23] They foresaw certain difficulties in getting independent psychiatric opinions, not least that 'it might be thought by some that this would deteriorate into a mere formality or at least that another doctor would be unwilling to question a colleague's clinical judgment'. The Interdepartmental Committee also felt that there might be reasons for considering whether the views of other professionals might not also be sought.

The Interdepartmental Committee also had in mind the recent decision in *Re D (a minor) (wardship: sterilisation)*.[24] This was an application to the High Court to exercise its wardship jurisdiction in relation to the proposed sterilisation of an eleven-year-old mentally handicapped girl. The clinical team, with the exception of the clinical psychologist whose intervention led to the matter coming to court, were agreed that the operation was in her best interests. Heilbron J. concluded that the girl's capacity to consent to the operation depended on her ability to understand and appreciate its implications. The court was also alert to the possibility that in the course of time her capacity to consent might improve and that she might subsequently become aware of what had happened and come to resent it deeply. On those grounds the court would not allow the operation to proceed. This case illustrated to the Interdepartmental Committee that other professionals along with the public did not accept that decisions about the use of a particular treatment should always be left to doctors. On the other hand, there were obvious difficulties in legislating for second opinions from different professionals depending on the treatment involved, since the appropriate professional would vary according to the circumstances of the case.[25] The Committee's report put forward three options:

 (i)   an independent psychiatrist's opinion;
 (ii) a report from a committee in each hospital charged with oversight of the rights of patients; and
 (iii) a report from a multidisciplinary panel especially established for the purpose.

In 1978 a further interdepartmental *Review of the Mental Health Act 1959* reported that, although much medical opinion had been in favour of a medical second opinion, there had been a good deal of support for the idea of a multidisciplinary panel, on the grounds that this would add a new and important safeguard in relation to contentious treatments.[26] The DHSS and the other departments concerned expressed the hope that the medical profession would 'feel able to go along with this proposal' and announced that it intended to establish such panels with a 'substantial medical involvement'.[27]

177

By the early 1970s psychosurgery was undergoing something of a renaissance. Anthony Clare noted, in 1976, that although the theoretical basis of psychosurgery may have appeared simplistic and vague, this did not prevent 'a veritable plethora of operations from being performed'.[28] At the Brook Hospital, surgeons claimed good results in severely and chronically depressed and obsessional patients from an operation on the frontal lobes involving the implantation of radioactive yttrium rods or pellets. Operations for depression, anxiety and obsessional neurosis were also performed at the Atkinson Morley Hospital in Wimbledon, whilst at the Queen Elizabeth Hospital and Edinburgh Royal Infirmary different operations including temporal lobectomies and amygdalotomies were performed in cases of severe persistent aggression. Clare found it difficult to judge how fast the operation rate was increasing, but as evidence that it was he cited the fact that the most established psychosurgeon of the day, Geoffrey Knight, presented statistical evidence for over 1,000 of his own cases at the 1970 Second International Conference of psychosurgery.

Sargant and Slater remained ardent propagandists of psychosurgery in the 1972 edition of their textbook, *Introduction to Physical Treatments in Psychiatry*. They continued to argue for its use in treating schizophrenia, even though all studies carried out after 1955 claimed that the effect of the operation on delusions and hallucinations was disappointing.[29] In 1971, during Slater's editorship of the *British Journal of Psychiatry*, an article was published by Walter Freeman, again propounding the virtues of early temporal lobectomy because 'in a dangerous disease such as schizophrenia it may prove safer to operate than to wait'. To those now firmly in the age of psychopharmacology, this seemed preposterous. Clare found it 'scarcely believable' that such a reputable journal would publish such a 'deplorable paper' consisting of four pages of casual anecdote, potted history and amateur statistics, arguing that the most serious irreversible treatment method open to psychiatry should be employed in schizophrenia and insisting that it could be more dangerous not to operate than to do so. Was it any wonder that the critics of psychosurgery tended to write it off as 'knife happy sorcery'?[30]

Indeed some of psychosurgery's supporters have provided more evidence against themselves from their own mouths and pens than a thousand showings of *One Flew Over the Cuckoo's Nest*. There is an infamous passage in the 1972 edition of Sargant and Slater's textbook where they discuss the usefulness of the operation in cases of reactive depression where irremediable environmental factors are involved:

> A depressed woman, for instance, may owe her illness to a psychopathic husband who cannot change and will not accept treatment. Separation might be the answer but is ruled out by other ties. ... Patients of this type are often helped by antidepressant drugs. But in the occasional case where they do not work, we have seen patients enabled by a leucotomy to return to a difficult environment and cope with it in a way which had hitherto been impossible.[31]

Not surprisingly, given this climate of controversy, psychosurgery occupied an important place in the discussions of the consent to treatment issue.

In the 1970s experiments were being carried out in Broadmoor Hospital with the implantation of hormones for the reduction of sex drive in male sex offenders. MIND investigated the possibility of a suit against the Responsible Medical Officer (RMO – the consultant in charge of the patients' medical treatment) on behalf of one of these patients who developed breasts, but no case ever reached court.[32] The patient claimed in a sworn statement that those who took part believed they would be released sooner if they agreed to the treatment. At least one man had to have a mastectomy to remove an enlarged breast.[33]

Unmodified ECT was also open to abuse, in the guise of an emergency treatment. Because of its unpleasant effects, it could be used as a deterrent or corrective. Writing in 1951, Partridge described the administration of ECT to a schizophrenic patient in the 'disturbed block' of Broadmoor. The patient was introspective but with an urge every few months to tear his clothes to pieces. Every few months when 'he was ripe for another bout of destruction' they would administer ECT.[34] In September 1979 a complaint was made to the DHSS concerning administration of unmodified ECT (without either an anaesthetic or a muscle relaxant) in Broadmoor. A student nurse who had witnessed the affair gave a sworn statement to MIND. The patient alleged that the doctor had got the staff to hold him down, and would shout 'let go' at the last minute and throw the switch. The patient is quoted as saying 'straight ECT hurts a lot for a few seconds after

179

they throw the switch. It scrambles your brains and for days you can't remember anything. I had 17 lots of ECT like this.'[35] When this case was raised with the DHSS in 1979, the then Secretary of State, Patrick Jenkin, said:

> The choice of drugs and the dosage and any application of medical treatment is essentially a matter of clinical judgement of the doctor. Unless there is prima facie evidence of substantial professional misconduct or malpractice (as distinct from generalised ill-defined allegations or complaints) management ought not to seek to concern itself in such matters as clinical judgement.[36]

The risks of unmodified ECT had been amply demonstrated more than twenty years previously with the *Bolam* case (see Chapter 9). There were some who argued, with no great conviction, that unmodified ECT was justified where a patient urgently needed ECT in a situation where anaesthetic was contraindicated or an anaesthetist was not available, but the consensus was that after 1960 it would have been totally unjustified to use it in any circumstances. Concerns were also growing that ECT was being given without consent before other therapies had been given time to work.

In 1980 the Boynton Report was published on allegations of abuses at Rampton made in the Yorkshire Television documentary 'The Secret Hospital'. They included an analysis of the pattern of seclusion during three months in 1979 which showed that, on any one day, between 7 and 9 per cent of the female population was likely to be secluded, compared with 1 per cent of the men. Seclusion was authorised by the nurse in charge of the ward. Although the duty doctor and the nursing officer were to be informed immediately of a seclusion, there was no requirement that they attend straight away. The Committee also found that when patients were secluded it was common practice for an intramuscular injection of a phenothiazine drug to be given. If the drug had already been prescribed *pro re nata* (as the circumstances required) it could be given without reference to a doctor. The Committee found that such injections were even given to patients who went voluntarily into seclusion. They asked the hospital to investigate the disparity in the use of seclusion between male and female blocks, and made three other specific recommendations. First, that when a patient went voluntarily into seclusion there

180

should rarely be a need for an injection; oral medicine should suffice. Second, that the rules should provide for an early visit for a doctor, and not just for a visit within twenty-four hours. Finally, that senior nurse management should carefully monitor the use of seclusion.[37]

By 1980 it was accepted that some controls must be imposed on the unbridled exercise of clinical judgment to give treatment without consent. The only question was the form which those controls should take. In 1979 the Labour Government fell and was replaced by the Conservatives under Margaret Thatcher. The steady stream of inquiries into abuses in psychiatric hospitals during the 1970s had also indicated a need for some effective complaints investigation machinery for patients and those who were legitimately concerned about patient care. The question was how this function would be performed. Should there be a central commission based on the exercise of visitatorial functions, or was there a need for the type of multidisciplinary committee proposed by Gostin, with patients represented by an advocacy service based in the hospitals?

One of the principal recommendations of the Boynton Report was that the DHSS should consider establishing an appointed body to inspect and monitor all institutions where people are subject to detention under the Mental Health Act.[38] In 1981 fresh government proposals for mental health law reform were issued, advocating the establishment of a central Commission and review of treatment by medical second opinion rather than the multi-disciplinary solution.[39] After a break of almost twenty-five years, the enshrinement of these recommendations in the Mental Health Act 1983 marked a return to the protection of patients' rights through the use of a central Commission. In this sense it was a return to tradition. However, a significant departure was that the new Commission was also to oversee a system of second opinions under Part IV of the 1983 Act with regard to psychosurgery, surgical implants of hormones for the reduction of male sex drive, ECT and medicines for mental disorder.

Although the 1983 Act is often described as representing a return to legalism, it builds on the basic framework of broad discretionary powers in the 1959 Act. Informal admission remains. The RMO's holding power for up to seventy-two hours also stays, but it is now delegable to a nominated deputy, and for the first time nurses of 'the prescribed class' have the power to hold the patient for up to six hours pending the arrival of a doctor.[40] The twenty-eight-day admission for observation is renamed admission for assessment (or for assessment followed by medical treatment), to make it clear that treatment may be given compulsorily. There is still an emergency power to admit for assessment for up to seventy-two hours on one medical recommendation. The periods of detention for patients compulsorily admitted for treatment or by a criminal court under a hospital order were halved by the 1983 Act, so that they are now six months, renewable initially for six months, and thereafter at twelve-monthly intervals.[41] This effectively doubled the frequency of patients' entitlement to review of their detention by a MHRT.

Section 141 of the 1959 Act had re-enacted the full protection given by section 16 of the 1930 Act, placing the burden on the complainant to seek leave for proceedings and the need to show substantial grounds that any person purportedly acting in pursuance of the Act had acted in bad faith or without reasonable care. This protection was construed widely by the House of Lords in 1976 in *Pountney* v. *Griffiths*[42] to extend to the use of force in exercising functions of control and restraint as well as to powers expressly conferred under the 1959 Act. The protection applied whether or not the plaintiff was a patient under the Act. The *British Medical Journal* welcomed the decision as offering 'reassurance to the medical profession that the five Law Lords were unanimously agreed that the protection of section 141 extends to acts both done and purportedly done by staff in the course of controlling ... patients in mental hospitals'.[43]

In section 139 of the 1983 Act the procedural hurdle is disapplied to proceedings against the Secretary of State or a health authority, and although actual liability may still only arise if bad faith or want of reasonable care is established in the main action, leave may now be granted without the plaintiff having to show substantial grounds for the contention.[44] For criminal proceedings, the leave of the Director of Public Prosecutions is now required. Since the passage of the 1983 Act, the courts have further reduced this obstacle to legal action by ruling that the requirement of leave does not apply to public law applications for judicial review.[45] In other civil proceedings the position is somewhat less certain. In *Winch* v. *Jones*, the Master of the Rolls held that a plaintiff is entitled to leave if he or she can show that the case deserves further examination,[46] but in *James* v. *Mayor and Burgesses of*

Havering,[47] Farquharson LJ held that it was necessary to establish a prima facie case of bad faith or lack of reasonable care.

The 1983 Act attempted to modify the procedures and safeguards in the 1959 Act in order to provide more effective protections for patients' rights by limiting clinical powers and immunities. However, the changes were modifications rather than wholesale reforms, and the underlying framework of broad professional discretion remains essentially intact. The significant departures from the 1959 legislation were the establishment of the Mental Health Act Commission and the introduction of express provisions in Part IV of the 1983 Act relating to consent to treatment.

The functions of the Mental Health Act Commission (MHAC) were summarised by Lord Elton for the government in the House of Lords debates on the Mental Health (Amendment) Bill:

> Its main functions will be to deal, first, with consent to treatment. ... Then there is the preparation of a code of practice covering treatment for detained patients ... your Lordships wanted it closely considered and were concerned to introduce a multidisciplinary element into the second opinion. That is a function which is allocated to this body because it is a multidisciplinary panel. There is also the monitoring of the powers of detention and generally acting as a watch-dog for detained patients.[48]

One of the most debated questions was whether the Commission should have jurisdiction over detained patients only, or also over informal patients. The government was firmly committed to giving the MHAC jurisdiction over detained patients only, on the basis that detained patients needed it more than others because, as Lord Elton put it, they were 'not free to leave the hospital when they wish, as other patients are'.[49] Government estimates were that, at any one time, there were 7,000 detained patients and 180,000 or so informal patients, 78,000 of whom had been in-patients for over three years.[50] The Secretary of State for Health, Kenneth Clarke, resisted all calls to extend the remit to cover informal patients, even those who had been in hospital for more than three years, on the grounds that the MHAC would have its work cut out to deal with patients who were detained. There were other bodies with the task of visiting hospitals whose work benefited informal patients, such as the Health Advisory Service and the National

Development Team for Mental Handicap. Powers were provided in the bill for the Secretary of State to decide 'in two or three years' whether informal patients could be brought within the remit, and Kenneth Clarke reassured the Special Standing Committee that if the Commission itself sought extension into this area, that would be 'quite a strong point [carrying] more weight than ... that of members of the public or even action groups which are trying to get the MHAC driven into the field'.[51]

In its *First Biennial Report* in 1985, the Commission expressed concern about the position of informal patients, particularly the long-stay patients who were incapable but not detained. The MHAC's concerns focused on two aspects of the treatment of informal patients: their treatment without consent and their '"*de facto* detention" in a locked ward or room, a physical form of detention which is outside the Act'.[52] In May 1986 the MHAC forwarded to the Secretary of State a draft proposal for a regulation to extend its remit to cover three aspects of the treatment of informal patients. These were:

(a) restraints which prevent informal patients from leaving hospital or any part of it including medication or denial of clothing;

(b) intentional deprivation of the company of other patients or deprivation of other amenities; and

(c) any form of medical treatment which includes the imposition on the patient of a stimulus which it is intended that s/he should find unpleasant or uncomfortable other than a treatment for a physical illness or a disability.

The MHAC also asked for the extension to cover children who are not normally detained under the Mental Health Act, but under child-care legislation or wardship. The Secretary of State declined the request.[53]

The 1983 Act actually confers the majority of the MHAC's functions on the Secretary of State, with a provision that he shall direct the Commission to perform them on his behalf.[54] This would not relieve the Secretary of State of responsibility for these functions. The MHAC has the legal status of a special health authority, and Lord Elton emphasised that this meant it was 'not a Quango' (quasi-autonomous non-governmental organisation).[55] Much emphasis was laid in debating the 1982 Bill on the importance of multi-disciplinariness in modern psychiatric care, and this was reflected in the MHAC's composition. The ninety members are appointed by the Secretary of State for Health and the Secretary of State for Wales, and they include psychiatrists, psychologists, social workers, nurses, lawyers and specialist category members. The MHAC's jurisdiction does not extend to Scotland which has its own legislation and Mental Welfare Commission. The MHAC is under a general duty to oversee the use of compulsory powers under the 1983 Act, and the more specific duties of investigating the handling of complaints made by or in relation to detained patients. Its first chair was Lord Colville of Culross (1983–1987), a former Home Office Minister. He was succeeded first by Sir Louis Blom Cooper QC (1987–1994), the barrister and author and then by Viscountess Runciman, Chair of the Prison Reform Trust.

A statutory duty is imposed directly on the MHAC to report biennially to Parliament. Secondary legislation conferred on the MHAC Central Policy Committee the task of advising the Secretary of State for Health on the preparation of a Code of Practice on the Mental Health Act.[56] The Code of Practice was issued in 1990, and substantially revised in 1993.[57] The Secretary of State has given the MHAC the task of monitoring its operation. The Commission visits hospitals regularly and interviews detained patients. The general pattern is for visits to be announced in advance, but more recently surprise visits have been carried out. One of the most important functions exercised by the MHAC is the administration and monitoring of the system of statutory second opinions established under Part IV of the Act.

Part IV identifies two groups of treatments for mental disorder, each requiring a different kind of second opinion. The first is 'the section 57 procedure' whereby special category treatments may only be given *with the valid consent of the patient*. It applies to all patients, detained or informal. The special treatments are psychosurgery and surgical implants of hormones to reduce male sex drive. The patient's consent is certified as genuine by a panel of three people appointed by the MHAC. Then the doctor member of the panel must approve it as being likely to alleviate or prevent deterioration in the patient's condition.

The other kind of second opinion allows treatment *without consent*. It is known as 'the section 58 procedure' and it applies to patients who are liable to be detained under the Act.[58] Where it is proposed to give ECT or medicines as treatments for mental disorder without the patient's consent, a second opinion must be sought from a psychiatrist appointed by the MHAC. Before treatment can be given, the second opinion doctor must certify that the patient is either incapable of consenting to the treatment or has refused it, but that it ought to be given, having regard to the likelihood that it will alleviate or prevent deterioration in the patient's condition. A detained patient can be compulsorily treated for three months with medicine before becoming entitled to a second opinion, but unless it is an emergency, involuntary ECT may never be given without a second opinion.[59]

The second opinions are binding, not advisory. There is recognition of the multidisciplinary principle, that the decision as to whether the treatment should be given is not purely medical. Before deciding that a treatment ought to be given, second opinion doctors must consult a nurse and another person who has been professionally concerned in the patient's treatment. The multidisciplinary principle was not warmly welcomed by doctors. Drs Hamilton and Udwin of Broadmoor Hospital wrote to the Special Standing Committee discussing the bill expressing strong opposition to the requirement to consult a 'second professional'.[60]

Second opinion appointed doctors (SOADs)[61] are appointed by the MHAC, whose secretariat responds to any request for second opinion visit, nominating a SOAD from the appointed doctor panel to undertake it. The panel consists of just over 150 consultant psychiatrists. Although the MHAC arranges regular training seminars for SOADs, it has no control over their decisions, nor does it operate as an appeal mechanism in individual cases. There is no appeal to the MHAC against a decision to refuse authority to treat. Dicta in *X* v. *A, B, and C and the Mental Health Act Commission* suggest that in deciding whether a treatment ought to be given, the SOAD owes a private law duty to the patient to take reasonable care whilst rendering a second opinion.[62] The relationship between the MHAC and the SOADs is 'at arm's length'. Members of the MHAC's National Standing Committee on Consent, which oversees the second opinion process, perceive their role as being to monitor clinical practice and clinical judgment, not to change it.

The 'section 57 procedure' must first be observed if it is proposed to carry out, as treatment for mental disorder, psychosurgery or surgical hormone implants for reducing male sex drive on any patient whether detained or informal. These treatments may only be given if the patient can understand their nature, purpose, and likely effects, and has consented. The decision as to capacity and the existence of valid consent is made by a team of three people – a psychiatrist and two others appointed by the MHAC – again recognition that this is not a purely medical decision. Even if the patient has given valid consent, the treatment may not proceed unless the medical member of the team certifies that it ought to be given, having regard to the likelihood that it will alleviate or prevent deterioration in the patient's condition.[63] Although the non-medical members of the appointed panel have no involvement in the second part of the decision, there is some concession to multidisciplinariness in that, before making it, the second opinion doctor must consult two other people who have been professionally concerned with the patient's medical treatment, one of whom must be a nurse, and the other neither a nurse nor a doctor.[64] The procedure is somewhat paternalistic in that, even if there is true consent from the patient and a doctor willing to give the treatment, the second opinion doctor may nonetheless decide that it should not be given.

Since the 1983 Act there have been between fifty and sixty-five applications under section 57 per two-year period from 1983 to 1991. This declined to forty-six between 1991 and 1993 because of difficulties during 1991 experienced by the main psychosurgery centre, the Geoffrey Knight Unit at the Brook Hospital, in obtaining yttrium rods with which to carry out the operations. Of the 274 referrals since 1983, psychosurgery was authorised in 218 cases (79.6 per cent), authority was refused in 10 cases (3.7 per cent), 42 (15.3 per cent) were withdrawn, and 4 (1.4 per cent) were pending at the end of 1993.[65]

Where authority to operate was refused, the reason was most often that the patient lacked the capacity to give valid consent. Applications may be withdrawn because the patient decides against the operation, or because it is decided to try other forms of treatment. The MHAC *Third Biennial Report (1987–1989)* refers to one case of authorisation for an amygdalotomy, used where aggression is a strong component of the patient's illness.[66] This case apart, the operations carried out were for depressive or obsessional disorders. This may be why, since 1985, almost twice the number of psychosurgery applications have been for women (135) as for men (76), a similar gender imbalance to that discovered in the Department of Health study of leucotomies in the 1950s.

There have been four applications since 1983 (only one of which was proceeded with) for surgical implants of hormones. This is probably because the most widely used sexual supressant, Cyproterone Acetate, is administered by mouth. In their *Second Biennial Report* the MHAC noted that they had considered the case for including the administration of depot injections of Cyproterone Acetate within the definition of surgical hormone implantation. They resolved that it was not for them 'to make additions to the treatments specified by the Act and Regulations by way of broad based interpretation; but that at the same time it must not flinch from applying section 57 to treatments which clearly fall within the relevant definitions.'[67] This unflinching attitude led them into trouble with the courts in *R* v. *Mental Health Act Commission ex parte W*.[68] The court held that the MHAC had been wrong in applying the section 57 procedure to injections, through a wide bore syringe, of Goserelin capsules. Goserelin is a hormone analogue used to treat prostate cancer, but on this occasion it was used experimentally to suppress the libido of a convicted paedophile. The consequence of the ruling was that, since the patient was consenting, the treatment could be given without a second opinion. The patient failed in a later attempt to obtain damages from the MHAC and the appointed team involved.[69] Because most sexual suppressant treatments are administered by depot injection and not surgically, this has been one of very few applications of section 57 to hormone implants, and there have been none since 1988.

Under section 61 of the Act, the psychiatrist in charge of treatment for a patient who has had psychosurgery may be required to furnish the MHAC with a progress report six months after the operation, and at regular intervals thereafter. The MHAC routinely asks for such reports, but the obligation to provide them has never been fully complied with by all psychiatrists. In 1993, the MHAC stated that no reports at all had been provided in approximately a quarter of cases, and those which had been provided varied considerably in their comprehensiveness. They announced that they were undertaking a systematic review of these reports and the associated procedures.[70] Section 61 reviews, if they were properly done, would provide a much needed comprehensive follow-up survey of patients' progress over a prolonged period.

The section 57 second opinion procedure requires valid consent before the special treatments specified may be given, but the bulk of Part IV relates to the circumstances in which treatment may be given without consent.

12

TREATMENT WITHOUT CONSENT UNDER THE 1983 ACT

Section 58 of the 1983 Act applies only to the treatment of detained patients with medicines and ECT, and authorises treatment without consent subject to a second opinion. This chapter draws on a survey of second opinions carried out in 1992. All second opinion appointed doctors (SOADs), whether or not they authorise the proposed treatment, must return the certificate authorising treatment (Statutory Form 39) to Commission headquarters, together with the Mental Health Act Commission's (MHAC) internal administrative form (MHAC 2). MHAC 2s contain biographical details and a brief case history of each patient, as well as information about the second opinion visit, such as whether the patient was capable of consenting; the identity of the other professionals consulted; whether the original treatment plan was changed; whether emergency treatment had been given under section 62 prior to the second opinion; and whether the doses of drugs are within the dose limits recommended in the British National Formulary (BNF). Where the SOAD gives authority to exceed the BNF recommended maximum dose, this must be specified on Form 39. The MHAC also receives section 61 progress reports from Responsible Medical Officers (RMOs) (Form MHAC 1) which give detailed descriptions of individual drugs and doses or the number of ECTs given, together with a general statement of the patient's progress.

The survey reported here was of 1,009 MHAC 2s returned to the Commission between December 1991 and August 1992, and 232 MHAC 1s returned during the first three months of 1992, which were made available for study following scrutiny by the MHAC National Standing Committee on Consent. Altogether, 276 hospitals were represented in the sample, with cases from all

190

the major psychiatric hospitals in England and Wales, private sector as well as NHS. There were eighty-eight special hospital patients; thirty-five from Broadmoor, thirty-eight from Rampton, and fifteen from Ashworth. A total of 839 of (83 per cent) of the MHAC 2 patients were detained following civil admission, of whom 764 were detained for treatment under section 3, and 75 under section 2, 'for assessment, or for assessment followed by treatment' for up to twenty-eight days. The remaining 164 were mentally disordered offenders.

Informal patients are entitled to refuse treatment, although if they refuse treatment that is deemed necessary in their own interests or for the protection of others, their RMO has the legal power to detain them with the agreement of an approved social worker or the nearest relative and another doctor.[1] Where a detained patient is to be given ECT at any time, valid consent or a second opinion from a consultant psychiatrist nominated by the MHAC is required.[2] During the debates on the 1982 Bill there was some lobbying to make ECT subject to the section 57 procedure, so that consent would be required before it could be given. The government responded by making ECT subject to section 58 by regulation rather than on the face of the Act. In this way, they left themselves the option to move it to the section 57 category if experience showed the need, without resort to amending legislation.[3]

Section 58 also applies to medicines for mental disorder, but the patient only becomes eligible for a second opinion if 'three months or more have elapsed from the first occasion in that period [of detention] when medicine was administered to him by any means for his mental disorder'.[4] This is the so-called 'stabilising period', a result of lobbying by the Royal College of Psychiatrists, during which medicine may be given at the direction of the RMO without consent or a second opinion. The Secretary of State, Kenneth Clarke, described its rationale in these terms:

> The danger against which everyone wished to protect patients was the continuing course of heavy drug therapy, which has to be resorted to and can be beneficial in some cases. There are different views about that sort of treatment and it was felt that some safeguards were required. If we start applying safeguards from the moment any drug treatment is embarked upon there will be difficulties. There will

be no time to see whether the treatment is working and the patient may object bitterly, because he does not understand that it will do him good.[5]

The section 58 procedure applies only to patients liable to be detained under the provisions of the 1983 Act which authorise detention for longer than seventy-two hours, except for the power of a criminal court to remand for reports under section 35. They also do not apply to offender patients subject to restriction orders who have been conditionally discharged from hospital, where acceptance of treatment may be made a condition of discharge.[6] The vast majority of psychiatric patients are informal.[7] Over 90 per cent of all admissions are informal. The most recent figures show that between 1 April 1992 and 31 March 1993, there were 242,044 informal admissions, and 21,356 compulsory admissions in NHS hospitals, and 5,703 admissions to private hospitals, of which 452 were compulsory. Formal admissions to NHS hospitals have risen by 31 per cent from the 1987–1988 figure of 16,276, whilst informal admissions have risen by 16 per cent over the same period, from 209,124 in 1987–1988.[8]

The official view of the importance of consent-seeking is that, although Part IV can be used to authorise treatment without consent, the RMO must always seek the patient's valid consent before giving treatment.[9] If the patient is capable of consenting and has consented to ECT or medicine, the RMO certifies this on Statutory Form 38.[10] Unlike the consent forms used in general medicine, Form 38 does not require the patient's signature, only that of the RMO. The RMO must certify that two criteria are met: that the patient is capable; and that he or she consents to the treatment. The statutory test of capacity under Part IV is that the patient is capable of understanding the nature, purpose and likely effects of the treatment. The MHAC advises SOADs that in assessing validity of consent they should look not just at capacity to understand in the abstract, but at actual understanding of the treatment proposal.

This raises the question of how much knowledge the patient must display of the treatment before being capable of understanding its nature, purpose and likely effects, and hence how much the patient is entitled to be told by the doctor who proposes that treatment. In the Goserelin judicial review case, Stuart Smith LJ stated that no doubt consent has to be 'informed consent in

192

that [the patient] knows the nature and likely effects of the treatment'.[11] In the particular case, where an anti-cancer drug was being put to novel use as a sexual suppressant, the judge held that it was important that the patient should know this. However, he went on to reject the proposition that 'a patient must understand the precise physiological process involved before he can be said to be capable of understanding the nature and likely effects of the treatment or can consent to it'.[12] The *Third Biennial Report* says that the

> knowledge communicated by the therapist may vary in detail from 'broad terms' to great detail, depending on the patient's ability and the complexity of the treatment being offered, with the final criteria ... being that the patient is capable of understanding the nature, purpose and likely effects of the treatment.[13]

The Code of Practice emphasises the doctor's personal responsibility to determine whether each patient whom he or she proposes to treat has capacity to give a valid consent. It also stresses that the assessment of capacity is a matter for 'clinical judgment, guided by current professional practice and subject to legal requirements'.[14] Mentally disordered people are not necessarily incapable, and capacity is to be assessed in relation to the patient in question, at the particular time, with relation to the treatment proposed. The explanation of the treatment given by the doctor should be appropriate to the level of the patient's assessed ability.[15]

As to the criteria to be used in assessing capacity, the Code requires understanding, not only of the likely effects of the treatment, but also of the likely consequences of not having it. An individual must have the ability to:

(a) understand what the medical treatment is and that somebody has said that he or she needs it and why the treatment is being proposed;

(b) understand in broad terms the nature of the proposed treatment;[16]

(c) understand its principal benefits and risks;

(d) understand what will be the consequences of not receiving the proposed treatment; and

(e) possess the capacity to make a choice.[17]

In addition to certifying that the patient is capable and has consented, the RMO must give a brief description of the treatment consented to. The Code of Practice requires the RMO to indicate on Form 38 the drugs prescribed by the classes described in the BNF, the method of their administration, and the dose range, indicating the dosages if they are above the BNF limit. The BNF is not the only prescribing guide available to doctors, but under DHSS Circular Letter DDL(84)4 and the Code of Practice it plays an important part in the second opinion process. Not only do RMOs describe the drugs consented to in terms of BNF categories, so too do the SOADs when they authorise treatment without consent. The BNF is published jointly by the British Medical Association and the Royal Pharmaceutical Society and updated biannually. It describes the effects and side effects of each drug, specifying recommended maximum dosage levels which are determined on the advice of medical advisers working mainly from the manufacturer's data sheet, and produced after the available information has been considered by the Committee for the Safety of Medicines when deciding to give the drug a product licence. Some of the less sedative antipsychotics have no BNF recommended maximum. The BNF is intended for the guidance of doctors, pharmacists and others who have the necessary training to interpret the information it provides. Each category (e.g. 4.2.1 antipsychotic drugs, or 4.2.2 depot antipsychotics) includes a large number of different drugs, and this method of describing treatment to which consent has been given confers considerable scope for the RMO to change medication within categories, or to give more than one drug within the same category at the same time.

The RMO is the gatekeeper of the system. Where a patient agrees to treatment, the decision about incapacity will determine whether there will be a second opinion, and where the patient disagrees a second opinion will only be needed if the RMO decides to persist with the treatment. It scarcely upholds the principle of self-determination if a RMO accepts the consent of a patient who does not understand the decision being made, or who has not been given information about the treatment's nature, purpose, and effects. Where commissioners who visit and interview detained patients in hospital come across someone who is described as capable and consenting by the RMO, but who is in their view incapable, they often ask the RMO to refer the case for a second opinion. If a second opinion is required because the patient cannot

Table 1 Total second opinions under section 58

Year	Second opinions
1983–5	4032
1985–7	5845
1987–9	7592
1989–91	7169
1991–3	8839

Source: MHAC, First–Fifth Biennial Reports

Table 2 Second opinions by gender of patient

Year	1983–5	1985–7	1987–9	1989–91	1991–3
Males	1781	2472	3152	3048	4010
Females	2251	3373	4440	4121	4829
Total	4032	5845	7592	7169	8839

Source: MHAC, First–Fifth Biennial Reports

Table 3 Second opinions under section 58 by type of treatment

Year	1983–5	1985–7	1987–9	1989–91	1991–3
Medicine	1886	2483	3138	3023	4627
ECT	2146	2455	4203	3978	4067
Both	—	907	251	166	145
Total	4032	5845	7592	7169[18]	8839

Source: MHAC, First–Fifth Biennial Reports

Table 4 Second opinions under section 58 by legal category of mental disorder

Year	1983–5	1985–7	1987–9	1989–91	1991–3
M illness	3667[a]	5477	7154	6830	8271
M impairment	365	335	408	345	340
S M impairment	—	—	—	—	80
Psychopathy	—	87	113	83	148
Total	4032	5899[b]	7675[c]	7258[d]	8839

Source: MHAC, First–Fifth Biennial Reports

a Includes psychopathic disorder   b 44 patients had a double diagnosis
c 83 patients had a double diagnosis   d 89 patients had a double diagnosis

consent or is refusing, it is the personal responsibility of the RMO to ensure that a second opinion visit is requested.[19]

The MHAC publishes statistics of second opinions biennially. The five MHAC biennial reports show a clear increase in the number of second opinions since the 1983 Act came into force.

Since 1983, compulsory civil admissions of women have ranged between 51 and 54 per cent of the total, whilst men constitute the vast majority of offender patients (1,442 males as opposed to 255 females in 1992–1993). This is reflected in the national second opinion figures (Table 2) and Table 3 shows the type of treatment.

Between 1991 and 1993, second opinions for medicines outnumbered those for ECT for the first time since the 1983 Act came into force. The vast majority of section 58 second opinions are for patients suffering from mental illness.

Of the 1,009 MHAC 2 cases surveyed, 963 patients were suffering from mental illness, 44 were mentally impaired, 17 were severely mentally impaired, and 19 were suffering from psychopathic disorder, with double diagnosis accounting for the excess over 1,009. The largest diagnostic categories within the mental illness group were schizophrenic psychosis with 445 patients, affective psychosis with 277, and depressive disorder with 216.[20]

Since 1989 the MHAC has produced statistics of second opinions for mentally ill patients by gender and type of treatment, showing that for ECT women far outnumber men, and the reverse is the case for medicines. Between 1989 and 1991, 71.4 per cent (2,827) of the mental illness second opinions for ECT were for women and 61.6 per cent (1,671) for medicines involved men. Between 1991 and 1993, women were 67.4 per cent (2,614) of the second opinions for ECT, whilst men were 59.6 per cent (2,546) of those for medicines.

The gender composition of the sample closely reflected the national figures for the period from 1991 to 1993 (55 per cent women, 45 per cent men) with 566 (56 per cent) women and 443 (44 per cent) men. The patients' ages ranged from a fifteen-year-old girl to a ninety-four-year-old woman, both having second opinions for ECT. 60 per cent of the male patients were forty or under, and 80 per cent of them were fifty-five or under. Women tended to be more concentrated in the older age groups, with 70 per cent over forty, and more than 50 per cent over fifty-five.

Ethnicity is a strong contemporary issue in psychiatry, with increasing acceptance that black people, particularly young people born in Britain, are more likely to be diagnosed schizophrenic,[21] more likely to be compulsorily admitted to psychiatric hospital, more likely to be treated in conditions of security,[22] and more likely to be given large doses of medication.[23] There are conflicting views about whether this reflects actual morbidity (which might well itself result from young black males' experience of racism), or is a result of racism or inability to understand cultural differences producing a predisposition on the part of psychiatrists to diagnose black people schizophrenic. The Special Hospitals Service Authority figures show that almost 10 per cent of patients in top security special hospitals are Afro-Caribbean,[24] although a more recently published estimate is that 15 per cent of the population of Broadmoor Hospital is Afro-Caribbean.[25] In 1991, the MHAC asked SOADs to record the ethnic origin of patients, based on self ascription, but some SOADs remained reluctant to do this, and in ninety-eight cases the information was missing.

More men had medicine, and more women had ECT second opinions. Medicine and ECT second opinions were evenly split in the sample, with 490 for ECT, 497 for medicines, and 22 for both. The gender split for ECT was 73 per cent (357) women and 27 per cent (133) men, whilst for medicines it was 61 per cent (301) men and 39 per cent (196) women. Nine men and thirteen women were having second opinions for both ECT and medicines. There was a steep increase in the number of women over forty having ECT, with high concentrations (208) in the sixty-one to eighty age group. In the over-eighty age group, the vast majority of second opinions for both sexes were for ECT (forty-two of the forty-eight women, and seven of the twelve men).

ECT is an established treatment for affective psychosis and depressive disorder, which are more prevalent in women. It is also used, albeit less frequently, in the treatment of schizophrenic psychosis. Women had proportionally more second opinions for ECT than men in all the largest diagnostic categories. Over 77 per cent (167) of the 216 patients with depressive disorder were women. Of these, 93.4 per cent (156) had ECT second opinions, 4.2 per cent (7) medicine, and 2.4 per cent (4) both. Of the men with this diagnosis, 85.7 per cent (42) had second opinions for ECT, 8.2 per cent (4) for medicines, and 6.1 per cent (3) for both. All depressive disorder second opinions in the over seventy age group were for ECT (including five for ECT and medicine).

Seventy per cent (196) of the 277 patients suffering from affective psychosis were women. Second opinions for ECT were given to 78.6 per cent (154), 17.9 per cent (35) for medicine, and 3.5 per cent (7) for both. Of the men, 67.9 per cent (55) had a second opinion for ECT, 28.4 per cent (23) for medicine, and 3.7 per cent (3) for both. When age was taken into account, the percentages having ECT after age sixty rose significantly (ranging between 90 and 100 per cent) for both sexes.

Although only small numbers of schizophrenic patients had ECT second opinions, there were some significant gender differences. Whilst 13.6 per cent (38) of the 279 men with schizophrenic psychosis had second opinions for ECT, or ECT and medicines, the level for women was 28.3 per cent (45). Second opinions for medicines were given to 86.4 per cent of the male schizophrenics (241), and 71.7 per cent of the women (119). ECT as a treatment for male schizophrenics seems to be used with young men. Twenty-two (63 per cent) of the thirty-five males were having ECT in the twenty-one to thirty-five age group. Interestingly, five of the seventeen schizophrenic men having ECT aged between twenty-one and thirty were Afro-Caribbeans.

Many more women than men have second opinions for ECT. Substantial numbers of middle-aged and elderly women are being detained under the Mental Health Act and are having ECT in circumstances where they are either refusing or are unable to consent. Opinion about ECT amongst those who have undergone it is deeply divided. Some patients say that it provides the only effective relief, whilst others say that it has done them positive harm. There is continuing controversy about the use of ECT with the very young and the elderly, with some doctors as well as survivors of the treatment asserting that it causes irreversible damage to the brain and mental function, whilst the bulk of the medical establishment insists that its use should not be ruled out on any age group on grounds that it may be essential to relieve acute depression.[26]

The physical hazards of ECT are substantially reduced if it is given with muscle relaxants and an anaesthetic, but anaesthetics carry increased dangers for elderly patients. The risk of death has been estimated at 4.5 deaths per 100,000 treatments, which is low compared to the rate from overdoses of anti-depressant drugs.[27] The side effects of ECT include loss of memory which is usually temporary, but which may last for up to three months. Memory loss is also a symptom of certain types of depression. Some patients complain that they have never regained their memory properly.

The MHAC *Third Biennial Report 1987–1989* suggested that a large proportion of the ECT work of second opinion doctors is for old people 'who have been detained because they cannot consent to ECT, even though they are already unprotestingly in hospital and the treatment is required because they are refusing food and fluids'. This survey reinforced that impression, since eighteen ECT visits took place on the day of detention, and 60 per cent (294) happened within the first seven days of detention.

Treatment which would in normal circumstances require a second opinion may be given in emergencies defined in section 62 of the 1983 Act, without prior compliance with the second opinion procedures. The intention behind this provision was that a second opinion should be obtained as soon after the emergency treatment as possible, that the emergency treatment and the reasons for it should be recorded, and the records made available to MHAC teams on their visits to hospitals. There was a surprisingly high use of section 62 for ECT; 112 of the 116 patients (11 per cent of the MHAC 2 cases) receiving emergency treatment under section 62 being ECT cases, eighty-four women and twenty-eight men. Forty-five of the women were over sixty years old, including twenty-five over seventy, six between eighty-one and ninety, and one over ninety-one. Seventeen of the men were over sixty, including eleven who were over seventy and three who were over eighty. Sixty-one per cent of second opinion visits for patients given emergency treatment occurred within five days of admission, and 73 per cent took place within seven days. This strongly suggested that many of these patients were detained in order to allow ECT to be given without consent, and treated once under section 62 pending the second opinion visit. As for the consent status of the section 62 ECT patients, twenty (three men and seventeen women) were capable and refusing; sixty-three (nineteen men and forty-four women) were incapable and refusing; and twenty-nine (six men and twenty-three women) were incapable of expressing any acceptance or refusal. MIND has recently issued a policy statement on physical treatments seeking legal change to ensure that no-one who is capable of giving informed consent has ECT against his or her will, and people who are incapable of consenting only ever have

ECT in cases of urgent necessity, and then not if they object.[28] This would have ruled out ECT for the sixty-three emergency cases in this sample who were deemed incapable and refusing, and the twenty who were capable and refusing.

In all the emergency ECT cases, the reason for the administration of emergency ECT was either the immediate need to save life, or to prevent serious deterioration in the patient's condition. Patients having emergency ECT were frequently described in terms such as 'refusing food and fluids, inaccessible, and beyond reassurance', and the treatment as 'necessary to save the life of the patient'. In one case the patient had been tube fed from admission, had lost fifteen pounds in the past week, and her physical state had become critical. The clear impression was that patients are already seriously deteriorated by the time they are admitted compulsorily for depressive illnesses.

Whereas the majority of second opinions for ECT were middle-aged and elderly women, the majority of medicines second opinions were for younger patients, particularly men. Of those receiving second opinions for medicines, 240 of the 301 men and 109 of the 196 women were aged between fifteen and forty-five. There were fourteen men and thirty-six women over sixty receiving second opinions for medicines.

The vast majority of medicines second opinions were for antipsychotic medication. Amongst the adverse effects described in the BNF for these drugs are:

> *parkinsonian symptoms* (including tremor) which may occur gradually, *dystonia* (abnormal face and body movements) which may appear after only a few doses, *akathisia* (restlessness) which may resemble an exacerbation of the condition being treated, and *tardive dyskinesia* (which usually takes longer to develop).[29]

Tardive dyskinesia, characterised by uncontrollable abnormal movements, is of particular concern because it may be irreversible on withdrawing therapy, and treatment may be ineffective. The BNF says it occurs 'fairly frequently' in patients on long-term therapy and with high dosage, and 'occasionally after short-term treatment with low dosage'. Malignant neuroleptic syndrome is a rare, but potentially fatal effect of some neuroleptic drugs, which has been reported in the United Kingdom for Haloperidol, Chlorpromazine, and Flupenthixol Decanoate.

When SOADs authorise treatment they do so by specifying the BNF category, the maximum number of drugs from each category, and whether BNF dose ranges may be exceeded. The BNF dosage ranges are recommended maxima. The BNF acknowledges that: 'In some patients it is necessary to raise the dose of an antipsychotic drug above that which is normally recommended', but warns that 'this should be done with caution and under specialist supervision'.[30] A similar warning is given with relation to depot antipsychotics. The BNF says that: 'Individual responses to neuroleptic drugs are very variable and to achieve optimum effect dosage and dosage interval must be titrated according to the patient's response', but warns that 'extra-pyramidal symptoms occur frequently'.[31]

In cases where antipsychotic medicines are ineffective in standard doses, there is a tendency to experiment with higher doses and combinations of different drugs. Many psychiatrists can produce a wealth of anecdotal evidence of cases where they have considered it necessary to exceed BNF limits, because of the patient's metabolism, or where normal doses produce little effect. Some doctors argue that the BNF dose ranges err too much on the side of caution, because they are based on manufacturers' data sheet assessments, drafted with an eye towards minimising their own potential legal liability. Views such as these have led to widespread use of high-dose medication and polypharmacy, both of which carry increased risk of side effects.

In 1993, after this research was carried out, the Royal College of Psychiatrists issued a *Consensus Statement on High Dose Medication* which admitted that the use of high-dose medication has increased over the past twenty years, and 'megadose treatment' has been used with treatment resistant patients. However, the statement emphasised that there is no evidence beyond the anecdotal to show its superior effectiveness, and megadoses have been associated with violent disturbed behaviour, making it difficult to determine whether such behaviour is triggered by the patient's illness or by the drugs.

With polypharmacy, since many of these medicines have the same side effects, when they occur it is difficult to determine which of the different drugs is causing them. The BNF emphasises that 'prescribing more than one antipsychotic at a time is *not* recommended; it may constitute a hazard and there is no significant evidence that side effects are minimized'.[32] The Royal College consensus statement agrees that polypharmacy is undesirable on a routine basis. It also states that there might be occasional patients for whom it has been proved necessary by experience over the years, where a patient may need another antipsychotic in a more concentrated form to combat an acute phase of the illness, or where high potency antipsychotics may need to be supplemented by more sedative antipsychotics to cope with a period of intense distress.

The BNF suggests that psychotic patients should be having either oral or depot antipsychotics, but not both at the same time, advising that when transferring from oral to depot therapy, dosage by mouth should be gradually phased out.[33] Fraser and Hepple, in their study of prescribing practice in Broadmoor, note that the use of more than one antipsychotic 'has generally been agreed to be an example of bad prescribing practice', but then talk of the potential for further research on this in secure hospitals such as Broadmoor, where clinicians give anecdotal reports of patients whose mental states can only be stabilised when a combination of antipsychotic drugs is used.[34] The theory of good prescribing is that polypharmacy and high-dose medication should be reserved for the most exceptional cases. What is the position in practice?

From the evidence of this survey, whilst the number of cases where side effects were expressly mentioned was small (five of the MHAC 1s and and fifteen MHAC 2s), polypharmacy was extensively practised. Second opinions for drugs were given to 519 MHAC 2 cases, 497 for medication alone, and 22 for ECT and medication. In 87 per cent (454) of cases treatment with antipsychotic drugs from BNF category 4.2.1 was authorised, and 82 per cent (425) were having depot antipsychotics from 4.2.2. A total of 363 patients (70 per cent) were having anticholinergic medication from 4.9.2 or 4.9.3. More than one antipsychotic was authorised in respect of 73 per cent of the patients having second opinions for medicines. By far the most common prescribing combination was antipsychotics from both categories 4.2.1 and 4.2.2 together with anticholinergic drugs for side effects, authorised for 292 (56 per cent) of the patients.

For the MHAC 1 patients, by far the most frequent prescribing combination was antipsychotic medication from BNF 4.2.1 and 4.2.2 neuroleptics with anticholinergic drugs (usually Procyclidine) to control side effects. A total of 218 (94 per cent) were having neuroleptic drugs from 4.2.1, 195 (84 per cent) were having depot neuroleptics, and 170 (73 per cent) were having anticholinergic drugs from BNF category 4.9.2. Of those having anticholinergic drugs, 144 were on a regular daily dose of the drug, and 26 were written up to receive it PRN, if side effects manifested themselves.

As Fraser and Hepple note, frequent concurrent prescription of anticholinergic medication with antipsychotics is a cause for concern in that 'the World Health Organisation consensus statement (1990) recommended that prophylactic use of these drugs may be justified early in treatment (after which it should be discontinued and its need be re-evaluated)'.[35] The BNF too clearly states that routine administration of these drugs is *not* justified as not all patients are affected, and because tardive dyskinesia may be worsened or masked by them.[36] The high level of use of these drugs indicates either that the WHO consensus statement and the BNF are not being adhered to in many cases, or that the use of anticholinergic medication is actually necessary in these cases to control side effects rather than as a prophylactic measure.

Given the high numbers of patients on combinations of drugs, it is perhaps surprising that there were only eight MHAC 2 cases where the SOAD expressed concern about polypharmacy, in only two of which did the SOADs time limit their approval.[37] Polypharmacy tended to concern SOADs when a patient was having drugs from four or five different BNF categories.

There were 154 SOADs on the MHAC list when this survey was carried out. All were consultants. The majority were attached to NHS or private hospitals, but twenty-five were retired. Retired doctors (one-sixth of the total) carried out 352 (over one-third) of the second opinions in the sample. Twelve doctors (less than 8 per cent) did almost 35 per cent of the work, and thirty-three (21 per cent) of the doctors carried out 672 (66 per cent) of the visits. Of the three doctors who did more than thirty visits, one (a retired consultant) did fifty-three, one thirty-six, and one thirty-five. It must be remembered that thirty-eight doctors did not appear in the sample, and this may have been because they had not sent in an expenses claim to the Commission during the study period, rather than because they had not carried out any visits. Nevertheless, since this research the MHAC Consent Committee has identified the high concentration of work with a few doctors as a question to be addressed.

DHSS circular letter DDL 84(4), issued in 1984 to all RMOs, described the purpose of the second opinion as 'to protect the patient's rights by ensuring that a treatment given without his consent is justified and in his interests'.[38] The legal question to be answered by the SOADs in deciding whether absence of consent should be overridden is 'Should the treatment be given, having regard to the likelihood that it will alleviate or prevent deterioration in the patient's condition?'[39] DDL(84)4 made it clear that SOADs' role is not to substitute their own decision as to what the treatment should be for that of the RMO making the treatment proposal. Where there is no consent, the question for the SOAD is 'whether or not the treatment plan is one which should be followed even if it is not necessarily the one which the appointed doctor would make himself'. The guidance goes on to say that 'doctors vary in their therapeutic approach and appointed doctors should feel able to support a consultant proposing a programme which others would regard as one which should be followed'.[40]

In many jurisdictions in the United States, proxy decision-makers are required to operate on the basis of substituted judgment when making decisions about the treatment of an incapacitated person. This means that they must take account of the patient's known views, religious and other beliefs, and general outlook on life in an attempt to make the decision that the person would have made. If such information is lacking, then the best interests test is applied. This is the favoured approach of English common law on treatment decisions. Whilst substituted judgment is patient-centred, best interests tests depend primarily on the views of doctors as to the patient's interests. They require that the likely benefits be weighed against the risks and may incorporate some concept of the least invasive alternative. The legal test of likelihood that the treatment will alleviate or prevent deterioration is much looser even than the best interests test, and it has been diluted further by DDL 84(4) to apply what are in effect *Bolam* principles. The treatment plan should be approved if there is a responsible body of psychiatric opinion which would support it in such a case.

The Code of Practice describes the SOAD's role as an additional safeguard to protect the patient's rights.[41] It also stresses that the SOADs act as individuals and must reach their own judgment as to whether the proposed treatment is reasonable in the light of the general consensus of appropriate treatment for such a condition, taking account not only of the therapeutic efficacy of the proposed treatment but also (where a capable patient is withholding his consent) the reasons for such withholding, which should be given their due weight.[42]

SOADs begin their visits by ensuring that the patient's detention papers are in order, since lawful detention is a prerequisite of a second opinion under section 58.[43] Although the 1983 Act does not specifically entitle the patient to be interviewed, DDL(84)4 says that the SOAD 'will visit the patient, consult the responsible medical officer and other staff'.[44] Under section 58, the SOAD must certify whether the patient is refusing the treatment or is incapable of understanding its nature, purpose and likely effects, and this cannot be judged without seeing the patient. The Code of Practice states that the patient should be interviewed in private, but others may be present if the patient and SOAD agree, or if the doctor would be at significant risk of physical harm from the patient.[45] In seven cases in the MHAC 2 study the patient was not interviewed. In four, treatment was authorised even though the patients' mental state made interview impossible, and in another, although the patient refused to be interviewed, the SOAD authorised twelve ECTs to treat 'acute schizophrenic illness with episodes of aggression'. In the other two, the patients had absented themselves from hospital and treatment was not authorised.

The Code states that the case should be discussed face to face with the RMO, with telephone consultation only in exceptional circumstances. Despite this, telephone consultation appeared to be more the norm than the exception. In some cases, however, no consultation of any kind was possible. In one, the SOAD refused to authorise treatment, following a visit on the day after Boxing Day, because the RMO, the senior registrar and the social worker were all unavailable. The SOAD said that he would not have insisted on ECT if it had been his patient, since the patient was clearly and adamantly refusing, and a nurse, the only professional available for consultation, agreed with him. In two other cases, the RMO was not available and the SOAD had to discuss the case with the senior house officer in one case and the registrar in the other.

The SOAD must consult a nurse and one 'other person' who has been professionally concerned with the patient's medical treatment, broadly defined in section 145(1) of the 1983 Act to include nursing, and care, habilitation and rehabilitation under medical supervision. This reflects Parliamentary concerns that the decision should have a multidisciplinary element. The consultees 'may expect a private discussion with the SOAD (again only in exceptional cases on the telephone), to be listened to with consideration, and should consider commenting upon':

(a) the proposed treatment and the patient's ability to consent to it;
(b) other treatment options;
(c) the way in which the decision to treat was arrived at;
(d) the facts of the case, progress, attitude of relatives etc.;
(e) the implications of imposing treatment on a non-consenting subject and the reasons for the patient's refusal of treatment;
(f) any other matter relating to the patient's care on which the consultee wishes to comment.[46]

The nurse consultee must be qualified. Nursing assistants, auxiliaries and aides are excluded. In one case a third year student nurse was consulted, contrary to the Code of Practice advice. In another, a senior nurse who had known the patient for little more than an hour was consulted for the sake of statutory form but, in the words of the SOAD, 'the most valuable contribution' came from a nursing assistant who was 'very sensible and knowledgeable' even though not eligible herself to be consulted.

The duty to consult the 'other person' professionally concerned with the patient's treatment has been much discussed. The RMO is responsible for ensuring that someone is available who must be professionally concerned with the patient's 'medical treatment'. The Act, DDL(84)4 and the Code of Practice all make it clear that the certificate (Form 39) cannot be issued unless the two people designated have been consulted.

Despite this, in one case a certificate was issued authorising ECT, even though no second consultee could be contacted. The SOAD recorded that there had been no occupational therapy or psychologist contact since admission and the approved social worker who applied for compulsory admission was not contactable. The patient was described as 'refusing food and fluids, losing weight and wants to die'. In another case, treatment was authorised illegally as a result of the SOAD consulting a doctor (a Senior House Officer) as the other person. The patient had eight ECTs before the RMO noticed the irregularity, which was not picked up during the monitoring by the National Standing Committee on Consent. In another case the SOAD had to return to the hospital to carry out the consultation three days after his original visit because the person originally proposed was not acceptable.

By far the largest category of 'other persons' in the sample was social worker, with 503 cases. Sometimes the social worker consulted was the approved social worker who had applied for compulsory admission and had not seen the patient since. Occupational therapists were the second largest group, with 356 (including five occupational assistants), followed by psychologists with fifty-one. Physiotherapists were consulted in thirty-three cases, pharmacists in twenty-four, dieticians in seven, and the chaplain in one case. The 'others' included physiotherapy assistants, teachers (including special needs teachers), housekeepers, adult education tutors, technical instructors, wardens of hostels, and training co-ordinators. In two cases involving the same hospital, a ward clerk was the person consulted. Although both patients had been in hospital for three months, he was said to be the only 'other person' who knew them.

Clearly, the reason for accepting people so tenuously connected with medical treatment, even broadly defined, was the difficulty in finding a qualified 'other person' to consult, a fact reported by 110 SOADs in the sample. In ninety-four of these cases, consultation was by telephone. In seven cases there was no other person available for consultation. Difficulties in finding someone to consult led to SOADs accepting people who had known the patient for only a very short time. Their knowledge of the patient would be scanty, or non-existent, and they could by no stretch of the imagination be said to have been 'professionally involved' in the patient's treatment. Where the patient had just been admitted, this was difficult to avoid, but not all cases fell into this category. Often the nurse and the other person had first met the patient no more than a couple of hours before the SOAD's visit, having been brought in specially 'to get to know the patient in order to fulfil the requirements of the Act'.

The MHAC *Fifth Biennial Report* states that 'to require the statutory other consultee to be invariably professionally qualified and included in a professional register would be unnecessarily restrictive'. However, referring to this research, they also express their grave doubts about the validity of some certificates which refer to consultation of ward clerks, 'gymnasium technicians' or 'occupational therapy aids'.[47] They propose that SOADs should endeavour to meet with somebody whose qualifications, experience and knowledge of the patient enable him or her to make an effective contribution to the work of the multidisciplinary team. The desire to have true multidisciplinary involvement in the treatment decision seems far from realisation, and indeed the difficulties in finding another person to consult call into question whether the multidisciplinary care which is part of the ethos of the 1983 Act is a myth or reality. The duty to consult the other professional is becoming seen as a tiresome formality, and if the other professionals consulted are too junior or too unfamiliar with the patient to express a valid view, the decision will effectively be left to doctors.

Every MHAC biennial report has mentioned the high level of agreement between RMOs and SOADs, estimating it to be between 94 and 96 per cent.[48] There were thirty-six (3.6 per cent) cases where the Form 39 was withheld. In seven cases, by the time the SOAD visited, the patient was consenting and a Form 38 certifying capacity and consent was issued. Six patients were ineligible for a second opinion, four because they had not been receiving medicine for three months, one because her detention was invalid, and one because he was remanded under section 35 of the Act.

In four ECT cases, authority was withheld for clinical reasons. Two were because anti-depressant medication had not been given adequate time to work, and the others were due to doubts about diagnosis. In one, the RMO diagnosed the patient as suffering from depression, whilst the SOAD thought he had a schizophrenic disorder and refused to authorise ECT. In the other, the SOAD wanted a further opinion as to 'the viability of using ECT for the patient's bizarre symptoms'.

Of the cases where objection influenced refusal, six involved ECT. In one the SOAD did not consider that there were adequate clinical grounds for giving ECT against the wishes of an an eighty-year-old man whose mental state was 'essentially normal'. In three cases, all involving women, the SOADs were impressed by the lucidly expressed opposition of the patients to ECT, and there had been no immediate danger to their lives. In the fifth case, the twenty-three-year-old patient's parents were unwilling for her to have ECT. The SOAD asked the RMO to discuss the question further with the parents, but noted that 'treatment without consent may have to be authorised later if the patient's condition deteriorates further'. In the sixth ECT case, the SOAD agreed with the nurse and the other consultee (an approved social worker) that ECT should not be given, but that the patient should be moved to a more stable and less threatening environment, such as a continuing care facility.

Two refusal cases concerned treatment with Clozapine (marketed in the UK as Clozaril by the manufacturer Sandoz), a powerful oral antipsychotic drug (BNF category 4.2.1), which has been on the scene since the 1960s. Clinical trials in the United Kingdom were stopped in 1975, when reports from abroad indicated a serious risk that patients might develop the potentially fatal side effect of agranulocytosis (a fall in the white cell count). However, its use went on in over twenty countries where it had already been approved, and it proved effective in giving relief from severe chronic schizophrenia to some patients who had previously shown little response to conventional antipsychotic medication. The drug underwent something of a rehabilitation in Britain in the late 1980s. It received a product licence in 1989 from the Committee on the Safety of Medicines, on condition that the manufacturers carry out a strictly controlled programme of haematological monitoring for each patient.[49] Sandoz will not release Clozapine in quantities above the BNF recommended maximum, which is currently 900 mg daily in divided doses, and restrict its use to patients registered with the Clozaril Patient Monitoring Service, requiring weekly blood sampling for the first eighteen weeks of treatment, and fortnightly sampling thereafter. If the early signs of agranulocytosis develop, the supply of tablets is immediately withdrawn.

The MHAC has issued a guidance note on Clozaril indicating that blood monitoring is authorised by section 58 as part and parcel of the treatment for mental disorder since 'it is necessary and appropriate to ensure that medicine for mental disorder is administered efficaciously and safely in accordance with good medical practice'.[50] The guidance says that the degree of resistance and its origins (for example religious objections), should be taken into account by RMOs and SOADs in deciding whether to authorise the treatment. Where the RMO is deciding whether to give Clozapine within the three month 'stabilising period', the decision to override an active refusal is one for his or her clinical judgment.[51]

In the first case where authority to give Clozapine was withheld, the full range of other drug therapy had not been tried, and there had been no attempt to work with the family. The SOAD felt that the patient's father's consent to the treatment was essential. In the other, the patient had a long history of not responding to neuroleptics. He accepted his current medication, but refused blood tests. Because of the uncertainties, 'the RMO agreed to postpone consideration of Clozapine pending further assessment and legal advice'.

In cases where a Form 39 is refused, the RMO can still ask for another second opinion within a short time, if the patient's condition deteriorates. The Code of Practice emphasises the importance of SOAD and RMO making every effort to reach agreement, and if they do not, for the SOAD to inform the RMO personally and to give reasons.[52] The SOADs' decisions are their own personal responsibility, and cannot be appealed against. However, if the patient's situation subsequently changes, the RMO may request a further second opinion, and the MHAC's policy is to ask the same SOAD to return.[53] There were five cases in this survey where Form 39 was issued on a revisit after an initial refusal of authority to treat.

In addition to the thirty-six cases where Form 39 was refused, there were seven where 'significant changes' were recorded in the treatment plan. In one, the SOAD authorised a more permissive plan than that requested by the RMO, who had proposed a course of up to three ECTs, anxiolytics and antipsychotic medication for a seventy-three-year-old woman. The SOAD suggested up to six ECTs to give 'extra flexibility' and the addition of antidepressant medication. The other six cases involved antipsychotic drugs. One concerned Pimozide, the others Clozapine.

Following thirteen sudden deaths from cardiac failure of patients being treated with Pimozide, the Committee for the Safety of Medicines recommends ECG before treatment in all patients, and periodic ECGs in patients having doses above 16 mg daily. The BNF maximum was reduced from 60 mg to 20 mg daily in August 1990. In the Pimozide case, the second opinion may have saved the patient's life, because the RMO had proposed to give the drug at up to one and a half times BNF maximum. Because the patient had heart problems, the SOAD was only prepared to approve it within BNF limits.

One of the five Clozapine cases involved an aggressive refusal by the patient who said he would fight blood monitoring. The SOAD believed, erroneously, that the manufacturers would not release the drug for use with non-consenting patients. In another, the RMO wanted permission for 12 ECTs and Clozapine. Authority was given for ECT and the antipsychotic drug Modecate at up to twice the BNF recommended maximum. The other three cases involved requests for Clozaril in conjunction with depot antipsychotic medication. The manufacturer's data sheet advises against using Clozaril with depot antipsychotics which cannot be removed from the body quickly in situations where this may be required. In one, the SOAD refused to add Clozapine to the anxiolytics and oral and depot antipsychotics already authorised, but advised the RMO that it might be considered in future if the patient's progress came to a halt. In the other two, where the patients had previously been on high doses of other neuroleptics, the SOADs authorised the addition of Clozapine to the treatment plan but required a reduction in the doses of the other neuroleptics.

There were sixty case of 'slight changes', but only eleven (eight drugs and three ECT) involved the SOAD authorising less than the RMO had asked for. Thirteen 'slight changes' were to a more permissive plan of treatment. The remaining thirty-five made no substantive difference, being technical changes, such as that the RMO had not asked for a maximum number of ECTs and the SOAD had authorised up to twelve, recording this as a slight change.

Allowing for refusals of Form 39 for technical legal reasons or because the patient had improved or was consenting, the concordance rate found by this study was 96 per cent. Although the significant changes were indeed significant, there was a tendency on the part of SOADs to record as slight changes alterations which were trivial or which had no effect on the treatment proposal. Such a high concordance rate is not really surprising, given the criteria to be applied by the SOADs. As the MHAC explained it in 1987:

> [S]econd opinions prove generally to be requested in respect of well-established and widely agreed treatment procedures, and the role of the appointed doctor is not to impose his own views as to which treatment can properly be supported as ... acceptable.[54]

211

The House of Commons Special Standing Committee expressed the view that when a second opinion had been given to authorise a course of treatment without consent, the authorisation should not, in Kenneth Clarke's words, be 'a timeless authorisation for the treatment to continue, but should be subject to a periodic review'.[55] The suggestion for periodic review came from representatives of the psychiatric profession themselves. Section 61 of the 1983 Act requires the RMO to furnish a progress report on Form MHAC 1 to the MHAC each time the detention of a patient who has had a second opinion is renewed.[56] The reports are then monitored by the MHAC National Standing Committee (NSC) on Consent, which decides whether to send another SOAD to visit the patient. A report may also be required at any other time if directed by the MHAC. In 1985 the MHAC announced that, 'to ensure a proper and independent assessment', on receipt of a MHAC 1 they would send a different SOAD 'to determine whether treatment ought to continue in the light of the facts at that time'.[57] Each time detention was renewed a SOAD would again be sent, unless a multidisciplinary committee of commissioners had good reasons for not doing so. The MHAC *Third Biennial Report* announced a change.[58] Although automatic revisits by SOADs on the first MHAC 1 continue, further revisits are at the discretion of the MHAC Consent NSC, which always has a doctor present. Current policy states that there may be a revisit if there have been 'several' MHAC 1s since the last SOAD visit.

The main obstacle to effective monitoring is that there seem to be many cases where no MHAC 1s are sent in. The *Fourth Biennial Report* noted that, whereas some hospitals had been submitting reports regularly every few months, others had submitted very few, and reminded hospital managers of their obligations.[59] If a second opinion is not followed by a MHAC 1 report, the MHAC has no way of knowing whether the patient has been discharged, is now consenting, or through an oversight has been denied the opportunity of further review. Commissioners visiting hospitals are asked to ensure that MHAC 1s have been sent in where necessary.

MHAC policy is that, where the dose is above BNF limits, there will not necessarily be a visit by a SOAD when the MHAC 1 is submitted, but the case must be referred to the MHAC Consent NSC for 'decision and action'. Of the 232 MHAC 1 cases examined as part of this study, 30 involved doses above BNF, and a

SOAD was asked to revisit in only 14 of these. In one of the cases where, strangely, no revisit happened, the patient was on a cocktail of different antipsychotic drugs, some at doses above BNF, and also Clozapine – which was not authorised on her Form 39.

SOADs may give a time limit to their approval for a treatment which requires a progress report before the next renewal of detention is due. In twelve cases from the MHAC 2 study, SOADs asked for a further review within three months. The reasons for this varied. In two cases it was due to the strength of the patient's refusal, one where the patient was described as needing several staff to hold her down while being given her depot injection. In eight cases (two of which involved polypharmacy as well as high doses) it was because the patient was receiving doses of medication in excess of BNF limits and there were worries about potential side effects. For the other two, although the doses were within the BNF range, the SOADs were concerned about polypharmacy and possible side effects. In the eight cases where the SOADs time-limited their approval of high-dose medication, the patients were receiving combinations of drugs from more than one BNF category in doses above BNF limits, and in four cases the doses were between three and six times BNF. Of the high-dose cases where treatment was authorised but early review was not asked for, two involved Clozapine with high doses of depot neuroleptics, which, as we have seen, the data sheet warns against.

SOADs asked for an early revisit in some cases, and others which merited a revisit because of high doses or polypharmacy were picked up by the 'automatic revisit on the first MHAC 1' rule. However, a significant number of high-dose cases (sixteen out of thirty) were not revisited. A prime concern behind the enactment of section 61 was to ensure that patients were not subject to heavy drug régimes for prolonged periods. There is, therefore, a strong case for tightening up the MHAC policy regarding revisits, so that they are more effectively targeted on the cases where a close review of the situation is warranted by the nature of the treatment, the dosage levels, or for other specific reasons.

The theory of the second opinion procedures is that they offer a safeguard for patients in respect of treatments deemed to carry particular risks. Whilst it is true that section 57 provides an important protection, in that the most controversial treatments cannot be given without consent, the main role of Part IV is to provide clear legal authority to treat detained patients without their consent. Section 63 provides that any 'medical treatment for mental disorder' not specifically identified as requiring a second opinion, may be given to a detained patient without consent by or under the direction of the RMO. 'Medical treatment for mental disorder' is defined broadly to include 'nursing, and care, habilitation and rehabilitation under medical supervision', extending beyond those treatments which require a second opinion. In Lord Elton's words, section 63 was included 'to put the legal position beyond doubt ... for the sake of the psychiatrists, nurses and other staff who care for these very troubled patients'.[60] When faced with the criticism that this provision might authorise a disturbingly wide range of interventions, Lord Elton emphasised that it did not apply to 'borderline' or 'experimental' treatments but 'things which a person in hospital for treatment ought to undergo for his own good and for the good of the running of the hospital and for the good of other patients ... perfectly routine, sensible treatment'.[61] In fact subsequent case law has established that forcible feeding of anorexic patients is treatment for mental disorder within the meaning of section 145(1) of the 1983 Act, and may therefore be given without the patient's consent under section 63 (see pp. 265–267).[62]

Despite the importance attached to consent seeking in the Code of Practice, the purpose of the section 58 second opinion is clearly not to uphold the autonomy of the patient, since detained patients' wishes may be overridden, and the treatment decision taken for them. But once we allow treatment decisions to be taken on behalf of patients rather than by patients themselves, we create problems of a different order from those normally associated with consent, which have to do with patients' rights to be given information. Whilst competent patients may be told about a risk and decide for themselves whether to run it, where proxy decision makers take decisions for patients they must decide where the patients' interests lie, and to how much risk it is legitimate to subject them in the interests of therapy. The debates show that what many Parliamentarians thought they were introducing was protection for patients against hazardous treatment, a mechanism to ensure that treatment was truly in their best interests. What they actually did was to introduce a system to ensure that treatments given without consent accorded with *a* body of psychiatric opinion, hence raising the question of the extent of risk of un-wanted effects of treatment which psychiatric opinion is prepared to accept on its patients' behalf.

There was evidence of surprisingly frequent use of high-dose medication. Sixty-three (12 per cent) of the 519 second opinions for medicine in the MHAC 2 sample involved dosage above BNF limits, forty-six males and seventeen females. Sixteen patients receiving above BNF were in special hospitals, and sixteen in Regional Secure Units.[63] The thirty-seven non-offender patients receiving doses above BNF were detained under section 3. In twenty-three cases the SOAD expressed the maximum permitted dose in terms of a multiple of the BNF limit, and in some cases authority was given for up to two or three times the limit. In five cases the treatment authorised was up to one and a half times BNF. In thirteen cases it was up to twice BNF. In one case, authority was given for up to three times and in two cases, four times the BNF limit. The record was held by a young man of unknown ethnicity having oral antipsychotics up to six times BNF, depot antispychotics up to four times BNF and anxiolytics at up to three times the limit, for whom the SOAD asked for a review in three months.[64]

Thirty of the MHAC 1 cases (12.9 per cent) involved doses above BNF.[65] Eleven were in special hospitals, ten in secure units, and nine in local NHS hospitals.[66] The majority (eighteen) were detained under section 3, and nine were subject to hospital orders, two with restrictions.[67] Where the authority to give drugs was expressed in multiples of the BNF maximum, two cases were up to one and a half times BNF,[68] nine were up to twice the limit,[69] and three were up to three times BNF.[70] In one case the SOAD authorised up to eight times BNF maximum doses of 4.2.1 anti-psychotics, and four times BNF of anxiolytics.[71]

The MHAC *Third Biennial Report* noted the views of some SOADs that black patients may be more likely than others to be given drug doses in excess of BNF recommended levels:

> [T]he Commission is concerned to find ... that the use of high levels of medication is more common than may be expected. A number of second opinion doctors in the Southern Region of the Commission have the impression that this is the case for some Afro-Caribbean patients in the hospitals they have visited.[72]

They recognised the public sensitivity of the issue and said they would be paying it attention in the next two years. However, the next Biennial Report simply records that the MHAC monitoring group reviews reports authorising compulsory treatments with higher than usual doses of medication and long courses of ECT with particular care, and that 'the Commission does not set any arbitrary limit to treatment, this being entirely a matter for the professional judgment of the patient's RMO and the appointed doctor'.[73]

The controversy has intensified following the deaths of three Afro-Caribbean patients in seclusion in Broadmoor Hospital after heavy doses of sedative medication, and also since the case of Randoph Ince, an Afro-Caribbean patient who was the subject of a television documentary in 1991, and who suffered severe side effects from very high doses of regular medication.[74] During 1985 this patient was given doses of the drugs Chlorpromazine and Haloperidol considerably in excess of the BNF recommended upper limits. He suffered serious physical side effects, including breast growth and lactation. In 1985, a SOAD, fearing that the patient's life might be at risk, refused the RMO permission for a further increase in the dose of Chlorpromazine to 6000 mg per day (six times the BNF recommended maximum) and Haloperidol Decanoate to 4000 mg per month (almost thirteen times the BNF recommended maximum). In this survey, because some of the SOADs did not return information about patients' ethnic origins, it was not possible to reach any firm conclusions about ethnicity and high-dose medication.

The most striking aspect of the medication cases was the surprisingly high number of occasions where BNF recommended dose limits were exceeded (12 per cent of the medicines cases), and in a small number of cases the very large margin by which they were exceeded. However, because of widespread use of polypharmacy and the way in which treatment is authorised, the cases where SOADs recorded doses in excess of BNF significantly underrepresent the extent of high-dose medication without consent. At the time of writing, the MHAC has asked SOADs to specify a maximum number of different drugs from each BNF category on the Form 39.

Clozapine, hailed in the same magazines and the same terms used for psychosurgery as the answer to schizophrenia, provides an interesting example of how a manufacturer can impose some control over the administration of a drug, to ensure that it is not given in doses above BNF limits, and to see that patients' blood count is monitored. This control is not complete, however. One aspect of concern is the potential interaction between Clozapine and other antipsychotic drugs. Where the Form 39 authorises treatment in terms of '4.2.1 including Clozapine within BNF limits' it permits giving Clozapine in conjunction with other antipsychotic drugs, as long as the doses of the individual drugs are within BNF limits. Some SOADs were not prepared to authorise Clozapine with depot antipsychotics. Others were. The clinical authority established so expansively by the 1959 Act may have been subjected to new decision-making procedures, but these are based on peer review according to *Bolam* criteria. The personnel involved in the decision to treat without consent have definitely changed. But has the substance of the decisions that are made also been altered? This is difficult to judge. It is often said that the existence of the second opinion procedures may deter doctors from putting up proposals for outlandish treatment plans. It does not seem to inhibit treatment plans which require megadoses of drugs, so it is difficult to judge whether the substance of decisions about treatment without consent has been altered by Part IV.

13

EMERGENCY SEDATION, SECLUSION AND RESTRAINT IN CONTEMPORARY PSYCHIATRY

In recent years concern has grown about the use of antipsychotic drugs as major tranquillisers for emergency sedation, and for behaviour control where patients have no psychotic symptoms. Some SOADs in the MHAC 2 study described antipsychotic medication for mentally impaired patients as being for 'behaviour control'. In January 1994 it was alleged that in Ashworth Hospital, patients diagnosed as personality disordered or mentally impaired were being given antipsychotic medication not as a treatment for illness but as a means of controlling behaviour by keeping them sedated.[1] These cases were drawn to the attention of the authorities by a team of MHAC visitors to the hospital. An independent consultant forensic psychiatrist brought in by the hospital recommended reduction in the drug doses. Nursing staff said that the patients' behaviour on high doses of medication had been aggressive and violent. When the medication was reduced, patients suffered severe withdrawal symptoms and became even more aggressive, suggesting that these are drugs of dependence.

The Code of Practice states that the control of behaviour by medication requires careful consideration, and warns that 'medication which begins as purely therapeutic may, by prolonged routine administration, become a method of restraint. . . . Medication should not be used as an alternative to adequate staffing levels.'[2] The Ashworth Committee of Inquiry, which reported in 1992, commented on the use of 'sledgehammer' medicines, acknowledging that there were 'no doubt occasions when patients will benefit', but 'in the absence of treatable psychotic symptoms, these medicines should surely play a very minor part in an overall treatment plan'.[3]

Since the mid-1980s there have been three highly publicised cases in Broadmoor special hospital where Afro-Caribbean patients have died in seclusion having been given injections of emergency sedative medication. Michael Martin's death in 1984 followed an injection of what was described in Broadmoor nursing slang as a 'five and two'; 500 mg of Sodium Amylobarbitone (Sodium Amytal) and 200 mg of Promazine (Sparine), both of which have a very powerful sedative effect. The BNF recommended maximum of Sodium Amylobarbitone is 500 mg, and for individual doses of Promazine 50 mg at six-hourly intervals. The inquiry into Michael Martin's death found that:

> The nurses acted in accordance with a general understanding that existed at the time between the RMO and nursing staff that in an emergency and in the case of particular patients the drug could be administered by senior nursing staff and their action ratified subsequently by the RMO.[4]

The medical director subsequently issued an instruction that any emergency medication had to be prescribed in advance, and could not be 'prescribed' after administration.

In 1988 Joe Watts died in seclusion following an injection of 200 mg of Chlorpromazine (four times the BNF recommended maximum of 50 mg every six to eight hours). There was some speculation at the inquest that the Chlorpromazine might have been accidentally injected into a vein and stopped his heart. In 1990, another black patient, Orville Blackwood, died in seclusion after having two injections, one of 150 mg of Promazine (Sparine), and the other of 150 mg of Fluphenazine Decanoate (Modecate).[5]

These cases raise the question of the level of protection afforded to patients by section 62, which is intended to allow treatment to be given if a second opinion cannot be arranged sufficiently speedily to cope with an emergency, whilst at the same time protecting patients against hazardous or irreversible treatments, unless their own lives are in serious danger or their health is about to suffer serious deterioration. Section 62 authorises emergency treatment to be given without prior compliance with the second opinion procedures, stating that sections 57 and 58 do not apply to any treatment:

(a) which is immediately necessary to save the patient's life; or
(b) which (not being irreversible) is immediately necessary to prevent a serious deterioration in his condition; or
(c) which (not being irreversible or hazardous) is immediately necessary to alleviate serious suffering by the patient; or
(d) which (not being irreversible or hazardous) is immediately necessary and represents the minimum interference necessary to prevent the patient behaving violently or being a danger to himself or others.

The MHAC has consistently maintained that, where it is invoked, a request should simultaneously be made for a second opinion, 'so that repeated use does not arise',[6] noting in their *First Biennial Report* a case where no fewer than twelve ECT treatments were given to a patient under section 62.[7]

The Code of Practice stresses that the treatment must be given by or under the direction of the RMO, and must be necessary to achieve one of the objects specified in the section. It is insufficient for it simply to be 'necessary' or 'beneficial'.[8] A treatment is deemed irreversible if it has unfavourable physical or psychological consequences which cannot be righted, and hazardous if it entails 'significant physical hazard'.[9] The Code of Practice states that the RMO is responsible for deciding whether a treatment is irreversible or hazardous, 'having regard to mainstream medical opinion'.[10] We have already seen how there is a long tradition in psychiatry of bias towards benefit over risk. Where a treatment is immediately necessary to prevent serious suffering on the part of the patient or to prevent him or her from acting violently or from endangering him- or herself or others, it must be neither irreversible nor hazardous.

Section 62 offered no protection to Michael Martin, Joe Watts or Orville Blackwood. Although the Code of Practice makes the RMO responsible for treatment under its provisions, the Prins Report on the death of Orville Blackwood found that a junior doctor considered himself to have the power to use the provision. Although the Committee thought that the associate specialist's decision to give drugs could be seen as a misuse of section 62, they felt that, in fairness to him, the Code was not 'as specific as it might be in relation to who is empowered to act in emergency in the RMO's absence'.[11] The cases which have ended in tragedy have tended to involve emergency medicine being given by junior medical staff or nurses.

In the Blackwood case it was not clear which of the heads of section 62 was being used to justify the treatment. If the purported reason for the emergency sedation was that the patient needed to be stopped from behaving violently or endangering himself or others, there must be doubt as to whether the limits imposed by section 62(1)(d) had been observed. First the treatment must be immediately necessary and represent the minimum interference necessary to prevent the patient from behaving violently or being a danger to him- or herself or others. The evidence before the Committee included case notes which said vaguely that Blackwood was 'again getting disturbed', whilst the nursing notes described him as uncommunicative. It was also suggested that he was lying on the bed and may even have been asleep when the doctor and the nurses entered the seclusion room. If this was so, it is hard to see how the treatment can have been immediately necessary to prevent him from behaving violently or being a danger to others, let alone how it can have been the minimum necessary to do so.

Treatment used to prevent violence must be neither hazardous nor irreversible. It is difficult to accept that a dose of intramuscular antipsychotic of three times the BNF recommended maximum, given in conjunction with a depot antipsychotic (when the BNF recommends that more than one antipsychotic should not be given at the same time) could be viewed as entailing anything other than a significant physical hazard. Of course, the doctor might have justified the treatment under section 62(1)(b) which allows treatment that is not irreversible to be given if it is immediately necessary to prevent serious deterioration in the patient's condition. This is what makes contemporaneous record keeping so important. It requires the doctor authorising the treatment to address his or her mind to the nature of the emergency, to judge whether the treatment he or she is giving is indeed immediately necessary, and to know whether it is hazardous or irreversible. Where there is no contemporaneous record, there is a danger that section 62 may be used as an *ex post facto* rationalisation. It also leaves open the possibility that restrictive interventions such as seclusion or even emergency medication may be resorted to as a means of teaching the patient a lesson.

The Code of Practice urges hospital managers to ensure that a form is devised to monitor the use of section 62, to be completed by the patient's RMO every time urgent treatment is given, recording details of the proposed treatment; why it is of urgent necessity to give it; and the length of time for which it is given.[12] The *Fifth Biennial Report* noted that although hospitals have been asked to do this for at least five years, 'many ... have still not instituted an effective recording system', particularly when the treatment involved is medicine.[13]

Concern has continued about patient deaths following the administration of major tranquillisers, and not just in Broadmoor or the other special hospitals. Two female patients have died in Horton Hospital following high doses of major tranquillisers.[14] In July 1990 Gina Ditchman died following high doses of major tranquillisers. The MHAC's request in January 1992 to the health authority to set up an independent inquiry into her death was turned down. In March 1993 came the inquest of Elizabeth Jenkinson, who died following several intravenous injections of Clopixol and Droperidol. She had 90 mg of Droperidol over a twelve-hour period, three times the amount recommended on the manufacturer's data sheet. The coroner forwarded a report to the Committee on the Safety of Medicines, the Secretary of State for Health, and the health authority.

The Prins Committee has recently called on the Department of Health to establish a research project to investigate the link between phenothiazine drugs (particularly Chlorpromazine and Promazine) and sudden death in psychiatric patients. They also expressed concern about the increased risk of an intra-muscular sedative entering the vein of a patient who is struggling, and recommended that wherever possible injecting struggling patients should be avoided. Where it could not be avoided, extreme caution should be exercised.[15]

The MHAC have expressed worries about treatment purportedly being given under section 62 when the patient is either not detained or is held under the short-term holding powers to which the section does not apply.[16] There were two cases in the MHAC 2 survey where informal patients were given ECT, purportedly under section 62. The MHAC also note cases of emergency treatment being given to disturbed patients by relatively unskilled staff under common law, and whilst they view such treatment as falling outside their statutory remit, they have urged 'a careful audit'. They have also invited the Royal College of Psychiatrists to extend its study of homicides and suicides to include the deaths of patients being treated in emergency situations.[17] A small survey of reports by commissioners who visited inquests of detained patients revealed two cases where patients had died in seclusion within the first week of admission following administration of doses of Chlorpromazine PRN of well over the BNF maximum (in one case 3000 mg, and in the other 1200 mg). In neither case had the patient been seen by a consultant psychiatrist.[18]

The limits on hazardous treatments in section 62 do not offer adequate protection for patients for three principal reasons. First, there appears to be a tendency on the part of doctors to see it as permissive rather than restrictive. Second, the section does not apply to patients who are detained under powers authorising detention for seventy-two hours or less, such as the doctor's holding power or the emergency admission for assessment under section 4.[19] In such cases, the Code of Practice suggests that authority for emergency treatment may be found in common law: 'on rare occasions involving emergencies where it is not possible immediately to apply the provisions of the . . . Act the common law authorises such treatment as represents the minimum necessary to avert behaviour by the patient that is an immediate serious danger to self or to other people'.[20] On this view, where patients are treated under common law the prohibition on hazardous treatments does not appear to apply. The third weakness of section 62 in medicine cases is that, where patients are detained under longer-term powers, medicines may be given without consent during the three-month 'stabilising period' at the direction of the RMO, and without the need for a second opinion. Only four of the 116 uses of section 62 in the MHAC 2 sample were for medicines; three by men and one by a woman. Two occurred because the three-month stabilising period period had elapsed and the RMO had not requested a second opinion in time, and in the other two the patients had withdrawn consent. Very often emergency sedation is given in the period immediately following admission. After three months, the MHAC view is that PRN medication for which the patient's consent cannot be anticipated should be included by the SOAD on the Form 39. Since Form 39 certificates are widely drafted to authorise treatment in terms of BNF categories of drug, this is not an effective safeguard. Once there has been a second opinion which includes the PRN medication, section 58 has been complied with and there is no need for recourse to section 62.

Sixty-nine of the 232 MHAC 1 patients were prescribed PRN sedation on the Form 39, forty-five were written up for Chlorpromazine, and 24 Haloperidol. In thirty-seven Chlorpromazine cases the dose was 100 mg, in four it was 150 mg, and in the remaining four it was 200 mg oral or intramuscular. In each case the MHAC 1 gave the dose with the indication 'O/IM', meaning that it could be given orally or by intramuscular injection. It is generally viewed as bad prescribing practice to specify the same dose for oral or intramuscular antipsychotic drugs, because intramuscular drugs are much more quick acting. This is reflected in the BNF recommended maxima for each route. If given orally, the BNF usual maintenance dose is 75–300 mg daily, but up to a gram may be required in psychosis. If given by intramuscular injection the BNF dose for relief of acute symptoms is 25–50 mg every six to eight hours. Haloperidol was also invariably prescribed as to be given 'O/IM'. In ten cases it was to be given in doses of 10 mg, in five cases the dose was 5–10 mg, in three cases 10–20 mg, and in the remaining six, 20 mg.

An important question in deciding the level of protection offered to patients by the law is the extent to which a doctor is legally liable after prescribing high-dose antipsychotic PRN medication which causes injury to the patient. The defence in section 139 of the 1983 Act would apply, so there could be no liability of any kind without bad faith or negligence. For criminal proceedings the leave of the Director of Public Prosecutions would be required, and there could be no criminal liability for homicide without intent to injure or gross negligence.[21] In a civil action the plaintiff would have to show that the death resulted from a breach of the RMO's duty to act in accordance with a responsible body of medical opinion that is skilled in the speciality. This would be difficult to establish, since high-dose neuroleptics appear to be in wide use as emergency sedation, and even the Consensus Statement admits of a significant number of exceptional cases. The Code of Practice has tried to tilt the common-law test in the patient's favour by saying that, in deciding whether a treatment is hazardous, doctors should have regard to 'mainstream' medical opinion. But there appear to be many streams of opinion, not just the one. There can be no doubt that section 62 is ineffective in protecting patients from high doses of emergency medication in circumstances where their wellbeing and even their lives may be just as seriously at risk from the treatment as they would be if they were left untreated. Although section 62 was intended to balance the need for treatment in emergencies with the protection of patients from dangerous treatments, it is seen by many doctors as a wide-ranging power. Its use is not subject to proper monitoring and, in many cases that involve medicine, authority to treat can be found in provisions which do not prohibit hazardous treatment.

The European Convention too offers little protection against chemical restraint if it is carried out in accordance with accepted medical practice. In *Herczegfalvy* v. *Austria*[22] Herczegfalvy complained to the Strasbourg Court that his treatment with heavy doses of sedative medication breached Articles 3 and 8 of the Convention. The Court declared that 'the position of inferiority and powerlessness which is typical of patients confined in psychiatric hospitals calls for increased vigilance in reviewing whether the Convention has been complied with',[23] and in principle, medical treatment without consent could amount to inhuman and degrading treatment contrary to Article 3 which permits of no derogation. However, it was for the medical authorities to decide, 'on the basis of recognised rules of medical science, on the therapeutic methods to be used, if necessary by force, to preserve the physical and mental health of patients who are entirely incapable of deciding for themselves'.[24] Whilst proclaiming that the principles of medicine were 'in principle decisive' and that a measure which was 'a therapeutic necessity' could not be inhuman or degrading, the court was nevertheless bound to satisfy itself that medical necessity had been convincingly shown to exist. In this case, Article 3 had not been breached. Moreover, the Court dismissed the complaint of infringement of the right of privacy under Article 8 by Herczegfalvy's treatment without consent, since he had not produced evidence to contradict the contention that he lacked capacity at the material times to make his own treatment decisions. Individuals who wish to show a breach of Article 8 must establish that they were treated without consent notwithstanding that they had the necessary capacity to decide for themselves.[25]

Seclusion continues to occupy a 'twilight zone' between medical treatment and coercion. After the 1959 Act it ceased to be defined and regulated in delegated legislation, but despite its disappearance from the statute book, seclusion was still widely practised. In 1974, in *A* v. *United Kingdom*,[26] a Broadmoor patient complained to the European Commission on Human Rights of an infringement of the prohibition on inhuman or degrading treatment in Article 3 of the European Convention. He stated that he had been kept in seclusion for five weeks with only limited opportunities for exercise and association. Treatment will be inhuman only if it reaches a level of gravity involving considerable mental or physical suffering, and degrading if the person has undergone humiliation or debasement involving a minimum level of severity.[27]

The Commission declared the complaint admissible and visited Broadmoor in 1977. A friendly settlement was reached. The UK Government undertook to introduce a new seclusion policy for the hospital, including an undertaking that seclusion rooms would have not less than 4.7 square metres floor space and would have natural lighting. Patients secluded for longer than three hours would have a programme of care drawn up for them, to be reviewed daily. Patients were to be observed at irregular intervals not exceeding fifteen minutes. Written records of the patient's condition were to be kept in a special book. If the patient was secluded for more than twenty-four hours, the hospital management team should be informed, and if the seclusion lasted for more than seven days, the hospital managers again had to be informed.[28]

The publication in 1990 of the first edition of the *Mental Health Act Code of Practice* marked an important step in the bringing of seclusion to the fold of central regulation. The Code contained detailed recommendations on the use of seclusion and the content of local seclusion policies. Seclusion was defined as the supervised confinement of a patient alone in a room which may be locked for the protection of others from serious harm. The Code emphasised that it should not be used as a punitive measure or to enforce good behaviour.[29] Although not prepared to consider seclusion as a treatment technique which might be included in any treatment programme, the authors of the Code viewed it as falling within the definition of medical treatment for the purposes of section 145 of the 1983 Act. If it is medical treatment in the legal sense, it may be carried out without consent at the direction of the RMO under section 63 of the Act. An alternative view is that the legal justification for seclusion arises from the common-law power to detain for the purposes of preventing a breach of the peace, a detention which must cease when the risk has passed.[30] Whatever view is taken, the problems of unravelling the punitive and the protective elements in seclusion remain as intractable as ever.

The Code specifies that hospitals should have clear written guidelines for the use of seclusion, 'to ensure the safety and wellbeing of the patient in a dignified and humane environment'.[31] Their content is remarkably similar to the guidelines promulgated by the Lunacy Commissioners and the Board of Control, declaring seclusion to be a last resort, insisting that the decision be taken by senior staff and requiring frequent observation. The decision to seclude may be made by a doctor, the nurse in charge of the ward, a nursing officer or a senior nursing officer. When the decision is taken by someone other than a doctor, arrangements must be made immediately for a doctor to attend. A nurse must be available within sight and sound of the seclusion room at all times, and present with a patient who has been sedated. The patient is to be observed at intervals not exceeding fifteen minutes, the aim being to ascertain the patient's condition and whether seclusion may be terminated. If it needs to continue, nursing reviews must be carried out every two hours and a doctor must review the case every four hours. After eight hours an independent review team must be brought in. The Code also requires that seclusion should be in a safe, secure and properly identified room, where the patient cannot harm him- or herself, with adequate heating, lighting, ventilation, opportunities for staff observation and protection of privacy from other patients. The patient should always be clothed. Detailed records are to be kept, and the use of seclusion is to be monitored by the managers of the hospital. The Code strategy is to set up a procedure to limit and monitor the use of seclusion.

The rights of people who are already lawfully detained to challenge their solitary confinement have been considered in a number of cases. At one point it seemed as though the courts might recognise that the lawfully detained still possess a residual liberty and could be protected against wrongful seclusion by an action for unlawful imprisonment. In *Furber* v. *Kratter* a special hospital patient who had been secluded for sixteen days following an attack on a nurse was given leave under section 139 of the 1983 Act to pursue her claim for unlawful imprisonment.[32] The case was based on the grounds that an imprisonment which was initially lawful could be rendered unlawful if the patient was kept in conditions which were seriously prejudicial to her health.

However, before the main action could come to trial, the House of Lords held in *R* v. *Deputy Governor of Parkhurst ex parte Hague*[33] that where a prisoner is segregated under rule 43 of the Prison Rules 1964, deterioration in the conditions in which a detainee is held cannot amount to false imprisonment. Moreover, the House held that in the absence of a clear intention in the Prison Act or the Prison Rules to create rights for prisoners, no action for breach of statutory duty could lie in respect of a failure to comply with their provisions. In a case where a prisoner or patient claims to have been secluded wrongfully, and to have suffered injury as a result, the correct cause of action is negligence.[34] Although a person's detention in intolerable conditions will not render the imprisonment unlawful if the custody itself is lawful, custodians owe a duty of care to detainees which will be breached if they negligently allow or deliberately cause the detainee's health to suffer. Moreover, if a lawfully detained person is kept in conditions which cause physical pain or give a degree of physical discomfort that could properly be described as intolerable even though it stops short of physical injury or impairment of health, damages may still be available for breach of the custodian's duty of care.[35]

Lord Goff accepted that an action in negligence was available in such circumstances, but 'only in respect of the types of damage which, on accepted legal principles, give rise to such an action'.[36] The need to show 'intolerable' conditions is a significant hurdle for potential plaintiffs, approaching the severity of the European Convention standard of inhuman or degrading treatment.[37] Even though there is no legal duty to comply with the Code of Practice,[38] failure to follow it may be referred to in an action for breach of the custodian's duty of care. The seclusion of a patient naked in an inadequately heated room would clearly amount to intolerable conditions. Seclusion in an unsafe room or failure properly to observe a patient who sustains injury as a result would also give rise to a negligence action. However, the availability of legal remedies does not address the problem that seclusion has serious psychological effects when it is prolonged, and even when it is not. Also, many of the patients who have died following high doses of major tranquillisers were in seclusion at the time.

It is difficult to control the use of seclusion for improper reasons. In 1987 and 1988 special hospital patients at Moss Side and Broadmoor were placed in seclusion as a result of industrial action by the Prison Officers' Association (POA).[39] Successive MHAC biennial reports refer to the extensive use of seclusion in Broadmoor, particularly for women on the high dependency wards who at times were spending long periods in isolation, in some cases more than a year.[40] MHAC teams of visitors to Broadmoor examined seclusion during 1991 and 1992, expressing their concern at its continued high incidence, and in particular the length of individual episodes.[41] The Code of Practice appeared not to have been followed. Records were not properly kept, and the required reviews by doctors were not evident. In many cases seclusion continued even though the patient was reported as 'quiet and co-operative', suggesting that it was not being used only when strictly necessary as a preventive measure.

There is a growing body of research evidence to prove what the Lunacy Commission knew in 1850, that the need for seclusion reduces with the provision of adequate staffing levels.[42] Just as, in the 1850s, the Lunacy Commission attempted to ensure that seclusion was not used as a means of achieving 'economy of attendants', the Code of Practice emphasises that it should not be used as a method of coping with staff shortages, reflecting concern that it may be used at times of industrial action in special hospitals as well as to combat inadequate staffing levels in general.

Concerns about the abuse of seclusion as a punishment have led to calls for its abolition. The committee of inquiry into complaints about Ashworth Special Hospital commented on its frequency and said that it appeared to be used as 'corrective isolation'.[43] They heard conflicting evidence from forensic psychiatrists as to the necessity for seclusion. Because there is no effective method of ensuring that it is not used punitively, the committee advocated that it be phased out as unnecessary, and because it should not be used in the care of mentally disordered people. They felt that it ought to be prohibited by statute.[44]

The prospects of achieving such a ban seem remote. In December 1993 the Special Hospital Services Authority (SHSA) issued guidelines stating that seclusion in a locked room should be rare, used only in response to disturbed behaviour and in a medical emergency. As an alternative, patients could be placed alone in a lockable room but not locked in. In April 1994 the POA announced that it intended to ballot its members on industrial action in protest at the new régime, which it said had been introduced without adequate staffing levels and had led to an increase in assaults on staff by patients.[45]

Although it remains an important issue in psychiatric care, physical restraint is not regulated by the 1983 Act. In 1987 the MHAC noted with 'surprise and misgivings' that restraint garments were in use at Moss Side Hospital, but did not express a corporate view. Altogether, eight patients were involved over a three-month period with a total, for all of them, of 130–135 periods of restraint per month.[46] In 1989 the MHAC reported that they had continued to examine carefully the occasions when such garments were used, and the policy governing their use. The number of patients restrained had reduced over the past two years, but one patient had been under restraint for 2,645 hours over a twelve-month period.[47] Again in 1991, the MHAC noted that four patients continued to be nursed for substantial periods in restraint garments and were pleased to learn of plans for an intensive therapy unit where these four patients could be cared for less restrictively.[48]

The 1990 version of the Code of Practice made reference to physical restraint of disturbed patients, emphasising that it should be used only as a last resort, and never as a matter of course. The type of restraint envisaged was to be carried out by nurses trained in safe methods of control and restraint, and that restraint garments or other devices should not be used on a continuing basis. In May 1992, Freda Latham, a learning disabled patient was strangled by her bib by which she had been left attached to a toilet pipe. In March 1994, the three nurses in whose care she had been were acquitted of ill treatment and wilful neglect and conspiracy to pervert the course of justice. In April 1994 the coroner recorded an open verdict.[49] The 1993 version of the Code adds an additional paragraph, clearly a response to this case, emphasising that: 'Restraint which involves tying or hooking a patient (whether by means of a tape or by using part of the patient's garments) to some part of a building or to its fixtures or fittings should never be used.'[50] The Code also envisages circumstances where restraint devices may legitimately be used, urging staff to 'make a balanced judgment between the need to promote an individual's autonomy by allowing him to move around at will, and the duty to protect him from likely harm' and stating that:

> In every case where the physical freedom of a patient is curtailed in his own interests, staff should record the decision and the reasons for it and state explicitly in a care plan under what circumstances restraint may be used, what form the restraint may take, and how it will be reviewed. Every episode of restraint must be fully documented and reviewed.[51]

The Code enjoins health authorities and NHS Trusts to have clear written policies on restraint, and to appoint a senior officer who should be informed of any patient subjected to any restraint which lasts for more than two hours. That person should see the patient as soon as is practicable and hold regular interviews thereafter to assist in putting forward any complaints which the patient may have.

Even though physical restraint by trained staff seems to be seen by the Code as less undesirable than restraint by mechanical devices it is not without its own hazards. Training in safe techniques of control and restraint has been carried out in special hospitals since the 1980s. In March 1994 an inquest jury at Nottingham returned an open verdict on the death in March 1992 of a Rampton patient, Brian Marsh, who suffered a heart attack after a struggle with nurses. 'Neck compression' and the effects of anti-depressant medication had been contributory factors. A Home Office pathologist who conducted a second post mortem on the patient said he had found bruising on his neck which indicated that he had been led in a neck lock for up to thirty seconds. The inquest heard from patients who said they saw one nurse, assisted by up to fifteen other staff, grab the patient in a neck lock and drag him backwards into the seclusion room where he died shortly afterwards.[52]

After an initial silence on continued restraint by garments or other devices, the Code of Practice has now followed the pattern adopted by the Lunacy Commission after 1890 of acknowledging that it may be necessary as a last resort, subject to observance of a procedure and to regular review. The Code's substantive provisions increase the possibility of legal redress in respect of restraint. *Pountney* v. *Griffiths*[53] established that nursing staff who exercise powers of control and restraint are acting pursuant to the Mental Health Act, so they can only be liable in criminal or civil proceedings if they act negligently or in bad faith. Prior to the 1993 revisions of the Code, it may have been possible to argue that it was not negligent to tie a patient by her clothing to a wall fixture, but such an argument would be difficult to sustain now.

In *Herczegfalvy* v. *Austria*[54] the patient was tied to a bed for a prolonged period. As with medical treatment, the court held that accepted medical practice at the time was in principle decisive, but the court would have to satisfy itself that medical necessity existed. On consideration of the facts, the court held that Article 3 had not been breached.

The ethical issues facing psychiatry at the end of the twentieth century are very similar to those facing it one hundred years ago. Although the law has abandoned direct legal regulation of seclusion and restraint, it has moved into the area of regulating treatment. There it has proved excellent at conferring broad clinical power to impose treatment. The current definition of medical treatment for mental disorder is a prime example of an 'open textured rule' capable of embracing a wide range of interventions. Once these are defined as medical treatment, their deployment becomes a matter of clinical judgment. Whilst seclusion and mechanical restraint are not treatment, they are nonetheless viewed as acceptable under the Code of Practice, provided certain procedures are observed, and in each case involving authorisation by a doctor. Accepted medical practice is the decisive factor both in a negligence action at national law, and in an action in respect of treatment or restraint based on Article 3 of the Convention. Although the Strasbourg Court will wish to verify the existence of medical necessity, the indications from *Herczegfalvy* are that quite extreme interventions may be accepted. The scope for a 'legalist' jurisprudence of treatment without consent similar to that developed by the Court of Human Rights under Article 5 in relation to detention on grounds of unsound mind appears limited at present. Statute law is proving excellent at authorising treatment without consent, and at accepting coercive practices into the fold of medical treatment. It shows no aptitude, however, for the business of ensuring that patients are not put seriously at risk by their treaters. The common law has shown itself to be no better. In the 1980s and early 1990s there was a series of cases in which common-law authority to treat incapacitated patients without consent was developed. They all involved sterilisation.

14

TREATMENT OF
INCAPABLE PATIENTS
WITHOUT CONSENT
UNDER COMMON LAW

Legislation plays a protective and empowering role for mental health professionals. It confers on them widely drawn discretionary powers, and shields doctors and others purportedly exercising compulsory powers under the legislation against any common law liability which they might otherwise incur. Common law has traditionally been seen as a 'safety net', enabling compulsory intervention for the protection of patients or other people where legislation does not provide the necessary powers. Although there were various common-law precedents on restraint of the furiously mad,[1] it was not until the late 1980s that the courts began to develop clear common-law principles governing treatment without consent, providing doctors with a flak jacket against legal liability. These developments need to be seen against the background of the more threatening guise in which the common law has traditionally been seen by mental health professionals in relation to treatment without consent, namely as a potential source of legal liability in battery or negligence.

Most of the few reported cases where doctors have been held liable in battery for treating patients without consent have involved sterilisation or depot contraception.[2] Because the tort of battery exists to protect the right of bodily autonomy, it may be committed even when the doctor believes that action is in the patient's best interests, and the plaintiff need not prove that he or she has suffered harm as a result of the treatment. Kennedy and Grubb detail the 'determined effort' by the courts in England and elsewhere to limit the scope of the tort of battery in modern medical law. Nevertheless, they also make the important point that: 'As a mechanism for compensating injured patients ... it remains a powerful symbolic and actual

233

deterrent against doctors ignoring the right of autonomy of their patients.'[3]

The limited role of battery became particularly clear in *Chatterton* v. *Gerson* (1980),[4] which established that liability existed only where the patient had been treated without any consent, or if the patient did consent that consent had been obtained by fraud or without the doctor having explained what was proposed in 'broad terms.' If there was consent following a broad explanation Bristow J. held that the correct form of action was not trespass, but negligence for failure to give sufficient information. The plaintiff had placed strong reliance on the 1972 American case of *Canterbury* v. *Spence* which established that doctors have a duty to disclose 'material risks',[5] and on the Canadian case of *Reibl* v. *Hughes*.[6] In the latter case, the Supreme Court held that a risk is material when a reasonable person, in what the physician knows or should know to be the patient's position, 'would be likely to attach significance to the risk or cluster of risks in deciding whether or not to forgo the proposed therapy'. Robertson has advanced two reasons for the emasculation of battery by the English courts. First, judicial policy 'in favour of restricting claims in battery to situations involving deliberate, hostile acts, a situation which most judges would regard as foreign to the doctor-patient relationship'.[7] Second, the 'attempt to restrict the scope of the doctrine of informed consent, principally by means of the requirement of causation, the use of expert evidence as to accepted medical practice, and emphasis of the "best interests" of the patient'.[8]

In 1985, in *Sidaway* v. *Bethlem Royal Hospital Governors*,[9] the House of Lords ruled on the test of liability in negligence where a doctor had failed to warn of risks associated with treatment. They held that the doctor-friendly *Bolam* test applied, namely that, in deciding what information to give about risks, a doctor was not negligent if he or she had acted in accordance with practice accepted at the time by a responsible body of medical opinion.[10] The courts reserve to themselves the ultimate right to decide whether a risk is so obviously material that it ought to be disclosed. However, application of the *Bolam* test means that a defendant doctor who can produce one or more responsible expert witnesses to say that they would not have disclosed the risk in question will escape liability for negligence. This is so even if the majority of doctors in the specialty would have acted differently. Accordingly,

English law rejected the 'transatlantic doctrine of informed consent'. Lords Keith and Bridge held that it was a matter for clinical judgment to decide on which risks to disclose, in order for a particular patient to make a rational choice whether or not to undergo the treatment recommended by a doctor. However, the disclosure of any risk with serious adverse consequences might be so obviously necessary for the patient to make an informed choice that no reasonably prudent doctor would fail to disclose it. A doctor was required, as part of the duty of care to the patient, to explain in a careful and responsible manner what he or she intended to do and the implications involved. However, the doctor only came under a duty to warn the patient if there was a real risk of misfortune inherent in the procedure, however well it was carried out. As long as the doctor could produce expert witnesses to show that the amount of information given or withheld accorded with a responsible body of medical opinion at the time, there would be no negligence.

The English courts have adopted a 'doctor oriented' test of disclosure, even where the patient asks questions. In 1985, in *Blyth* v. *Bloomsbury*, Leonard J. applied the dicta of Lords Keith and Bridge and held that the defendants had been negligent in not advising the plaintiff of the risks in treatment with Depo Provera, in the light of her manifest and reasonable request to be advised.[11] However, the decision was overturned in 1987 by the Court of Appeal, where it was held that the information which should be given in response to a patient's general inquiry could not be divorced from the *Bolam* test, any more than when no such inquiry is made.[12]

It seems that the United Kingdom will be the last common-law bastion of *Bolam* type tests in information disclosure. In the 1992 case of *Rogers* v. *Whitaker*, the High Court of Australia adopted the patient-oriented 'informed consent' standard of disclosure rather than the *Sidaway* approach, declaring that:

> The law should recognise that a doctor has a duty to warn a patient of a material risk inherent in the proposed treatment; a risk is material if, in the circumstances of the particular case, a reasonable person in the patient's position, if warned of the risk, would be likely to attach significance to it or if the medical practitioner is or should be aware that the particular patient, if warned of the risk, would be likely to attach significance to it.[13]

The *Bolam* standard is important not only as a yardstick in making the retrospective decision as to whether a doctor has acted negligently. It has also been introduced as the standard to be observed prospectively by doctors in deciding whether a specific treatment is in the best interests of an incapacitated patient, and whether they may therefore exercise their power to give it without consent. The power to treat incapacitated adult patients without consent in their best interests was laid down by the House of Lords in *Re F*, where a health authority applied for a High Court declaration that the sterilisation of a thirty-five-year-old mentally handicapped woman would not be unlawful because she was incapable of consenting.[14] *Re F* has provided the basis for the development of a new role for the English courts in authorising treatment without consent.

The case law on consent in the 1970s and early 1980s, and the introduction of the second opinion procedures in the 1983 Act led to increased awareness of consent issues among those treating mentally disordered people. It was also realised that the provisions of Part IV apply only to treatment for mental disorder, and do not authorise the treatment of informal patients without consent, giving rise to considerable disquiet about the legal position when treatment for mental or physical disorder was given to informal, incapacitated patients without consent. These factors undoubtedly created a climate in which test cases concerning treatment without consent at common law would inevitably be brought. The cases through which this development occurred involved sterilisations of mentally handicapped patients, and the opening up of the *parens patriae* jurisdiction in the United States had a clear influence on the process.

In the United States, the challenge concocted by the pro-sterilisation lobby in *Buck* v. *Bell*[15] clothed state eugenic sterilisation laws with constitutional authority. In 1942, after the Nazi atrocities had become fully apparent, another constitutional challenge marked a sea change in the attitude of the Supreme Court to the eugenics movement. In *Skinner* v. *Oklahoma* the Supreme Court struck down Oklahoma's law authorising the sterilisation of thrice convicted felons.[16] Although the *Skinner* ruling did not overrule *Buck* v. *Bell*, and eugenic sterilisation laws continued to operate in many states through the 1960s, and even into the 1970s,[17] the opinions of Justices Douglas and Jackson emphasised that these laws deprived individuals of their 'fundamental constitutional right to procreate'. This right weighed most heavily with Heilbron J. in her decision in 1975, in *Re D*, where the patient was made a ward of court to stop a sterilisation operation.[18]

As Reilly notes, '[a]lthough legal scholars have asserted that *Buck* v. *Bell* is no longer "good law", it has never been overturned, and the few courts that have considered the constitutionality of involuntary sterilisation statutes have upheld them'.[19] Nevertheless, by the late 1970s, uncertainties about the legality of sterilising incompetent patients without their consent led to judicial involvement on a different basis. The courts were no longer asked to consider whether non-consensual sterilisation infringed rights to security of the person. Instead, a new wave of applications was made by carers and relatives asking the courts to exercise their *parens patriae* jurisdiction to authorise sterilisation on the grounds that it was in the best interests of the patient. The legal bases for these applications have been the right of the patients to receive treatment which is in their best interests, the right of privacy, entailing the right to control of one's own body, and rights of reproductive choice. These applications have been founded on the principle that mentally incapacitated people are as entitled to these rights as anyone else, and where they are unable themselves to choose how to exercise them, it is for the courts to make the necessary decision.

The United States courts have traditionally employed one of two bases for proxy decision making. The first is 'substituted judgment', where the court or proxy decision maker attempts to make the decision which the incapacitated person would make, in the light of evidence about the person's known beliefs, values and previous statements of opinion. For patients who have been permanently mentally handicapped this approach is open to the criticism that it involves the court in a highly speculative exercise, since the person will not have expressed any views and there will be little or no evidence of what he or she would have wanted. The second approach is to act in the 'best interests' of the incapacitated person. Here, one of the key questions is whether the court will employ a narrow definition of best interests – confining it to medical interests – or a wide one where a much broader range of factors including social and general welfare interests is taken into account. In 1986, in *Re Eve*, the Canadian Supreme Court stated that the courts only had jurisdiction to authorise a therapeutic sterilisation.[20]

The wider view of best interests was taken by the New Jersey Supreme Court in *Re Grady*, a leading United States precedent, where the parents of a young learning disabled woman applied to the court to authorise her sterilisation.[21] They were concerned that, when she left school and entered a sheltered workshop, she would be seduced and become pregnant. The judge at first authorised the operation and the state attorney general appealed to the New Jersey Supreme Court, which ruled that it had jurisdiction to order the operation, but that the prior sanction of the court was necessary in all cases. The court also ordained certain minimum procedural and substantive safeguards. A guardian had to be appointed to represent the incapacitated person, her case had to be evaluated by independent medical experts and there had to be a personal meeting between the patient and the judge. The judge should not approve a sterilisation unless it was established that the person permanently lacked the capacity to decide for herself, and that there was clear and convincing evidence that sterilisation was in her best interests. The court listed the factors which were to be taken into account in determining the best interests question, including:

(a) the likelihood of pregnancy;
(b) the likelihood that pregnancy would cause damage to physical or mental health;
(c) the likelihood of sexual activity;
(d) the person's ability to care for a child;
(e) her ability to understand about reproduction and contraception;
(f) the practicability of other methods of contraception;
(g) the advisability of sterilisation now rather than at a later date;
(h) the likelihood that therapeutic advances might improve the person's condition or remove the need for sterilisation; and finally
(i) that the proponents are seeking sterilisation in good faith and their primary concern is for the best interests of the incapacitated person, not for their own or the public's convenience.

These North American cases revealed the potential of the *parens patriae* jurisdiction to authorise treatment without consent and opened up the possibility that the courts could be used to provide doctors with protection against legal action when treating patients without consent. A similar development would soon take place in England and Wales, but first the courts had to overcome a significant obstacle, namely the absence of a *parens patriae* jurisdiction for adults.

In 1975, at the time of the decision in *Re D (a minor) (wardship: sterilisation)* where a girl was warded to prevent sterilisation,[22] the Department of Health published figures showing that in 1973 and 1974, thirteen boys and thirty-eight girls under the age of eighteen were sterilised.[23] Commenting on *Re D*, the legal correspondent of the *British Medical Journal* (BMJ) regretted that Mrs Justice Heilbron had not been 'a little bolder' and laid down general guidance as to whether sterilisation was ever lawful when performed on a minor or on an adult whose consent might be invalid because of mental disorder. The BMJ went on to argue that 'some sort of independent body was required so that the merits of proposed non-therapeutic sterilisations can be vetted', and it felt that legislation was 'particularly vital on account of the number of minors sterilised in the recent past'. 'Above all,' the article concluded, 'doctors are entitled to know where they stand on the law. At the moment there is a serious risk of actions for assault brought by minors sterilized for non-therapeutic reasons once they reach their majority.'[24]

The desired mechanism for vetting sterilisations did not develop for another decade. The first English case where the courts were asked to use wardship to authorise sterilisation, rather than to prevent it, was decided in 1987, *Re B (a minor) (wardship: sterilisation)*.[25] B was nearing her eighteenth birthday, after which she would be beyond the reach of wardship, and this was an important reason why authority for sterilisation was being sought at that point rather than later. It also explains the unusually fast progress of the case, from the initial decision of Bush J. on 20 January 1987 to authorise sterilisation as 'the only possible decision for her future welfare', to the upholding of that decision by the House of Lords on 30 April 1987.

B was described as having a 'moderate degree of mental handicap'. She could dress herself, could carry out simple domestic duties, and had been taught to cope with menstruation. Her ability to communicate was limited to sentences of one or two words, and she could not be allowed out alone because she did not understand about traffic or money. The local council applied for the wardship and sterilisation, and the Official Solicitor appeared as guardian *ad litem* for B to oppose the application. It was agreed that she would always be incapable of giving informed consent to sterilisation, abortion or marriage. This proved the crucial distinction between *Re B* and *Re D (a minor) (wardship: sterilisation)*,[26] where Heilbron J. had said that sterilisation deprived a woman of a 'basic human right, namely that of a woman to reproduce, and therefore it would, if performed on a woman for non-therapeutic reasons and without her consent, be a violation of such right'.[27] Bush J. said that depriving B of this right was 'in effect depriving her of nothing at all, because she will never desire the basic human right to reproduce, and indeed, far from it being a question of not desiring it, on the facts of this case it would be positively harmful to her'.[28]

Bush J.'s decision was based on his acceptance that B would have no maternal feelings and none were likely to develop, that there would be serious management problems during her pregnancy and it would not be in her best interests to allow it to go full term. The only alternative to sterilisation was oral contraception which, taken over a long period might have detrimental side effects, and which, because of her proneness to mood swings, might give rise to 'difficulty' in 'enforcing over the years that it is taken on each and every day'. B's social worker had said that if B was 'in one of her moods', there was no way she would try to give the pill. The risk of side effects, and the likely difficulty of enforcing compliance, led one of the expert witnesses to put the chances of devising a successful regime of oral contraception at only 30 to 40 per cent, whereas the chances of harm from a sterilisation operation (by occlusion of the Fallopian tubes, not hysterectomy) were minimal.

In the Court of Appeal, Dillon LJ delivered the leading judgment upholding the judge's decision, and holding that the loss of the right to reproduce would mean nothing to B. He said this:

> Not that many years ago the risk [of pregnancy] would have been avoided because a girl with her disabilities would have been strictly institutionalised all her life. Now the best opinion is that such a person should be allowed as much freedom as possible to enjoy such a quality of life as her limited abilities will permit. . . . but the greater freedom is allowed, the greater obviously is the risk of pregnancy.[29]

This statement is reminiscent of the trade-off between sterilisation and increased freedom for the feeble minded that was urged unsuccessfully by local authorities and the eugenics movement in the 1920s and 1930s. As *Re B* continued its ascent of the court hierarchy, parallels were drawn with the experience of eugenic sterilisation. There were, of course, key differences. The project of sterilising the feeble minded was aimed at a very wide group who were capable of leading independent lives in the community. The justification for eugenic sterilisation had then been cast in terms of the alleged interests of society in racial perfection and not having to bear the burden of looking after incapacitated people. However, implicit in the decision about B's interests was her inability to provide parental care for any potential offspring and that it would not be in their interests that they be brought into the world. If this could be described as eugenic at all, it was 'Christian Democrat social engineering' rather than 'Nazi racial purity' eugenics. In the House of Lords, Lords Hailsham LC, Bridge and Oliver strongly emphasised that the appeal had 'nothing to do with eugenics' and that the sole question was the 'welfare and best interest of B herself'.[30]

One reason why *Re B* had caused controversy was the rejection of the distinction between therapeutic and non-therapeutic sterilisations which was so important in the debates of the 1930s, and which had formed the basis of the Canadian decision in *Re Eve*.[31] In that case, La Forest J. concluded that sterilisation should never be authorised by a court exercising *parens patriae* jurisdiction for non-therapeutic purposes. In *Re B* Lord Hailsham found the conclusion that sterilisation should never be authorised for non-therapeutic purposes 'unconvincing, and in startling contradiction to the welfare principle which should be the first and paramount consideration in wardship cases'.[32] Lord Bridge felt that if the wardship court could only intervene to authorise a sterilisation when it is 'therapeutic' as opposed to 'non-therapeutic', then its attention was being diverted from the true issue, which is whether the operation is in the ward's best interests. He declined to be drawn into 'arid semantic debate' as to where the line is drawn between 'therapeutic' and 'non-therapeutic treatment'.[33] Lord Oliver felt that it was 'entirely immaterial' whether measures to protect against 'future and foreseeable injury are properly described as therapeutic'.[34] Thus the House of Lords rejected a distinction which had strongly influenced British thinking in the

1920s and 1930s about the legality of sterilising incapacitated people.

The decision in *Re B* provoked concerns about the lawfulness of sterilising mentally incapacitated adults. No equivalent jurisdiction to wardship appeared to exist for adults. The *parens patriae* jursidiction of the High Court over people of unsound mind had lapsed in 1960, the last delegation of the power under the sign manual having been revoked, and although not abolished, the jurisdiction was in abeyance because no one had been entrusted with the authority to exercise it.[35] *Re B* was followed in 1987 and 1988 by two cases seeking the authority of the courts to proceed with abortion and sterilisation operations on mentally handicapped adult women. These were *Re X* (an abortion)[36] and *T* v. *T and another* (a sterilisation).[37] The procedural device chosen to authorise the treatment and to provide protection for the doctors was a request for a declaration that these operations would not be unlawful by reason only of the absence of consent from the patients. These cases were to mark the beginnings of a dramatic development of the declaratory jurisdiction of the High Court as a mechanism for authorising treatment of incapacitated adults without consent.

In both cases the High Court granted the declarations sought because it was in the best interests of the patients that the operations be performed. However, doubts remained whether the declaration was the appropriate mechanism to authorise treatment without consent. The Official Solicitor, as B's guardian *ad litem*, had appealed *Re B*, thus enabling the law relating to under-eighteens to be declared authoritatively by the House of Lords as the final appeal court. Because, in the adult cases, there was no mechanism to appeal against these decisions, neither the Court of Appeal nor the House of Lords had been given the opportunity to lay down an authoritiative ruling. This was soon remedied.

In 1988, in *Re F*, Scott Baker J. granted a declaration that it would be lawful to sterilise a thirty-five-year-old informal mentally handicapped patient despite her inability to consent.[38] F's mother had made the application to the Family Division of the High Court. The court heard evidence that F had formed an attachment of a sexual nature with another patient, that all concerned with her care we're agreed that pregnancy would be a disaster for her, and that other forms of contraception were either impracticable or medically contra-indicated. Hurried arrangements were made whereby the Lord Chancellor, Lord Mackay, issued a directive under section 90 of the Supreme Court Act 1981, amending the Rules of Court to allow the Official Solicitor to represent the patient's interests in such cases and in doing so to appeal to the Court of Appeal and House of Lords, if necessary. The aim of the rule change was twofold: to ensure that the arguments against the operation were fully put, and to obtain from the Law Lords an authoritative statement of the law.

Argument in the Court of Appeal and the House of Lords was addressed primarily to two questions: (a) whether there was a legal principle justifying operations in such cases; and (b) now that the *parens patriae* jurisdiction had gone, whether the courts had jurisdiction to authorise treatment without consent. In a classic piece of judicial law-making, the House of Lords declared the principle that doctors have the power and, in certain circumstances, the duty to give treatment to incapacitated adults which is necessary in their best interests. Treatment is necessary in a patient's best interests if it is carried out in order to save life or to ensure improvement or prevent deterioration in his or her health.

In deciding whether a treatment is necessary in a patient's best interests, the doctor must act in accordance with a responsible and competent body of medical opinion; the *Bolam* standard.[39] So, the test used to determine the liability in negligence of doctors regarding past acts would in future be used to determine the scope of their power to treat incapacitated patients. If, acting in accordance with a responsible body of medical opinion, the doctor decides that treatment is in the patient's best interests, there is not only a power, but in certain circumstances there may also be a duty to give it, and there can be no liability in battery. The corollary is that if the doctor, again according with the *Bolam* standard, believes the treatment not to be necessary in the patient's best interests, to give it is a battery.

The application of the *Bolam* test in this context has been strongly criticised. David Carson has asked whether it is imaginable 'that any other group of people could have their *best* interests restated as merely the right not to have others make negligent decisions in relation to them.'[40] Larry Gostin has argued that incapable patients should be entitled to 'insist not merely on non-negligent treatment, but treatment which is in all the circumstances in his or her best interests', and the application of *Bolam* leaves little room for safeguards against treatment whose efficacy, safety or morality is open to question.[41]

As to the mechanism to authorise treatment, the House of Lords decided that, since sterilisation was not a treatment for mental disorder, the procedures to authorise treatment without consent in Part IV of the 1983 Act did not apply, nor did the Court of Protection's jurisdiction over property and affairs of incapacitated patients extend to medical treatment. After extensive argument on the subject, the Law Lords found that the *parens patriae* jurisdiction was effectively in permanent abeyance. Moreover, they viewed the creation of novel heads of jurisdiction as being for Parliament, not the courts. This meant that the only mechanism left was a declaration that the operation would not be unlawful despite the absence of consent from the patient, providing the doctor with what Lord Donaldson MR would later call a 'flak jacket' against legal liability. This being the only possibility to 'authorise' the operation, the Law Lords upheld Scott Baker J.'s decision at first instance.

One problem with the declaration is that it does not alter the legal position of the parties, it simply declares what it is. With wardship, the House of Lords in *Re B* had been able to follow the lead given in *Re Grady* and require all proposed sterilisations of incapacitated minors to be brought before the Family Division of the High Court.[42] All the Law Lords in *Re F* agreed on the need for court validation of certain types of treatment without consent, including sterilisation and organ donation, referred to as 'special category treatments' in the Court of Appeal and in argument in the House of Lords. However, with the exception of Lord Griffith, they all accepted that under the present law those wishing to sterilise an adult incapacitated patient without consent could not be obliged to seek a declaration, although they would be strongly advised to do so.

Under the common-law regime, one of the principal new figures involved in treating incapacitated people is the Official Solicitor. Shortly after the ruling in *Re F* in 1989, the Official Solicitor issued *Practice Note (Official Solicitor) (sterilisation)*[43] on the procedure for applying for declarations. It also contained guidance on substantive questions, closely modelled on the criteria listed in *Re Grady*, which counsel for the Official Solicitor had vainly attempted to persuade the Law Lords in *Re F* to incorporate in their speeches.

The Note stressed that the purpose of the proceedings was to establish whether the proposed sterilisation was in the patient's best interests and that 'the judge will require to be satisfied that those proposing sterilisation are seeking it in good faith and that their paramount concern is for the best interests of the patient, rather than for their own or the public's convenience'. The Official Solicitor 'anticipated' that the judge would require evidence clearly establishing that the following criteria are met. First, the patient must be incapable of making her own decision about sterilisation and be unlikely to develop sufficiently to make an informed judgment in the foreseeable future. Second, that there is a need for contraception because the patient is physically capable of procreation and is likely to engage in sexual activity at the present or in the near future from which there is a 'real danger', as opposed to a mere chance, that pregnancy is likely to result. Third, that the patient will experience substantial trauma or psychological damage if she becomes pregnant – a trauma greater than that resulting from the sterilisation itself – and that she is permanently incapable of caring for a child, even with reasonable assistance from a future spouse where the patient may have the capacity to marry. Finally, evidence would be required establishing that there is no practicable less-intrusive means of solving the anticipated problem than immediate sterilisation. As well as the need to show that all less drastic contraceptive methods have proved unworkable or inapplicable and that the operation could not be postponed until some time in the future, the evidence would include a proportionality requirement that sterilisation would not of itself cause physical or psychological damage greater than the intended beneficial effects.[44]

In February 1990, in *J* v. *C* and at the invitation of the Official Solicitor, Thorpe J. gave guidance on the appropriate procedure in such applications.[45] Emphasising that the Practice Note was intended as guidance, not as a mandatory code, Thorpe J. stressed that all evidence, including expert evidence, should be submitted in affidavit form, indicating that an answer to the questionnaire issued by the Official Solicitor to applicants' solicitors was not obligatory. In 1993 a new note was issued, *Official Solicitor: Practice Note (sterilisations: minors and mental health patients)*.[46] The new note states that whilst 'the proceedings will normally involve a thorough adversarial investigation of all possible viewpoints and alternatives to sterilisation, nevertheless, straightforward cases proceeding without dissent may be disposed of at a hearing for directions without oral evidence'.[47]

The role of the Official Solicitor in these proceedings is either as an independent guardian representing the interests of the patient, or as an *ex officio* defendant. He carries out his own investigations, calls his own witnesses and takes whatever steps appear to him necessary in order to ensure that all relevant matters are fully aired before the judge, including cross-examining the expert and other witnesses, and presenting all reasonable arguments against sterilisation. In all cases where the patient is able to express any views – however limited – about parenthood, sterilisation or the legal proceedings, the Official Solicitor meets and interviews the patient in private.[48]

Undoubtedly, the Official Solicitor has played an important role in seeking to use Practice Notes to import the *Re Grady* criteria into English decisions about sterilisation, but his success in doing so has been somewhat limited. *J* v. *C* was a clear signal that they were not to be regarded as mandatory but as guidance. In *Re W (an adult: mental patient) (sterilisation)*[49] Hollis J. further weakened the *Re Grady* position by granting a declaration authorising sterilisation, even though the Official Solicitor had produced evidence that the risk of pregnancy was small, because in the light of the medical opinion it was in the patient's best interests that the sterilisation be performed.

Although the concept of best interests is broad, extending to social as well as medical interests, medical opinion is given a privileged position in determining what those interests are. In discharging his role of putting the reasonable arguments against sterilisation, the Official Solicitor is in the position of representing a concept of individual freedom based primarily on the right of bodily integrity and the right to reproduce. This inevitably appears partial, extreme and Utopian to a judiciary more alert to the limits of the abilities of the patients concerned. They are more inclined to consider sterilisation as freeing mentally handicapped people from a liability, or as enhancing their developmental potential than as a deprivation of fundamental rights and freedoms. During the Lords hearing of *Re F*, for example, the observer was left with the abiding impression that the advocates for all the parties were agreed that sterilisation was the best course for F, and that the arguments of counsel for the Official Solicitor based on autonomy, bodily integrity, and the right to reproduce were viewed as unrealistic in a case involving a profoundly learning disabled person.

The ruling in *Re F* did not *require* those seeking authority to treat incapacitated patients without consent to apply to the court. However, by strongly advising those contemplating abortion, sterilisation or organ donation to seek a declaration, it effectively left little alternative but a court appearance for those seeking a legal flak jacket against liability for assault in those cases. Inevitably this presented the Family Division of the High Court with the task of deciding which cases involved routine medical treatment, which could be given without the need to come to court, and which cases would require a declaration.

In 1991 the therapeutic/non-therapeutic distinction was raised again in three judgments by the president of the Family Division. These removed the requirement of court involvement in abortions and therapeutic sterilisations of mentally incapacitated patients. In *Re S.G. (a patient)* – a case where the patient's father, as her next friend, sought a declaration to the effect that an abortion was necessary in the applicant's best interests – the president, Sir Stephen Brown held that the specific approval of the High Court was not a necessary condition precedent to the termination of the pregnancy of a severely mentally handicapped patient.[50] In his Lordship's opinion the Abortion Act 1967 provided fully adequate safeguards for doctors who were to undertake this treatment, provided that the conditions of section 1 were complied with. Section 1 provides that a doctor is not guilty of an offence under the law relating to abortion when two medical practitioners have formed the opinion in good faith:

(a) that the continuance of the pregnancy would involve risk to the life of a pregnant woman or of injury to the physical or mental health of the pregnant woman or any existing children of her family, greater than if the pregnancy were terminated; or

(b) that there is substantial risk that if the child were born it would suffer from such physical or mental abnormalities as to be seriously handicapped.

As Douglas has noted, these procedures are designed to authorise abortion with consent, and are not apt to consider the different issues arising from abortions without it, such as the level of capacity of the patient and whether the treatment is in her best interests.[51]

Re E (a minor) (medical treatment) was an application in wardship to authorise the sterilisation of a mentally handicapped seventeen-year-old suffering from excessive menstruation.[52] Sir Stephen Brown P. held that it was not necessary for the responsible doctor to seek the formal consent of the court before carrying out the operation. Even though its inevitable effect would be to sterilise the patient, where its purpose was to render therapy rather than achieve sterilisation, the approval of the court was not necessary. In April 1991, in *Re G. F. (medical treatment)*, Sir Stephen Brown P. extended the effect of his ruling in *Re E* to incapacitated adults.[53] He held that it was not necessary to seek a declaration authorising the sterilisation of a a twenty-nine-year-old woman with severe mental and physical handicap who was suffering from excessive menstruation, as the purpose of the operation was essentially therapeutic. The president laid down a procedure, reminiscent of section 1 of the Abortion Act, for deciding when a sterilisation was therapeutic and therefore need not trouble the court. It required the agreement of two doctors that the operation is:

(1) necessary for therapeutic purposes;
(2) in the best interests of the patient; and
(3) that there is no practicable, less intrusive alternative.

The first refinement of the 'special category' was a strategic retreat of the courts from involvement in abortions and therapeutic sterilisations of incapacitated adults. In the latter case, this left behind a judicially prescribed decision-making process modelled on section 1 of the Abortion Act 1967. By July 1992 it had also been made clear, in *Re H (mental patient)*[54] that the medical treatment which could be carried out without consent, and without need for a High Court declaration under the *Re F* principle, included diagnostic procedures. Sir Nicholas Wilson QC held that there was no reason to distinguish between diagnostic and therapeutic procedures because, as the proposed procedures were clearly in the best interests of the patient, it was lawful for the doctors to subject the patient to them. This was not one of those special cases identified in *Re F* where it was necessary or desirable to grant a declaration. Had a declaration been granted in this case, that might have been an unfortunate signal to others in that it was appropriate as a matter of good medical practice for the implementation of such procedures to be delayed, pending the outcome of a costly application to the court.

Wardship and the jurisdiction to grant declarations not only enable the courts to pronounce upon the position of the parties to the proceedings, they have also provided a vehicle for judicial development of the substantive law relating to consent. Chapter 15 considers recent case law on consent and the proposals of the Law Commission on the treatment of mentally incapacitated adults.

15

CODIFYING CLINICAL AUTHORITY

In 1992 the procedure developed in *Re F* was applied in two cases, *Re T (adult) (medical treatment)*[1] and *Re S (adult) (refusal of medical treatment)*,[2] to override clear refusals by patients who were not mentally disordered, where there was a strong likelihood that they would die if their treatment decisions were upheld. In *Re T*, Lord Donaldson MR gave a strong statement of the rights of competent adults to refuse treatment:

> An adult patient who ... suffers from no mental incapacity has an absolute right to choose whether to consent to medical treatment, to refuse it or to choose one rather than another of the treatments being offered.... This right of choice is not limited to decisions which others might regard as sensible. It exists, notwithstanding that the reasons for making the choice are rational, irrational, unknown, or even non-existent.[3]

The Court of Appeal accepted that an anticipatory refusal made while the patient is competent that is sufficient in scope to cover the situation which has later arisen will bind the doctor. On this occasion, however, the refusal had been made when the patient, a lapsed Jehovah's Witness, was in a weakened state and was acting under the undue influence of her mother who remained a devout adherent of the faith. The court also doubted whether her refusal was sufficient in scope since it was not clear whether she had intended to refuse all blood transfusions, or only those which were not necessary to keep her alive. In *Re S* a Caesarean section was authorised on a refusing woman because her own life and that of her foetus were found to be in immediate danger. These two decisions have not altered the concept of incapacity.

They indicate the circumstances in which an apparently capable refusal may be overridden using the declaratory procedure.

As the Law Lords were deciding *Re F*, the Law Commission began what would become a five-year examination of decision making on behalf of mentally incapacitated adults, issuing their first consultation paper in 1991,[4] and in 1993, following wide consultation, three further papers outlining their provisional proposals for decision making regarding property and affairs, personal care, and medical treatment.[5] Their final report, entitled simply *Mental Incapacity*,[6] published in March 1995, includes a Mental Incapacity Bill based on the following three principles:

(i) that people are enabled and encouraged to take for themselves those decisions which they are able to take;

(ii) that where it is necessary in their own interests that someone else should take decisions on their behalf, the intervention should be as limited as possible and should be concerned to achieve what the person himself would have wanted; and

(iii) that proper safeguards should be provided against exploitation and neglect and against physical, sexual or psychological abuse.[7]

There would be no place in the Law Commission's scheme for the making of decisions which would protect other persons, but would not be in the best interests of the person without capacity. The protection of others is seen by the Commission as the proper preserve of the Mental Health Act 1983. The Commission's draft Bill largely follows the framework of the provisional proposals outlined in *Consultation Paper No 129: Mentally Incapacitated Adults and Decision-Making: Medical Treatment and Research*.[8] These included a statutory scheme of decision making to replace the current common-law principles, which would apply to treatment for both mental and physical disorders, covering incapacity and treatment decisions other than those which are already subject to Part IV of the 1983 Act. The intention is that the scope of Part IV will not be changed.[9] People would be able, while they are still capable, to make provision for legal recognition of decisions about their medical treatment in the event of their future incapacity by way of advance directives or enduring powers of attorney for medical treatment. The common-law rule in *Re F* would be replaced by a statutory authority allowing treatment to be given which is 'reasonable in all the circumstances to safeguard and promote the best interests of an incapacitated person'.[10] The suggested statutory scheme would be under the supervision of a 'judicial forum', a revamped Court of Protection, with jurisdiction over health, welfare and property decisions. Some may see a certain irony in the fact that, as the Commission started its work, the House of Lords in *Re F* rejected the argument that the Court of Protection's existing jurisdiction over 'property and affairs' could extend to treatment decisions. However, the Court of Protection as currently organised is ill-suited to deal with health and welfare decisions, and when it was put to her in 1989, the Court's Master viewed the prospect with severe misgivings. The new court would be reconstituted with selected Family and Chancery Division, circuit and district judges. In contrast to the current court which is based in London, and is seen as remote, the new court would have a base in each judicial circuit. It would have jurisdiction to make certain treatment decisions. It could pronounce on a person's capacity or on the scope or validity of advance refusals and continuing powers of attorney over property, affairs and health. It could also appoint a manager for an incapacitated person. The court would operate under a general presumption, again based on the least restrictive alternative, that 'single issue' orders are to be preferred to the appointment of a manager, and that the manager should be given authority only over those areas where the person is incapable of deciding for him- or herself.

It is interesting to compare the new court's role with the *parens patriae* jurisdiction of the Chancery Division. Under the nineteenth-century procedure a trial was held to determine whether the person was of unsound mind. If this was proved a committee of the person was appointed, 'committee' meaning the one to whose care the incapacitated person was committed. The committee could administer property and affairs and could decide to put the patient in a hospital or asylum. Complete power was obtained over the subject. *Parens patriae* or 'Chancery lunatic' cases were often held in public before a special jury of twenty-four. The procedure was amended under the Lunacy Act 1891, and proceedings were held privately before masters rather than judge or judge and jury after several well-publicised cases in the 1880s and early 1890s.[11] They appealed to the press for a number of reasons. They were full public proceedings where an individual was fighting for his or her liberty, and provided an opportunity for public celebration of common-law safeguards. There was a heavy element of sexual politics since the majority of cases involved well-to-do women and the proposed committee was usually the husband. Finally, the adversarial nature of the proceedings could be relied on to unearth a certain amount of interesting domestic detail. When the Court of Protection took over the jurisdiction over property and affairs, it operated by appointing 'receivers', the term used for the administrator of the affairs of a bankrupt. In keeping with the new language of community care (care managers, budget managers, etc.) the Commission's proposal is that the new Court of Protection would act through the appointment of managers. Unlike the purely Chancery based adult *parens patriae*, the new Court of Protection would operate within a new hybrid paradigm of Family and Chancery procedures, evoking parallels with the scheme of protective orders in the Children Act 1989.

The Commission's draft Bill would bring together under one legislative umbrella all health, welfare and property decisions for people who lack mental capacity, and would also confer new functions on local authorities in relation to mentally vulnerable people in need of care and protection. Part 1 of the Bill would confer statutory authority to make health care, financial and personal welfare decisions for people over 16 who are without capacity. It would also enable decisions to be made on their behalf by the donee of a power of attorney, by the new Court of Protection or by a court-appointed manager, repealing and replacing Part VII of the Mental Health Act 1983 and the Enduring Powers of Attorney Act 1985.

A key task facing the Commission was to develop a working definition of incapacity. They made their proposals subject to the general presumption that an adult has capacity until the contrary is shown. Under their original proposals and under the draft Bill, people who were not mentally disordered would only be treated as incapacitated if, because they are unconscious or for any other reason, they are unable to communicate a treatment decision to others even though all practicable steps to enable them to do so have been taken without success.[12]

As for people with mental disorder, the presumption of competence would still apply, but a different test would operate. It was provisionally proposed that they would be considered incapable of taking a specific medical treatment decision for themselves if they were 'unable to understand an explanation in broad terms and simple language of basic information relevant to taking it, including information about the reasonably foreseeable consequences of taking it or failing to take it, or [we]re unable to retain the information for long enough to take an effective decision'.[13]

There has been strong criticism of using mental disorder as a gatekeeper concept in this way.[14] Campbell and Heginbotham argue that making special provision for mentally disordered people is discriminatory because it entails treating mental disorder as 'a specific compulsion inviting condition', leading to 'modes of adjudication, treatment and disposal along lines which differ quite markedly from the manner in which other people are dealt with'.[15] They suggest that the reason we are alarmed by proposals to eliminate special legislation for mental disorder is because they open up the possibility of intervention in the lives of all citizens, of a sort which is presently confined to those with a mental disorder. The unspoken presumption is that:

> such powers are all very well for the mad, but not for the rest of us. Once we put aside that assumption, we may find that in framing protectionist and paternalistic laws, we are more scrupulous in examining the basis and evidence on which such practices proceed at present with respect to those with a mental disorder.[16]

The Commission emphasise that mentally disordered people will not automatically be presumed to be incompetent, and decisions will still have to be made about their level of understanding and cognitive abilities: 'A finding of mental disorder would only be a first stage in the assessment of capacity and the presumption of competence would still apply.'[17]

In their final report the Commission have abandoned the mental disorder threshold in favour of one based on mental disability, meaning 'any disability or disorder of the mind or brain, whether permanent or temporary, which results in an impairment or disturbance of mental functioning'. Their thinking is that using mental disability would provide a significant protection in terms of Article 5 of the European Convention in that where infringement of the person's liberty was concerned this would be based on a finding of mental disability and incapacity resulting from it. The Commission considered that, unlike the definition of mental disorder in the Mental Health Act 1983 with its connotations of detention, 'mental disability' would in no sense prejudice or stigmatise those who 'are in need of help with decision making'.[18]

Even if mentally disordered patients could understand the information relevant to taking the decision, under the Commission's provisional proposals they would have been considered incapable of taking the treatment decision in question if they were 'unable because of mental disorder to make a true choice in relation to it'.[19] The potential scope of the 'true choice' criterion was very wide, but it was intended to extend to those who have a deluded perception of the purpose of the treatment, or as a result of an illness such as anorexia have a compulsion to refuse treatment, rather than those who understand it and wish to refuse it, whether for 'rational' reasons such as worries about side effects, or for reasons which others might find irrational. Even in such cases the presumption of competence would still apply, and the burden would be on those alleging incapacity.

After the Commission's provisional proposals were published, the case of *Re C (mental patient: medical treatment)*[20] came before Thorpe J. The central issues were the test of capacity, and the validity of an advance refusal of treatment. Judicial dicta in *Re T (adult) (medical treatment)* and *Airedale NHS Trust* v. *Bland* had already indicated that advance refusals of specific treatment could in certain circumstances be binding,[21] but this was the first occasion where an English court had been invited to rule directly on the validity of an advance directive. The plaintiff, a sixty-eight-year-old Broadmoor patient with paranoid schizophrenia, sought court recognition of his current capacity to refuse amputation of a gangrenous leg and prospective validation of his advance directive. He refused to consent to amputation in any circumstances, even if it meant death. The immediate danger to his health was averted by surgery to remove the area of infected tissue without amputation. The hospital authorities refused the undertaking sought by his solicitor that they would recognise C's repeated refusals and would not amputate in any future circumstances, so he sought a declaration that he was capable of refusing amputation and an injunction restraining Heatherwood Hospital from amputating his right leg without his express written consent.

Thorpe J. granted the orders sought, holding that the High Court has power, exercising its inherent jurisdiction, to rule by way of injunction or declaration that an individual is capable of refusing or consenting to medical treatment, and to determine the effect of a purported advanced directive as to the future medical treatment. He also held that a refusal could take the form of a declaration of intention never to consent in the future or never to consent in some future circumstances. The question to be decided here was whether C's capacity was so reduced by his chronic mental illness that he did not sufficiently understand the nature, purpose and effects of the proffered amputation. Thorpe J. held the presumption that C had the right to self determination not to have been displaced, despite the fact that he was detained and his general capacity was impaired by schizophrenia. He had delusions of a successful international career in medicine. He felt that he would not die if his leg was not amputated, because God would protect him. In Law Commission terms, it was questionable whether he could make 'a true choice'. Dr Nigel Eastman, a consultant forensic psychiatrist who appeared as an expert witness for the plaintiff, was asked at short notice in the course of proceedings to outline the criteria by which capacity could be determined and, as he has subsequently admitted, did so on the basis of his recollection of the Law Commission's provisional proposals. In his view, three elements had to be considered: (1) whether the patient could comprehend and retain the treatment information; (2) whether he believed it; and (3) whether he could weigh it in the balance to arrive at a choice. Thorpe J. adopted this test, and found that it had not been established that C did not understand the nature, purpose and likely effects of the amputation he was refusing. He understood and retained the relevant treatment information and 'in his own way' he believed it, even though he did not accept the doctors' assessment that the vascular disease of his foot would lead to a return of his gangrene and threaten his life. In fact, he is still alive two years after the court action. He had arrived at a clear choice. So although it was questionable whether C 'believed' the relevant treatment information, in the sense that he did not accept the doctors' assessment of the likely consequences of not having his leg amputated, he was nevertheless found not to be incapable because 'in his own way he believed it'. The validity of his advance directive was upheld.

Re C is an important reminder that it is for those alleging incapacity to displace the presumption of capacity, and that the mere fact that someone is suffering from mental disorder does not necessarily mean they are incapable of making a treatment decision. It has also enshrined the 'Eastman' test of incapacity as part of the common law. This may be difficult to implement in practice because of the second criterion, that the patient must believe the relevant treatment information. It does not mean that, in order to be capable, the patient must accept the medical evaluation of the likely outcome of having the treatment or not having it and of the trade-off between risks and benefits. As Thorpe J. would later put it in *B* v. *Croydon District Health Authority*,[22] there is a difference between outright disbelief (due to mental disorder) which meant being 'impervious to reason, divorced from reality, or incapable of adjustment after reflection', and 'the tendency which most people have when undergoing medical treatment to self assess and then to puzzle over the divergence between medical and self-assessment'.[23]

In their final report and recommendations the Law Commission have built on the *Re C* test, and have sought to resolve any potential contradiction between the 'belief' requirement and the right of refusal for irrational reasons mentioned in *Re T*. Persons with a mental disability would be considered 'without capacity' under their draft Bill if they were at the material time unable by reason of mental disability to make a decision for themselves on the matter in question.[24] A person would be deemed unable to make a decision by reason of mental disability if the disability is such that:

(a) he or she is unable to understand or retain the information relevant to the decision, including information about the reasonably foreseeable consequences of deciding one way or another or of failing to make the decision; or

(b) he or she is unable to make a decision based on that information.

The second of these criteria is to replace their original 'true choice' test. In the Commission's view, requiring the person to be able to make a decision based on the information 'deflects the complications of asking whether a person needs to "appreciate" information as well as understand it. A decision based on a compulsion, the overpowering will of a third party or any other inability to act on relevant information as a result of mental disability is not a decision made by a person with decision-making capacity.'[25] In other words the fact that persons have understood the relevant information, but that their appreciation in the sense of their evaluation of the risks and benefits does not accord with that of the doctors, will not be enough to remove their decision-making capacity. There would be a presumption that a person has capacity and decisions about capacity would be made on the balance of probabilities.

Two further limits apply to the scope of incapacity by reason of mental disability. First, a person would not be regarded as unable to understand the relevant information if able to understand an explanation of that information in broad terms and simple language, implying entitlement to such an explanation. Second, the right of 'refusal' for irrational reasons from *Re T (adult) (medical treatment)*[26] would be preserved, in that a person would not be regarded as unable to make a decision by reason of mental disability merely because he makes a decision which would not be made by a person of ordinary prudence.

Central to the Law Commission's proposals is the statutory authority to treat incapacitated patients subject to a general duty to act in their best interests. This would not simply be an enactment of the *Re F* principle. The authority would not extend only to doctors. The original proposals would have conferred it on 'treatment providers'. Under the draft Bill it could be claimed by anyone, to do anything for the personal welfare or health care of a person who is, or is reasonably believed to be, without capacity in relation to the matter in question, 'if it is in all the circumstances reasonable for it to be done by the person who does it'.[27] The person claiming statutory authority is protected from legal liability if he reasonably believes that the person is without capacity, and that he is acting in the best interests of the person concerned, a narrower protection than the defence in section 139 of the Mental Health Act 1983.

The statutory authority to treat would also operate with a more sophisticated concept of best interests than that currently applied by the common law. In *Airedale NHS Trust* v. *Bland*,[28] where the *Re F* principle was applied to grant a declaration that it would be lawful to discontinue naso-gastric feeding of a young man in a persistent vegetative state, the Law Lords rejected substituted judgment in favour of best interests. The Law Commission provisionally proposed a list of factors to be taken into account in deciding whether a treatment is in the patient's best interests, combining aspects of both traditional 'best interests' criteria and 'substituted judgment'. These represent a noble attempt to get treatment providers to approach the best interests question not simply from their own perspective of what is best for the patient in narrowly defined medical terms, but in terms of the patient's known wishes and what he or she could be expected to want to uphold his or her freedom, dignity and well-being. Consideration was to be given to:

(1) the ascertainable past and present wishes and feelings (considered in the light of his or her understanding at the time) of the incapacitated person;

(2) whether there is an alternative to the proposed treatment, and in particular whether there is an alternative which is more conservative or less intrusive or restrictive; and

(3) the factors which the incapacitated person might be expected to consider if able to do so, including the likely effect of the treatment on the person's life expectancy, health, happiness, freedom and dignity.[29]

This best interests test contrasted markedly with both the common law *Bolam*-based test and the Mental Health Act test of the likelihood that the treatment will alleviate or prevent deterioration in the patient's condition. The proposals build in a concept of the least restrictive alternative and, in contrast to the common law, they would require a much more patient-centred consideration of best interests.

Under the draft Bill, in forming a reasonable belief that he was acting in the person's best interests, a person claiming the statutory authority would have to consider:

(a) so far as ascertainable, the person's past and present wishes and feelings, and the factors which he would consider if he were able to do so;

(b) the need to permit and encourage that person to participate, or to improve his ability to participate, as fully as possible in anything done for and any decision affecting him; and

(c) whether the purpose for which any action or decision is required can be as effectively achieved in a manner less restrictive of his freedom of action.[30]

Of these (a) imports an element of substituted judgment into the best interests test, (b) requires decisions to be taken for the promotion of personal autonomy, and (c) introduces a principle of proportionality or least restrictive alternative. They largely reflect the Commission's interim proposals except that they have left out their suggested requirement from their provisional proposals to consider the factors which the incapacitated person might be expected to consider if able to do so, including the likely effect of the treatment on the person's life expectancy, health, happiness, freedom and dignity.[31] These criteria would be elaborated in a statutory code of practice. In addition to the above factors, where practicable, the views of one or more of the following as to what is in the person's best interests would have to be considered:

(i) any person named by the person as someone to be consulted on these matters;
(ii) anyone, whether his spouse, a relative, friend or other person, engaged in caring for him or interested in his welfare;
(iii) the donee of any continuing power of attorney granted by him;
(iv) any manager appointed for him by the court.

The general authority would be available without recourse to a court, but it would be subject to three general restrictions. First, unless necessary to avert a substantial risk of serious harm to the person concerned, the general authority does not authorise: (a) the use of or threat of force to enforce the doing of anything to which the person concerned objects; or (b) the detention or confinement of that person whether or not he objects. This means that forcible injection, restraint, seclusion, or other treatment involving touching an informal patient would not be available unless necessary to avert a substantial risk of serious harm to the person concerned. Measures for the protection of others would require recourse to the Mental Health Act. This limitation should be read in the context of the Mental Health Act Code of Practice, which states that:

> On rare occasions involving emergencies, where it is not possible immediately to apply the provisions of the Mental Health Act, a patient suffering from mental disorder which is leading to behaviour that is an immediate serious danger to himself or to other people may be given such treatment as represents the minimum necessary to avert that danger.[32]

The second general restriction is that, unless necessary to prevent the death of the person concerned or serious deterioration in his condition while an order on the matter is sought from a court, the general authority does not authorise any step which is contrary to directions given or inconsistent with a decision made, within the scope of his authority, by the donee of a continuing power of attorney granted by him or by a manager appointed for him by the 'judicial forum'. Finally, the statutory authority would not be able to take any step which contravenes an advance refusal, made when the patient was capable and which is applicable in the circumstances of the case.[33]

In addition to the general limits on the statutory authority to treat, certain treatments would not be able to be given without either a judicial or medical second opinion or delegated consent. Non-therapeutic sterilisations (i.e. those done for reasons other than to relieve disease of the reproductive organs or menstrual management), and any treatment or procedure to facilitate the donation of non-regenerative tissue or bone marrow would require either court sanction or 'delegated consent' from the donee of a continuing power of attorney granted by the person concerned or by a manager appointed for him by a court. The Secretary of State for Health would be empowered to extend these requirements to other treatments by regulation.

The concept of 'delegated consent' is central to the Law Commission's proposals. Whilst it may have been widespread practice in the past to accept delegated consent from a relative of the patient, the case law on consent from the 1980s and 1990s has made it clear that relatives' consent on behalf of incapacitated people has no legal standing, and the Law Commission endorses this. The power to consent must be expressly conferred, either by the persons themselves prior to the onset of incapacity through a continuing power of attorney, or by the Court through the appointment of a manager.

The following treatments would require a statutory second medical opinion or delegated consent: (a) Electro Convulsive Therapy; (b) medicines for mental disorder (although these could be given without consent for three months); (c) abortion; (d) sterilisation for relieving existing detrimental effects of menstruation; and (e) any other treatment prescribed by regulations to be made by the Secretary of State. Part IV of the 1983 Act would not be changed, but the second opinion for ECT and medicines after three months would be extended to the non-detained. Like their Mental Health Act counterparts, the second opinion doctors would be appointed by the Secretary of State. However, unlike the Mental Health Act, the criteria by which the treatment would be allowed to proceed would not be the likelihood of alleviation or prevention of deterioration in the patient's condition. For the treatment to proceed, the opinion would have to certify: (a) that the person concerned is without capacity to consent; and (b) that the treatment is in his or her best interests.

The main exception to the principle that all decisions must be in the best interests of the incapacitated person alone applies in relation to discontinuance of artificial hydration and nutrition to patients in Persistent Vegetative States (PVS). Clause 10(1) provides that it shall be lawful to discontinue artificial nutrition or hydration of a person who is unconscious, has no activity in his cerebral cortex and has no prospect of recovery if: (a) the court approves; (b) the donee of a continuing power of attorney, acting within the scope of his authority, has consented; or (c) a manager appointed by the court has consented. One potentially controversial provision is that a power would be conferred on the Secretary of State to make regulations to authorise any surgical or medical procedure in relation to a person without capacity to consent which, although not carried out for his benefit, will in the opinion of the Secretary of State, not cause him significant harm and will be of significant benefit to others. The treatments envisaged by the Commission are elective ventilation where a person who is about to die anyway is kept alive to preserve organs for donation, and genetic screening where the information obtained may be of benefit to others but not the incapacitated person. These would be authorised subject to the consent of the court, of the attorney, of a manager or of a second opinion doctor. The second opinion would have to certify that the person concerned is without capacity. This would not apply to procedures carried out for research, and nothing could be done if the person objects or it would be contrary to an advance refusal.

The Bill deals with non-therapeutic research procedures where the subject lacks capacity to consent, and the research is unlikely to be of benefit to him or her, or the benefit is likely to be long delayed. It makes such non-therapeutic research lawful if it is into an incapacitating condition with which he is or may be affected. In addition to this a Mental Incapacity Research Committee (MIRC) to be appointed by the Secretary of State would have to have approved the research as ethical. Finally, unless the

Committee designates the research as not involving direct contact with the person concerned, there must be consent to the subject's participation from the court, a continuing attorney acting within the scope of his authority, or a medical second opinion to the effect that the person concerned is without capacity and that his or her participation in the research is appropriate. When making their decision, the court, the attorney, the manager and the second opinion doctor would not be required to act in the best interests of the person, but would be required to have regard to the person's past or present wishes, the need to encourage him to participate or to improve his ability to participate, as fully as possible in anything done for and any decision affecting him, and the views of those closely involved with the person as to what he or she would have wanted and what his or her best interests are. No non-therapeutic research could be carried out contrary to a valid advance refusal or if the person objects. We have already seen how in experimenting with treatments for mental disorder there is a tendency on the part of clinicians to focus on potential benefit, however speculative, even when the risk of detriment is high, so if this regulation of research is to protect patients effectively, the MIRC will have to have the power to decide when research is genuinely therapeutic.

The most dramatic developments in upholding patient autonomy have occurred in the recognition of advance refusals of treatment. In 1992 the BMA issued a statement supporting the principle of advance directives, but resisting the idea of legislation to make them binding. The House of Lords Select Committee on Medical Ethics which reported in January 1994, after the decision in *Re C*, also commended advance directives but did not see any need for legislation, recommending instead that the colleges and faculties of the health-care professions should jointly develop a code of practice.[34] Following *Bland* and *Re C*, the BMA issued a new statement in January 1994 supporting 'limited legislation to translate the common law into statute and clarify the non-liability of doctors who act in accordance with an advance directive'.[35] In April 1995 the BMA published *Advance Statements about Medical Treatment*,[36] a response to the House of Lords invitation to develop a code of practice on advance directives for health professionals, defining different types of advance statement and explaining their legal and ethical status. The Commission propose legislation for the recognition and enforceability of advance

263

refusals of treatment. Their draft Bill would recognise advance refusals by anyone over 18. These would be presumed to be valid if made in writing and signed by the person and at least one other person as a witness to his signature, and could be revoked or altered by the person at any time while he has the capacity to do so. The BMA's request for a statutory defence would be met by the Law Commission's Bill which would provide that:

> No person should incur liability for (1) the consequences of withholding any treatment or procedure if he or she has reasonable grounds for believing that an advance refusal of treatment applies; or (2) for carrying out any treatment or procedure to which an advance refusal applies unless he or she knows or has reasonable grounds for believing that an advance directive exists.[37]

In the absence of any evidence to the contrary, it would be presumed that an advance refusal does not apply where those having the care of the person consider that the refusal (a) endangers that person's life; or (b) if that person is a woman who is pregnant, the life of the foetus. This would mean that women in the position of the patient in *Re T (adult) (medical treatment)* or *Re S (adult) (refusal of medical treatment)*[38] would have to specify clearly that they did not want blood transfusions or Caesarean sections even if the result would be their death and/or that of their foetus. An advance refusal would not preclude the taking of any action to prevent the person's death or a serious deterioration in his or her condition, pending a decision of the court on the validity or applicability of an advance refusal or on the question whether it has been withdrawn or altered. Nor would it preclude the provision of 'basic care' for the person who made it, basic care meaning care to maintain body cleanliness and to alleviate severe pain and the provision of direct oral nutrition and hydration.[39] Most important in the present context, an advance refusal of treatment for mental disorder would not be binding once a patient is detained under the 1983 Act.[40] Hence, whilst the detained patient in *Re C* could validly execute an advance refusal of a treatment for physical illness, even if he would die as a result, had he been refusing psychiatric treatment, his refusal would have been overridden by Part IV of the 1983 Act, even if the likely consequences were much less drastic than loss of his own life or serious danger to others. The contradiction between the rights of patients at common law and their statutory position as detained psychiatric patients was starkly posed in a series of recent cases involving force feeding.

The decision in *Bland*, that naso-gastric feeding was medical treatment, was soon followed by cases concerning the circumstances in which force feeding is lawful. Following *Re T* and *Bland* it seemed certain that force feeding of a competent patient who is not detained under the Mental Health Act was unlawful and this has since been confirmed in *Secretary of State for the Home Department* v. *Robb*.[41] *Leigh* v. *Gladstone*,[42] where it was held that a mentally competent hunger-striking suffragette prisoner could lawfully be force fed, is no longer good law. However, patients who are detained under the 1983 Act are in a different position because of section 63, which provides that:

> The consent of a patient shall not be required for any medical treatment given to him for the mental disorder for which he is suffering, not being treatment falling within section 57 or 58 above, if the treatment is given by or under the direction of the responsible medical officer.

Force feeding of anorexic patients by naso-gastric tube is practised as a treatment of last resort. In 1993 Lancely and Travers reported in the *Bulletin of the Royal College of Psychiatrists* a case where a health authority was granted declarations to the effect that anorexia nervosa was a form of mental disorder and artificial feeding was medical treatment for mental disorder within the meaning of section 63, and therefore might be given to a detained patient without consent under the direction of the RMO.[43]

In *F* v. *Riverside Health Trust*,[44] Stuart White J. held that force feeding of an anorexic patient, if needed, would be medical treatment for mental disorder under section 63, that spoon feeding with or without restraint would be lawful, and that if the respondent refused to accept spoon feeding or sufficient food to improve her weight that it was lawful to sedate her and feed her by naso-gastric tube. This order was overturned because the patient had not been given an adequate opportunity to voice her objections, but there have been two subsequent reported cases on force feeding detained patients, one involving anorexia nervosa, and the other a refusal to eat by a patient with a borderline personality disorder. In January 1994 in *Re K. B. (adult) (mental patient:*

medical treatment),[45] Ewbank J. held that feeding by naso-gastric tube of an anorexic patient detained under section 3 of the 1983 Act was treatment for mental disorder which, because of section 63, did not require the consent of the patient. In this case an SOAD had been authorising the treatment on a Form 39 under section 58 until told to stop by the MHAC on the basis that what was being administered was food, not medicine.

With anorexia, there is an argument that the patient is incapable by reason of mental disorder of making a 'true choice' because refusal of food is a recognised symptom of the disease, or that it renders her unable to understand the relevant information about the treatment and make a decision on the basis of it. In July 1994 the question was raised of the applicability of section 63 where the patient suffers not from anorexia but a personality disorder. In *B* v. *Croydon Health Authority* Thorpe J. granted a declaration that force feeding was medical treatment for mental disorder under section 63 in respect of a twenty-four-year-old detained patient suffering from a 'borderline personality disorder' coupled with post-traumatic stress disorder resulting from sexual abuse as a child.[46] Her symptoms included depression and a compulsion to self-harm, stemming from an irrationally low self-regard for which the only known treatment is psychoanalytic psychotherapy. Initially she expressed her compulsion by cutting or burning herself, but after she was placed under strict nursing surveillance, she stopped eating. At the end of March 1994 she wrote a letter to the hospital which, as Hoffmann LJ put it in the Court of Appeal, showed 'great intelligence and self-awareness',[47] refusing the two treatment options then on offer, namely tube feeding and ECT and asking for a transfer to another hospital. In it she said 'my basic need is to be understood why I feel the need to punish myself, and at present this is by not eating'.

Thorpe J. outlined the three stages of decision making from *Re C*: receiving and retaining the relevant information, believing it, and weighing it in the balance so as to arrive at a true choice.[48] He rejected the submission that the assessment of capacity was primarily a medical matter for the medical practitioner with clinical responsibility. Where the decision as to capacity or lack of it is finely balanced and not manifest one way or the other, the clinician should seek an assessment from an authoritative medical expert if not a ruling from the court. In B's case he found that the presumption of capacity had not been displaced, but then arrived at, for him, the 'disquieting' conclusion that section 63 of the 1983 Act authorised what common law would not, the treatment of a competent detained patient against her will.

B's appeal to the Court of Appeal turned on the interpretation of section 63, and her capacity at common law was not the primary issue. Nevertheless Hoffmann LJ said that it was B's 'very self-awareness and acute self analysis' which led him to doubt 'whether she could be said to have made a true choice in refusing to eat'.[49] He found it hard to accept that:

[S]omeone who acknowledges that in refusing food at the critical time she did not appreciate the extent to which she was hazarding her life, was crying out inside for help but unable to break out of the routine of punishing herself, could be said to be capable of making a true choice as to whether to eat.[50]

Neill LJ also expressed doubt as to B's capacity at common law. Whatever the Law Commission's latest views on the determination of capacity, the widely drawn 'true choice' criterion seems to be becoming entrenched in the common-law test.

The Court of Appeal held that medical treatment for mental disorder could include a range of treatments ancillary to the core treatment, not all of which had to be in themselves likely to alleviate or prevent deterioration in that disorder. The Court of Appeal also rejected a submission by B's counsel that, if force feeding using liquid food through a naso-gastric tube was a treatment for mental disorder, it was an administration of a medicine, and therefore a second opinion under section 58 would be necessary. Even if section 58 had applied, a patient is only entitled to a second opinion for medicines after three months, so it would have provided scant protection for B in this case.

The five years since the *Re F* ruling have seen a dramatic development in the role of the common law and the courts *vis-à-vis* medicine. The common law has been traditionally remedies-based rather than strictly rights-based. Prior to 1989 the common law developed on the basis of a small number of damages actions brought by patients against doctors. Only the brave or the reckless doctor would have offered him- or herself as a defendant in a test case in the days when the role of courts was limited to dealing with civil disputes or, more rarely still, criminal prosecutions, arising from cases where patients had been treated without consent. *Re F* opened up the possibility of remedies for doctors and health authorities, remedies in the shape of the declaration of right. The Law Lords in *Re F* took the view that a declaration of right could only be granted if the incapacitated patient had a right to the treatment, which is why they went out of their way to emphasise that a doctor not only has the power, but also in certain circumstances, a duty to give necessary treatment.[51] If there is a duty on the doctor, then there must be a correlative right in the patient. Since then, with rare exceptions such as *Re C*, the jurisdiction to grant the declaratory remedy has been primarily used by doctors or health authorities to seek authority to treat or to withhold treatment in the absence of consent, or to define the scope of medical treatment itself. Driven by these test cases, the common law of treatment without consent has developed with astonishing rapidity. At the heart of that development has been a rhetoric of rights, of the ascendency of the right of self determination over the principle of the sanctity of life. However, in terms of practical results, remedies granted, the common-law proof of the pudding, again with the notable exception of *Re C*, the prime thrust of the case law has been towards defining the scope of doctors' powers to treat without consent. The burgeoning common law and the Law Commission's proposals may be seen as reflecting legalism, requiring courts to decide publicly questions which had often previously been matters of clinical judgment, and making those decisions within a framework of rights, powers, duties and legally defined criteria. This has without doubt led to gains in terms of patients' rights, such as the right of capable adults to make binding advance refusals of treatment. But the common-law declaratory jurisdiction has privileged a medical conception of individual rights, where the right of incapacitated patients to be treated in what a substantial body of medical opinion regards as their best interests prevails over all others, leaving patients with few effective safeguards against controversial treatments. Despite the portrayal of these proceedings in the Official Solicitor's practice notes as a 'thorough adversarial examination' and therefore as representing the common-law apotheosis of safeguards for individual rights, cases where there is no conflict may be decided on the basis of affidavit evidence, and the proceedings are inherently parental in nature, geared towards concepts of best interests as determined by the *Bolam* test. Because these hearings are expensive and time-consuming, there has been a clear movement by the judges to restrict the need to come to court to those cases where they consider the controversial nature of the proposed treatment to warrant it.

The Law Commission's proposals to codify clinical authority to treat without consent, and to provide a range of new procedural safeguards presided over by a more accessible judicial forum than the High Court, are therefore to be welcomed. Their most welcome feature will be that, if enacted, they will eliminate the contagion of *Bolam* from the determination of patients' best interests. On the negative side, their enactment would result in three potentially overlapping regimes of treatment without consent: Mental Health Act second opinions operating according to a likelihood of medical benefits; the new Court of Protection and Incapacity Act second opinions using a best interests test, and a residual role for the declaratory jurisdiction of the High Court. If the Commission's proposals are enacted without an overhaul of the Mental Health Act 1983, there is a substantial risk of arbitrary differences in the level of safeguard available for patients, depending upon whether they are detained or informal. Before concluding it is important to consider the situation of yet another group who are subject to a different legal regime of powers to treat without consent, children under eighteen.

16

INFORMAL COMPULSION:
TREATING CHILDREN
WITHOUT CONSENT

Children are people under eighteen.[1] There are 629 mental illness in-patient beds for children in England, but the service for children and adolescents has been described as unplanned, patchy and variable in quality and composition.[2] In 1991 the United Kingdom Government ratified the 1989 United Nations Convention on the Rights of the Child. Article 25 of the Convention requires State Parties to recognise the right of the child who has been placed by the competent authorities for the purposes of care, protection or treatment of his or her physical or mental health, to a periodic review of the treatment provided, and all other circumstances relevant to his or her placement. In 1994 the Government reported to the UN Committee on the Rights of the Child to the effect that children who are detained under the 1983 Act have the same rights as adults to challenge their detention and treatment without consent. Then, somewhat disingenuously, they declared that the vast majority of children in psychiatric hospitals are informal patients.[3] Whilst true, this statement takes no account of the fact that informal does not necessarily mean voluntary, that under English law children may be admitted informally against their will, and when this happens they are *de facto* detained but have none of the safeguards which accompany detention under the Act.

This situation arises because health-care professionals are reluctant to detain children, even if they are clearly refusing treatment. Common practice is to admit children informally and to seek consent for treatment from the person with parental responsibilities, or from the local authority if the child is in care. The reason most often given is to avoid the stigma of detention and any adverse consequences which might ensue for the juvenile in later life as a result of having been detained, although much of that stigma comes from having been a psychiatric patient or from having been in care, rather than having been detained under mental health legislation. The Mental Health Act Code of Practice and the Guidance on the Children Act both encourage the use of the compulsory powers under the Mental Health Act where a juvenile is refusing necessary psychiatric medication. The advice in these codes is based on the idea that detained patients have access to statutory safeguards not available if the patient is admitted informally.

Article 12 of the United Nations Convention on the Rights of the Child provides that States Parties shall assure to the child who is capable of forming his or her own views the right to express those views freely in all matters affecting the child, the views of the child being given due weight in accordance with [his or her] age and maturity . . .'. The rights of children between sixteen and eighteen to make their own treatment decisions were enhanced by section 8(1) of the Family Law Reform Act 1969 which provides that:

> the consent of a minor who has attained the age of sixteen years to any surgical, medical or dental treatment which, in the absence of consent, would constitute a trespass to the person, shall be as effective as it would be if he were of full age; and where a minor has given an effective consent to any treatment, it shall not be necessary to obtain any consent for it from his parent or guardian.

Section 8 became widely regarded as conferring complete power both to consent to and to refuse medical treatment to everyone over sixteen. The capacity of children under sixteen to make treatment decisions was an important issue in the 1985 ruling of the House of Lords in *Gillick* v. *West Norfolk and Wisbech Health Authority*,[4] where Lord Fraser said he was not disposed to hold that a girl aged less than sixteen lacks the power to give valid consent to medical treatment merely on account of her age. He concluded that there was no statutory provision which compelled him to hold that a girl under the age of sixteen lacked the legal capacity to consent to contraceptive advice, examination and treatment 'provided that she has the necessary understanding and intelligence to know what they involve.'[5] Lord Scarman described the power of a competent child under sixteen not just as a power to consent, but a power to decide, implying both consent and refusal. He said this:

Parental right yields to the child's right to make his own decisions when he reaches a sufficient understanding and intelligence to be capable of making up his own mind on the matter requiring decision.[6]

Thus in retrospect, the speeches in *Gillick* give a narrow and a broad view of 'Gillick competence': Lord Fraser does not go beyond competence to consent; and Lord Scarman confers on those with sufficient understanding and maturity the power to consent and to refuse. Lord Scarman's view became the more widely held, forming the basis of rights in the Children Act 1989 to refuse medical examinations and being adopted in Guidance on the Children Act on consent to treatment in residential settings.[7]

Events in 1991 brought to prominence the question of the legal safeguards which are available to guarantee that psychotropic medication is only given to juvenile patients when it is strictly necessary in their best interests. In June 1991 the MHAC published criticisms of the sedation and seclusion of young persons without consent at Langton House, a private home for disturbed adolescents,[8] and a week later the report was published of an inquiry instituted by the Department of Health into the forced medication of a sixteen-year-old girl in St Charles' Youth Treatment Centre.[9] The inquiry found that intramuscular injections of neuroleptic medication (Largactil) had been administered against the girl's will, and that she had been kept in solitary confinement for seven weeks. It also noted that there was confusion among the staff as to the circumstances in which such treatment without consent might be justified. Guidance issued in the wake of these events suggested that, where it was intended to give a juvenile compulsory psychiatric treatment, consideration should be given to using the powers under the 1983 Act with its concomitant safeguards. This approach was to be undermined by a body of case law which has developed since 1992, and which has removed the rights of children to refuse treatment, if a doctor thinks it is in their best interests and a parent, or the local authority if the child is in care, consents to it.

The first of these was *Re R (a minor) (wardship: medical treatment)*,[10] an appeal against a decision to ward a girl aged fifteen years ten months who was prone to attacks of mental disorder and violent mood swings resulting in dangerous behaviour to herself and to others. The purpose of the wardship proceedings was to enable psychiatric medication to be given despite her refusal. Although R had in the past accepted injections of seda- tive medication (from BNF 4.1 'minor tranquillisers'), she said this was because she felt she had no choice as if she refused she would be injected anyway. The proposal was now to give her antipsychotic medication (BNF 4.2.1 'major tranquillisers'). Waite J. granted the application and authorised the medication to be given, finding that R lacked the mental capacity to make her own decision. The Official Solicitor appealed to the Court of Appeal, which dismissed the appeal, on the basis that the judge had been right to find her incapable. Lord Donaldson accepted that '*Gillick* competent' patients under sixteen have the right to *agree* to treat- ment proposed by a doctor, whether or not those with parental rights and duties agree, but then said that their right to refuse treatment proposed by a doctor had to give way to the power of those with parental rights and responsibilities to consent on their behalf.

The Children Act 1989 aimed to create a comprehensive frame- work of statutory powers and court orders to cover every foreseeable eventuality, leaving only the unexpected to be dealt with by the High Court. Since the 1989 Act came into force local authorities can no longer use wardship where a child is in care, although the inherent jurisdiction of the High Court remains avail- able for the resolution of issues concerning the child's future. Local authorities must have the leave of the High Court before they may invoke the inherent jurisdiction, and leave may only be granted where the desired result cannot be achieved without resort to it.[11]

The inherent jurisdiction was invoked by a local authority in 1992 to authorise the compulsory placement and treatment of an anorexic girl of sixteen in a psychiatric unit specialising in eating disorders in *Re W (a minor) (medical treatment: court's jurisdic- tion)*,[12] the case where Lord Donaldson MR delivered his famous 'flak jacket' judgment. The primary issue before the court was whether, in the light of section 8 of the Family Law Reform Act 1969, and the fact that W was over sixteen, the court had any jurisdiction to make an order concerning W's medical treatment which conflicted with her wishes. Her condition had deteriorated to the point in 1991 when for a short time she had to be fed by naso-gastric tube and her arms had been encased in plaster.

The Court of Appeal held that not only did the High Court have the power under the inherent jurisdiction to override the refusal of a minor, even one who is over sixteen, to undergo necessary treatment, but so too did those who had parental responsibility. The effect of section 8 of the 1969 Act was to give a minor who has attained the age of sixteen a right to consent to surgical medical or dental treatment, but not an absolute right to veto such treatment. Only the court could override the consent of a sixteen- or seventeen-year-old. Consent could not be overridden by those with parental responsibility for the minor, but refusal could.

Re R was followed by Thorpe J. in *Re K, W, and H (minors) (medical treatment)*.[13] In November 1991 the Northampton Area Health Authority set up an inquiry into practices in the adolescent unit at St Andrew's Hospital Northampton, following a number of complaints from former patients, one of which concerned the use of emergency sedation. Children were only admitted to the unit if their parents or the local authority having care of them consented in writing to the regime adopted by the unit, including the emergency use of medication. The committee's report recommended that in cases of doubt about a child patient's consent the hospital would be wise to apply for a specific issue order under section 8 of the Children Act 1989, which is what the authority did. Thorpe J. held that the applications were 'misconceived and unnecessary', and that *Re R* had 'made it plain' that a child of '*Gillick* competence' could consent to treatment but that, if he or she declined to do so, consent could be given by someone else with parental rights or responsibilities. Even if they had been '*Gillick* competent', it was manifest that their refusal of consent would not have exposed the doctor at the unit to the risk of civil or criminal proceedings if he had proceeded to administer medication in emergency and in the face of such refusal, since in each instance he had parental consent.

The 1993 version of the Mental Health Act Code of Practice notes the changes introduced as a result of the Children Act 1989, stating the consequences of *Re R* and *Re W* in the following terms:

> No minor of any age has power, by refusing consent to treatment, to override a consent to treatment by anyone who has parental responsibility for the minor including a local authority with the benefit of a care order or consent by the court.[14]

The Code describes refusal as a very important consideration in making clinical judgments and for parents and the court in deciding whether themselves to give consent. Its importance increases with the age and maturity of the minor.[15] The Code is here seeking to adopt an approach which is consistent with Article 12 of the UN Convention on the Rights of the Child. In cases involving emergency protection orders, child assessment orders, interim care orders and full supervision orders under the Children Act 1989, competent children have the right to refuse consent to such examination, assessment and in certain circumstances treatment, and their refusal cannot be overridden. Where a child is informally admitted by parents or guardians, the Code warns against assuming that the parents have consented to any treatment 'regarded as necessary'. Consent should be sought for each aspect of the child's care as it arises, and 'blanket' consent forms should not be used.[16]

Compulsory placement without formal detention of minors in psychiatric hospital by those with parental rights has been held to be lawful under the European Convention in the *Nielsen* case.[17] The applicant had been admitted at the age of twelve to a Danish psychiatric hospital by his mother who was the sole holder of parental rights. Because his mother had consented to the admission, he had no rights under Danish law to challenge his detention. His application to the European Commission of Human Rights alleged breach of Articles 5(1) and 5(4), in that he had been detained without evidence of unsoundness of mind and had been afforded no opportunity to challenge the lawfulness of his detention. The European Court of Human Rights held that the hospitalisation did not amount to a deprivation of liberty within the meaning of Article 5, but was 'a responsible exercise by the mother of her custodial rights in the interests of the child'.[18]

The position is similar at English law. In *R* v. *Kirklees Metropolitan Council ex parte C* (1992),[19] a girl challenged the decision of the local authority to admit her at the age of twelve against her will to a psychiatric hospital without using the powers of compulsory detention under the 1983 Act. C had been violent and disruptive at an assessment centre. Kennedy J. held that, just as an adult could lawfully agree to enter a psychiatric hospital for assessment, the position was no different in relation to a child, save that there must be a valid consent. This could come from a parent or the local authority. The local authority had consented, and were entitled to conclude that C was not 'Gillick competent' on account of her age and her general behaviour problems at the time. The decision to dismiss the application was upheld by the Court of Appeal,[20] which held that juveniles could be admitted informally against their will with the consent of the parents, or, where appropriate, the local authority.

In the cases on treating juveniles decided since Re R in 1991, the widely held view of the Gillick ruling as having established the 'Scarman' version of Gillick competence has been completely overturned. Wardship and the inherent jurisdiction have been used in much the same way as the jurisdiction to grant declarations to establish, often by way of obiter 'guidance', a new body of rules laying down the rights and duties of doctors and patients. It seems now that legislation will be necessary if a young person who is 'Gillick competent' is to have complete autonomy in the field of medical treatment, as was previously thought by many to be the position. The courts have also upheld the practice of local authorities or parents admitting juveniles informally, with the result that they are actually detained but deprived of all the safeguards available to detained patients. Whatever criticisms may be levelled at the safeguards relating to the psychiatric treatment of adults without consent, juvenile patients who are 'de facto detained' may be denied even that basic protection. It was for this reason that the MHAC sought in 1986 to extend its remit to the treatment of mentally disordered juveniles who were detained under 'any order, authority or power other than one arising under the 1983 Act'.[21] The Code of Practice and the Children Act Guidance which advise detention of juveniles to provide safeguards are swimming against an overwhelming tide of professional unwillingness to use compulsory powers under the 1983 Act. If child patients are to be given adequate protection against potentially hazardous treatments, the only practicable alternative would appear to be to extend the second opinion procedures and the remit of the MHAC to cover children who are informal patients receiving treatment for mental disorder. The Royal College of Psychiatrists Consensus Statements on High Dose Medication (1993) and ECT (1995) suggest that, before giving these treatments to a young person, two (non-statutory) second opinions from other doctors should be obtained.

The rhetoric of autonomy has been notably absent from the case law on treating children without consent. The question which must now be addressed is whether the correct balance has been struck between children's rights to make their own treatment decisions and the need to protect their health. It is suggested that it has not. Much of the case law has concerned extreme situations where treatment has been necessary to prevent a threat to the life of the child or lasting damage to his or her health. Consideration should be given to amending section 8 of the Family Law Reform Act 1969 to clarify the rights of sixteen- and seventeen-year-olds to refuse medical treatment, to restore the status quo ante *Re W* and ensure that overriding the refusal of a child will be based on a finding of incapacity. As a bare minimum, in order to comply fully with Article 25 of the UN Convention, the jurisdiction of the MHAC to hear complaints, of MHRTs to review detention, and the second opinion procedures in section 58 of the 1983 Act should all be extended to child patients, whether they are detained or subject to informal compulsion.

CONCLUSION

Historically, periods of major psychotherapeutic change have coincided with attempts to remake the image of psychiatry and psychiatrists. Law and legal institutions have played an important role, not only in the ideological sense of facilitating changes in public perception of what psychiatrists do, but also in the practical sense of providing them with the legal authority to do it. This history shows that, in examining law's role *vis-à-vis* psychiatry, it is important to adopt a wider conception of law than simply legislation and case law. Because psychiatric patients have traditionally been denied access to the courts it is necessary to mine deeper, in what may be described as the legal substrata. These include the rules and guidance issuing from the commissioners who have traditionally presided over the mental health system, as well as their decisions (sometimes non-decisions) in cases where patients have been mistreated or lost their lives, but which have never reached a court. Decisions by commissioners in these cases may have as much impact on psychiatric practice as any court ruling. Looking at law and psychiatry in terms of treatment without consent rather than powers of detention reveals more clearly the central aspect of the psychiatric professional project; the preservation and expansion of clinical authority, both in the sense of discretion as to which treatments to give, and the power to give them without consent. Official bodies like the Lunacy Commission, the Board of Control and latterly the courts have played a key role in this process.

The 'abolition' of restraint, in which the Lunacy Commissioners played an important role, enabled psychiatry to take on a new guise as a professional and humanitarian discipline. A key factor enabling the medical profession to achieve professional domination of the mental disorder market was their ability to use drugs to replace restraint. Engravings of the hapless Norris chained in the Bethlem dungeon or Pinel liberating the maniacal patients have become powerful symbols of the dark age from which psychiatry emerged in the mid-nineteenth century. Victory over mechanical restraint was not claimed until the late 1850s, and if we are searching for technological breakthroughs which enabled this to take place, good candidates would be opium, the bromides, chloral and the invention of the hypodermic syringe.

The Lunacy Acts also enshrined the clinical and legal authority of doctors, subjecting them to central regulation by the Lunacy Commission. The Lunacy Commission fostered the idea that seclusion and restraint were medical interventions by requiring doctors to authorise them. During this time, under the superintendence of the Lunacy Commission, a moral calculus of psychiatric intervention was developed. Although not prohibited in legislation, merely required to be recorded, mechanical restraint was viewed as bad. Seclusion was grudgingly accepted as a necessary intervention, as long as it was not used for 'economy of attendants'. Drug treatment, although recorded in the case books, was a matter of medical judgment.

By the 1870s it was abundantly clear that mechanical restraint had been replaced by chemical restraint. There appear to have been two schools of how chemical restraint was best achieved. The 'perpetual sedation' school used chloral, the bromides, and other debilitating drugs of dependence to keep patients in a state approaching stupor. This was opposed by the 'short sharp shock' school, which included George Savage and Henry Maudsley, who felt that prolonged administration of sedatives destroyed the person's health, but who were not averse to deploying a heavy dose of hyoscyamine as a corrective and a deterrent. Of course there were also the empiricists who used both.

The 1880s saw a revolt against the new moral order of non-restraint. Savage championed the view that certain forms of restraint, such as padded gloves and wet packs, should be regarded as a legitimate exercise of clinical authority and part of psychiatry's armamentarium. Savage would later claim to have made a self-conscious decision to seek to free himself and psychiatry from central prescription of treatment methods. The resultant provisions of the Lunacy Act 1890 were a compromise. Mechanical restraint was not outlawed, but permitted for medical reasons and with a medical certificate, as long as it was in a form permitted by the Lunacy Commission. Medical authority to impose restraint, although limited and subject to a requirement to report to the Commission, was confirmed in the 1890 legislation. This model would be used again under the Mental Health Act 1983 to authorise treatment without consent.

During the last twenty years of the Lunacy Commission's life, and until the 1930s, few breakthroughs were made in British psychiatry, and it continued to rely strongly on sedatives like chloral, the bromides and paraldehyde, and extensive use of seclusion in side rooms. The Board of Control, which replaced the Lunacy Commission, became a willing ally in the profession's desire to promote the view of psychiatry as fit to take its place in mainstream medicine. The Mental Treatment Act 1930 reflected this, remodelling the Board as a medically dominated body, and conferring extensive immunity from suit on doctors. Even before 1930 the Board had been promoting experimentation with new forms of treatment, but after 1930 this really took off.

Elliot Valenstein has emphasised that the wave of experimentation with physical treatments like comas, shocks and psychosurgery was a mainstream phenomenon, and this was certainly true of Britain, where the Board of Control actively promoted physical treatment. Physical treatment was radical both in its physical effects on patients and in its effect on psychiatry. It marked a rebellion against therapeutic conservatism which relied on tried and tested methods; sedatives accompanied by painstaking, lengthy, and often fruitless efforts to open patients up to analysis. Physical treatment promoted the desired view of psychiatry in the fold of physical medicine. This equation was further reinforced by the fact that patients could now come in for a short burst of radical treatment and be discharged 'cured', which, as we have seen, could cover a multitude of states. There must have been some whose cures were the result of the great lengths to which they went to avoid readmission, having been so terrorised by their experience. These treatments also relieved the pressure on overcrowded institutions. Although they provided a 'quick fix', the problem with the physical treatments was that (*pace* Walter Freeman's motel-room lobotomies) they were so radical that they had to be carried out in hospitals.

The age of experimentation was important in paving the way for the 'psychopharmacological revolution' for a number of reasons. First it reinforced the experimental ethos of psychiatry, and reintroduced a radical pioneering spirit, and a respect for eccentric devil-may-care genius, not seen since the days of the whirligig chair and baths of surprise. Risks to patients could easily be seen as minimal when the stakes were so high: a possible cure for their own illness, and the advancement of science. Consent seeking, although carried out by some, was not a priority for most, and regarded as of no importance by others. The experimental ethos carried on into the 1950s and was instrumental in establishing a new sheet anchor for psychiatry – Chlorpromazine.

In 1954 the breakthrough into the age of psychopharmacology was widely proclaimed in medical journals across the world, and psychiatrists began carrying out clinical trials in psychiatric hospitals across the country. Again, consent seeking was not a priority, and many were experimented on without their consent. Just as the age of experimentation with physical treatments had brought experiments with high doses of barbiturates, it was not long before the initial worries about the pronounced side effects of phenothiazines subsided, and experiments began with their use in megadoses. Valenstein has argued that the reason why psychosurgery lasted so long was that there were so many different types to evaluate. Much the same could be said of the neuroleptics. They have undoubtedly contributed to the relief of much mental distress, but they are ineffective in some cases and have serious side effects in others. However, new drugs are being developed all the time with a view to minimising this or that side effect, and they can be tried in endless different permutations. If one drug does not work, higher doses can be tried. Or another can be tried, and another, and another. The 1959 Act continued the favourable legal climate for experimental treatment without consent, with re-enactment of the immunities and defences in section 16 of the 1930 Act, and a concept of clinical authority which devolved power to the newly created ranks of 'consultant psychiatrists'. In the age of psychopharmacology, intramuscular injections of Chlorpromazine were soon established as the standard method of restraining a disturbed patient, and combinations of different major tranquillisers and barbiturates (for example the Broadmoor five and two) were still in use (with fatal results) to restrain in the 1980s and 1990s. Injections of major tranquillisers, used in combination with seclusion, became the 'sheet anchors' of modern psychiatry. Because of their unpleasant effects, these treatments were open to abuse for punishment or deterrence. The only physical treatment to survive the 1950s in wide use was ECT.

Concerns of the 1970s and early 1980s led to the introduction of express legal provision for treatment without consent, which had previously been so much taken for granted as part of clinical authority that mentioning it did not even occur to legislators. By the 1980s it was necessary to spell it out. Part IV upheld the position of the RMO as in charge of a detained patient's treatment, and defined powers to treat without consent, subject to a second opinion procedure. If the personnel with power to decide whether or not to treat without consent had changed, did Part IV result in a change in the substance of these decisions? One clear incursion on clinical authority was that psychosurgery would no longer be allowed without valid consent. Another was that the decision of the SOAD to refuse permission was binding on the RMO and there was no appeal to the MHAC. Set against this is the fact that the second opinion is medical. Although there is a duty on the SOAD to consult other professionals, on occasion these are staff in occupations with little to do with patient care, and often nurses and others were brought in to 'get to know' the patient before being consulted. The test for giving the treatment, likelihood of benefit or prevention of deterioration, used in combination with the *Bolam* test, creates a presumption in favour of the RMO's judgment. Not surprisingly, the concordance rate for section 58 opinions is high. The 1992 survey showed that the main cases where authority was withheld for clinical reasons involved ECT or the 'new' antipsychotic Clozaril, because it was felt that other less drastic treatments should be given time to work. There was even one case, the Pimozide case, where the second opinion may have been a life saver. The survey also shows the extent of psychiatry's continued reliance on ECT, and in particular the strikingly high numbers of middle-aged and elderly women who have the treatment. In this the pattern of the past is being followed, for women have traditionally been in the majority of those receiving radical treatment, whether it be clitoridectomy, ovariotomy, lobotomy, chemical shock, comas or ECT.

Perhaps the most important indicator of the effect on the substance of clinical decisions, and of the resilience of the experimental spirit, is the extent to which SOADs authorised high dose medication. The BNF recommended dose levels, used loosely as a yardstick in the second opinion process, are viewed by some psychiatrists as too low, and resistance to central prescription remains strong. The fact that 12 per cent of medicine second opinions involved doses above BNF limits does not suggest a significant interference with clinical authority. A poignant reminder of psychiatry's limitations were the numbers of patients in the MHAC 1 survey who had been on high doses of medication for years and who showed no improvement, remaining totally inaccessible (61 out of 232). Could it be that their medication contributed to their poor mental state?

Clinical authority was reinforced in another way under the 1959 and then the 1983 legislation. Medical treatment was defined broadly, the principal defining characteristic being that it is done under medical supervision. This made possible its expansive interpretation in the 1990s force-feeding cases. In fact recognised treatments of psychiatric patients today include restraint (only rarely and in very limited circumstances), seclusion (subject to local procedures and requirements for observation), ECT and medicines (subject to the second opinion procedures). ECT, as a hangover from the days of physical treatments, still attracts greater controversy than drug treatment, although concerns about high doses and polypharmacy are on the increase. Large doses of major tranquillisers are used to restrain the very disturbed patient, and there is evidence that some patients are subject to heavy sedation on a routine basis. The Victorians would have called this chemical restraint.

Concerns about consent seeking for physical surgery on psychiatric patients emerged as early as the mid-nineteenth century with the Baker Brown affair, even if 'consent', or more accurately, permission, could be given by the patient's relatives or the Lunacy Commission. Legal and ethical awareness of issues of consent has largely been developed through cases where doctors have sought to perform surgery on the sexual or reproductive organs of women. The sterilisation debates of the 1930s were important for a number of reasons. They showed that consent was important. They also raised the ethical issue of the acceptability of consent based on the promise of discharge from hospital if sterilisation is agreed to. The Brock Committee's recommendation of 'voluntary sterilisation' subject to the oversight of the Board of Control foundered largely because of the Nazi example, but also because the view prevailed that the operation could only be performed if it was in the patient's medical interests. These did not include social interests such as the possibility of living a freer life, or the distressing effects of pregnancy on a learning disabled woman, or 'eugenic' matters like the possibility of producing disabled offspring. The possibility was left open for contraceptive sterilisation without consent based on double effect, if it were done primarily for medical reasons. The absence of legislation meant that law was cast in the guise of predator awaiting any doctor who strayed beyond the consensus view of acceptable bounds.

Since the 1980s the law has appeared in a different guise in sterilisation cases. Inspired by North American developments in the *parens patriae* jurisdiction, we see the British courts overcoming the absence of an equivalent here by using the jurisdiction to grant declarations. Law's new role is to authorise treatment without consent before the event, and to develop clinical authority to treat incapacitated people if it is in their best interests according to a responsible doctor standard. In sterilisation cases best interests can include non-medical interests, such as the opportunity for a freer life outside an institution, or that the person would not understand pregnancy and would be distressed by the bodily changes. Having rushed into this area of decision making, the courts have since sought to make a strategic retreat. The rejection of the therapeutic/non-therapeutic distinction as the distinguishing factor between legal and illegal sterilisation without consent was followed by its revival in 1991 as the means of distinguishing between those treatments which were necessary for the health of the patient, where court approval is not needed, and those which were based on broader notions of best interests. These developments have certainly altered (and made more costly) the process by which decisions requiring court approval are made. Whether they have altered the substantive outcome of medical decision-making is more doubtful. Prospective, permission-seeking uses of the courts have provided vehicles to issue authoritative legal statements of clinical authority to treat incapacitated adults without consent if it is in their medical best interests, to override the refusal of '*Gillick* competent' juveniles, to define the scope of medical treatment under the 1983 Act, and even at the suit of a patient to pronounce on his capacity and the validity of an advance directive. Through these law-making activities the common law too has played an important part in the legal definition and construction of clinical authority.

British psychiatry is again at a crucial turning point. The current issue is the extension of clinical authority to psychiatric patients in the community. By the time the Mental Health Act 1959 came into force, psychiatry had one important new weapon in its armamentarium. This was the depot antipsychotic drug, whereby an injection of neuroleptic could last for two weeks by slow absorption from a depot formed at the injection site. This made it possible to maintain patients in the community. It also brought into the language the 'revolving door patient' who would be detained, become well on medication, be discharged, would cease medication, would relapse, and be readmitted.

Under the 1890 and 1930 legislation clinical authority to treat without consent was closely related to in-patient status. The debates prior to the 1959 Act saw increasing emphasis placed on care in the community, and bound up in this was a concern to ensure that patients who were in the community could be required to comply with medication. The Percy Commission placed mental health guardianship at the centre of their policy of fostering the re-orientation of psychiatric care towards the community. This was reflected in the 1959 Act which opened guardianship to mentally ill as well as mentally handicapped people, with the guardian having all the powers of a parent over a child under sixteen. By the 1970s guardianship had become a social services rather than a health authority function, with applications being made to the local social services authority. By the late 1970s there was widespread concern that it had never been much used and was a failure.

Why did mental health guardianship fail as a vehicle of compulsion in the community? Although it was finally doomed when it became a social services rather than a health authority function, mental deficiency guardianship under the 1913 Act declined steeply from the late 1940s when it ceased to be used as a way of providing finance for caring relatives.[1] The principal reason it never took off was that the psychiatric profession quickly developed an alternative which did not involve the laborious process of applying for guardianship, with its abdication of control to the social services authority.

The solution was the 'long leash',[2] a creative use of extended leave. The 1959 Act transferred clinical authority from Medical Superintendents to RMOs, including the power to grant conditional leave. RMOs fashioned this community power by granting leave to detained patients on condition that they continued their medication. Even if they complied, patients would be recalled to hospital at regular intervals for one night by the RMO to renew the detention. They would then be sent out on leave again under a continued obligation to continue taking medication, on pain of recall to hospital by the RMO if they did not. This could be repeated *ad infinitum*, so that patients remained subject to long term compulsion to take medicine in the community. It had the advantage that the RMO retained effective control, and the decision to readmit was a matter for his or her clinical judgment alone. The 1978 Interdepartmental *Review of the Mental Health Act 1959* referred to it as 'a misuse of powers'.[3]

In 1985 the MHAC found the 'long leash' to be in extensive use and expressed serious doubts about its legality.[4] These were shown to be well founded by *R* v. *Hallstrom and another ex parte W (No. 2)* and *R* v. *Gardner and another ex parte L*.[5] Both cases involved patients with long histories of chronic schizophrenic illness. The patient in *Hallstrom* was detained 'notionally' for one night and leave of absence was granted the next day, on condition that she accepted her medication. *Gardner* concerned a patient who had been given leave of absence in February 1985. In May 1985 the RMO renewed the authority to detain for a further six months even though the patient continued to live in the community throughout. McCullough J. rejected the 'medicalist' argument that any ambiguity in the statute should be resolved so as to enable doctors to do what was in accordance with good psychiatric practice, namely to require patients in the community to accept medication which was in their best interests. Instead he adopted the legalist approach that:

> [U]nless clear statutory authority to the contrary exists, no one is to be detained in hospital or undergo medical treatment ... without his consent. This is as true of a mentally disordered person as of anyone else.[6]

The 'long leash' was unlawful.

These decisions led to an outcry on the part of many psychiatrists and the Royal College of Psychiatrists proposed introducing a 'community treatment order'.[7] For five years the Department of Health showed no great enthusiasm for this, and the question was shelved until the appointment in 1992 of Virginia Bottomley as Secretary of State for Health. She expressed her concern that vulnerable mentally ill people were 'slipping through the net', and that the 'pendulum' of mental-health law had swung too far in the direction of civil liberties.[8] During 1992 the Royal College was busy preparing a new set of proposals for 'Community Supervision Orders', effectively guardianship under the control of the RMO. On the last day of 1992, Ben Silcock, a young schizophrenic, jumped into the lions' enclosure at London Zoo. Although badly mauled, he survived. The incident was captured on amateur video and appeared on network news. It would gradually emerge that, despite providing a powerful image, the case was not ideal proof of the need for compulsory community treatment, first because Ben Silcock had in fact taken his medication, and, what was not revealed at the time, was awaiting trial for assault on a police officer, the stress of which may well have been a major cause of the tragic episode.

Immediately following the incident, the Secretary of State held meetings with the Royal College and other interested parties, and a Department of Health Working Party was appointed to examine the question. No sooner had the review team begun work than public attention was focused on another case where a formerly detained schizophrenic patient had been discharged, had ceased taking his medication and killed a young musician, Jonathan Zito. The patient was Christopher Clunis, a paranoid schizophrenic with a long history of violence, who had been released from hospital three months before the attack. He had been supposed to attend Friern Barnet Hospital as a voluntary out-patient but had not turned up. An inquiry was instituted by the health authorities concerned which reported in February 1994, finding that there had been no aftercare plan for Clunis, as required for formerly detained patients by section 117 of the 1983 Act, and that the authorities had failed to manage or oversee provision of health and social services for him.[9]

In August 1993, the Secretary of State for Health announced a a 'ten point plan' including the introduction of a new statutory power of 'supervised discharge', and a series of shorter term measures to make greater use of existing powers. The *Code of Practice* was amended to emphasise that patients may be detained under the 1983 Act solely in the interests of their own health, even if there is no risk to their own or other people's safety. Those doing the assessment must consider any evidence that the patient's mental health will deteriorate if he does not receive treatment, including 'the known history of the individual's mental disorder.'[10]

The Department of Health also announced the introduction of supervision registers, described by the Secretary of State as the equivalent of 'at risk registers' for children, to keep track of patients who are 'at risk to themselves or others'. These have been introduced without legislation and, unlike the changes to the Code, without the need for any Parliamentary approval, by Health Service Guidance HSG(94)5, issued by the NHS Management Executive. This required the introduction of supervision registers by 1 April 1994. Under the new National Health Service market reforms, health authorities as purchasers must contract with provider units, including private sector hospitals, for patient care. The Guidance informs health authorities that, when purchasing mental health care services from NHS Trusts or other bodies, they are required to include terms in their contracts ensuring that provider units set up supervision registers which identify and provide information on mentally disordered patients in the community who are liable to be at risk. These represent a firm push away from legalism, limiting the rights of privacy of psychiatric patients. They have been introduced without any Parliamentary debate by administrative circular rather than by legislation. Although the circular is couched in mandatory terms requiring inclusion of registers in contracts, as Kate Harrison has pointed out, its legal status is ambiguous:

> The Secretary of State for Health has the power to make directions under s. 17 of the National Health Service Act 1977, but the guidance was not made under that section. It is not possible to direct through guidance, and the Government has conceded that [it] does not have the force of law.[11]

It is also open to question whether the guidance meets the requirements of Article 8 of the European Convention which precludes interference with the right of privacy by a public authority unless it is in accordance with the law and necessary in a democratic society. This entails the existence of a procedure to regulate the holding of personal information about individuals and to enable the person's interest in keeping it private to be weighed against competing public interests. The decision as to the inclusion or removal of a patient is one for the RMO, advised by the care team. Patients have no effective rights of appeal against inclusion on the register.

The final piece of the jigsaw is the application for after care under supervision proposed in the Mental Health (Patients in the Community) Bill 1995.[12] This represents a significant coup for psychiatric clinical authority, a medicalisation of guardianship. The power would apply to patients detained for treatment. Applications would be made by RMOs, not social workers, to the health authority subject to consultation with the patient and others involved in aftercare. Supervision would have to be justified on the grounds of risk of harm to the patient or others. Patients would be required to live at a specified address, and to attend specified places for medical treatment or training, but they could not be required to accept medication against their will. But if patients 'neglect to receive' or refuse any services offered to them (this really means medication) the health and social services authorities will be required 'to review the services provided and consider whether his condition warrants re-admission' under the revised authoritative interpretation in the Code of Practice. The Bill envisages that patients under supervision could not be forcibly medicated in the community, but could be taken and conveyed (forcibly) by the supervisor to any place where they are required to attend for medical treatment. This, together with the power to reassess for compulsory admission, will be able to be used as bargaining tools to obtain the consent of patients in the community. Far from being insignificant, as Thorold has argued,[13] this is an important new direction in the extension of clinical authority. As psychiatric hospitals are closed on a large scale, so psychiatry loses its traditional base, the territory within which it can exercise clinical authority, and care is predominantly in the community. We would expect calls to extend clinical authority to treat without consent into the community. This is not, strictly speaking, what is happening, because patients will consent. However, psychiatrists' ability to pressure patients to consent has been greatly strengthened, and consent obtained by pressure is not true consent.

Although in some senses this represents an extension of clinical authority into the community, in other ways it represents a potential threat, since the original Bill provided for a community RMO who could be any registered medical practitioner, not necessarily a consultant psychiatrist. The community RMO could be the patient's own general practitioner, although the Bill expressly provides that there would be nothing to prevent the RMO, the community RMO and the supervisor being the same person. It was no surprise when the Royal College of Psychiatrists tabled an amendment, adopted in modified form by the Government in the House of Lords, to ensure that the community RMO is approved under section 12 of the 1983 Act as having experience in the diagnosis and treatment of mental disorder.

The extension of compulsory community powers raises the question of the extent to which they will be counterbalanced by entitlement to support and services in the community. How far will Gostin's 'new legalist' principle of the 'ideology of entitlement' to accommodation and community support services be recognised? Section 47 of the National Health Service and Community Care Act 1990 requires local social services authorities to carry out an assessment of the needs of any person who appears to be in need of community care services and, having regard to the results of the assessment to decide whether his or her needs call for the provision by them of any such services. Section 117 of the 1983 Act puts a joint duty on the local district health authority and the local social services authority to provide, in co-operation with relevant voluntary agencies, aftercare services for patients who cease to be detained and leave hospital following detention under the 1983 Act for treatment, under a hospital order made by a criminal court, or following transfer from prison.[14] The duty continues until the authorities are satisfied that the individual patient no longer needs aftercare. Patients who are covered by section 117 of the 1983 Act are entitled to assessment and, if appropriate, provision under section 47 of the 1990 Act. Limited successes have been achieved in enforcing these provisions through the courts.[15]

Can effective safeguards be devised to ensure that patients who are required to accept psychotropic medication on a long term basis are not required to do so unnecessarily and are not harmed by their treatment? Under English law the juridical bases of the right to bodily integrity are the tort of battery and the criminal law of assault. Liability for all but 'bad faith' battery will effectively be eliminated by the fact that the defence in section 139 will apply to patients subject to supervised discharge. Article 5 of the European Convention on Human Rights protects against arbitrary detention on grounds of unsoundness of mind, and the Strasbourg Court has developed an extensive jurisprudence regarding the need for objective evidence of mental disorder justifying detention: rights to be informed of the fact of detention and the reasons for it, and rights to periodic review of the lawfulness of detention. However, these do not entitle patients to review of supervised discharge. The Bill will entitle patients to apply to a MHRT for discharge from supervision, but the burden is on them to show that they are not mentally disordered or that supervision is not necessary to ensure that they receive appropriate aftercare under section 117.[16]

The right of bodily integrity is protected by Articles 3 and 8 of the European Convention, neither of which is ideally adapted to protect patients from hazardous treatments, as the *Herczegfalvy*[17] ruling showed. Supervised patients will not have rights to second opinions under section 58, although as formerly detained patients they will be entitled to complain to the MHAC in relation to the exercise of powers and duties under the Act. Many features of this power and the regime of registers and the like show a clear rejection of legalism in favour of medicalism. The power to put on the register and apply for supervision is conferred on the RMO. There would be little opportunity for effective independent review. Individual rights are overridden by administrative direction rather than legislation. Moreover, the proposals emphasise a primarily medical model of care and treatment for mentally disordered people in the community, placing compliance with drug regimes above all other forms of intervention and support, and ignoring patient's concerns about the side effects of long term use of depot neuroleptics. In Castel's terms this is an extension of tutelary power beyond the walls of the institution, entailing the extension to the community of new forms of institutional control and segregation which allow for the imposition of treatment in the community. To stop patients who are labelled as at risk from escaping the net of community control or 'falling through the network of care' in the Department of Health's phrase, the supervision guidance has an elaborate system, reminiscent of the Poor Law, for transferring patients to another authority's register when they move from one area to another. Registers are to provide the web of the network of care, the fabric for the institutionalisation of the community.

There has been great resistance by psychiatrists and nurses to any suggestion that they should be empowered to give medication forcibly to patients in their own homes. Supervised discharge avoids this by providing for assessment for readmission rather than forcible medication to be the consequence of non-compliance.

291

However, the introduction of supervised discharge may be merely the first stage of an inevitable extension of these powers, where the requirement of prior detention would be removed and, instead of defaulting patients being assessed for readmission, they would simply be taken to 'treatment centres' to be forcibly medicated and then returned home. The risk is that National Health Service in-patient provision will be so scarce that it is available only for those who need detention, with everyone else subject to supervision in the community or in private nursing or residential care homes.

Consent has undergone significant redefinition over the past 150 years. In the nineteenth century the consent of a relative or the Lunacy Commission was accepted as sufficient. The Law Commission's proposals alter our concept of consent and who can give it. They promote new concepts of 'delegated consent' whereby others can be nominated by the patient or by a court to consent on the patient's behalf. They allow for recognition of new types of legal instrument whereby decisions to refuse treatment may be made before the onset of incapacity and remain binding thereafter, or the power to consent may be conferred on another. They would establish new tests for incapacity and new tests for best interests, and would be backed up by codes of practice. They would set a new ethical and legal context for medical decision making in relation to incapacitated patients. They are hard to evaluate in terms of legalism and medicalism because they extend clinical authority to the informal patient, but they also reflect a colonisation of medical decision making by lawyers (academic and professional) and legal procedures.

Perhaps the central legal issue in Britain today is the basis on which the right to make one's own treatment decision should be suspended. This has changed radically since 1845. From a position where it was simply presumed that mental patients were incapable of deciding for themselves about anything, we moved to a situation by 1930 where it was detained patients who were presumed incapable, but voluntary patients could always be detained if treatment without consent was thought necessary. Under the 1959 legislation it was again assumed that detained patients could be treated without consent, but treatment was often given to informal non-volitional patients without true consent. The 1983 Act still allows for the treatment without consent of detained patients, and the Government's proposed reforms will effectively extend clinical authority over patients in the community to those who have been detained. We now have a number of intersecting and overlapping legal regimes in relation to treatment without consent. Quite apart from the potential for confusion which this creates, there is a clear need to produce a single coherent legal basis on which peoples' right of treatment decision-making can be removed. The approach adopted by the common law and the Law Commission is to use incapacity as the gatekeeper concept with a presumption in favour of capacity. The case law of the European Court of Human Rights also suggests a move in this direction, but seems to suggest that where patients are claiming unlawful treatment without consent, the onus is on them to demonstrate capacity. Ideas of incapacity are also employed as the gatekeeper concept by the Council of Europe Draft Bioethics Convention, which states that:

> Patients whose ability to decide what is in their best interests is impaired by mental disorders may be subjected, without their consent, and on the protective conditions prescribed by law, to an intervention aimed at treating their mental disorders where, without such treatment, serious harm is likely to result to their health. The protective conditions prescribed by law shall include supervisory, control, and appeal mechanisms.[18]

Could this herald a new role for a finding of incapacity, not only as the basis of treatment without consent, but also of detention itself?

Many legal and ethical issues face psychiatry as it enters the twenty-first century. They include ethnic and gender bias in treatment without consent, and the question of whether patients are better served by advocacy schemes than by panoptical bodies like the MHAC. There can be no denying that psychiatry has made immense progress over its 150-year history. Despite their side effects, neuroleptics and antidepressants offer relief to many from the torment of mental illness, and depot neuroleptics the prospect of long term treatment in the community rather than in hospital. Invasive treatments previously in widespread use, such as force feeding, are now rarely employed. Restraint and seclusion are to be used only as a last resort. Despite these advances, patients or, as some prefer to be known, users or survivors of psychiatry, are critical of psychiatry's dependence on drugs and ECT, and argue for the right to be treated without drugs. They claim that major tranquillisers are dependence-forming and that the psychotic episode which almost invariably follows cessation of the drug is a withdrawal symptom. One theory of how this may occur is that neuroleptics block the dopaminergic receptors in the brain and that withdrawal leads to those receptors being exposed, but in a more sensitised form than before, since they have expanded to counter the effect of the neuroleptic. Users argue that they should not be forced on a long term basis to take drugs with such high risks of adverse effects. Other controversial issues, such as reliance on high doses of sedative medication as the 'sheet anchor', dog modern psychiatry just as much as they did in the past.

The answer to the question about what makes the mentally ill so vulnerable to medical experimentation should be clear. In tracing the history of treatment without consent, we uncover the prime importance of consent seeking. The right to make one's own treatment decisions is, as the American courts put it at the beginning of the century, a fundamental democratic right. It is also a check on unbridled clinical power, that the doctor must explain what is intended and secure agreement. Statements from users emphasise how central the power to give or withhold consent is to personal dignity. Once that right is taken away, there is a duty on society to protect patients from experimental treatment which may profoundly and possibly permanently alter a patient's personality, and where the hazards outweigh the potential bene-fits. Law has so far proved to be of limited use in achieving this. Nevertheless, there are encouraging signs that psychiatrists are at last taking seriously patients' concerns about side effects and are showing increasing willingness to treat their patients as partici-pating partners in a therapeutic relationship rather than as passive recipients of treatment ordered by doctors. The development of high ethical standards and a culture of consent-seeking among psychiatrists are much more likely to improve the position of patients than any amount of legislative reform.

TABLE OF STATUTES

TABLE OF STATUTORY
INSTRUMENTS

TABLE OF CASES

A v. *United Kingdom Application No 6840/74* European Commission of Human Rights Decisions and Reports vol. 10, p. 5, and vol. 20, p. 5.

Airedale NHS Trust v. *Bland* [1993] AC 789.

Associated Provincial Picture Houses v. *Wednesbury Corporation* [1948] 1 KB 223.

B v. *Croydon Health Authority* (1994) 22 BMLR 13 (QBD and CA) [1995] 1 All ER 683 (CA only).

Beatty v. *Cullingworth* (1896) 2 BMJ 1525.

Blyth v. *Bloomsbury Health Authority and Another* [1993] 4 Med LR 151 (CA).

Bolam v. *Friern Barnet Hospital Management Committee* [1957] 1 WLR 582.

Bravery v. *Bravery* [1954] 1 WLR 1169; [1954] 3 All ER 59.

Buck v. *Bell* (1927) 274 US 200.

Canterbury v. *Spence* (1972) F. 2d 722.

Chatterton v. *Gerson* [1981] 1 QB 432.

Commission v. *Ireland* Judgment of 18 January 1978, Reports of the European Court of Human Rights, Series A, vol. 25.

Cull v. *Chance, The Times,* 15–18 June 1932.

Davies v. *Barking and Brentwood Health Authority,* unreported, 2 November 1992 (QBD).

Everett v. *Griffiths* [1920] 3 KB 161.

F v. *Riverside Health Trust* (1993) 20 BMLR 1.

F v. *West Berkshire Health Authority* [1989] 2 All ER 545.

Furber v. *Kratter, The Times,* 21 July 1988.

Gillick v. *West Norfolk and Wisbech Health Authority* [1986] AC 112.

Gold v. *Haringey Health Authority* [1988] QB 481.

H v. *Home Office, The Independent,* 6 May 1992.

Hamilton v. *Birmingham Regional Hospital Board* (1969) 2 BMJ 456.

Harnett v. *Bond* [1924] 2 KB 517.

Hatcher v. *Black, The Times,* 2 July 1954.

Herczegfalvy v. *Austria* (1993) 15 EHRR 437.

J v. *C* (1990) 5 BMLR 100.

NOTES

INTRODUCTION

1 Quoted in Rothman, D.J., *Strangers at the Bedside: A History of How Law and Bioethics Transformed Medical Decision-Making*, New York, Basic Books, 1991, pp. 96–97.
2 (1914) 105 NE 92.
3 Jones, W.L., *Ministering to Minds Diseased: A History of Psychiatric Treatment*, London, Heinemann, 1983.
4 Valenstein, E., *Great and Desperate Cures: The Rise and Decline of Psychosurgery and Other Radical Treatments for Mental Illness*, New York, Basic Books, 1986.
5 Weiner, D.B., 'Le geste de Pinel: The history of a psychiatric myth', in M. Micale and R. Porter (eds) *Discovering the History of Psychiatry*, Oxford, Oxford University Press, 1994, pp. 232–247, especially p. 244.
6 Hunter, R. and McAlpine, I., *Three Hundred Years of Psychiatry 1535–1860, A History Presented in Selected English Texts*, London, Oxford University Press, 1963.
7 *Re W (a minor) (medical treatment: court's jurisdiction)* [1993] Fam 64, especially p. 76.
8 Unsworth, C.R., 'Law and lunacy in psychiatry's "Golden Age"', *Oxford Journal of Legal Studies*, 1993, vol. 13, pp. 479–507.
9 Scull, A.T., 'Psychiatry in the Victorian era' in A. T. Scull (ed.) *Madhouses, Mad Doctors and Madmen: The Social History of Psychiatry in the Victorian Era*, London, Athlone Press, 1981, pp. 5–32, especially p. 6.
10 The Circulars of the Lunacy Commissioners and the Board of Control can be found in PRO Files MH51/236–242 at Kew. Between 1845 and 1959 a total of 1,021 circulars were issued, 405 by the Lunacy Commission and 616 by the Board.
11 Department of Health and the Welsh Office, *Code of Practice on the Mental Health Act 1983*, London, HMSO, 1993, para. 18.15.
12 Katz, J., *The Silent World of Doctor and Patient*, New York, Free Press, 1984; Pernick, M.S. 'The patient's role in medical decision-

making: a social history of informed consent in medical therapy', in President's Commission for the Study of Ethical Problems in Medicine and Biomedical and Behavioural Research, *Making Health Care Decisions*, Washington, DC, US Government Printing Office, 1982, vol. 3, p. 3; Faden, R.R. and Beauchamp, T.L., *A History and Theory of Informed Consent*, New York, Oxford University Press, pp. 56–61.

13 (1767) 2 Wils. KB 359, especially 360; 95 ER 860, especially 861.

14 (1767) 2 Wils. KB 362, 95 ER 862.

15 Perceval, J., 'A narrative of the treatment experienced by a gentleman during a state of mental derangement', in D. Peterson (ed.) *A Mad People's History of Madness*, Pittsburgh, PA, University of Pittsburgh Press, 1982, 106–7.

16 Castel, R., *L'Ordre Psychiatrique: L'age d'or de l'alienisme*, Paris, Editions de Minuit, 1976; Castel, R., Castel F. and Lovell, A., *The Psychiatric Society*, New York, Columbia University Press, 1982; Castel, R., *The Regulation of Madness: The Origins of Incarceration in France*, trans. W.D. Halls, Berkeley and Los Angeles, CA,University of California Press, 1988.

17 Unsworth, C.R., 'Mental disorder and the tutelary relationship: from pre- to post-carceral legal order', *Journal of Law and Society*, 1991, vol. 18, pp. 254–278.

18 The Brock Committee, *Report of the Departmental Committee on Sterilisation*, Cmd 4485, 1933.

19 See Unsworth, C.R., *The Politics of Mental Health Legislation*, Oxford, Oxford University Press, 1987.

20 Jones, K., 'The limitations of the legal approach to mental health', *International Journal of Law and Psychiatry*, 1980, vol. 3, pp. 1–14, especially pp. 10–11.

21 ibid., p. 14. For a more recent expression of Jones' views, see 'Law and mental health: sticks or carrots?', in G.E. Berrios and H. Freeman (eds) *150 Years of British Psychiatry 1841–1991*, London, Gaskell/Royal College of Psychiatrists, 1991, pp. 98–102.

22 Unsworth, C.R., 'Law and lunacy', p. 501.

23 ibid.

24 Gostin, L.O., 'Perspectives on mental health reforms', *Journal of Law and Society*, 1983, vol. 10, pp. 47–70 and 'The ideology of entitlement: the application of contemporary legal approaches to psychiatry', in P. Bean (ed.) *Mental Illness: Changes and Trends*, 1983, Chichester, John Wiley, pp. 27–54. Gostin estimated that approximately two-thirds of the provisions of the 1982 Mental Health (Amendment) Act derived from proposals of MIND (the National Association of Mental Health) contained in his book *A Human Condition* vols I and II; see 'Perspectives', p. 67.

25 *Van der Leer* v. *The Netherlands* (1990) 12 EHRR 567; *Winterwerp* v. *The Netherlands* (1979) 2 EHRR 387; *X* v. *United Kingdom* (1981) 4 EHRR 181.

26 *X* v. *United Kingdom* (1981) 4 EHRR 181, para. 40; *Winterwerp* (1979) 2 EHRR 387, para. 39; *Luberti* v. *Italy*, Judgment of 23 February 1984.

301

27 *Winterwerp* (1979) 2 EHRR 387, para. 37.
28 *X* v. *United Kingdom* (1981) 4 EHRR 181, para. 52.
29 Gostin, L.O., 'The ideology of entitlement', pp. 49–50.
30 ibid., p. 30.
31 Gostin, L.O., 'Perspectives', p. 61.
32 Law Commission, *Mental Incapacity*, Law Com. no. 231, London, HMSO, 1995.

1 1845–1853: THE BIRTH OF THE LUNACY COMMISSION

1 Hunter, R. and McAlpine, I., *Three Hundred Years of Psychiatry 1535–1860, A History Presented in Selected English Texts*, London, Oxford University Press, 1963, p. 701.
2 For a fuller account of Higgins' activities in exposing the abuses at York Asylum see Jones, K., *A History of the Mental Health Services*, London, Routledge & Kegan Paul, 1974, pp. 66–75.
3 Allderidge has explained that it was found necessary to enclose Norris in this device because in the years following admission in 1800 he had been extremely violent and dangerous. He used to escape from traditional manacles and use them as weapons. The decision to confine him in his iron harness was made in 1804, and he remained in it for nine years. Allderidge, P., 'Bedlam: fact or fantasy?', in W.F. Bynum, R. Porter and M. Shepherd (eds) *The Anatomy of Madness: Essays in the History of Psychiatry, vol. II, Institutions and Society*, London, Tavistock, 1985, pp. 17–33, especially pp. 24–26. See also: Jones, op. cit., pp. 75–78.
4 Hervey, N., 'A slavish bowing down: the Lunacy Commission and the psychiatric profession 1845–60', in Bynum, Porter and Shepherd, op. cit., pp. 98–131.
5 Madhouses Act 1828, 9 Geo. IV, c. 41.
6 5 & 6 Vict., c. 87.
7 8 & 9 Vict., c. 100.
8 Quoted in the evidence of the National Council for Civil Liberties to the *Royal Commission on the Law Relating to Mental Illness and Mental Deficiency*, 1957 Cmnd 169, p. 840, para. 49.
9 8 & 9 Vict., c. 126, s. 2.
10 48 Geo III, c. 96. The 1845 Act followed a report by the Lunacy Commissioners that there were only seventeen county asylums in England and Wales and that twenty-one counties had no provision of any kind, whether private or public.
11 8 & 9 Vict., c. 100, s. 14.
12 ibid., s. 17.
13 ibid., s. 28.
14 ibid., s. 52.
15 ibid., ss. 90–91.
16 Lunatics Act 1845, 8 & 9 Vict., c. 100, s. 112.
17 ibid., s. 56.
18 Jones, K., *Lunacy, Law and Conscience*, London, Routledge & Kegan

Paul, 1955, pp. 190–194.

19 Lunatics Act 1845, 8 & 9 Vict., c. 100, s. 59.

20 Lunacy Commissioners Circular Letter No. 8, 19 Jan 1846, Book No. 1, PRO File MH51/236, Kew.

21 The Lunatics Act 1845, 8 & 9 Vict., c. 100, s. 61.

22 The Lunatics Act 1853, 16 & 17 Vict., c. 96, s. 64.

23 ibid., s. 100.

24 ibid., ss 76–77.

25 Hervey, op. cit., pp. 98–131, especially p. 119.

26 Bentham, J., *Panopticon; or the Inspection House*, 3 vols, London, T. Payne, 1791. See also Burns, J.H. and Hart, H.L.A., *Collected Works of Jeremy Bentham: A Comment on the Commentaries and a Fragment of Government*, London, Athlone Press, 1977, p. 531.

27 Conolly, J., *On the Construction and Government of Lunatic Asylums and Hospitals for the Insane*, London, Churchill, 1847.

28 Rees Thomas, W., 'The unwilling patient', twenty-seventh Maudsley Lecture, *Journal of Mental Science*, 1953, vol. 99, pp. 191–201.

29 Bynum, W.F., Porter, R. and Shepherd, M., (eds) *The Anatomy of Madness: Essays in the History of Psychiatry, vol. III, The Asylum and its Psychiatry*, London, Routledge, 1988, p. 7.

30 For an excellent study of the retreat, see Digby, A., *Madness, Morality and Medicine: A Study of the York Retreat 1796–1914*, Cambridge, Cambridge University Press, 1985.

31 Jones, W.L., *Ministering to Minds Diseased: A History of Psychiatric Treatment*, London, Heinemann, 1983, p. 105.

32 Select Committee on Madhouses, *First Report. Minutes of Evidence Taken before the Select Committee Appointed to Consider of Provision Being Made for the Better Regulation of Madhouses in England*, ordered by the House of Commons to be printed, 25 May 1815, in Hunter and McAlpine, op. cit., p. 702.

33 *Report of the Metropolitan Commissioners in Lunacy to the Lord Chancellor* (1844), pp. 145–6.

34 Lunatics Act 1845, 8 & 9 Vict., c. 100, s. 59.

35 For details of this episode, see *Seventh Annual Report of the Commissioners in Lunacy . . . for the year ending 30 June 1852*, 1853, HC 285; *The Observations of the Governor upon the report of the Commissioners in Lunacy on Bethlem Hospital*, and *Return for copies of all reports of the Commissioners in Lunacy as to the state and management of Bethlehem Hospital, and of all correspondence thereon*, both in PRO File MH50/5, Kew, Minute Books of the Lunacy Commission, April 1851–Aug 1852.

36 PRO File MH50/5, Kew, Minute Books of the Lunacy Commission, April 1851–Aug 1852.

37 *Report and Evidence of the Lunacy Commission to the Home Secretary on Bethlehem Hospital*, 7 February 1852, p. 14. The report was laid before Parliament on 12 December 1852.

38 Hervey, op. cit., p. 110 says the commissioners observed 'only the barest decencies in their assault on the hospital'.

39 The Lunatics Act 1853, 16 & 17 Vict., c. 96, s. 90.

40 ibid., s. 53.
41 See for example Lunacy Commission Circular No. 180 (1879) 'Precedents of general rules for the government of Lunatic Asylums pursuant to s. 53 of Lunatic Asylums Act 1853', PRO File MH51/237, Kew, Lunacy Commissioners Circular Letters Book No. 2, Circulars 102–229, 1864–1889.
42 Hunter and McAlpine, op. cit., p. 634, where there is an illustration of Haslam's key.
43 ibid.
44 ibid.
45 Diarmid, J.M., 'The hypodermic injection of morphia in insanity', *Journal of Mental Science*, 1876, vol. 22, pp. 18–42.
46 Perceval, J., A narrative of the treatment experienced by a gentleman during a state of mental derangement, in D. Peterson (ed.) *A Mad People's History of Madness*, Pittsburgh, PA, University of Pittsburgh Press, 1982, pp. 106–107.

2 1853–1880: THE TRIUMPH OF NON-RESTRAINT?

1 Tomes, N.J., 'The great restraint controversy', in W.F. Bynum, R. Porter and M. Shepherd (eds) *The Anatomy of Madness: Essays in the History of Psychiatry, vol. III, The Asylum and its Psychiatry*, London, Routledge, 1988, pp. 190–225, especially p. 196.
2 ibid., p. 201.
3 Bucknill, J.C., 'The restraint system', *Asylum Journal*, 1854, vol. 1, pp. 81–83 and 97–99.
4 Lunacy Commission Circular No. 54 to Medical Superintendents, 15 Feb 1854.
5 Conolly, J., 'Notice of the eighth report of the Commissioners in Lunacy', *Asylum Journal*, 1854, vol. 1, pp. 134–137; Conolly, J., 'Second notice of the eighth report of the Commissioners in Lunacy', *Asylum Journal*, 1855, vol. 1, pp. 144–149; Conolly, J., 'Third notice of the eighth report of the Commissioners in Lunacy', *Asylum Journal*, 1855, vol. 1, pp. 164–166; 'Fourth Notice of the Eighth Report of the Commissioners in Lunacy', *Asylum Journal*, 1855, vol. 1, pp. 180–185.
6 Conolly, J., *The Treatment of the Insane Without Mechanical Restraint*, London, Smith Elder & Co., 1856.
7 Conolly, 'Fourth notice', p. 181.
8 Conolly, 'Second notice', p. 148.
9 Bucknill, J.C., 'On the employment of seclusion in the treatment of the insane', *Asylum Journal*, 1855, vol. 1, pp. 186–189, especially p. 187.
10 Quoted in Conolly, 'Fourth notice', p. 181.
11 Bucknill, J.C., 'The annual reports of the county lunatic asylums and hospitals of the insane in England and Wales published during the year 1855', *Asylum Journal of Mental Science*, 1856, vol. 1, pp. 257–283, especially pp. 267–268.
12 ibid., p. 283.
13 Tomes, op. cit. p. 201.

14 *Eleventh Annual Report of the Commissioners in Lunacy*, 1857, HC 157, pp. 24–37.

15 ibid., p. 37.

16 ibid.

17 *Twelfth Annual Report of the Commissioners in Lunacy*, 1858, HC 340, pp. 9–11.

18 *Annual Report of Bethlem Royal Hospital*, Bethlem Archive, 1870, p. 42.

19 *Sixteenth Annual Report of the Commissioners in Lunacy*, 1862, HC 417, pp. 20–21.

20 ibid., pp. 187–189

21 Tomes, op. cit., p. 201.

22 *Twenty-Seventh Annual Report of the Commissioners in Lunacy*, 1873, HC 256, pp. 19–20.

23 ibid., p. 22.

24 Robertson, C.L., 'On the sedative action of the cold wet sheet in the treatment of recent mania' (address to the Brighton and Sussex Medico-Chirurgical Society in April 1861), *Journal of Mental Science*, 1861, vol. 7, pp. 265–277.

25 *Journal of Mental Science* 1862, vol. 8, p. 281.

26 Robertson, C.L., 'The case of James Snashall', *Journal of Mental Science*, 1864, vol. 10, pp. 77–81.

27 Minute on wet packs, Minute Book of the Lunacy Commission, PRO File MH50/15 1868–9, Kew, 24 August 1868.

28 *Thirteenth Report of the Commissioners in Lunacy*, 1859, HC 204, pp. 67–8.

29 See their 10 March 1873 criticism of the medical superintendent of Newcastle borough asylum for neglecting to complete records of the time and duration of seclusion, PRO File MH50/18, Kew, 1873–5.

30 *Annual Report of Bethlem Royal Hospital*, Bethlem Archive, 1870, p. 34.

31 At the meeting of 7 April 1873, on reading visiting comissioners' entry No. 1525 at Lancashire county asylum in Prestwich, it was ordered that the medical superintendent be informed of the great regret felt by the Board at the large amount of seclusion used, with an expression of their hope that means would be found to remedy this in the future.

32 *Twenty-Seventh Annual Report of the Commissioners in Lunacy*, 1873, HC 256, p. 23.

33 *Annual Report of Bethlem Royal Hospital*, Bethlem Archive, 1876, pp. 33–34.

34 PRO File MH50/21, 1879–1881, Kew, Minute of 31 May 1880.

35 Lunacy Commission Circular No. 180, 'Precedents of general rules for the government of lunatic asylums pursuant to s. 53 of Lunatic Asylums Act 1853', 1879, PRO File MH51/237, Lunacy Commissioners Circular Letters Book No. 2, Circulars 102–229, 1864–1889.

36 Digby, A., *Madness, Morality and Medicine: A Study of the York Retreat 1796–1914*, Cambridge, Cambridge University Press, 1985, pp. 127–129.

3 CHEMICAL RESTRAINT

1 *Journal of Mental Science*, 1859, vol. 5, pp. 172–173.
2 *Annual Report of Bethlem Hospital*, Bethlem Archive, 1857, p. 38.
3 Diarmid, J.M., 'The hypodermic injection of morphia in insanity', *Journal of Mental Science*, 1876, vol. 22, p. 26.
4 Hunter, R. and McAlpine, I., *Three Hundred Years of Psychiatry 1535–1860, A History Presented in Selected English Texts*, London, Oxford University Press, 1963, p. 1049; Tourney, G., 'Psychiatric therapies 1800–1968', in T. Rothman (ed) *Changing Patterns in Psychiatric Care*, London, Vision Press, 1971.
5 Medawar, C., *Power and Dependence: Social Audit on the Safety of Medicines*, London, Social Audit Ltd, 1992, p. 48.
6 *Journal of Mental Science*, 1865, vol. 11, pp. 363–371 and 598–602.
7 Medawar, op. cit., p. 49.
8 ibid., pp. 50–51.
9 *Journal of Mental Science*, 1869, vol. 15, p. 630.
10 *Journal of Mental Science*, 1872, vol. 18, pp. 118–119.
11 ibid., p. 136.
12 Quoted in Tomes, N.J., *The Persuasive Institution: Thomas Story Kirkbride and the Art of Asylum Keeping 1841–1883*, PhD thesis, University of Pennsylvania, 1978, p. 253.
13 *Journal of Mental Science*, 1872, vol. 18, pp. 596–597.
14 ibid., p. 598.
15 Tomes, op. cit., p. 253.
16 Hughes, J., *Letters of a Victorian Madwoman*, Columbia, University of South Carolina Press, 1993.
17 Jones, W.L., *Ministering to Minds Diseased: A History of Psychiatric Treatment*, London, Heinemann, 1983, p. 106.
18 Woolf, V., *Mrs Dalloway*, London, Hogarth Press, 1925. See also Trombley, S., *All That Summer She Was Mad: Virginia Woolf and her Doctors*, London, Junction Books, 1981.
19 Savage, G.H., 'Uses and abuses of chloral hydrate', *Journal of Mental Science*, 1879, vol. 25, pp. 4–8.
20 Pritchard Davies, F., 'Chemical restraint and alcohol', *Journal of Mental Science*, 1881, vol. 26, pp. 526–530.
21 ibid., p. 529.
22 ibid. Rendering a patient unconscious by garotting was regarded by some surgeons at the time as a safer alternative to chloroform.
23 ibid., p. 530.
24 *Journal of Mental Science*, 1881, vol. 27, pp. 305–341.
25 ibid., p. 332.
26 ibid., p. 8.
27 Cameron, R.W.D., 'Restraint in the treatment of the insane', *Journal of Mental Science*, 1883, vol. 28, pp. 353–356 and 519–531, especially p. 353.
28 ibid., p. 521.
29 ibid., p. 530.
30 ibid.

31 *Journal of Mental Science*, 1883, vol. 29, pp. 92–97 and 138.
32 ibid., p. 95.
33 Bethlem Hospital Case Book No. 127, Females 1885, Patient L.R., admitted February 1885.
34 ibid., patient E.H., admitted 3 March 1885.
35 *Fifty-Ninth Annual Report of the Commissioners in Lunacy*, 1905, HC 220, pp. 37–41.
36 *Sixty-Eighth Annual Report of the Commissioners in Lunacy*, 1914, HC 264, pp. 58–59.

4 1880–1913: THE RETURN OF RESTRAINT

1 *Annual Report of Bethlem Royal Hospital*, Bethlem Archive, 1879, p. 44.
2 *Annual Report of Bethlem Royal Hospital*, Bethlem Archive, 1880, p. 44.
3 *Annual Report of Bethlem Royal Hospital*, Bethlem Archive, 1881, p. 41.
4 *Thirty-Sixth Annual Report of the Commissioners in Lunacy*, 1882, HC 219, p. 91.
5 Minute books of the Lunacy Commission, PRO File MH50/23, Kew, 1883–1884, 23 April 1884.
6 *The Times*, 22 August 1888, p. 6.
7 *The Times*, 23 August 1888, p. 10.
8 *Forty-Third Annual Report of the Commissioners in Lunacy*, 1889, HC 207, pp. 97–98.
9 Minute Book, PRO File MH50/25, Kew, 1887–1889, 31 July 1888.
10 *Annual Report of Bethlem Royal Hospital*, Bethlem Archive, 1888, pp. 38–40.
11 ibid., pp. 39–40.
12 ibid., p. 40.
13 *The Times*, 11 September 1888, p. 5.
14 *The Times*, 10 September 1888, p. 4.
15 ibid.
16 Jones, K., *A History of the Mental Health Services*, London, Routledge & Kegan Paul, London, 1974, p. 165.
17 See Jones, K., 'Law and mental health: sticks or carrots?', in G.E. Berrios and H. Freeman (eds) *150 Years of British Psychiatry 1841–1991*, London, Gaskell/Royal College of Psychiatrists, 1991, pp. 98–102, especially pp. 94–95; and Unsworth, C.R., *Politics of Mental Health Legislation*, Oxford, Oxford University Press, 1987, pp. 96–97.
18 'Increase in lunacy', *The Times*, 11 July 1889.
19 *Titbits*, 28 January 1888.
20 Minute books of the Commissioners in Lunacy, PRO File MH50/25 1887–1889, Kew, 20 March 1889.
21 *The Times*, 8 May 1890.
22 Lunacy Act 1890, 53 Vict. c 5, s. 315.
23 ibid., s. 38.
24 ibid., s. 75.

25 Jones, op. cit., 1972, pp. 153–181.

26 Lunacy Act 1890, 53 Vict. c. 5, s. 330(1).

27 In *Shackleton* v. *Swift* [1913] 2 KB 304, especially 314 (an action for false imprisonment) Kennedy LJ declared that: 'The object of this Act is to protect people who are trying to do their duty ... even though they may not have exactly complied with the regulations'. For a similar statement from Scrutton LJ in a negligence action see *Everett* v. *Griffiths* [1920] 3 KB 161, especially 197.

28 Lunacy Act 1890, 53 Vict. c. 5, s. 40 (1).

29 ibid., s. 40(4).

30 *Forty-Fourth Annual Report of the Commissioners in Lunacy*, 1890, HC 274, Appendix M, p. 358; Regulation as to instruments and appliances for the mechanical and bodily restraint of lunatics, 9 April 1890, Lunacy Commission Circular No. 233, 1890.

31 *Forty-Ninth Annual Report of the Commissioners in Lunacy*, 1895, HC 311, p. 122.

32 ibid.

33 ibid., p. 123.

34 PRO File MH51/238 Lunacy Commission circular Letters Book No. 3, Circular Nos 230–405, Statutory Rules and Orders (S.R. & O.) 1913 No. 712, Board Circular 404, 25 June 1913.

35 ibid., Circular 270.

36 *Forty-Ninth Annual Report*, op. cit., p. 124.

37 ibid., pp. 124–125.

38 Minute books of the Lunacy Commissioners, PRO File MH50/29, 1896–1897, Kew.

39 ibid., 29 September 1897.

40 *Fifty-Sixth Annual Report of the Commissioners in Lunacy*, 1902, HC 71.

41 *Fifty-Third Annual Report of the Commissioners in Lunacy*, 1899, HC 355, pp. 46–47.

42 PRO File MH51/238, op. cit., Circular 304. The definition was drawn from the commissioners' 54th annual report to the Lord Chancellor, p. 12.

43 Partridge, R., *Broadmoor*, London, Chatto & Windus, 1953, p. 89.

44 ibid., p. 90.

45 Parker, E., 'The development of secure provision', in Gostin, L.O., *Secure Provision*, London, Tavistock, 1985, pp. 15–65, especially p. 25.

46 *Sixty-First Annual Report of the Commissioners in Lunacy*, 1907, HC 225, p. 65.

47 ibid., p. 66.

48 *Sixty-Second Annual Report of the Commissioners in Lunacy*, 1908, HC 200, pp. 59–61.

49 PRO File MH51/238, op. cit., Commission Circular 368, Local Government Board Circular 1910.

50 *Sixty-Fifth Annual Report of the Commissioners in Lunacy*, 1911, HC 207, p. 57.

51 (1909) 26 TLR 139, especially p. 142.

52 ibid.
53 In D. Peterson (ed), *A Mad People's History of Madness,* Pittsburgh, PA, University of Pittsburgh Press, 1982, pp. 187–193.
54 *Sixty-Fifth Annual Report,* op. cit., p. 58.
55 S.R. & O. 1913, No. 712.
56 The rules were again amended by S. R. & O. 1925, No. 76.
57 Rees Thomas, W., 'The unwilling patient', twenty-seventh Maudsley Lecture, *Journal of Mental Science,* 1953, vol. 99, pp. 191–201.

5 SURGICAL TREATMENT AND CONSENT

1 *The Times,* 15 December 1866, p. 5.
2 Baker Brown, I., *On the Curability of Certain Forms of Epilepsy, Catalepsy and Hysteria in Females,* London, Hardwicke, 1866.
3 *The Lancet,* 5 May 1866, p. 487.
4 *The Lancet,* 9 June 1866, pp. 639–640.
5 *The Lancet,* 16 June 1866, p. 663.
6 *The Lancet,* 23 June 1866, p. 699.
7 ibid.
8 *The Lancet,* 17 November 1866, pp. 560–561.
9 *The Lancet,* 8 December 1866, p. 639.
10 ibid.
11 *The Lancet,* 15 December 1866, p. 679.
12 *The Times,* 26, 28, 31 January and 15 February 1867.
13 *Journal of Mental Science,* 1867, vol. 13, pp. 129–131.
14 *The Lancet,* 9 February 1867, p. 175.
15 *British Medical Journal,* 6 April 1867, p. 395.
16 ibid., p. 402.
17 ibid., p. 408.
18 For other discussions of clitoridectomy and the Baker Brown affair see Showalter, E., 'Victorian women and insanity', in A.T. Scull (ed.), *Madhouses, Mad Doctors and Madmen: The Social History of Psychiatry in the Victorian Era,* London, The Athlone Press, 1981, pp. 313–331; Ehrenreich, B. and English, D., *For Her Own Good: 150 Years of the Experts' Advice to Women,* London, Pluto Press, 1979, pp. 111–112; Barker Benfield, G.J., *The Horrors of the Half-Known Life: Male Attitudes Towards Women and Sexuality in Nineteenth Century America,* New York, Harper & Row, 1976; and Shepherd, J.A., *Spencer Wells: The Life and Work of a Victorian Surgeon,* Edinburgh, E. & S. Livingstone, 1965.
19 *British Medical Journal,* 6 April 1867, p. 387.
20 *Journal of Mental Science,* 1868, vol. 14, pp. 272–273.
21 Shortt, S.E.D., *Victorian Lunacy: Richard M. Bucke and the Practice of Late Nineteenth Century Psychiatry,* Cambridge, Cambridge University Press, 1986, p. 126.
22 *Journal of Mental Science,* 1880, vol. 26, p. 470.
23 *Journal of Mental Science,* 1886, vol. 32, p. 287.
24 *Annual Report of Bethlem Royal Hospital,* Bethlem Archive, 1885, p. 37; *Case Book,* 127, 1885.

25 *British Medical Journal*, 1896, vol. 2, pp. 1525–1526.
26 ibid.
27 (1906) 79 NE 562.
28 37 *Chicago Legal News* 213; referred to in *Mohr* v. *Williams* (1905) 104 NW 12, especially p. 14.
29 ibid., pp. 14–15.
30 *Schloendorff* v. *Society of New York Hospitals* (1914) 105 NE 92, especially p. 93.

6 THE BOARD OF CONTROL AND STERILISATION OF 'THE UNFIT'

1 Mental Deficiency Act 1913, 3 & 4 Geo. V, c. 28, ss. 21–26.
2 The Radnor Commission, *Report of the Royal Commission on the Care of the Feeble Minded*, London, HMSO, 1908, Cd 4202.
3 PRO File MH51/239, Board of Control Circular Letters, Nos 406–577, 30 March 1914–1 January 1921. Home Office Circular, 22 December 1913.
4 Mental Deficiency Act 1913, 3 & 4 Geo. V, c. 28, s. 25.
5 Mental Treatment Act 1930, 20 & 21 Geo. V, c. 23, ss. 11 and 13.
6 National Health Service Act 1946, 9 & 10 Geo. VI, c 81, ss. 49–50. Since 1959 the licensing of private nursing homes has been carried out by health authorities on behalf of the Secretary of State for Health and Social Security. For a general account of licensing of private mental nursing homes see Jones, R.M., *Registered Homes Act Manual*, 3rd ed., London, Sweet & Maxwell, 1993.
7 PRO File MH50/67, Kew.
8 The Radnor Commission, op. cit., 1908.
9 Cabinet Minute 37/108 No. 189 1911, PRO, Kew.
10 Letter of 2 February 1917. Memorandum of cases referred to the Board of Control concerning sterilisation, made by F. Caswell for the Board on 1 August 1932, PRO File MH51/546 Individual Cases where Sterilisation Considered, Kew.
11 ibid.
12 Board of Control, Minute Book, 28 June 1919, PRO File MH50/48, Kew.
13 ibid.
14 Binney, C., 'The law as to sterilization', published by the Eugenics Education Society, PRO File MH51/546, Kew, p. 22.
15 ibid., pp. 14 and 22.
16 ibid., p. 22.
17 *British Medical Journal*, 13 June 1925, p. 842.
18 Supplement to *British Medical Journal*, 27 June 1925.
19 ibid.
20 ibid., p. 2.
21 Trombley, S., *The Right to Reproduce: A History of Coercive Sterilisation*, London, Weidenfeld & Nicolson, 1988, p. 85.
22 ibid.
23 ibid., emphasis added.

24 PRO File MH51/240, Board of Control Circular Letters Nos 578–741,
    10 January 1912–October 1930, Circular No. 659.
25 ibid.
26 *The Times*, 18 January 1926.
27 *The Times*, 20 January 1926.
28 Minute of a meeting between the Minister of Health and the Board
    of Control PRO File MH80/8, Kew, p. 6.
29 PRO File MH51/546, Kew.
30 The Mental Deficiency Act 1927, 17 & 18 Geo. V, c. 33, received
    the Royal assent on 27 December.
31 The correspondence between Darwin and Willis, and the various
    draft Bills which passed between them are to be found in PRO File
    MH51/547 'Sterilisation Draft Bill of the Eugenics Society – 1927',
    Kew.
32 See, for example, *The Seventeenth Annual Report of the Board of
    Control for the Year 1930*, London, HMSO, 1931, p. 77, where the
    Board reiterated their strong recommendation of previous reports
    'that the marriage of defectives under order should be banned'. In
    the following annual report, the board asserted that: 'Everyone was
    agreed as to the desirability of trying to prevent the marriage of
    defectives', *The Eighteenth Annual Report of the Board of Control
    for the Year 1931*, London, HMSO, 1932, p. 79.
33 PRO File MH51/547, Sterilisation Draft Bill of the Eugenics Society,
    1927.
34 Trombley, op. cit., p. 97.
35 Lord Riddell, *Sterilisation of the Unfit*, London, H.K. Lewis & Son,
    1929.
36 *Journal of Mental Science*, 1931, vol. 77, pp. 263–267.
37 PRO File MH51/546.
38 ibid.
39 ibid., letter of 4 December 1931.
40 ibid., memo of 9 December 1931.
41 ibid., letter of 9 December 1931.
42 ibid., letter of 15 January 1932.
43 PRO File MH51/541 (Board of Control), 'Deputation to Ministry
    of Health concerning the Sterilisation of Mental Defectives', Kew.
44 ibid.
45 Hansard, H.C. Debs, Ser. 5, vol. 266, col. 2115; PRO File MH51/541,
    Kew.
46 PRO File MH51/210, Chairman's Memorandum and Draft Report,
    Kew.
47 Report of the Quarterly Meeting of the Royal Medico-Psychological
    Association, *Journal of Mental Science*, 1936, vol. 82, p. 13.
48 *The Times*, 15–18 June 1932.
49 PRO File MH51/212, Minute of the Proceedings of the First Meeting
    of the Brock Committee, p. 1, Kew.
50 ibid., p. 7.
51 PRO File MH51/210, Letter from Brock to Maude of 16 October
    1933, Kew.

52 ibid.
53 (1927) 274 US 200.
54 Cynkar, R.J., '*Buck* v. *Bell*: "Felt Necessities" v. "Fundamental Values"', *Columbia Law Review,* 1981, vol. 81, pp. 1418–1461.
55 (1927) 274 US 200.
56 Reilly, P.R., *The Surgical Solution – A History of Involuntary Sterilisation in the United States*, London, Johns Hopkins University Press, 1991, p. 88.
57 ibid., p. xiii.
58 Brock was disparaging about the biologists, saying that 'many of them had never seen a defective, and ... appear to proceed on the basis that what is true of the Californian fruit fly, or of the armadillo, must apply also to defectives'. Letter of 14 November 1932, PRO File MH51/221, Kew.
59 Sir Hubert Bond of the Board of Control nevertheless compiled a list of members of the association for Brock as possible further witnesses. See also letter to Professor Bolton from Brock, 2 December 1932, PRO MH51/221, Kew. See also Bolton, J.S., *Journal of Mental Science*, 1931, vol. 77, pp. 264–269.
60 PRO File MH51/542, Kew.
61 ibid., Memorandum of Evidence to the Brock Committee, 29 January 1932.
62 The Brock Committee, *Report of the Departmental Committee on Sterilisation*, 1933, Cmd 4485, 1933, p. 6, Para. 3.
63 ibid., pp. 5–6.
64 ibid., pp. 6–7.
65 ibid., p. 9.
66 ibid.
67 ibid., p. 31
68 ibid., p. 39.
69 ibid., p. 37.
70 Note of meeting of the Brock Committee, 19 December 1932, PRO File MH51/220, Kew, p. 8. Memorandum of Evidence of W.F. Menzies, p. 4, PRO File MH51/223, Kew.
71 Brock Committee, p. 42.
72 ibid., p. 43.
73 ibid., p. 45.
74 ibid., pp. 45–47.
75 Weindling, P., *Health, Race and German Politics between National Unification and Nazism 1870–1945*, Cambridge, Cambridge University Press, 1989, p. 525.
76 ibid., pp. 526–528.
77 *The Times,* 20 January 1934.
78 *Empire News*, 21 January 1934.
79 *Sunday Express*, 21 January 1934.
80 26 January 1934, p. 94.
81 Hansard, HC Debs, 28 February 1934, Cols 1178–1184.
82 *The Lancet,* 27 January 1934, pp. 193–194.
83 *Passing Show*, 10 March 1934.

84 *Catholic News*, 7 April 1934.
85 *News Chronicle*, 16 May 1934.
86 *Daily Herald*, 4 July 1934.
87 *Catholic News*, 14 July 1934; *Catholic Times*, 6 July 1934.
88 *The Lancet*, 23 June 1934, p. 1343.
89 *Morning Post*, 29 November 1934.
90 *Empire News*, 29 July 1934.
91 Report of Quarterly meeting of the Medico-Psychological Association to discuss the Report of the Departmental Committee on Sterilisation, 22 November 1935, *Journal of Mental Science*, 1936, supplement to vol. 82, pp. 1–18, especially p. 13.
92 Hansard, 13 April 1937, Cols 817–855.
93 Trombley, op. cit., p. 161.
94 Marshall, F., 'Sterilisation and the Law', *Birmingham Gazette*, 31 January 1950.
95 Trombley, op. cit., pp. 164–166.
96 Association of Municipal Corporations and the County Council's Association, *Memorandum of the Incidence of Mental Deficiency and Sterilisation*, February 1952, PRO File MH51/541/177689, Kew. Emphasis added.
97 ibid.
98 [1954] 1 WLR 1169; [1954] 3 All ER 59.
99 Douglas, G., *Law, Fertility and Reproduction*, London, Sweet & Maxwell, 1991, p. 47.
100 (1975) 2 BMJ 775.

7 THE BOARD OF CONTROL AND THE MENTAL TREATMENT ACT 1930

1 London County Council (General Powers) Act 1915, 5 & 6 Geo V, c. iii, s. 23.
2 Unsworth, C.R., *The Politics of Mental Health Legislation*, Oxford, Oxford University Press, 1987, pp. 184–185.
3 ibid., p. 172.
4 ibid.
5 ibid., p. 67.
6 ibid., pp. 67–68.
7 For an example of this see *Eighth Annual Report of the Board of Control for the Year 1921*, London, HMSO, 1922, Appendix B.
8 Lomax, M., *The Experiences of an Asylum Doctor*, London, George Allen & Unwin, 1921, p. 78.
9 ibid., pp. 99–103.
10 ibid., p. 102.
11 The research sections of the annual reports of the Board of Control in the 1920s and early 1930s are replete with abstracts of papers on the subject of 'asylum dysentery'. See, for example, *Eighth Annual Report*, op. cit., pp. 87–92. The disease seemed to diminish in the 1930s. Whether this was due to the declining use of croton oil which took place then, or because of improved hygiene, is impossible to tell.

12 'The trend of psychiatry in England and Wales', *Journal of Mental Science*, 1922, vol. 68, p. 174.

13 *Ninth Annual Report of the Board of Control for the Year 1922*, London, HMSO, 1923, Appendix A, pp. 89–94.

14 ibid., p. 89.

15 ibid.

16 ibid., p. 90. Emphasis added.

17 ibid., p. 94.

18 Grant-Smith, R., *Experiences of an Asylum Patient*, London, George Allen & Unwin, 1922, p. 85.

19 ibid., p. 127.

20 ibid., pp. 128–129.

21 *Report on the Administration of Public Mental Hospitals*, London, HMSO, 1922, Cmd 1730.

22 *Ninth Annual Report*, op. cit., p. 2.

23 Nolan, P., *A History of Mental Health Nursing*, London, Chapman & Hall, 1993, p. 77.

24 See for example *Eleventh Annual Report of the Board of Control for the Year 1924*, London, HMSO, 1925, p. 2.

25 Unsworth, op. cit., p. 126.

26 [1924] 2 KB 517.

27 Unsworth, op. cit., p. 187.

28 The Board's main recommendations to the Macmillan Commission are summarised in the *Thirteenth Annual Report of the Board of Control for the Year 1926*, London, HMSO, 1927, pp. 2–4.

29 Minute Books of the Commissioners in Lunacy, PRO File MH50/58 1930, Kew.

30 Unsworth, op. cit., p. 121.

31 The Macmillan Commission, *Report of the Royal Commission on Lunacy and Mental Disorder*, London, HMSO, 1926, Cmd 2700, para. 214.

32 Jones, K., *A History of the Mental Health Services*, London, Routledge & Kegan Paul, 1974, p. 239, and Unsworth, op. cit., p. 191.

33 Jones, op. cit., p. 239.

34 Unsworth, op. cit., p. 191.

35 *Thirteenth Annual Report*, op. cit., p. 2. The Macmillan Commission, op. cit., para. 209.

36 The Macmillan Commission, op. cit., para. 45.

37 ibid., para. 263.

38 Mental Treatment Act 1930, Geo. V, c. 23, s. 5.

39 Board of Control Circular, No. 805, January 1935. PRO File MH51/241, Kew. Board of Control Circular Letters, Nos 751–886, October 1930–November 1940.

40 Mental Treatment Rules 1930, S.R. & O. 1930, No. 1083, r. 60.

41 PRO File MH51/610, Kew.

42 Unsworth, op. cit., p. 213.

43 The Percy Commission, *Report of the Royal Commission on the Law Relating to Mental Illness and Mental Deficiency*, Cmnd 169, 1957: *Minutes of Evidence, Answer* 2,532: Royal College of Physicians.

44 Macrae, D., Presidential Address to the Medico-Psychological Association, *Journal of Mental Science*, 1937, vol. 83, pp. 489–504.
45 Unsworth, op. cit., p. 132.

8 THE BOARD OF CONTROL AND TREATMENT FOR MENTAL DISORDER, 1913–1930

1 Sargant, W., *The Unquiet Mind*, London, Pan Books, 1971, p. 13.
2 Sargant, W. and Slater, E., *Introduction to Physical Treatment in Psychiatry* (5th edn), Edinburgh, Livingstone, 1972.
3 Sargant, W., 'On chemical tranquillisers', *British Medical Journal*, 28 April 1956, pp. 939–943.
4 Unsworth, C.R., *The Politics of Mental Health Legislation*, Oxford, Oxford University Press, 1987, p. 180.
5 Saxty Good, T., 'History and progress of Littlemore Hospital', *Journal of Mental Science*, 1930, vol. 76, pp. 602–621, especially p. 616.
6 Fisher, J.W., *Modern Methods of Mental Treatment: A Guide for Nurses*, London, Staples, 1948, p. 15.
7 *Seventeenth Annual Report of the Board of Control for the Year 1930*, London, HMSO, 1931, p. 48.
8 *Eighteenth Annual Report of the Board of Control for the Year 1931*, London, HMSO, 1932, p. 48.
9 Hunter, W., 'Oral sepsis as a cause of disease', *British Medical Journal*, 1900, ii, pp. 215–216.
10 Hunter, W., 'Chronic sepsis as a cause of mental disorder', *Journal of Mental Science*, 1927, vol. 73, pp. 563–566.
11 Scull, A.T., 'Desperate remedies: a Gothic tale of madness and modern medicine', in R.M. Murray and T.H. Turner (eds) *Lectures on the History of Psychiatry* (The Squibb Series), London, Gaskell/Royal College of Psychiatrists, 1990, pp. 145–169, especially p. 152.
12 Quoted in Scull, ibid.
13 Cotton, H.A., 'The relation of chronic sepsis to so-called functional mental disorder', *Journal of Mental Science*, 1923, vol 69, pp. 435–465, especially p. 457.
14 ibid., p. 160.
15 Graves, T.C., 'Chronic sepsis and mental disorder', *Journal of Mental Science*, 1923, vol 69, pp. 465–471, especially p. 470.
16 *Journal of Mental Science*, 1927, vol. 73, pp. 716–728, especially p. 722. See also Kopeloff, N., and Kirby, G.H., 'Focal infection', *Journal of Mental Science*, 1929, vol. 75, pp. 267–270, especially p. 268.
17 Rambaut, D.F., 'Some recent forms of mental treatment', *Journal of Mental Science*, 1934, vol. 80, pp. 630–638, especially p. 637.
18 Circular 631 of 27 Feb 1924. Malarial Treatment of General Paralysis of the Insane MH51/240, Board of Control Circular Letters, Nos 578–749 (10 Jan 1921–Oct 1930).
19 Muhlens, P., 'The dangers of fever treatment of paralysis', *Klinische Wochenschrift*, 24 December 1923, p. 2340.
20 MH51/240 Malarial Treatment Circular 680, 8 February 1926.

21 Meacher, E.T., *General Paralysis and its Treatment by Induced Malaria*, London, HMSO, 1935.
22 *Twenty-Fourth Annual Report of the Board of Control for 1937–1938*, London, HMSO, HC 174, 1938, reviewed in the *Journal of Mental Science*, 1939, vol. 85, pp. 1055–1057.
23 MH51/240 Circular 948, April 1944.
24 Dove Cormack, H., 'The position of the medical superintendent of the future', *Journal of Mental Science*, 1940, vol. 86, supplement, pp. 8–14, quoting from the standard asylum rules issued in 1910.
25 *The Fifteenth Annual Report of the Board of Control for the Year 1928*, London, HMSO, 1929, pp. 3–4.
26 Scull, A.T., 'Somatic treatments and the historiography of psychiatry', *History of Psychiatry*, 1994, vol 5, pp. 1–12.
27 Dove Cormack, op. cit., p. 3.

9 THE AGE OF EXPERIMENTATION: THE BOARD OF CONTROL AND TREATMENT FOR MENTAL DISORDER, 1930–1959

1 Medawar, C., *Power and Dependence: Social Audit on the Safety of Medicines*, London, Social Audit Ltd, 1992, pp. 56–57.
2 ibid.
3 ibid., p. 59.
4 Meerloo, A.M., 'On the action of barbituric acid compounds', *Journal of Mental Science*, 1933, vol. 79, pp. 336–367.
5 Macleod, N., 'The bromide sleep: a new departure in the treatment of acute mania', *British Medical Journal*, 1900, vol i, p. 134; Ragg, P.M., 'The bromide sleep in a case of acute mania', *British Medical Journal*, 1900, vol i, p. 1309.
6 Rudolph, G. de M., 'Experimental treatments of schizophrenia', *Journal of Mental Science*, 1931, vol 77, pp. 766–776.
7 Müller, M., 'Prolonged narcosis with somnifaine in psychiatry', *Zeitschrift für die Gesamte Neurologie und Psychiatrie*, 1925, vol 96, p. 653.
8 Jones, W.L., *Ministering to Minds Diseased: A History of Psychiatric Treatment*, London, Heinemann, 1983, p. 4.
9 City of Cardiff, *Cardiff Asylum 26th Annual Report for the Year 1933*, Cardiff, Glossop & Sons, 1934, pp. 16–17; City of Cardiff, *Cardiff Asylum 31st Annual Report for the Year 1938*, Cardiff, Glossop & Sons, 1939, p. 12.
10 Ström Olsen, R. and McCowan, M.L., 'Prolonged narcosis in mental disorder', *Journal of Mental Science*, 1934, vol. 80, pp. 658–669.
11 City of Cardiff, *Cardiff Asylum 27th Annual Report for the Year 1934*, Cardiff, Glossop & Sons, 1935, pp. 14, 16–17.
12 Palmer, H.A., 'The value of continuous narcosis', *Journal of Mental Science*, 1937, vol. 83, pp. 636–678, especially p. 663.
13 Wilson, R.S. and Gillman, S.W., 'Medinal luminal prolonged narcosis', *Journal of Mental Science*, 1938, vol. 84, pp. 991–994.
14 Berrington, W.P., 'A psychopharmacological study of schizophrenia',

Journal of Mental Science, 1939, vol. 90, p. 415.

15 *Australian Health and Medical Law Reporter*, 1991, paras 75–081–751–1095.
16 Sargant, W., *The Unquiet Mind*, London, Pan Books, 1971, p. 78.
17 ibid.
18 Jones, op. cit., p. 23.
19 Partridge, R., *Broadmoor*, London, Chatto & Windus, 1953, p. 233.
20 Ackner, B., Harris, A. and Oldham, A.J., 'Insulin treatment of schizophrenia: a controlled study', *Lancet*, 1957, vol. i, p. 607.
21 Sargant, op. cit., p. 81.
22 Wilson, I., *A Study of Hypoglycaemic Shock Treatment in Schizophrenia*, London, HMSO, 1935.
23 MH51/240 Circular No. 832 March 1937.
24 *Twenty-Fourth Annual Report of the Board of Control for the Year 1937*, London, HMSO, 1938, HC 174, p. 3.
25 ibid.
26 Quoted in *Journal of Mental Science*, 1939, vol. 85, pp. 1055–1057, especially p. 1056.
27 *Twenty-Fifth Annual Report of the Board of Control for the Year 1938*, London, HMSO, 1939, HC 171.
28 Kennedy, A.M., 'Convulsion therapy in schizophrenia', *Journal of Mental Science*, 1937, vol. 88, pp. 609–629, especially p. 613.
29 *Annual Report to the Governors of Bethlem Royal Hospital*, London, 1938, Physician Superintendent's Report, p. 8.
30 ibid.
31 ibid.
32 *Annual Report to the Governors of Bethlem Royal Hospital*, London, 1939, Physician Superintendent's Report, p. 9.
33 ibid., p. 10.
34 Partridge, R., op. cit., p. 223.
35 Kennedy, op. cit., pp. 610–629.
36 ibid.
37 Tourney, G., 'Psychiatric therapies 1800–1968', in T. Rothman (ed.) *Changing Patterns in Psychiatric Care*, London, Vision Press, 1971, pp. 3–42, especially p. 25.
38 Valenstein, E., *Great and Desperate Cures: The Rise and Decline of Psychosurgery and Other Radical Treatments for Mental Illness*, New York, Basic Books, 1986, p. 52.
39 Cerletti, U., 'Electroshock therapy', in F. Marti-Ibanez, A.A. Sackler and R.R. Sackler (eds) *The Psychodynamic Theories in Psychiatry*, New York, Hoeber–Harper, 1956, pp. 258–270, especially p. 259.
40 Medawar, op. cit., p. 44.
41 ibid., p. 27.
42 Valenstein, op. cit., p. 52.
43 *Annual Report to the Governors of Bethlem Royal Hospital*, London, 1940, Physician Superintendent's Report, p. 7.
44 Sargant, op. cit., p. 109.
45 Clare, A., *Psychiatry in Dissent: Controversial Issues in Thought and Practice*, London, Tavistock, 1976, pp. 257–262.

46 [1957] 1 WLR 582.
47 ibid., p. 590.
48 Valenstein, op. cit., p. 5.
49 ibid.
50 Fulton, J.F., *Frontal Lobotomy and Affective Behaviour*, New York, W.W. Norton, 1951, pp. 97–98.
51 Pressman, J.D., 'Sufficient promise: John F. Fulton and the origins of psychosurgery', *Bulletin of the History of Medicine*, 1988, vol. 68, pp. 1–22.
52 Moniz, E., *Tentativées Opératoires dans le Traitement de Certaines Psychoses*, Paris, Masson et Cie, 1936.
53 Valenstein, op. cit., p. 109.
54 ibid., p. 108.
55 Review of Moniz, E., 'Prefrontal leucotomy in the treatment of mental disorders', *American Journal of Psychiatry*, 1937, vol 93, p. 1379, in *Journal of Mental Science*, 1938, vol. 84, p. 441.
56 Valenstein, op. cit., p. 142.
57 Freeman, W. and Watts, J. 'Prefrontal lobotomy in the treatment of mental disorders', *Southern Medical Journal*, 1937, vol. 38, pp. 23–31.
58 Pressman, op. cit., p. 17.
59 Valenstein, op. cit., p. 159.
60 Sargant, op. cit., p. 93.
61 Clare, op. cit., p. 294.
62 Sargant, op. cit., p. 112.
63 Crossley, D., 'The introduction of leucotomy: a British case history', *History of Psychiatry*, 1993, vol. 4, pp. 553–564.
64 Rees, T.P., 'The indications for a pre-frontal leucotomy', *Journal of Mental Science*, 1943, vol. 89, pp. 161–163, especially p. 161.
65 See, for example, the 'Warlingham Park leucotomes', Nos I and II, reproduced in J.S. McGregor and J.R Crumbie, 'Prefrontal leucotomy', *Journal of Mental Science*, 1942, vol. 88, pp. 534–545.
66 Cunningham Dax, E. and Radley Smith, E.J., 'The early effects of pre-frontal leucotomy on disturbed patients with mental illness of long duration', *Journal of Mental Science*, 1943, vol. 89, pp. 182–185.
67 McGregor and Crumbie, op. cit., p. 537.
68 *Journal of Mental Science*, 1943, vol. 89, p. 187.
69 ibid.
70 Circular No. 958 (Prefrontal Leucotomy) issued to hospitals in March 1945 and to licensed houses in August 1945.
71 *Thirty-Third Annual Report of the Board of Control for the Year 1946*, 1947, HC 126, p. 3.
72 Valenstein, op. cit., p. 173.
73 Ministry of Health, *Leucotomy in England and Wales 1942–54*, (Report No. 104), London, HMSO, 1961.
74 ibid.
75 ibid., pp. 5–6.
76 Valenstein, op. cit., pp. 193–194.
77 ibid., p. 213.
78 Fisher, J.W. *Modern Methods of Mental Treatment: A Guide for*

Nurses, London, Staples, 1948, p. 81.
79 Medawar, op. cit., pp. 12–13.
80 Sargant, W., 'Discussion on sedation in man', *Proceedings of the Royal Society of Medicine*, 1958, quoted in Medawar, op. cit., pp. 68–69.

10 THE AGE OF PSYCHOPHARMACOLOGY

1 *Journal of Mental Science*, 1933, vol. 79, p. 784.
2 Guttmann, E., 'Artificial psychosis produced by mescaline', *Journal of Mental Science*, 1936, vol. 82, pp. 203–221.
3 Sandison, R.A., Spencer, A.M. and Whitelaw, J.J.D.A., 'The therapeutic value of Lysergic Acid Diethylamide', *Journal of Mental Science*, 1954, vol. 100, pp. 491–507; Sandison, R.A., 'Psychological aspects of the LSD treatment', *Journal of Mental Science*, 1954, vol. 100, pp. 508–515.
4 ibid., p. 503.
5 Pukas, A., 'Patients haunted by LSD treatment', *The Sunday Times*, 12 February 1995.
6 Charatan, F.B.E., 'An evaluation of chlorpromazine (largactil) in psychiatry', *Journal of Mental Science*, 1954, vol. 100, pp. 883–884.
7 Anton Stephens, D., 'Psychiatric uses of chlorpromazine', *Journal of Mental Science*, 1954, vol. 100, pp. 548–549.
8 ibid.
9 ibid., p. 547.
10 Charatan, op. cit., p. 887.
11 Anton Stephens, op. cit., p. 550.
12 ibid.
13 ibid.
14 Charatan, op. cit., p. 893.
15 Malitz, S., 'A two year evaluation of chlorpromazine in clinical research and practice', *American Journal of Psychiatry*, 1956, vol. 113, pp. 540–546.
16 Robb, H.P., 'The use of chlorpromazine in a mental deficiency institution', *Journal of Mental Science*, 1959, vol. 105, pp. 1029–1031.
17 Jones, W.L., *Ministering to Minds Diseased: A History of Psychiatric Treatment*, London, Heineman, 1983, p. 43.
18 Tourney, 'Psychiatric therapies 1800–1968', in T. Rothman (ed.) *Changing Patterns in Psychiatric Care*, London, Vision Press, 1971, pp. 28–29.
19 Stengel, E., 'The patients' attitudes to leucotomy and its effects', *Journal of Mental Science*, 1952, vol. 98, pp. 382–388.
20 S. R. & O. 1925 Nos 75 and 76.
21 Mental Deficiency Regulations S. R. & O. 1925 No. 76, later replaced by S. R. & O. 1948 No. 1000, r 34.
22 *Fourteenth Annual Report of the Board of Control for the Year 1927*, London, HMSO, 1928, pp. 73–77.
23 ibid., p. 75.
24 ibid., pp. 73 and 77.
25 PRO File MH51/281, Kew.

26 ibid.
27 ibid., Letter of 12 February 1931 to the medical superintendent of Bracebridge Mental Hospital, near Lincoln.
28 PRO File MH50/66 Minute Book of the Board of Control for 1937, 5 August and 15 September 1937.
29 PRO File MH51/281, Kew file on death of patient M.I.C., 26 January 1953.
30 ibid.
31 ibid.
32 The Mental Deficiency Regulations, 1948 SI 1948 No. 1000.
33 Hansard H.C. Debs, Ser. 5, vol. 518, cols 2153–2156.
34 Unsworth, C.R., *The Politics of Mental Health Legislation*, Oxford, Oxford University Press, 1987, pp. 253–258.
35 PRO File MH51/610, Kew.
36 Freeman, H., 'In conversation with A.K. Ross', *Psychiatric Bulletin*, 1992, vol. 16, pp. 193–200.
37 *R* v. *Board of Control ex parte Kathleen Rutter* [1956] 2 QB 109.
38 PRO File MH51/610, Kew.
39 Unsworth, op. cit., p. 266; K. Jones, *A History of the Mental Health Services*, London, Routledge & Kegan Paul, 1972, pp. 304–305.
40 Sargant, W., *The Unquiet Mind*, London, Pan Books, 1971, p. 74.
41 Unsworth, op. cit., p. 231.
42 Mental Health Act 1959, 7 & 8 Eliz. II, c. 72, s. 25.
43 ibid., s. 26.
44 ibid., s. 29.
45 Unsworth, op. cit., p. 271.
46 Percy Commission, *Report of the Royal Commission on the Law relating to Mental Illness and Mental Deficiency*, London, HMSO, 1957, Cmnd 169, Evidence of Socialist Medical Association, p. 686, para. 18.
47 For a full discussion of the current powers of tribunals see Gostin, L.O. and Fennell, P., *Mental Health: Tribunal Procedure* (2nd edn), London, Longman, 1992.
48 Unsworth, op. cit., p. 288.
49 Percy Commission, op. cit., *Minutes of Evidence*, Answer 2,303.
50 ibid., Memorandum of Evidence of the BMA p. 1043, para. 94; Memorandum of Evidence of the Royal Medico-Psychological Association, p. 277, para. 84.
51 ibid., Memorandum of Evidence of the BMA p. 1043, para. 93; Memorandum of Evidence of the Royal Medico-Psychological Association, p. 277, para. 83.
52 Rule 6 of the Mental Deficiency Regulations 1948 (S.R. & O. 1948 No. 1000) already allowed the medical superintendent to delegate his functions in relation to submission of reports.
53 Mental Health Act 1959, 7 & 8 Eliz. II, c. 72, s. 59(1).

11 THE MENTAL HEALTH ACT COMMISSION AND THE MENTAL HEALTH ACT 1983

1 Rothman, D.J., *Strangers at the Bedside: A History of How Law and Bioethics transformed Medical Decision-Making*, New York, Basic Books, 1991, pp. 15–16.
2 Manchester Mental Patients' Union, *Your Rights In Mental Hospital*, Manchester, Moss Side Community Press, 1976, p. 32.
3 Hansard HC Debs, Ser. 5, vol. 849, p. 77, 23 January 1973.
4 The Davies Committee, *Report of the Committee on Hospital Complaints Procedure*, London, HMSO, 1973, para 7.35.
5 ibid.
6 ibid., para 7.36.
7 *Report of the Committee of Inquiry into Allegations of Ill-treatment of Patients and other Irregularities at the Ely Hospital, Cardiff*, London, HMSO, 1969, Cmnd 3975.
8 *Report of the Farleigh Hospital Committee of Inquiry*, London, HMSO, 1971, Cmnd 4557.
9 *Report of the Committee of Inquiry into Whittingham Hospital*, London, HMSO, 1972, Cmnd 4861.
10 The Butler Committee, *Report of the Committee on Mentally Disordered Offenders*, London, HMSO, 1975, Cmnd 6244, paras 3.50–3.62, especially para. 3.53.
11 ibid.
12 ibid., para 3.54.
13 ibid., para 3.56.
14 Manchester Mental Patients' Union, op. cit., p. 32.
15 Jones, J.H., *Bad Blood: The Tuskegee Syphilis Experiment*, New York, Free Press, 1981, p. 2.
16 Valenstein, E., *Great and Desperate Cures: The rise and Decline of Psychosurgery and Other Radical Treatments for Mental Illness*, New York, Basic Books, 1986, p. 285.
17 Rothman, op. cit., p. 186.
18 Valenstein, op. cit., p. 289.
19 Gostin, L.O., *A Human Condition Vol. I*, London, MIND, 1975, p. 122.
20 ibid., pp. 123–130.
21 Jacob, J., 'The right of the mental patient to his psychosis', *Modern Law Review*, 1976, vol. 39, pp. 17–42, especially p. 40.
22 DHSS, *A Review of the Mental Health Act 1959*, London, HMSO, 1976, para. 8.23.
23 ibid., para 8.24.
24 [1976] Fam 185.
25 DHSS, *Review 1959*, para 8.25.
26 DHSS, Home Office, Lord Chancellor's Department and Welsh Office, *Review of the Mental Health Act 1959*, London, HMSO, 1978, Cmnd 7320, paras. 6.28–6.29.
27 ibid.
28 Clare, A., *Psychiatry in Dissent: Controversial Issues in Thought and Practice*, London, Tavistock, 1976, pp. 290–291.

29 Sargant, W. and Slater, E., *Introduction to Physical Treatments in Psychiatry* (5th edn), Edinburgh, Livingstone, 1972, p. 117.
30 Clare, op. cit., p. 298.
31 Sargant and Slater, op. cit., pp. 105–106.
32 Gostin, op. cit., p. 116.
33 Further details of these cases emerged as a result of the television documentary 'Special Treatment' in the *Cutting Edge* series screened on 7 December 1992. See also *The Independent*, 7 December 1992, p. 6.
34 Partridge, R., *Broadmoor*, London, Chatto & Windus, 1953, p. 224.
35 *The Independent*, 7 December 1992, p. 6.
36 ibid.
37 The Boynton Report, *The Report of The Review of Rampton Hospital*, London, HMSO, 1980, Cmnd 8073, paras 13.2.1–13.2.9.
38 ibid., para. 4.7.
39 *Reform of Mental Health Legislation*, London, HMSO, 1981, Cmnd 8405, 1981.
40 Mental Health Act 1983, s. 5.
41 ibid., ss 2, 3, 4, 20.
42 [1976] AC 314.
43 *British Medical Journal*, 1975, vol. 2, p. 378.
44 Mental Health Act 1983, s. 139.
45 *R* v. *Hallstrom and another ex parte W* [1985] 3 All Er 775 (CA).
46 [1986] QB 296.
47 (1992) 15 BMLR 1.
48 Hansard H.L. Debs, Ser. 5, Vol. 426, col. 1137, 1 Feb 1982.
49 ibid.
50 Special Standing Committee on the Mental Health (Amendment) Bill Reports of Standing Committees, Session 1981–1982 ,Vol. Xl, col. 576, 17 June 1982.
51 ibid., col. 577.
52 Mental Health Act Commission (MHAC), *First Biennial Report 1983–1985*, London, HMSO, 1985, para. 6.2.
53 MHAC, *Second Biennial Report 1985–1987*, London, HMSO, 1987, para. 17.1.
54 Mental Health Act 1983 ss. 120(1), (4), and 121(2); The Mental Health Act Commission (Establishment and Constitution) Order 1983, SI 1983, No. 892, r 3(2)(c).
55 Hansard H.L. Debs, Ser. 5, Vol. 426, col. 1150, 1 February 1982.
56 Mental Health Act 1983 ss. 119–121; Department of Health and the Welsh Office, *Mental Health Act 1983 Code of Practice*, London, HMSO 1989, revised in 1993.
57 Department of Health and the Welsh Office, *Mental Health Act 1983 Code of Practice*, London, HMSO, 1993.
58 Mental Health Act, s. 56.
59 ibid. ss. 58 and 62.
60 HC Debs, 22nd Sitting, 29 June 1982, Col 812.
61 For the avoidance of infelicitous acronyms, a decision was made early in the life of the MHAC to refer to second opinion doctors (SODs) as second opinion appointed doctors (SOADs).

322

62 (1991) 9 BMLR 91, especially p. 99, per Morland J.
63 Mental Health Act 1983, s. 57 and the Mental Health (Hospital, Guardianship and Consent to Treatment) Regulations, 1983, SI 1983, No. 893, r 16(1).
64 Mental Health Act 1983, s. 57(3).
65 The sources for these figures are the MHAC First–Fifth Biennial Reports 1985, 1987, 1989, 1991, 1993.
66 MHAC, *Third Biennial Report 1987–1989*, London, HMSO, 1989, p. 23.
67 MHAC, *Second Biennial Report 1985–1987*, London, HMSO, 1987, p. 20.
68 *The Guardian*, 27 May 1988; *The Independent* 27 May 1988; *The Times* 27 May 1988. Reported *sub nomine R* v. *Mental Health Act Commission ex parte X* (1988) 9 BMLR 77. For a fuller discussion of the issues in this case see Fennell, P., 'Sexual suppressants and the Mental Health Act', *Criminal Law Review*, 1988, pp. 660–676.
69 *X* v. *A, B and C and the Mental Health Act Commission* (1991) 9 BMLR 91, especially p. 99, per Morland J.
70 ibid.

12 TREATMENT WITHOUT CONSENT UNDER THE 1983 ACT

1 Mental Health Act 1983, s. 5(2).
2 Mental Health Act 1983, s. 58.
3 Speech of Kenneth Clarke, Hansard H.C. Debs, ser 6, vol. 29, col. 87, 18 October 1982.
4 Mental Health Act 1983, s. 58(1)(b).
5 Speech of Kenneth Clarke, op. cit., col. 86.
6 Mental Health Act 1983, s. 56.
7 ibid., s. 131, which provides that patients may '[be] admitted ... without any application, direction or order rendering [them] liable to be detained'.
8 Department of Health, *Statistical Bulletin In-patients Formally Detained in Hospitals under the Mental Health Act 1983 and other Legislation, England: 1987–88 to 1992–93*, Statistical Bulletin 95/4, London, Department of Health 1995. Bean, P., *The Nature and Extent of Compulsory Admissions to Mental Hospitals within the Four London Regional Health Authorities*, Report to the King's Fund, 1993, suggests that the figures collected centrally by the Department of Health are not reliable.
9 Department of Health and the Welsh Office, *Mental Health Act 1983 Code of Practice*, London, HMSO, 1993, paras 16.9, 16.11, 16.13.
10 Mental Health (Hospital, Guardianship and Consent to Treatment) Regulations, 1983, SI 1983 No. 893, r. 16(2)(b) and Schedule 1.
11 ibid., p. 86.
12 ibid., p. 87.
13 MHAC, *Third Biennial Report 1987–1989*, London, HMSO, 1989, p. 25.

14 Dept of Health and Welsh Office, op. cit., as revised by amendments laid before Parliament on 19 May 1993, para. 15.9.

15 ibid., para. 15.11.

16 The origin of the term 'broad terms' is *Chatterton* v. *Gerson* [1981] 1 QB 432.

17 Dept of Health and Welsh Office, op. cit., para. 15.10.

18 These figures are from MHAC, *Fourth Biennial Report 1989–1991*, London, HMSO, 1991, p. 34. The total is correct, but they do not add up correctly.

19 ibid., paras. 16.23 and 16.26.

20 World Health Organisation, *Glossary and Guide to the Classification of Mental Disorder in accordance with the Ninth Revision of the International Classification of Diseases (ICD–9)*, Geneva, World Health Organisation, 1978, replaced in 1993 by ICD–10.

21 Harrison, G, Owens, D. and Halton, A., 'A prospective study of severe mental disorder in Afro–Caribbean patients', *Psychological Medicine*, 1988, vol. 18, pp. 643–657 and Lewis, D., Croft Jeffries, C. and David, A., 'Are British psychiatrists racist?', *British Journal of Psychiatry*, 1990, vol. 157, pp. 410–415.

22 McGovern, D. and Cope, R., 'The compulsory detention of males of different ethnic groups, with special reference to offender patients', *British Journal of Psychiatry*, 1978, vol. 150, pp. 505–512.

23 Chen, E.Y.H., Harrison, G. and Standen, P., 'Management of first episode psychiatric illness in Afro–Caribbean patients', *British Journal of Psychiatry*, 1991, vol. 158, pp. 517–522.

24 Written Answer (Parliamentary Debates, 20 January 1993, vol. 217, col. 324). The percentages given were: Broadmoor 10.9 per cent, Ashworth 8.0 per cent, Rampton 11.1 per cent, overall 9.9 per cent.

25 Special Hospitals Service Authority, *Report of the Committee of Inquiry into the Death in Broadmoor Hospital of Orville Blackwood and a Review of the Deaths of Two other Afro–Caribbean Patients: 'Big, Black and Dangerous'* (The Prins Report), Special Hospitals Service Authority, 1993.

26 Breggin, P. R., *Electroshock: Its Brain Disabling Effects*, New York, Springer, 1979; Morgan, R.F., *Electroshock: The Case Against*, Toronto, IPI Publishing, 1991; Siddall, R., 'A shock in the dark', *Community Care*, 26 May–1 June 1994, pp. 23–24.

27 Royal College of Psychiatrists, *The Use of Electro-Convulsive Therapy*, London, Royal College of Psychiatrists, 1977.

28 MIND, *Policy on Physical Treatments*, London, MIND, 1994, p. 4.

29 British Medical Association and Royal Pharmaceutical Society of Great Britain, *British National Formulary* (No. 25), March 1993, p. 148.

30 British Medical Association and Royal Pharmaceutical Society of Great Britain, *British National Formulary* (No. 21), March 1991, p. 132. This was the current edition at the time of the research. See now *British National Formulary* (No. 25), op. cit., p. 149.

31 *British National Formulary* (No. 21), op. cit., pp. 138–139.

32 ibid., p. 132.

33 ibid., p. 139.

34 Fraser, K. and Hepple, J. 'Prescribing in a special hospital', *Journal of Forensic Psychiatry*, 1992, vol. 3, pp. 311–320.
35 ibid., p. 316.
36 ibid.
37 Cases 83, 153, 183, 344, 153, 446, 565 and 715
38 MHAC, *Guidance for Responsible Medical Officers: Consent to Treatment*, London, Department of Health and Social Security, 1984, DDL(84)4, para. 16. DDL stands for Dear Doctor Letter.
39 Mental Health Act 1983, s. 58(3)(b).
40 MHAC, *Guidance for Responsible RMOs*. DDL (84)4, para. 17.
41 Dept of Health and the Welsh Office, *Mental Health Act 1983 Code of Practice*, London, HMSO, 1993, para. 16.38.
42 ibid., para. 16.39.
43 DDL(84)4, para. 23, states that this is to ensure that 'the consent to treatment procedures concern a person who is correctly detained.'
44 DDL(84)4, para. 24f. Emphasis added.
45 *Code of Practice*, 1993, para. 16.28b.
46 *Code of Practice*, 1993, para. 16.36–16.37.
47 MHAC, *Fifth Biennial Report 1991–1993*, London, HMSO, 1993, p. 38.
48 MHAC, *First Biennial Report 1983–1985*, London, HMSO, 1985, para. 11.4; *Second Biennial Report 1985–1987*, London, HMSO, 1987, p. 22; *Third Biennial Report*, p. 5; *Fourth Biennial Report*, p. 31; *Fifth Biennial Report*, p. 37.
49 MHAC, *Guidance on the Administration of Clozapine and Other Treatments Requiring Blood Tests Under Provisions of Part IV of the Mental Health Act*, Practice Note 1, June 1993.
50 ibid., Summary and Conclusions, para. 1.
51 ibid., p. 3.
52 *Code of Practice*, 1993, para 16.31.
53 ibid., para. 16.32.
54 MHAC, *Second Biennial Report*, p. 22.
55 Hansard H.C. Debs, Ser. 6, vol. 29, cols 57–60, 18 October 1982.
56 For restricted patients this must take place after the first six months, and thereafter at twelve-monthly intervals.
57 MHAC, *First Biennial Report*, p. 41.
58 MHAC, *Third Biennial Report*, p. 41.
59 MHAC, *Fourth Biennial Report*, para. 6.4.
60 Hansard H.L. Debs, Ser. 5, Vol. 426, cols 1064–1065, 1 February 1982.
61 ibid., col. 1071.
62 *F* v. *Riverside Health Trust* (1993) 20 BMLR 1; *Re K.B.* (1994) 19 BMLR 144.
63 Five patients detained in private secure facilities are included in the RSU total.
64 Case 576.
65 Cases 2001, 2011, 2013, 2017, 2027, 2039, 2041, 2047, 2050, 2080, 2122, 2123, 2126, 2127, 2129, 2139, 2141, 2144, 2164, 2166, 2172, 2173, 2176, 2178, 2181, 2188, 2201, 2206, 2207 and 2225.
66 This includes private sector medium secure provision.

67 In the other three cases information about the section of detention was not available.
68 Cases 2013 and 2141.
69 Cases 2001, 2011, 2014, 2039, 2126, 2172, 2173, 2206 and 2207.
70 Cases 2047, 2129 and 2201.
71 Case 2164.
72 MHAC, *Third Biennial Report*, p. 25.
73 MHAC, *Fourth Biennial Report*, p. 31.
74 'Randolph's Story', shown in the Channel 4 *Black Bag* series in March 1991.

13 EMERGENCY SEDATION, SECLUSION AND RESTRAINT IN CONTEMPORARY PSYCHIATRY

1 *The Independent*, 31 January 1994.
2 Department of Health and the Welsh Office, *Mental Health Act 1983 Code of Practice*, London, HMSO, 1993 revision, para. 18.14.
3 *The Report of the Committee of Inquiry into Complaints about Ashworth Hospital*, London, HMSO, 1992, Cm 2028–1, p. 209.
4 The Ritchie Committee, *Report to the Secretary of State for Social Services Concerning the Death of Mr Michael Martin at Broadmoor Hospital on 6th July 1984 (The Ritchie Report)*, London, DHSS, 1985, Paragraph E5, p. 9.
5 The Prins Committee, *Report of the Committee of Inquiry into the Death in Broadmoor Hospital of Orville Blackwood and a Review of the Deaths of Two Other Afro–Caribbean Patients: 'Big, Black and Dangerous'*, London, Special Hospitals Service Authority, 1993, *passim*.
6 MHAC, *Second Biennial Report 1985–1987*, London, HMSO, 1987, p. 23.
7 MHAC, *First Biennial Report 1983–1985*, London, HMSO, 1985, p. 40.
8 *Code of Practice*, para. 16.18.
9 Mental Health Act 1983, s. 62(3).
10 *Code of Practice*, para. 16.18b.
11 The Prins Committee, op. cit., pp. 40–41. The doctor concerned did not know what the abbreviation 'RMO' meant.
12 *Code of Practice*, para. 16.19.
13 MHAC, *Fifth Biennial Report 1991–1993*, London, HMSO, 1993, p. 37.
14 Kingman, S., 'Deaths fuel calls for more scrutiny of tranquillizers', *The Independent*, 26 May 1992; 'Woman's hospital death fuels concern over drugs', *The Independent*, 13 March 1993.
15 The Prins Committee, op. cit., p. 47.
16 MHAC, *Fifth Biennial Report*, p. 37.
17 ibid., p. 37. The Royal College of Psychiatrists is undertaking a 'Confidential Inquiry into Homicides and Suicides of Mentally Ill People'.
18 Murphy, E., 'Inquests Involving Detained Patients Attended by Mental Health Act Commissioners', unpublished, 1993.

19 Treatment without consent under Part IV may only be given to a patient admitted under section 4 if the admission has been converted to a section 2 by the furnishing of a second medical report.
20 *Code of Practice*, para. 15.24
21 *R* v. *Prentice and Sullman* and *R* v. *Adomako* [1993] 4 All ER 935 (CA); [1994] 3 All ER 79 (HL).
22 (1993) 15 EHRR 437.
23 ibid., para. 82 of the judgment.
24 ibid.
25 ibid.
26 Application No. 6840/74, European Commission of Human Rights Decisions and Reports, vol. 10, p. 5, and vol. 20, p. 5.
27 *Commission* v. *Ireland*, Judgment of 18 January 1978, Reports of the European Court of Human Rights, Series A vol. 25, paras 162, 167 and 179–181.
28 A was given an *ex gratia* payment of £500.
29 *Code of Practice*, paras. 18.15–18.23.
30 Fennell, P.W.H., 'Detention and control of informal mentally disordered patients', *Journal of Social Welfare Law*, 1985, pp. 345–349.
31 *Code of Practice*, para. 18.16.
32 *The Times*, 21 July 1988.
33 [1992] 1 AC 58.
34 ibid., pp. 165–166, 167, 177, 179.
35 ibid., per Lord Bridge at p. 166.
36 ibid., p. 167.
37 See Richardson, G., *Law, Process and Custody: Prisoners and Patients*, London, Weidenfeld & Nicolson, 1993, pp. 145–146, and *H* v. *Home Office*, *The Independent*, 6 May 1992.
38 *Code of Practice*, para. 1.1.
39 MHAC, *Third Biennial Report 1987–1989*, London, HMSO, 1989, pp. 38–40.
40 ibid., p. 38; *Fourth Biennial Report 1989–1991*, London, HMSO, 1991, p. 23; *Fifth Biennial Report*, p. 40.
41 *Fifth Biennial Report*, p. 25.
42 Morrison, P. and le Roux, B., 'The practice of seclusion', *Nursing Times*, 1987, vol. 83, pp. 62–66.
43 Ritchie Committee, op. cit., p. 205.
44 ibid., p. 206.
45 *The Guardian*, 5 April 1994.
46 *Second Biennial Report*, p. 63.
47 *Third Biennial Report*, pp. 39–40.
48 *Fourth Biennial Report*, p. 25.
49 *The Guardian*, 26 May 1994.
50 *Code of Practice*, para. 18.9.
51 ibid.
52 Brindle, D., 'Jurors give open verdict on patient who struggled with Rampton nurses', *The Guardian*, 22 March 1994.
53 [1976] AC 314.
54 (1993) 15 EHRR 437.

14 TREATMENT OF INCAPABLE PATIENTS WITHOUT CONSENT UNDER COMMON LAW

1 Fennell, P.W.H., 'Detention and control of informal mentally disordered patients', *Journal of Social Welfare Law*, 1985, pp. 345–349.
2 *Hamilton* v. *Birmingham Regional Health Board*, (1969) 2 BMJ 456; *Evening Standard*, 30 April 1969; *Devi* v. *West Midlands Regional Health Authority,* unreported judgment of Justice Kilner Brown, 7 May 1980 (Digested [1980] *Current Law* 687, CA (1981) unreported transcript 491; *Potts* v. *North Western Regional Health Authority*, *The Guardian*, 23 July 1983, p. 24.
3 Kennedy, I., and Grubb, A., *Medical Law: Text and Materials* (2nd edn) London, Butterworths, 1994, p. 171.
4 [1981] 1 QB 432.
5 (1972) F. 2d 772, especially 780.
6 (1980) DLR (3d) 1.
7 Robertson, G., 'Informed consent to medical treatment', *Law Quarterly Review*, 1981, vol. 97, pp. 102–126, especially p. 116.
8 ibid.
9 [1985] AC 871.
10 *Bolam* v. *Friern Barnet Hospital Management Committee* [1957] 1 WLR 582.
11 *The Times*, 24 May 1985 (QBD).
12 Per Lords Justice Kerr and Neill [1993] 4 Med LR 151 (CA). See also *Gold* v. *Haringey Health Authority* [1988] QB 481, and *Davis* v. *Barking & Brentwood Health Authority*, unreported, 2 November 1992 (QBD). For a full discussion of the ethical and legal issues relating to the duty to inform the patient in England and Wales and elsewhere, see Kennedy and Grubb, op. cit., pp. 172–245.
13 *Rogers* v. *Whitaker* (1992) 67 ALJR 47.
14 *Re F*, [1990] 2 AC 1; *Sub nomine F* v. *West Berkshire Health Authority*, [1989] 2 All ER 545.
15 274 US 200 (1927).
16 316 US 527 (1942).
17 Eugenic sterilisation programmes continued into the 1970s in Iowa and Minnesota. Reilly, P.R., *The Surgical Solution – A History of Involuntary Sterilisation in the United States*, London, Johns Hopkins University Press, 1991, pp. 128–165.
18 [1976] Fam 185; [1976] 1 All ER 326.
19 Reilly, op. cit., p. 152.
20 (1986) 31 DLR (4th) 1.
21 (1981) 426 NE 2d 467.
22 [1976] Fam 185.
23 *The Times*, 18 September 1975.
24 *British Medical Journal*, 1975, vol. 2, pp. 775–777.
25 [1988] AC 199.
26 [1976] Fam 185.
27 ibid., p. 193.
28 (1987) 2 BMLR 126, 129.

29 ibid., p. 13.
30 [1988] 1 AC 199, especially pp. 202, 204 and 212.
31 (1986) 31 DLR (4th) 1.
32 [1988] AC 199, especially p. 203.
33 ibid., p. 205.
34 ibid., p. 211.
35 Hoggett, B.M., 'The Royal Prerogative in relation to the mentally disordered: resurrection, resuscitation or rejection', in M.D.A. Freeman (ed.), *Medicine Ethics and Law*, London, Stevens, 1988, pp. 85–102; Unsworth, C.R., 'Mental disorder and the tutelary relationship: From pre- to post-carceral legal order', *Journal of Law and Society*, 1991, vol. 18, pp. 254–278, especially p. 261. See also A. Grubb and D. Pearl, 'Sterilisation and the courts', *Cambridge Law Journal*, 1987, vol. 46, pp. 439–464, especially p. 463.
36 *The Times*, 4 June 1987.
37 [1988] Fam 52.
38 [1990] 2 AC 1; *Sub nomine F* v. *West Berkshire Health Authority*; [1989] 2 All ER 545; (1989) 4 BMLR 1; (1989) All ER, pp. 200–206.
39 *Bolam* v. *Friern Barnet Hospital Management Committee*, [1957] 1 WLR 582.
40 Carson, D., 'The sexuality of people with learning difficulties', *Journal of Social Welfare Law*, 1989, pp. 355–372, especially p. 372.
41 Gostin, L.O., *Mental Health Services – Law and Practice*, London, Shaw & Sons, 1986, para. 20.16.4. See also Law Commission, *Consultation Paper No. 129, Mentally Incapacitated Adults and Decision-Making: Medical Treatment and Research*, London, HMSO, 1993, para. 3.39.
42 Indeed Lord Templeman went into some detail as to what the procedure should be; [1988] AC 199, especially pp. 204–205.
43 [1989] 2 FLR 447.
44 ibid.
45 (1990) 5 BMLR 100.
46 [1993] 2 FLR 222; [1993] 3 All ER 222.
47 ibid., para. 7.
48 ibid., para. 8.
49 [1993] 1 FLR 381.
50 [1991] 2 FLR 329; (1990) 6 BMLR 95.
51 Douglas, G., Note on *Re S.G. (a patient)*, [1991] FLR 329.
52 (1991) 7 BMLR 117.
53 [1992] 1 FLR 293, *orse F* v. *F* (1991) 7 BMLR 135.
54 [1993] FLR 29.

15 CODIFYING CLINICAL AUTHORITY

1 [1993] Fam 95.
2 [1993] Fam 123.
3 [1993] Fam 95, at p. 102.
4 The Law Commission, *Consultation Paper No. 119, Mentally Incapacitated Adults and Decision-Making*, London, HMSO, 1991.

5 The Law Commission, *Consultation Paper No. 128, Mentally Incapacitated Adults and Decision-Making: A New Jurisdiction; Consultation Paper No. 129, Mentally Incapacitated Adults and Decision-Making: Medical Treatment and Research; Consultation Paper No. 130, Mentally Incapacitated Adults and Decision-Making: Public Law Protection*, London, HMSO, 1993.

6 The Law Commission, *Mental Incapacity*, Law Com. No. 231, London, HMSO, 1995.

7 ibid., para 2.46.

8 The Law Commission, *Consultation Paper No. 129, Mentally Incapacitated Adults and Decision-Making: Medical Treatment and Research*, London, HMSO, 1993.

9 ibid., paras 7.7 and 7.10.

10 ibid., para. 3.40.

11 Examples are the cases of Constance Jane Maunders, *The Times*, 10 January 1890, 6e, found to be insane and incapable by a jury; Mary Ann Jones, *The Times*, 17 February, 12 and 30 April 1890, found to have fallen under the influence of one Badger, a former policeman, then a detective and landlord of the Bell Inn Canterbury, and adjudged to have been under the influence of insane delusions so as to be incapable of managing her property and affairs; and Mrs Mary Cathcart, heard between 16 June and 24 July 1890, *The Times*, 16–20 June and 4–7 July 1890, and found by a jury not to be insane, although in February 1890 she had been removed to an asylum under an urgency order.

12 Law Commission, Consultation Paper No. 129, op. cit., p. 8, paras 2.6 and 2.21. The Law Commission, *Mental Incapacity*, Law Com. No. 231, London, HMSO, 1995, Draft Mental Incapacity Bill, cl. 2.

13 The Law Commission, *Consultation Paper No. 129*, para. 2.12. This test is based on the Department of Health and Welsh Office, *Mental Health Act Code of Practice*, para. 15.10.

14 See especially Carson, D., 'Disabling progress: the Law Commission's proposals on mentally incapacitated adults', *Journal of Social Welfare and Family Law*, 1993, vol. 15, pp. 304–320.

15 Campbell, T. and Heginbotham, C., *Mental Illness: Prejudice, Discrimination and the Law*, Aldershot, Dartmouth, 1991, p. 93.

16 ibid., p. 95.

17 The Law Commission, *Consultation Paper No. 129*, para. 2.7.

18 The Law Commission, *Mental Incapacity*, Law Com. No. 231, London, HMSO, 1995, para. 3.8.

19 The Law Commission, *Consultation Paper No. 129*, para. 2.20.

20 [1994] 1 WLR 290.

21 For a discussion of the issues in *Bland* see Fennell, P.W.H., 'Medical Law', in *All England Law Reports Annual Review*, 1993, pp. 292–303.

22 (1994) 22 BMLR 13 at p. 21.

23 ibid., p. 20.

24 The Law Commission, *Mental Incapacity*, Law Com. No. 231, London, HMSO, 1995. Draft Mental Incapacity Bill, cl. 2.

25 ibid., para 3.17. See also Gunn, M., 'The Meaning of Incapacity',

Medical Law Review, 1994, vol. 2, pp. 8–28.
26 [1993] Fam 95; [1992] 3 WLR 782; [1992] 4 All ER 649; (1992) 9 BMLR 46.
27 Draft Bill, cl.
28 [1993] AC 789.
29 The Law Commission, *Consultation Paper No. 129*, para. 3.56.
30 The Law Commission, No. 231, Draft Mental Incapacity Bill, cl. 3.
31 The Law Commission, *Consultation Paper No. 129*, para. 3.56.
32 Department of Health and Welsh Office, The Mental Health Act Code of Practice, London, HMSO, 1993, para. 15.24.
33 The Law Commission, No. 231, Draft Mental Incapacity Bill, cl. 9(2).
34 House of Lords, *Report of the Select Committee on Medical Ethics*, London, HMSO, 1994, p. 54.
35 British Medical Association, *Statement on Advance Directives*, January 1994, para. 1.
36 British Medical Association, *Advance Statements About Medical Treatment*, London, BMJ Publications, 1995.
37 The Law Commission, No. 231, Draft Mental Incapacity Bill, cl. 9(4).
38 [1993] Fam 123.
39 The Law Commission, No. 231, Draft Mental Incapacity Bill, cl. 9(7)–(8).
40 The Law Commission, *Consultation Paper No. 129*, para. 7.9; British Medical Association, *Advance Statements About Medical Treatment*, London, BMJ Publications, 1995, para. 4.3.
41 [1995] 1 All ER 677.
42 (1909) 26 TLR 139.
43 C. Lancely and R. Travers, 'Anorexia nervosa: force feeding and the law', *Bulletin of the Royal College of Psychiatrists*, 1993, p. 835.
44 (1993) 20 BMLR 1.
45 (1994) 19 BMLR 144.
46 (1994) 22 BMLR 13 (Fam D and CA); [1995] 1 All ER 683 (CA only). C. Dyer, 'Judge sanctions force feeding', *Guardian*, 26 July 1994.
47 [1995] 1 All ER 683 at 689.
48 (1994) 22 BMLR 13 at 18.
49 ibid.
50 [1995] 1 All ER 683 at p. 689.
51 [1990] 2 AC 1, per Lord Brandon at pp. 55–56, Lord Griffiths at p. 69, and Lord Goff at p. 77. This point is discussed in Fennell, P.W.H., 'Inscribing paternalism in the law: consent to treatment and mental disorder', *Journal of Law and Society*, 1990, vol. 17, pp. 29–51, especially p. 43.

16 INFORMAL COMPULSION: TREATING CHILDREN WITHOUT CONSENT

1 Children Act 1989, s. 105(1), United Nations Convention on the Rights of the Child, Article 1.
2 Audit Commission, *Finding a Place: A Review of Mental Health Services for Adults*, London, HMSO 1994, p. 82; Health Advisory

Service, *Child and Adolescent Mental Health Services: Together We Stand*, Summary, London, HMSO, 1995, p. 3.

3 United Kingdom Government, *The UK's First Response to the United Nations Committee on the Rights of the Child*, London, HMSO, 1994, para. 5.147.

4 [1986] AC 112.

5 ibid. pp. 169–170.

6 ibid., p. 186.

7 Fennell, P.W.H., 'Informal compulsion: the psychiatric treatment of juveniles at common law' *Journal of Social Welfare and Family Law*, 1991, vol. 13, pp. 311–333.

8 *Guardian*, 18 June 1991.

9 *Evening Standard*, 25 June 1991.

10 [1992] Fam 11.

11 Children Act 1989, s. 100 (3) and 100 (4)(a).

12 [1992] Fam 1.

13 (1992) 15 BMLR 60.

14 Department of Health and Welsh Office, *Mental Health Act 1983 Code of Practice*, para. 30.7d.

15 ibid.

16 ibid., para. 30.8.

17 European Court of Human Rights Judgments and Decisions Series A vol. 144, Judgment of 28 November 1988.

18 ibid., para. 73.

19 (1992) 8 BMLR 110.

20 (1992) 15 BMLR 6. On the use of the inherent jurisdiction to admit compulsorily, see *South Glamorgan County Council* v. *W and B* (1992) 11 BMLR 162.

21 Mental Health Act Commission, *Second Biennial Report 1985–7*, London, HMSO, 1987, p. 51.

CONCLUSION

1 'Balancing Care and Control: Guardianship, Community Treatment Orders and Patient Safeguards', *International Journal of Law and Psychiatry*, 1992, vol 15, pp. 205–235.

2 Mental Health Act Commission, *First Biennial Report 1983–1985*, London, HMSO, 1985, pp. 25–27.

3 Department of Health and Social Security, Home Office, Welsh Office, and the Lord Chancellor's Department, *Review of the Mental Health Act 1959*, London, HMSO, 1978, Cmnd 7320, pp. 38–39.

4 Mental Health Act Commission, *First Biennial Report 1983–1985*, London, HMSO, 1985, p. 26.

5 [1986] 1 QB 1090.

6 ibid., p. 1104.

7 The term 'order' is a misnomer since under the 1983 Act only courts can make orders in respect of offender patients. Non-offender patients are admitted under applications made to the hospital managers.

8 Department of Health, *Report of the Internal Review of Legal Powers*

on the Care of Mentally Ill People in the Community, August 1993, p. 3.

9 Ritchie J.H., QC, Dick, D. and Lingham, R., *The Report of the Inquiry into the Care and Treatment of Christopher Clunis,* London, HMSO, 1994, p. 106.

10 Department of Health, *Code of Practice on the Mental Health Act 1983,* London, HMSO, 1993, para. 2.9.

11 Harrison, K., 'Supervision in the Community', *New Law Journal,* 1994, no. 144, p. 1017.

12 For a fuller analysis of the Bill and its history, see P.W.H. Fennell, 'Community care, community compulsion and the law', in S. Ritter and N. Hervey (eds) *Collaborative Community Health Care,* London, Edward Arnold, 1996, Chapter 6.

13 O. Thorold, 'Compulsory community care', *Guardian,* 21 February 1995.

14 That is, those detained under Mental Health Act 1983, ss. 3, 37, 47 or 48. On section 117 see the Code of Practice (2nd edn) (1993), paras. 27.1–27.11.

15 *R* v. *Ealing District Health Authority ex parte Fox* [1993] 1 WLR 373; *R* v. *Avon County Council ex parte Mark Hazell,* CO/659/92, unreported 5 July 1993, QBD.

16 Mental Health (Patients in the Community) Bill 1995, Sched. 1, para. 10(3).

17 (1993) 15 EHRR 437.

18 Convention for the Protection of Human Rights and the Dignity of the Human Being with regard to the Application of Biology and Medicine, Council of Europe, Strasbourg, July 1994, Article 10.

BIBLIOGRAPHY

Ackner, B., Harris, A. and Oldham, A.J., 'Insulin treatment of schizophrenia: a controlled study', *Lancet*, 1957, vol.i, p. 607.

Allderidge, P., 'Bedlam: fact or fantasy?' in W.F. Bynum, R. Porter and M. Shepherd (eds) *The Anatomy of Madness: Essays in the History of Psychiatry, Vol. II, Institutions and Society* London, Tavistock, 1985, pp. 17–33.

Anton Stephens, D., 'Psychiatric uses of chlorpromazine'; *Journal of Mental Science*, 1954, vol. 100, pp. 543–558.

Audit Commission, *Finding a Place: A Review of Mental Health Services for Adults*, London, HMSO, 1994.

Baker Brown, I., *On the Curability of Certain Forms of Epilepsy, Catalepsy and Hysteria in Females*, London, Hardwicke, 1866.

Barker Benfield, G.J., *The Horrors of the Half-Known Life: Male Attitudes Towards Women and Sexuality in Nineteenth Century America*, New York, Harper & Row, 1976.

Bean, P., *The Nature and Extent of Compulsory Admissions to Mental Hospitals Within the Four London Regional Health Authorities*, Report to the King's Fund, 1993.

Bean, P. and Mouncer, P., *Discharged from Mental Hospitals*, London, MIND, 1992.

Beauchamp, T.L. and Childress, J.F., *Principles of Biomedical Ethics* (3rd edn.), Oxford, Oxford University Press, 1989.

Bentham, J., *Panopticon; or the Inspection House*, 3 vols, London, J. Payne, 1791.

Berrington, W.P., 'A psychopharmacological study of schizophrenia', *Journal of Mental Science*, 1939, vol. 90, p. 406.

Bethlem Hospital, *Annual Reports of Bethlem Hospital*, London, Bethlem Hospital Governors, 1857–1940.

Binney, C., 'The law as to sterilization', published by the Eugenics Education Society, PRO File MH51/546, Kew.

Board of Control, *Eighth–Twenty-Third Annual Reports of the Board of Control*, non-Parliamentary papers published in London by HMSO.

Board of Control, *Twenty-Fourth Annual Report of the Board of Control for the Year 1937*, London, HMSO, 1938, HC 174.

Board of Control, *Twenty-Fifth Annual Report of the Board of Control for the Year 1938*, London, HMSO, 1939, HC 171.

Board of Control, *Thirty-Third Annual Report of the Board of Control for the Year 1946*, London, HMSO, 1947, HC 126.

The Boynton Report, *The Report of The Review of Rampton Hospital*, London, HMSO, 1980, Cmnd 8073.

Breggin, P.R., *Electroshock: Its Brain Disabling Effects*, New York, Springer, 1979.

Breggin, P.R., *Toxic Psychiatry: Drugs and Electro-Convulsive Therapy: The Truth and the Better Alternatives*, London, Fontana, 1993.

British Medical Association, *Code of Guidance on Advance Directives*, April 1995.

British Medical Association and the Royal Pharmaceutical Society of Great Britain, *British National Formulary* (No. 21), March 1991.

British Medical Association and the Royal Pharmaceutical Society of Great Britain, *British National Formulary* (No. 25), March 1993.

Brock Committee, *Report of the Departmental Committee on Sterilisation*, 1933 Cmd 4485.

Bucknill, J.C., 'The restraint system', *Asylum Journal*, 1854, vol. 1, pp. 81–83 and 97–99.

Bucknill, J.C., 'On the employment of seclusion in the treatment of the insane', *Asylum Journal*, 1855, vol. 1, pp. 186–189.

Bucknill, J.C., 'The annual reports of the county lunatic asylums and hospitals of the insane in England and Wales published during the year 1855', *Asylum Journal of Mental Science*, 1856, vol. 1, pp. 257–283.

Burns, J.H. and Hart, H.L.A., *Collected Works of Jeremy Bentham: A Comment on the Commentaries and a Fragment of Government*, London, Athlone Press, 1977.

Butler Commitee, *Report of the Committee on Mentally Disordered Offenders*, London, HMSO, 1975, Cmnd 6244.

Bynum, W.F., Porter, R. and Shepherd, M., (eds) *The Anatomy of Madness: Essays in the History of Psychiatry, Vol. I, People and Ideas*, London, Tavistock, 1985.

Bynum, W.F., Porter, R. and Shepherd, M. (eds) *The Anatomy of Madness: Essays in the History of Psychiatry, Vol. II, Institutions and Society*, London, Tavistock, 1985.

Bynum, W.F., Porter, R. and Shepherd, M. (eds) *The Anatomy of Madness: Essays in the History of Psychiatry, Vol. III, The Asylum and its Psychiatry*, London, Routledge, 1988.

Cameron, R.W.D., 'Restraint in the treatment of the insane', *Journal of Mental Science*, 1883, vol. 28, pp. 353–356 and 519–531.

Campbell, T. and Heginbotham, C., *Mental Illness: Prejudice, Discrimination and the Law*, Aldershot, Dartmouth, 1991.

Carson, D., 'The sexuality of people with learning difficulties', *Journal of Social Welfare and Family Law*, 1989, pp. 355–372.

Carson, D., 'Disabling progress: the Law Commission's proposals on mentally incapacitated adults', *Journal of Social Welfare and Family Law*, 1993, vol. 15, pp. 304–320.

Carson, D. and Wexler, D., 'New approaches to mental health law: will the UK follow the US lead, again?', *Journal of Social Welfare and Family Law*, 1994, pp. 79–96.

Castel, R., *L'Ordre Psychiatrique: L'age d'or de l'alienisme*, Paris, Editions de Minuit, 1976.

Castel, R., *The Regulation of Madness: The Origins of Incarceration in France*, trans. W.D. Halls, Berkeley and Los Angeles, CA, University of California Press, 1988.

Castel, R., Castel, F. and Lovell, A., *The Psychiatric Society*, New York, Columbia University Press, 1982.

City of Cardiff, *Cardiff Asylum 26th Annual Report for the year 1933*, Cardiff, Glossop & Sons, 1934.

City of Cardiff, *Cardiff Asylum 27th Annual Report for the year 1934*, Cardiff, Glossop & Sons, 1935.

City of Cardiff, *Cardiff Asylum 31st Annual Report fot the year 1938*, Cardiff, Glossop & Sons, 1939.

Cerletti, U., 'Electroshock therapy', in F. Marti-Ibanez, A.A. Sackler and R.R. Sackler (eds) *The Psychodynamic Theories in Psychiatry*, New York, Hoeber–Harper, 1956, pp. 258–270.

Charatan, F.B.E., 'An evaluation of chlorpromazine (largactil) in psychiatry', *Journal of Mental Science*, 1954, vol. 100, pp. 882–893.

Clare, A., *Psychiatry in Dissent: Controversial Issues in Thought and Practice*, London, Tavistock, 1976.

Cobb Committee, *Report on the Administration of Public Mental Hospitals*, London, HMSO, 1922, Cmd 1730.

Commissioners in Lunacy, *Report and Evidence of the Lunacy Commission to the Home Secretary on Bethlehem Hospital*, 7 February 1852.

Commissioners in Lunacy, *Annual Reports of the Commissioners in Lunacy to the Lord Chancellor 1845–1913*, First Report 1846–Sixty-Eighth Report 1914.

Conolly, J., *On the Construction and Government of Lunatic Asylums and Hospitals for the Insane*, London, Churchill, 1847.

Conolly, J., 'Notice of the eighth report of the Commissioners in Lunacy', *Asylum Journal*, 1854, vol. 1, pp. 134–137; 1855, vol. 1, pp. 144–149, 164–166 and 180–185.

Conolly, J., *The Treatment of the Insane Without Mechanical Restraint*, London, Smith Elder & Co., 1856.

Cotton, H.A., 'The relation of chronic sepsis to so-called functional mental disorder', *Journal of Mental Science*, 1923, vol. 69, pp. 435–465.

Council of Europe, Recommendation No. R(83)2 *Concerning the legal protection of persons suffering from mental disorder placed as involuntary patients*, 22 February 1983.

Council of Europe, *Draft Convention for the Protection of Human Rights and the Dignity of the Human Being with Regard to the Application of Biology and Medicine: Bioethics Convention and Explanatory Report*, Strasbourg, Council of Europe Directorate of Legal Affairs, 1994.

Crossley, D., 'The introduction of leucotomy: a British case history', *History of Psychiatry*, 1993, vol. 4, pp. 553–564.

Cunningham Dax, E. and Radley Smith, E.J., 'The early effects of pre-frontal leucotomy on disturbed patients with mental illness of long duration', *Journal of Mental Science*, 1943, vol. 89, pp. 182–185.

Cynkar, R.J., '*Buck* v. *Bell*: "Felt Necessities" v. "Fundamental Values"', *Columbia Law Review*, 1981, vol. 81, pp. 1418–1461.

Davies Committee, *Report of the Committee on Hospital Complaints Procedure*, London, HMSO, 1973.

Department of Health, *In-patients Formally Detained in Hospitals under the Mental Health Act and other Legislation 1984–1989/90*, Statistical Bulletin 2(7)92.

Department of Health and Social Security (DHSS), *A Review of the Mental Health Act 1959*, London, HMSO, 1976.

DHSS, Home Office, Lord Chancellor's Department and Welsh Office, *Review of the Mental Health Act 1959*, London, HMSO, 1978, Cmnd 7320.

DHSS, Home Office, Lord Chancellor's Department and Welsh Office, *Reform Of Mental Health Legislation*, London, HMSO, 1981 Cmnd 8405.

Department of Health and the Welsh Office, *Mental Health Act 1983 Code of Practice*, London, HMSO, 1989, revised 1993.

Department of Health and the Welsh Office, *Report of the Internal Review of Legal Powers on the Care of Mentally Ill People in the Community*, London, Department of Health, 1993.

Department of Health and the Welsh Office, Health Circular HC(90)23/LASSL(90)11, Care Programme Approach for People with a Mental Illness Referred to the Specialist Psychiatric Services.

Diarmid, J.M., 'The hypodermic injection of morphia in insanity', *Journal of Mental Science*, 1876, vol. 22, pp. 18–42.

Digby, A., *Madness, Morality and Medicine: A Study of the York Retreat 1796–1914*, Cambridge, Cambridge University Press, 1985.

Douglas, G., *Law, Fertility and Reproduction*, London, Sweet & Maxwell, 1991.

Douglas, G., Note on *Re S.G. (a patient)*, [1991] Family Law 310.

Dove Cormack, H., 'The position of the medical superintendent of the future', *Journal of Mental Science*, 1940, vol. 86, supplement, pp. 8–14.

Ehrenreich, B. and English, D., *For Her Own Good: 150 Years of the Experts' Advice to Women*, London, Pluto Press, 1979.

Faden, R.R. and Beauchamp, T.L., *A History and Theory of Informed Consent*, New York, Oxford University Press, 1986.

Fennell, P.W.H., 'Detention and control of informal mentally disordered patients', *Journal of Social Welfare Law*, 1985, pp. 345–349.

Fennell, P.W.H., 'Sexual suppressants and the Mental Health Act', *Criminal Law Review*, 1988, pp. 660–676.

Fennell, P.W.H., 'Beverley Lewis – Was the Law to Blame?', *New Law Journal*, 1989, vol. 139, pp. 1557–1559.

Fennell, P.W.H., 'Inscribing paternalism in the law: consent to treatment and mental disorder', *Journal of Law and Society*, 1990, vol. 17, pp. 29–51.

Fennell, P.W.H., 'Double detention under the Mental Health Act 1983 –

a case of extra-Parliamentary legislation', *Journal of Social Welfare and Family Law*, 1991, p. 206.

Fennell, P.W.H. 'Balancing care and control: guardianship, community treatment orders and patient safeguards', *International Journal of Law and Psychiatry*, 1992, vol. 15, pp. 205–235.

Fennell, P.W.H., 'Informal compulsion: the psychiatric treatment of juveniles under common law', *Journal of Social Welfare and Family Law*, 1992, pp. 311–333.

Fennell, P.W.H., (1993) 'Arrest or injection?', *New Law Journal*, 1993, vol. 143, pp. 395–398.

Fennell, P.W.H., 'Medical law', *All England Law Reports Annual Review*, 1993, pp. 292–311.

Fennell, P.W.H., 'Community care, community compulsion and the law', in S. Ritter and N. Hervey (eds) *Collaborative Community Health Services: Together We Stand*, London, Edward Arnold, 1996.

Fisher, J.W., *Modern Methods of Mental Treatment: A Guide for Nurses*, London, Staples, 1948.

Fisher, M., 'Guardianship under the mental health legislation: a review', *Journal Of Social Welfare Law*, 1988, pp. 316–327.

Fraser, K. and Hepple, J., 'Prescribing in a special hospital', *Journal of Forensic Psychiatry*, 1992, vol. 3, pp. 311–320.

Freeman, H., 'In conversation with A.K. Ross', *Psychiatric Bulletin*, 1992, vol. 16, pp. 193–200.

Freeman, W. and Watts, J., 'Prefrontal lobotomy in the treatment of mental disorders', *Southern Medical Journal*, 1937, vol. 38, pp. 23–31.

Fulton, J.F., *Frontal Lobotomy and Affective Behaviour*, New York, W.W. Norton, 1951.

Gostin, L.O., *A Human Condition Vol. I*, London, MIND, 1975.

Gostin, L.O., *A Human Condition Vol. II*, London, MIND, 1977.

Gostin, L.O., *Mental Health Services – Law and Practice*, London, Shaw & Sons, 1986.

Gostin, L.O., 'Perspectives on mental health reforms', *Journal of Law and Society*, 1983, vol. 10, pp. 47–70.

Gostin, L.O., 'The ideology of entitlement: the application of contemporary legal approaches to psychiatry', in P. Bean (ed.) *Mental Illness: Changes and Trends*, 1983, Chichester, John Wiley.

Gostin, L.O., 'Psychosurgery: a hazardous and unestablished treatment? A case for the importation of American safeguards to Britain', *Journal of Social Welfare Law*, 1982, pp. 83–95.

Gostin, L.O., *Secure Provision*, London, Tavistock, 1985.

Gostin, L.O. and Fennell, P., *Mental Health: Tribunal Procedure* (2nd edn) London, Longman, 1992.

Grant-Smith, R., *Experiences of an Asylum Patient*, London, George Allen & Unwin, 1922.

Graves, T.C., 'Chronic sepsis and mental disorder', *Journal of Mental Science*, 1923, vol. 69, pp. 465–471.

Grubb, A. and Pearl, D., 'Sterilisation and the courts', *Cambridge Law Journal*, 1987, vol. 46, pp. 439–464.

Gunn, M.J., 'Mental Health Act guardianship, where now?', *Journal of*

Social Welfare Law, 1986, pp. 144–152.

Gunn, M.J., 'The meaning of incapacity', *Medical Law Review*, 1994, vol. 2, pp. 8–28.

Guttmann, E., 'Artificial psychosis produced by mescaline', *Journal of Mental Science*, 1936, vol. 82, pp. 203–221.

Harrison, G., Owens, D. and Halton, A., 'A prospective study of severe mental disorder in Afro–Caribbean patients', *Psychological Medicine*, 1988, vol. 18, pp. 643–657.

Harrison, K., 'Supervision in the community', *New Law Journal*, 1994, vol. 144, p. 1017.

Health Advisory Service, *Child and Adolescent Mental Health Services: Together We Stand*, London, HMSO, 1995, Summary, p. 3.

Hervey, N., 'A slavish bowing down: the Lunacy Commission and the psychiatric profession 1845–60', in W.F. Bynum, R. Porter and M. Shepherd (eds) *The Anatomy of Madness: Essays in the History of Psychiatry, Vol. II, Institutions and Society*, London, Tavistock, 1985, pp. 98–131.

Hervey, N., 'The Lunacy Commission 1845–60, with special reference to the implementation of policy in Kent and Surrey', Unpublished PhD thesis, University of Bristol, 1987

Hoggett, B.M., 'The Royal Prerogative in relation to the mentally disordered: resurrection, resuscitation or rejection', in M.D.A. Freeman (ed.), *Medicine Ethics and Law*, London, Stevens, 1988, pp. 85–102.

Hoggett, B.M., *Mental Health Law* (Third Edition), London, Sweet and Maxwell, 1990.

House of Lords, *Report of the Select Committee on Medical Ethics*, London, HMSO, 1994.

Hughes, J., *Letters of a Victorian Madwoman*, Columbia, University of South Carolina Press, 1993.

Hunter, R. and McAlpine, I., *Three Hundred Years of Psychiatry 1535–1860, A History Presented in Selected English Texts*, London, Oxford University Press, 1963.

Hunter, W., 'Oral sepsis as a cause of disease', *British Medical Journal*, 1900, ii, pp. 215–216.

Hunter, W., 'Chronic sepsis as a cause of mental disorder', *Journal of Mental Science*, 1927, vol. 73, pp. 563–566.

Jacob, J., 'The right of the mental patient to his psychosis', *Modern Law Review*, 1976, vol. 39, pp. 17–42.

James, F.E., 'Insulin treatment in psychiatry', *History of Psychiatry*, 1992, vol. 3, pp. 221–235.

Jones, J.H., *Bad Blood: The Tuskegee Syphilis Experiment*, New York, Free Press, 1981.

Jones, K., *Lunacy, Law and Conscience*, London, Routledge & Kegan Paul, 1955.

Jones, K., *A History of the Mental Health Services*, London, Routledge & Kegan Paul, 1974.

Jones, K., 'The limitations of the legal approach to mental health', *International Journal of Law and Psychiatry*, 1980, vol. 3, pp. 1–14.

Jones, K., 'Law and mental health: sticks or carrots?', in G.E. Berrios and H. Freeman (eds) *150 Years of British Psychiatry 1841–1991*, London, Gaskell/Royal College of Psychiatrists, 1991, pp. 98–102.

Jones, R.M., *Mental Health Act Manual* (3rd edn), London, Sweet & Maxwell, 1993.

Jones, W.L., *Ministering to Minds Diseased: A History of Psychiatric Treatment*, London, Heinemann, 1983.

Katz, J., *The Silent World of Doctor and Patient*, New York, Free Press, 1984.

Kennedy, A.M. 'Convulsion therapy in schizophrenia', *Journal of Mental Science*, 1937, vol. 83, pp. 609–629.

Kennedy, I. and Grubb, A., *Medical Law: Text and Materials* (2nd edn), London, Butterworths, 1994.

Kingman, S., 'Deaths fuel calls for more scrutiny of tranquillizers', *The Independent*, 26 May 1992.

Kingman, S., 'Woman's hospital death fuels concern over drugs', *The Independent*, 13 March 1993.

Kopeloff, N. and Kirby, G.H., 'Focal infection', *Journal of Mental Science*, 1929, vol. 75, pp. 267–270.

Lancely, C. and Travers, R., 'Anorexia nervosa: force feeding and the law', *Bulletin of the Royal College of Psychiatrists*, 1993, p. 835.

Law Commission, *Consultation Paper No. 119, Mentally Incapacitated Adults and Decision-Making*, London, HMSO, 1991.

Law Commission, *Consultation Paper No. 128, Mentally Incapacitated Adults and Decision-Making: A New Jurisdiction*, London, HMSO, 1993.

Law Commission, *Consultation Paper No. 129, Mentally Incapacitated Adults and Decision-Making: Medical Treatment and Research*, London, HMSO, 1993.

Law Commission, *Consultation Paper No. 130, Mentally Incapacitated Adults and Decision-Making: Public Law Protection*, London, HMSO, 1993.

Law Commission, *Mental Incapacity*, Law Com. No. 231, London, HMSO, 1995.

Leigh, D., *The Historical Development of British Psychiatry: Volume One, 18th and 19th Century*, Oxford, Pergamon, 1961.

Lewis, D., Croft Jeffries, C. and David A., 'Are British psychiatrists racist?', *British Journal of Psychiatry*, 1990, vol. 157, pp. 410–415.

Lomax, M., *The Experiences of an Asylum Doctor*, London, George Allen & Unwin, 1921.

McGovern, D. and Cope, R., 'The compulsory detention of males of different ethnic groups', *British Journal of Psychiatry*, 1987, vol. 150, pp. 550–512.

McGregor, J.S. and Crumbie, J.R., 'Prefrontal leucotomy', *Journal of Mental Science*, 1942, vol. 88, pp. 534–545.

Maclay, W.S., 'Death due to treatment', *Proceedings of the Royal Society of Medicine*, 1953, vol. 46, pp. 13–20.

McLean, S.A.M., *A Patient's Right to Know: Information Disclosure, the Doctor and the Law*, Aldershot, Dartmouth, 1989.

Macleod, N., 'The bromide sleep: a new departure in the treatment of acute mania', *British Medical Journal*, 1900, vol. i, p. 134.

Macmillan Commission, *Report of the Royal Commission on Lunacy and Mental Disorder*, London, HMSO, 1926, Cmnd 2700.

Macrae, D., Presidential Address to the Medico-Psychological Association, *Journal of Mental Science*, 1937, vol. 83, pp. 489–504.

Malitz, S., 'A two year evaluation of chlorpromazine in clinical research and practice', *American Journal of Psychiatry*, 1956, vol. 113, pp. 540–546.

Manchester Mental Patients' Union, *Your Rights In Mental Hospital*, Manchester, Moss Side Community Press, 1976.

Marshall, F., 'Sterilisation and the law', *Birmingham Gazette*, 31 January 1958.

Meacher, E.T., *General Paralysis and its Treatment by Induced Malaria*, London, HMSO, 1935.

Medawar, C., *Power and Dependence: Social Audit on the Safety of Medicines*, London, Social Audit Ltd, 1992.

Meerloo, A.M., 'On the action of barbituric acid compounds', *Journal of Mental Science*, 1933, vol. 79, pp. 336–367.

Mental Health Act Commission (MHAC), *Guidance for Responsible Medical Officers: Consent to Treatment*, London, Department of Health and Social Security, 1984, DDL(84)4.

MHAC, *First Biennial Report 1983–1985*, London, HMSO, 1985.

MHAC, *Second Biennial Report 1985–1987*, London, HMSO, 1987.

MHAC, *Third Biennial Report 1987–1989*, London, HMSO, 1989.

MHAC, *Fourth Biennial Report 1989–1991*, London, HMSO, 1991.

MHAC, *Fifth Biennial Report 1991–1993*, London, HMSO, 1993.

MHAC, *Guidance on the Administration of Clozapine and Other Treatments Requiring Blood Tests Under Provisions of Part IV of the Mental Health Act*, Practice Note 1, June 1993.

Metropolitan Commissioners in Lunacy, *Report to the Lord Chancellor*, 1844, pp. 145–146.

MIND, *Policy on Physical Treatments*, London, MIND, 1994.

Ministry of Health, *Leucotomy in England and Wales 1942–1954* (Report No. 104), London, HMSO, 1961.

Moniz, E., *Tentativées Opératoires dans le Traitement de Certaines Psychoses*, Paris, Masson et Cie, 1936.

Morgan, R.F., *Electroshock: The Case Against*, Toronto, IPI Publishing, 1991.

Morrison, P. and le Roux, B., 'The practice of seclusion', *Nursing Times*, 1987, vol. 83, pp. 62–66.

Muhlens, P., 'The dangers of fever treatment of paralysis', *Klinische Wochenschrift*, 24 December 1923, p. 2340.

Müller, M., 'Prolonged narcosis with somnifaine in psychiatry', *Zeitschrift für die Gesamte Neurologie und Psychiatrie*, 1925, vol. 96, p. 653.

Murphy, E., 'Inquests involving detained patients attended by Mental Health Act Commissioners', unpublished, 1993.

National Health Service Executive, Guidance on Supervision Registers, HSG(94)5.

BIBLIOGRAPHY

NHS Executive, Guidance on the Discharge of Mentally Disordered People and their Continuing Care in the Community, HSG(94)27.

Nolan, P., A History of Mental Health Nursing, London, Chapman & Hall, 1993.

Palmer, H.A., 'The value of continuous narcosis', Journal of Mental Science, 1937, vol. 83, pp. 636–678.

Parker, E., 'The development of secure provision', in Gostin, L.O., Secure Provision, London, Tavistock, 1985, pp. 15–65.

Partridge, R., Broadmoor, London, Chatto & Windus, 1953.

Perceval, J., 'A narrative of the treatment experienced by a gentleman during a state of mental derangement', in D. Peterson (ed.) A Mad People's History of Madness, Pittsburgh, PA, University of Pittsburgh Press, 1982, pp. 106–107.

Percy Commission, Report of the Royal Commission on the Law Relating to Mental Illness and Mental Deficiency, London, HMSO, 1957, Cmnd 169.

Pernick, M.S., 'The patient's role in medical decision-making: a social history of informed consent in medical therapy', in President's Commission for the Study of Ethical Problems in Medicine and Biomedical and Behavioural Research, Making Health Care Decisions, Washington, DC, US Government Printing Office, 1982, vol. 3.

Peterson D., (ed.), A Mad People's History of Madness, Pittsburgh, PA, University of Pittsburgh Press, 1982.

Pressman, J.D., 'Sufficient promise: John F. Fulton and the origins of psychosurgery', Bulletin of the History of Medicine, 1988, vol. 68, pp. 1–22.

Pritchard Davies, F., 'Chemical restraint and alcohol', Journal of Mental Science, 1881, vol. 26, pp. 526–530.

Pukas, A., 'Patients haunted by LSD treatment', The Sunday Times, 12 February 1995.

Radnor Commission, Report of the Royal Commission on the Care of the Feeble Minded, London, HMSO, 1908, Cd 4202.

Ragg, P.M., 'The bromide sleep in a case of acute mania', British Medical Journal, 1900, vol. i, p. 1309.

Rambaut, D.F., 'Some recent forms of mental treatment', Journal of Mental Science, 1934, vol. 80, pp. 630–638.

Rees, T.P., 'The indications for pre-frontal leucotomy', Journal of Mental Science, 1943, vol. 89, pp. 161–165.

Rees Thomas, W., 'The unwilling patient', twenty-seventh Maudsley Lecture, Journal of Mental Science, 1953, vol. 99, pp. 191–201.

Reilly, P.R., The Surgical Solution – A History of Involuntary Sterilisation in the United States, London, Johns Hopkins University Press, 1991.

Report of the Committee on the Age of Majority, London, HMSO, 1967, Cmnd 3342.

Report of the Committee of Inquiry into Allegations of Ill-treatment of Patients and other Irregularities at the Ely Hospital, Cardiff, London, HMSO, 1969, Cmnd 3975.

Report of the Farleigh Hospital Committee of Inquiry, London, HMSO, 1971, Cmnd 4557.

BIBLIOGRAPHY

Report of the Committee of Inquiry into Whittingham Hospital, London, HMSO, 1972, Cmnd 4861.

Report of the Committee of Inquiry into Complaints about Ashworth Hospital, London, HMSO, 1992, Cm 2028–I & II.

Report of the House of Commons Health Committee, 'Community Supervision Orders', Fifth Report, vol. 1, HC 667–671 (23 June 1993).

Richardson, G., *Law, Process and Custody: Prisoners and Patients*, London, Weidenfeld & Nicolson, 1993.

Lord Riddell, *Sterilisation of the Unfit*, London, H.K. Lewis & Son, 1929.

Ritchie Committee, *Report to the Secretary of State for Social Services Concerning the Death of Mr Michael Martin at Broadmoor Hospital on 6th July 1984*, London, DHSS, 1985.

Robb, H.P., 'The use of chlorpromazine in a mental deficiency institution', *Journal of Mental Science*, 1959, vol. 105, pp. 1029–1031.

Robertson, C.L., 'On the sedative action of the cold wet sheet in the treatment of recent mania', *Journal of Mental Science*, 1861, vol. 7, pp. 265–277.

Robertson, C.L., 'The Case of James Snashall' (1864) *Asylum Journal of Mental Science*, 1864, vol. 10, pp. 77–81.

Robertson, G., 'Informed consent to medical treatment', *Law Quarterly Review*, 1981, vol. 97, pp. 102–126.

Rothman, D.J., *Strangers at the Bedside: A History of How Law and Bioethics Transformed Medical Decision-Making*, New York, Basic Books, 1991.

Royal College of Psychiatry, *The Use of Electro-Convulsive Therapy*, London, Royal College of Psychiatrists, 1977.

Rudolph, G. de M., 'Experimental treatments of schizophrenia', *Journal of Mental Science*, 1931, vol. 77, pp. 766–776.

Sandison, R. A., 'Psychological aspects of the LSD treatment', *Journal of Mental Science*, 1954, vol. 100, pp. 508–515.

Sandison, R.A., Spencer, A.M. and Whitelaw, J.J.A., 'The therapeutic value of Lysergic Acid Diethylamide', *Journal of Mental Science*, 1954, vol. 100, pp. 491–507.

Sargant, W., 'On chemical tranquillisers', *British Medical Journal*, 28 April 1956, pp. 939–943.

Sargant, W., 'Discussion on sedation in man', *Proceedings of the Royal Society of Medicine*, 1958, quoted in Medawar, C., *Power and Dependence*, 1992.

Sargant, W., *The Unquiet Mind*, London, Pan Books, 1971.

Sargant, W. and Slater, E., *Introduction to Physical Treatment in Psychiatry*, (5th edn), Edinburgh, Livingstone, 1972.

Savage, G.H., 'Uses and abuses of chloral hydrate', *Journal of Mental Science*, 1879, vol. 25, pp. 4–8.

Saxty Good, T., 'History and progress of Littlemore Hospital', *Journal of Mental Science*, 1930, vol. 76, pp. 602–621.

Scull, A.T., (ed.), *Madhouses, Mad Doctors and Madmen: The Social History of Psychiatry in the Victorian Era*, London, The Athlone Press, 1981.

BIBLIOGRAPHY

Scull, A.T., 'Desperate remedies: a Gothic tale of madness and modern medicine', in R.M. Murray and T.H. Turner (eds) *Lectures on the History of Psychiatry* (The Squibb Series), London, Gaskell/Royal College of Psychiatrists, 1990, pp. 145–169.

Scull, A.T., 'Somatic treatments and the historiography of psychiatry', *History of Psychiatry*, 1994, vol. 5, pp. 1–12.

Select Committee on Madhouses, *First Report. Minutes of Evidence Taken Before the Select Committee Appointed to Consider of Provision Being Made for the Better Regulation of Madhouses in England*, ordered by the House of Commons to be printed, 25 May 1815.

Shepherd, J.A., *Spencer Wells: The Life and Work of a Victorian Surgeon*, Edinburgh, E. & S. Livingstone, 1965.

Shortt, S.E.D., *Victorian Lunacy: Richard M. Bucke and the Practice of Late Nineteenth Century Psychiatry*, Cambridge, Cambridge University Press, 1986.

Showalter, E., 'Victorian women and insanity', in A.T. Scull (ed.), *Madhouses, Mad Doctors and Madmen: The Social History of Psychiatry in the Victorian Era*, London, The Athlone Press, 1981, pp. 313–331.

Showalter, E., *The Female Malady: Women, Madness and English Culture, 1830–1980*, London Virago Press, 1988.

Siddall, R. 'A shock in the dark', *Community Care*, 26 May–1 June 1994, pp. 23–24.

Special Hospitals Service Authority, *Report of the Committee of Inquiry into the Death in Broadmoor Hospital of Orville Blackwood and a Review of the Deaths of Two other Afro-Caribbean Patients: 'Big, Black and Dangerous'*, London, Special Hospitals Service Authority, 1993.

Stengel, E., 'The patients' attitudes to leucotomy and its effects', *Journal of Mental Science*, 1952, vol. 98, pp. 382–388.

Ström Olsen, R., and McCowan, M.L., 'Prolonged narcosis in mental disorder', *Journal of Mental Science*, 1934, vol. 80, pp. 658–669.

Tomes, N.J., *The Persuasive Institution: Thomas Story Kirkbride and the Art of Asylum Keeping 1841–1883*, PhD thesis, University of Pennsylvania, 1978.

Tomes, N.J., 'The great restraint controversy', in W.F. Bynum, R. Porter and M. Shepherd (eds) *The Anatomy of Madness: Essays in the History of Psychiatry, Vol. III, The Asylum and its Psychiatry*, London, Routledge, 1988, pp. 190–225.

Tourney, G., 'Psychiatric therapies 1800–1968', in T. Rothman (ed.) *Changing Patterns in Psychiatric Care*, London, Vision Press, 1971.

Trombley, S., *All That Summer She Was Mad: Virginia Woolf and her Doctors*, London, Junction Books, 1981.

Trombley, S., *The Right to Reproduce: A History of Coercive Sterilization*, London, Weidenfeld & Nicholson, 1989.

Tuke, D.H., 'Presidential address on the occasion of the fortieth anniversary of the Medico-Psychological Society', *Journal of Mental Science*, 1881, vol. 27, pp. 305–341.

United Kingdom Government, *The UK's First Response to the United Nations Committee on the Rights of the Child*, London, HMSO, 1994.

BIBLIOGRAPHY

Unsworth, C.R., *The Politics of Mental Health Legislation*, Oxford, Oxford University Press, 1987.

Unsworth, C.R., 'Mental disorder and the tutelary relationship: from pre- to post-carceral legal order', *Journal of Law and Society*, 1991, vol. 18, pp. 254–278.

Unsworth, C.R., 'Law and lunacy in psychiatry's "Golden Age"', *Oxford Journal of Legal Studies*, 1993, vol. 13, pp. 479–507.

Valenstein, E., *Great and Desperate Cures: The Rise and Decline of Psychosurgery and Other Radical Treatments for Mental Illness*, New York, Basic Books, 1986.

Wachenfeld, M.C., *The Human Rights of the Mentally Ill in Europe under the European Convention on Human Rights*, Copenhagen, Danish Centre for Human Rights in Collaboration with the Nordic Journal of International Law, 1992.

Welsh Office, *Mental Health Statistics for Wales, No. 11*, 1991.

Weindling, P., *Health, Race and German Politics Between National Unification and Nazism 1870–1945*, Cambridge, Cambridge University Press, 1989.

Weiner, D.B., 'Le geste de Pinel: the history of a psychiatric myth', in M. Micale and R. Porter (eds) *Discovering the History of Psychiatry*, Oxford, Oxford University Press, 1994, pp. 232–247.

Wilson, I., *A Study of Hypoglycaemic Shock Treatment in Schizophrenia*, London, HMSO, 1935.

Wilson, R.S. and Gillman, S.W., 'Medical luminal prolonged narcosis', *Journal of Mental Science*, 1938, vol. 84, pp. 991–994.

Woolf, V., *Mrs Dalloway*, London, Hogarth Press, 1925.

World Health Organisation, *Glossary and Guide to the Classification of Mental Disorder in Accordance with the Ninth Revision of the International Classification of Diseases (ICD–9)*, Geneva, World Health Organisation, 1978.

World Health Organisation, *Glossary and Guide to the Classification of Mental Disorder in Accordance with the Tenth Revision of the International Classification of Diseases (ICD–10)*, Geneva, World Health Organisation, 1994.

INDEX